An Italian Passage

John W. Briggs

An Italian Passage

Immigrants to Three American Cities, 1890–1930

New Haven & London
Yale University Press 1978

Published with assistance from the foundation established in memory of Philip Hamilton McMillan of the Class of 1894, Yale College.

Designed by Thos. Whitridge and set in IBM Selectric Baskerville type. Printed in the United States of America by Vail-Ballou Press, Binghamton, N.Y.

Published in Great Britain, Europe, Africa, and Asia (except Japan) by Yale University Press, Ltd., London. Distributed in Latin America by Kaiman & Polon, Inc., New York City; in Australia and New Zealand by Book & Film Services, Artarmon, N.S.W., Australia; and in Japan by Harper & Row, Publishers, Tokyo Office.

Library of Congress Cataloging in Publication Data

Briggs, John Walker, 1937–
   An Italian passage.

   Bibliography: p.
   Includes index.
   1. Italian Americans—New York (State)—History.
2. Rochester, N.Y.—History. 3. Utica, N.Y.—History.
4. Kansas City, Mo.—History. 5. Italian Americans—
Missouri—Kansas City—History. I. Title.
F130.I8B74   974.7'004'51   77-22006
ISBN 0-300-02095-3

CONTENTS

ILLUSTRATIONS
(following page 140)

Ecce Homo Society, Rochester, ca. 1928

Rochester's 1910 Labor Day Parade

The Red Band, Utica, 1921

Hucksters loading their wagons, 1911

Women shopping at Rochester public market, 1913

A wading pool in an immigrant area of Rochester, 1913

Children at the Rochester Truant School, ca. 1900

A typical residence on Frank Street, Rochester

A business district in the Italian colony, Rochester, 1911

The first block of Frank Street, Rochester, 1915

Old School No. 6, Rochester

Old School No. 5, Rochester, 1926

TABLES

ACKNOWLEDGMENTS

As is true of all scholars, I have benefited from the assistance and guidance of many persons in the course of writing this book. It is a pleasure to have the opportunity to acknowledge their help. Members of the staffs of forty archives in Italy and America freely extended themselves to further my research. A list of these institutions may be found in the Bibliographical Note below. Personnel of the public libraries of Rochester and Utica, New York, and Kansas City, Missouri, the libraries of the University of Minnesota, The Johns Hopkins University, the University of Rochester and the Biblioteca Nazionale in Palermo were equally helpful. I regret that I cannot recognize them individually for their courtesies to me. Much of the research for this book was made possible by a fellowship from the Fund for the Advancement of Education.

Eugene D. Genovese, Philip Gleason, Herbert G. Gutman, Francis Horler, Rudolph Vecoli, and Virginia Yans-McLaughlin, read one or another version of this book as it progressed through several revisions and were generous in their counsel. Perhaps to my detriment I was not always able to follow their advice. Indeed, they were not always in accord as to what should be done. Thus, they share credit for the virtues others may find in the work but are not to be held culpable for its deficiencies. Thomas R. Knapp and John K. Miller helped me solve problems involving data analysis. Sidney Hawkes, Willie Jackson, Ron Hein, and Robert Massa carefully transcribed and coded data from various sources for quantitative analysis. Margaret Zaccone typed succeeding drafts of the manuscript without complaint.

The opportunity to share one's research experiences with others of similar interests is a most valuable privilege. Josef Barton, Oksana Dragan, William Galush, Yeshayahu Jelinek,

Mark Stolerik, Rudolph Susel, and I, constituted the staff of a
research project on immigration, education, and social change.
In frequent daily contact with them over two years, I acquired
many insights into the meaning of the materials before me. I
still may not fully appreciate all of their contributions to my
understanding of immigration. Timothy L. Smith directed the
project and served as my thesis advisor. In the intervening years
he has remained a valued friend and counselor. The magnitude
of his contribution to my scholarly life can only, I suspect, be
appreciated by others of his students who have similarly benefited from his tutelage, leadership, and generosity.

I owe my family special thanks for their good-natured
tolerance of this extrapresence in our household. My wife Chari
took time from her own professional activities to read, discuss,
and edit the manuscript as it progressed to its final form.

INTRODUCTION

In the period between 1887 and the outbreak of the First World War more than 3,900,000 Italians passed through United States immigration stations. They tended to concentrate in the industrial East and Midwest and rapidly set about the business of community building. Scholars have subjected the large settlements in New York City and Chicago to considerable study. These cities represent one tradition of Italian settlement. But there is another pattern. Many Italians passed up the major metropolises to settle in medium-sized and smaller cities and towns. Here the colonies grew to their fullest expression in the years 1890–1930. This book explores this less-well-covered segment of the immigrant experience.

The three cities I have studied represent, individually and collectively, many of the characteristics found in numerous similar cities. Rochester, New York, was a medium-sized city with a large Italian-born population. Utica, New York, was a smaller city with a large population of Italian immigrants. During the four decades covered by this study, the foreign-born in these two colonies increased from under 1 percent to over 7 and 8 percent of the cities' populations respectively. In 1960, persons of Italian stock, the census designation for immigrants and their children, constituted over 9 percent of the populations of the Rochester and Utica-Rome metropolitan areas. Kansas City, Missouri, was a medium-sized city with a smaller Italian-born population which never exceeded 1 percent of the population during the years of the study. Fewer than 1 percent of its residents were of Italian stock in 1960.[1]

These Italian colonies met several methodological and design considerations, in addition to representing three common combinations of size of city and size of Italian population.

They were large enough to support a fairly complete range of community institutions, and yet were small enough to allow intensive and inclusive community studies. Each has preserved sufficient primary source materials to support historical research. Extant Italian newspapers and records from Italian parishes and public schools provide an indispensable base for the study. There are no major studies of the Italian settlement in any of the three cities to date. During the initial stages of this work, I had hoped I might find significant contrasts resulting from the varying sizes of the cities and their colonies. This plan for a major comparative dimension had to be abandoned when the similarities in the colony building of each city far outweighed the differences. Readers familiar with the literature on Italian-Americans will find that my book, while not neglecting the family, places less emphasis on this institution, which is usually given center stage. Initially I planned a more focused considera-tion of the family. However, as my research revealed novel insights into the character of emigrants, the nature of the emi-gration process, the variety of community life in Italian-American colonies, the degree of initiative taken by immigrants in attempt-ing to control their own destinies, and the place of education in this process, I came to see that these themes merited indepen-dent and extended exposition. Thus, I temporarily set aside my plans for an extended consideration of the place of the family in immigrant adjustments to the New World in order to give these less common findings fuller consideration.

Scholars have long recognized that immigrant efforts at community building were in part a reconstruction of their past and in part a construction of new and, for them, unique insti-tutions. The particulars of this blending of the new and old, of cultural baggage carried from Europe and influences from the American environment, constitute a popular theme in immigra-tion studies. Historians working along these lines have been hindered in identifying exactly who these emigrants were, and therefore what their cultural heritage was, by their remoteness from documents in the Old World. As a result, most studies have based their descriptions of the immigrant and his Old World backgrounds on published Italian sources which range from the superb eight-volume parliamentary study of conditions among the agricultural classes in the early twentieth century to the generally impressionistic work of Luigi Villari.

Villari illustrates a second limitation of works of history in this area. Whether historians intend to do so or not, they are often led into talking about emigrants as an undifferentiated group of peasants and employing descriptions of their culture that are so general and contradictory that they say nothing. Villari's depiction of the various regional character types in Italy illustrates the kind of generalization historians have often worked with:

> The Piedmontese is aristocratic, reserved, hospitable, steady and industrious, while the Lombard is quick, businesslike, rather noisy and fond of chatter, and active. The Venetian is gossipy, lazy, artistic and not particularly honest. The Tuscan is hard-working, skeptical, courteous, slow, conservative, but not exclusive, full of family affection, and frugal to the point of niggardliness. The Roman is reserved and dignified, but averse to hard work, and his passions frequently lead him to deeds of violence. In the South, there is a considerable difference between the Neapolitans and the Sicilians. The former are gay, of great natural intelligence and adaptability, artistic, loquacious, superstitious, utterly wanting in self-respect, vicious, fond of a quarrel, especially if it ends in the law courts, and given to outward show. They are often cruel and cowardly, but in great emergencies they can rise to a height of self-abnegation and heroism which has rarely been equalled. The Sicilian, on the other hand, is silent, has more dignity than the Neapolitan; he is more gentlemanly in manners and appearance, but he is vindictive and savage, and intolerant of all restraint.[2]

A related problem associated with Italian observations involves the tendency of contemporaries of the emigrants to denigrate the southerners for ideological or political reasons. Denis Mack Smith, among others, has observed that Italian national leaders, facing the reality of the failure of the enlightened

and liberal government of a newly united Italy to advance the
South as rapidly as the North, assigned the fault to a slothful
and corrupt southern population. The accusation rested upon a
myth that the South was a rich, fertile region. A second myth
of an inherently backward, if not barbarian, native population
then became necessary to explain the failure of the South to
blossom after release from the inefficient and despotic Bourbon
rule. The work of several German social scientists stressed the
mixed and heavily African racial background of southerners,
thus providing a convenient "scientific" veneer for the second
myth. This indictment reappeared after World War II, as the
national government again faced the problem of the South.[3]

Much of the traditional literary evidence about Italian
immigrants was written by men sharing this bias toward southern
Italians. Recent developments in social history have promoted
the use of alternative types of evidence which are somewhat
more resistant to distortion from such prejudice. An important
part of my portrayal of the Italian backgrounds of the immigrants comes from rarely used material in communal and
provincial archives.

Another popular source of information on the nature of the
Italian heritage comes from studies of immigrants done in this
country. Phyllis Williams conducted an often-cited investigation of the persistence of Italian culture among immigrants in
the mid-1930s. Leonard Covello's important analysis of the
social backgrounds of Italian immigrants and of the educational
adjustments they made in America also relies heavily on evidence
collected here for its description of Old World culture. Both
these works are flawed as sources for general statements about
the premigration culture by the special concerns of the authors.
Williams wrote what was to be a handbook for social workers,
while Covello sought an explanation for the poor school performance of a portion of the Italo-American children. Thus, both
authors tended to concentrate on the maladaptive and pathological aspects of immigrant life and to reinforce the general
distortions common among observers in Italy. Covello, in
describing his study, states that "the use of the questionnaire
as a sociological technique served, in the main, the purpose of

verification rather than discovery." He started with the premise that the Italo-American student was "squeezed between two worlds." His approach, then, was not likely to shed light on areas where the two worlds may have overlapped or where there was a great deal of diversity and internal contradiction in one or both worlds.[4]

Partly because of such obstacles, no doubt, recent scholarship on Italians in America has not advanced the knowledge of Italian backgrounds far beyond the point of understanding reached thirty years ago. Despite Rudolph Vecoli's strong warning of the danger in underemphasizing the importance of the particular culture of immigrants, historians have been content to ignore this aspect, to view it as inconsequential, or simply to borrow the general, undifferentiated portrayal of immigrants as backward peasants—what Vecoli calls the "mudsill" of Italian society. The challenge to answer the questions which Marcus Lee Hansen raised thirty years ago remains. Who emigrated? Who stayed behind? Why were choices made as they were? Only by seeking some answers to these questions can the impact of the selection process on the immigrants' New World experience be probed.[5]

Answers to Hansen's queries set important constraints on the kinds of interpretations that may be employed in subsequent analyses of the immigrants' experiences. If the emigrants were the mudsill of Italian society, as Vecoli believes, and if the social, intellectual, and psychological resources brought from the Old World were nearly all antagonistic—or at best irrelevant—to the new situation, then the immigrant experience in America has one set of meanings: success can be attributed to the new environment and the advantages it offers; alternatively, failure can be assigned to the European-spawned deficiencies in the newcomers which prevented them from grasping the opportunities America offered. Old World minds and souls either clung irrationally and at unreasonable cost to an irrelevant past, or they submitted passively to the powerful forces shaping their future.

Conversely, the belief that the emigrants were rational, confident, capable, and talented individuals dictates much greater care in interpreting their subsequent experience. The simplistic environmental explanation of success and the blame-the-victim approach to failure are no longer tenable. Interpretations now require a sensitive balancing of the character of the individuals involved and the nature of the social, economic, and political environments in which the process took place. The immigrants were not chameleons totally dependent on their surroundings for their character. They contributed to shaping their future rather than receiving their destinies wholly defined and packaged by others.[6]

Chapter 1 of this book addresses the question of who emigrated, while chapters 2 and 3 explore aspects of individualism and illiteracy, two areas of Italian culture which are reputed to have provided serious obstacles to successful adaptation to the American environment. Research in communal and provincial archives yielded important new evidence which is presented here. I determined the locus of these researches after a careful study of the Italian origins of the immigrants in the three American cities. Each archive visited served an area which supplied substantial numbers of immigrants to one or more of the American cities. Old World conditions imposed some compromises, however. Disorganization caused by an earthquake in western Sicily shortly before my visit there prevented any work in communal archives in the province of Trapani, the origin of many migrants to Kansas City. Such restrictions do not seriously affect the representativeness of the evidence, however, since I was able to glean sufficient material from a variety of types of villages in Sicily and in the mainland South.

While the relevance of this book to the field of immigration history and the resurgent interest in ethnicity will be obvious, other issues of scholarly interest it touches may be less evident at the outset. Historians and social scientists have increasingly questioned the sharp dichotomies previously drawn between traditional and modern social and cultural forms. This is partly the result of new discoveries of complexity and variety in traditional societies, and partly the realization that modernity does not immediately and in every instance of interaction eradicate and replace traditional forms. A new understanding of what

is involved in the movement from nonindustrial to industrial
societies is slowly emerging. In labor history the recent work of
Herbert Gutman, Peter Stearns, and E. P. Thompson—among
others—explores the cultural and social impact of exposure to
modernization on people from traditional societies. Virginia
Yans-McLaughlin, following a similar tack, is developing a
dialectical perspective in her work on the conjunction of
traditional Italian family life and the American industrial order.
The Italians studied here experienced a transition from traditional to modern society through their migrations. Their story
at many points speaks to issues now being hotly debated.[7]

Recently, social scientists have revived their interest in
voluntary associations. This form of group behavior has popularly been thought to be especially characteristic of Americans.
One historian, perhaps prompted by this assumption, reasoned
erroneously that if Italians in America formed voluntary associations, this activity must have been the result of new cultural
habits learned here; thus he interpreted it as a sign of their
Americanization. Anthropologists and sociologists have demonstrated that voluntary group activity exists in many kinds of
societies, both traditional and modern. Some have turned their
attention to determining the conditions under which voluntary
associations appear prominently in a society. Comparisons and
contrasts in the forms and activities of voluntary associations
in Italy and the United States will provide important insights
into the Italian immigrants' experience. A by-product of this
analysis is information which speaks to issues prominent in the
resurgent interest in voluntary group activity.[8]

A decade of criticism has questioned every aspect of schooling in America. Historians of education eagerly joined in dis-
mantling the earlier interpretation of the historical role of
schooling. The activities of school reformers, which had previously been presented as altruistic, in the work of revisionists
became action-calculated to preserve class or narrow professional self-interests. Far from sponsoring widespread opportunity, the schools, in this view, were intended to protect the class
structure, secure the future of the children of the already privi-
leged, and prepare the rest to function efficiently and quietly in

their preassigned places in the industrial order. Rather than gratefully accepting this racist and class-biased institution imposed from above, many lower-class parents and children, according to the revisionists, recognized the school as a cultural weapon and resisted its influence. The Italian immigrants whose story is recounted below represent one segment of the "victims of the system" (immigrants, blacks, and the poor) on which the revisionists rest their case. The record of their attitudes toward education and the actions they took concerning their own educations and those of their children speaks strongly to the points at issue among educational historians.[9]

WHO VENTURED TO LEAVE:
EMIGRATION FROM SOUTHERN ITALY

The forces which separated the emigrants from their homelands, setting them off on their migrations, have long been seen as central to the definition of the emigrant's character and potential. Were they men and women pushed unwillingly from their homes by powers beyond their control? Or were they opportunists pulled by the lure of greater prospects in other lands? Few scholars adopt one approach to the total exclusion of the other, but most have given greater importance to one. Interpretations that emphasize the "push" forces tend to present those dislodged from their homes as desperate, demoralized members of the lowest strata of society, the meanest sort, poorly prepared to make their way in another environment. Those fleeing religious or political persecution generally are considered to be exceptions.

Advocates of the "pull" thesis project a more favorable image of the immigrants. They are intelligent, motivated, and ambitious—welcome additions to the countries receiving them. My investigation begins in the Old World but takes a different tack from the simple "push" approach. It tests the hypothesis that emigration was a selective process tapping the more energetic and resourceful, not the most depressed and impoverished, elements of the working classes. The raw materials for a deeper understanding of the cultural and social resources of the immigrants lie in the answers to two questions. Therefore, Who left? and Why did they go? are the first issues to be addressed.[1]

Recently several studies have pointed to strong correlations between rates of emigration and the nature of the social structure in a given area. John S. MacDonald, in his study of Italians in Australia, laid the groundwork for a reevaluation of the popular equation between poverty, malaria, and oppression, and emigration from Italy. He sought to demonstrate that Italians did not choose emigration "for strictly economic reasons" but as "an alternative to striving for socioeconomic change at home." He thus rejected the simple arguments of ecological causation which have been so popular in writing on Italian emigration. For example, he notes that while malaria has often been suggested as a cause for emigration, the disease was most prevalent in Apulia, the southern region with the least out-migration. Likewise, poverty was more or less equally widespread among working classes in areas of both high and low emigration, and thus cannot be a sufficient explanation.[2]

Josef Barton has expanded and refined MacDonald's analysis of the relationship between varying socioeconomic structures and emigration in southern Italy and has tested the analysis by reference to migration from eastern Europe as well. Rates of emigration were most closely associated with a complex of social and psychological factors resulting from the concentration or dispersion of the landholding patterns. In areas of mixed property distribution, with a large proportion of small landholders and with tenants participating through share-farming contracts in the capitalization and management of the enterprise, rates of emigration were high. In areas of highly concentrated landholding, large and rather discrete classes of landless laborers were at odds with the magnates and developed greater laboring-class solidarity. The poor in these areas resorted to militant defensive activities, such as strikes and political organization, and had low rates of transoceanic migration.

Barton's study of the Hungarian principality of Transylvania and the sixteen Slovak counties of northern Hungary reveals the same strong correlation as in southern Italy between heavy emigration and property distribution, mixed and generally backward agricultural systems, and a greater degree of equality than elsewhere in the distribution of income. In short, high rates of emigration prevailed in areas where small and subtle gradations of income, property holding, and status were the rule. Similarly, low rates of emigration were charactistic where concentrated landholding, capital-intensive agricultural operations, and a lopsided distribution of income provoked landless cultivators to adopt a more militant stance and to choose some associative means to deal with their plight.[3]

Although MacDonald suggests that a complex interaction between land tenure and culture prompted emigration, he does not push on to a full consideration of cultural factors. His analysis suggests two interpretations. Was the choice between emigration or labor solidarity and resistance a simple, rational one made by impoverished men whose involvement in differing socioeconomic systems made one or the other alternative unrealistic? Or did the choice result from a complex interplay of structure and cultural ethos which shaped different kinds of aspirations and, at a deeper and more permanent level, fundamentally different world views? MacDonald seems to favor the former and simpler formulation when he suggests a sequence of events in which economic problems in Sicily led to labor organization in the form of the *Fasci* movement, which provoked strong government suppression and finally resulted in mass emigration.[4]

MacDonald also tends to minimize the continuity between the economic activities of specific immigrant groups in Australia and their Italian backgrounds. For example, he found that the Lipari Islanders in Sydney were in "great preponderance . . . retailers and caterers, in general, and fruit and vegetable vendors, in particular." They were almost all petty entrepreneurs; skilled or unskilled laborers were few. Fruit shops, milk bars, florist shops, fish shops, wine saloons, mixed businesses, and market commission agents' stalls were the most popular types of business establishments among the islanders. He considered that these occupations represented a major change, since very few engaged in fishing, market gardening, quarrying, or seafaring, the four occupations most closely resembling the work they were engaged in before leaving Italy.

By thus searching for direct "transplanting" of specific skills, business services, crops, and market classifications, MacDonald ignores more likely transfers of skills and attitudes in the new occupations. Parallels between the Lipari Islanders' heavy concentration in petty wholesale and retail operations and their

earlier experiences as market gardeners and fishermen are obvious, however. The latter two occupations in Sicily often involved
both production and marketing functions, and required familiarity with an exchange economy. The movement by the immigrant wholly into the marketing of produce would appear to be
a logical adjustment in keeping up with the realities of life in an
urban environment. Moreover, the concentration in petty bourgeois activities is entirely consistent with an Old World culture
which MacDonald's own evidence suggests stressed individual
mobility, accumulation of property, and proprietorship.[5]

J oseph Lopreato has done a convincing study of the impact of
emigration on and social change in one village in southern Italy
after World War II. His work reveals the paradox that, although
the people at the bottom of the social order "displayed the
strongest desire to emigrate and talked incessantly of it, they did
not often do so." Like the upper strata of the village he studied,
who also did not emigrate, the poorest families seldom experienced the social and cultural change or the economic improvement which middle-range families derived from emigration. The
families of "old emigrants," those who left before World War
II, clustered in the middle and lower strata. Less than 6 percent
were from the very bottom stratum. Those who did go to America and then returned, enjoyed a pronounced upward movement
into the upper-middle stratum as a consequence of their previous
emigration. Lopreato concluded that "emigration, or the more
specific factors which flow from it, [has] moved most of these
families from what might be called an 'upper lower class' to an
'upper middle class.' " The point to be stressed here is that contemporary emigration, and that of the past which was still alive
in the memories of his informants, was not open as a viable
option to those in the lowest ranks, some 17 percent of the families in the village he studied.[6]

Close examination of records in the areas of high emigration
will help to identify those who left and to define a set of beliefs
and circumstances commonly associated with the choice to move.
Historical evidence about the status of persons on the eve of
their emigration is very hard to find. One cannot ask informants
to rank and categorize individuals or families as Lopreato did.

The best the historian can do is muster evidence on occupation, property holdings, and, occasionally, education. Yet, from this meager and often incomplete data it is clear that the emigrants were a heterogeneous group. The Sicilian passport clerk in Termini Imerese, who carefully recorded the occupations of outbound agriculturists as *pastori, contadini, giardinieri, agricoltori, rustichi,* and *braccianti,* was making distinctions that had great social and economic meaning in his community.

He served in a coastal town with a diversified economy that included sizable numbers of truck farmers, *giardinieri,* who were highly skilled in the technology of intensive agriculture and in merchandising their crops in nearby urban markets. Along with these small incipient entrepreneurs, the list of persons engaged in agriculture extends through various gradations of small landowners and tenant or sharecropping farmers to the rural day laborer with no stake in the product of his toil. Fishermen represented another important occupational grouping in the town, which also had its complement of artisans, town laborers, and small merchants. Each of these groups was represented in the emigration from the commune in the period between 1901 and 1914.

The *contadini,* a category including a variety of relationships to the land and its produce, represented the largest occupational classification, comprising about 36 percent of the passport applicants. The 5 percent figure for agricultural day laborers, or *braccianti,* is almost equaled by the truck farmers, who represented over 4 percent of the migration stream. In total, all varieties of agriculturalists combined made up only 46 percent of the male population emigrating from this commune. The second largest group, comprising over 18 percent of the whole, was a listing which usually indicated town laborers and industrial workers. Fishermen represented 12 percent of the total, while the skilled trades contributed over 17 percent. Large and small merchants and "gentlemen" accounted for an additional 6 percent. Thus, 54 percent of the adult male passport recipients were in nonagricultural occupations.[7]

Termini was typical of a greater part of coastal Sicily, the area of the island with the most complex population changes. One historian likened the Sicilian population movements to rivers rushing from the hinterland to the sea. The interior provinces steadily lost inhabitants to the zones of truck farming and intensive agriculture along the coast. The provinces bounding on the sea experienced, therefore, both a moderate overall growth in population and at the same time sustained the heaviest emigration rates. By the time emigration approached its peak of intensity, 73 percent of the Sicilians lived in communes of 10,000 or more and at elevations close to sea level. The social structures of nearly all of these towns were as complex as that of Termini. Each had its complement of mariners and fishermen. The latter either collectively owned boats or worked on a share basis with an individual owner. Long lists of individuals with certified weights or measures, preserved because such instruments were subject to an annual tax, offer graphic evidence of the number and variety of petty commerical establishments existing in these communes. The registration lists probably comprise only a minimum of the total number of weights and measures used in local commerce.[8]

Variety also characterized the agricultural contracts operative in these coastal districts. In the early 1870s, Sidney Sonnino, a careful and sympathetic student of peasant life, found the giardinieri to be very numerous and well-off. They were supplying a part of the capital for their enterprises and were sharing powers and obligations of proprietorship with the landowners. In Sicily's famous citrus district around Palermo, called the "cone of gold," the general strength of the giardinieri was such that the large landowners resorted to extralegal means to control them, the application of "mafia" violence. By the 1870s the area around the Gulf of Termini was noted for its advanced methods of manufacturing high-quality olive oil. Arboreal culture there was being expanded under long-term improvement contracts which gave the cultivator exclusive rights for fifteen or sixteen years to the production of the land in return for development of vineyards on it. In Valle di Castellbuono the olive groves were operated under a scheme where one or more cultivators owned the trees and the landowner could only take full control of his land if all the trees died.[9]

Peasant life in Sicily was not idyllic, to be sure. Pressures from large proprietors and their middlemen (the *gabellotti*), rising taxes, the increasing cost of services such as milling, and the disastrous agricultural depression brought on by Francesco Crispi's trade war with France, combined to oppress and impoverish all small agriculturalists. By the 1890s, as Sicilian socialist Giuseppe De Felice observed, the situation was so bad that "the little proprietors melt like the snow before the sun."[10]

Nevertheless, small status differences among the active cultivators were numerous and varied, and were primary factors in shaping their aspirations and decisions. Observers as distant in time as Sonnino and Lorenzoni testify to the persistence of the system of values which stressed individual advancement through varying levels of dependency toward the goal of proprietorship. This essentially conservative pattern of economic values was a cultural vexation to Sicilian socialists. While they were talking of collectivization and socialization of the land, the contadini thought of improving agricultural contracts and dividing large estates so as to gain small holdings for themselves.[11]

The activity of returned emigrants is further testimony to the hardiness of this pattern of aspiration. The repatriated "Americani" were often reported to be disruptive influences in the home communes, using their newly accumulated capital to become proprietors or to enlarge and secure their holdings. MacDonald's statistical analysis supports the view that emigration tended to reinforce the values that induced it in the first place. His strongest correlations are between pre–World War I emigration and postwar measures of average income, agricultural income, inequality, and political radicalism. This suggests that while emigration was a natural outgrowth of a world view, once established, it worked to reinforce and strengthen that system of beliefs and values. Lopreato's work demonstrates that the choice to emigrate broadened the social structure to make room for upwardly mobile individuals and made them more secure and resolute in their achievements. His "old Americani," those families whose members emigrated in the early twentieth century, clearly gained long-term benefits from their venture.[12]

Industrial organization in Sicily was extremely decentralized. The famous Sicilian carts, the staple transport vehicle for the

agriculture and wine industries in Trapani, were seldom constructed wholly in one shop. Rather, each tradesman remained
autonomous. Separate and independent master artisans did the
wood work, metal work, and decorative painting on a single cart
in their various shops. Their 150 workshops in Trapani averaged
only two workers per unit. Outside of one Palermo furniture
establishment employing forty-seven workers, most manufacturing resided in the hands of individual craftsmen, remaining traditional, unrationalized, and unmechanized. Although the
artisans, like the agriculturalists, suffered increasing economic
insecurity as railroad construction opened the island to competition from outside industrial goods, they were not stripped of
their trades or forced into an industrial proletariat.[13]

Termini and the other large communes that dot the coasts
of Sicily may have been somewhat unusual in the diversity of
their economic structure. Yet, while interior communes lacked
fishermen and often truck farmers as well, they frequently had
an important contingent of miners who added another dimension
to the occupational structure.

Serradifalco, a mining community in central Sicily, provides
an interesting contrast to Termini. Here sulfur miners comprised
56 percent of the adult male emigrants for the years 1904-14.
In 1904 they contributed 77 percent of the year's total. Skilled
artisans and other townsmen made up about 12 percent of the
totals during the same ten years, while those employed in agriculture constituted no more than 32 percent. The braccianti,
probably including both town and rural day laborers in this
particular list, made up 25 percent of the 32 percent identified
here as agriculturalists.[14]

In 1890 the mining region of Sicily encompassed forty-eight
communes and had a labor force of close to 28,000. The mines
were not technologically rationalized, heavily capitalized, nor
worked with a large wage-labor force, as was the case in the
Sardinian mines. The Sicilian sulfur mining operations remained
small and were largely dependent on human labor. The miners
steadfastly resisted attempts to alter the system of petty entre-
preneurship under which each miner hired his own labor force,
provided a portion of the capital in the form of his own mules

and tools, and received remuneration on the basis of his work unit's production. Despite brutal and unhealthy conditions, these *picconieri* tended to think of themselves as equivalent to master artisans. Agricultural laborers, at first contemptuous of the miners, soon came to recognize their status as being equivalent to that of small proprietors. As in agriculture, workers expressed their aspirations in terms of individual mobility rather than seeking advancement through measures requiring class solidarity.[15]

Even in a small, simple agricultural village, migration was a selective process. The emigrants from Villa Vallelonga in the province of L'Aquila to Rochester, New York, came from a distinctive group of families. A special portion of the contadini households provided the majority of migrants. These households tended to be larger than others and their heads were more likely to be literate and holders of an elective franchise. Larger size and high incidence of literacy and franchise holding also characterized the families of emigrants of the artisan class, a group that provided more than their proportional share of the emigrants. Significantly, among the well-to-do and middle-class families literacy and franchise holding disappear as discriminators and the proportion of families with emigrants drops. Reluctance by the ruling classes to allow the lower classes access to literacy and the franchise makes these sensitive measures of an individual's position in the society. The emigrants, then, came largely from the upper levels of the working classes in the town and from the middle range of the agriculturalists.[16]

How representative of the total Italian emigration was that from communes such as Termini, Serradifalco, and Villa Vallelonga? Nearly every source of evidence on the occupational composition of Italian emigrants, except for the United States immigration figures, presents them as a diverse group. Italian government statistics reveal that from 1878 to 1909 workers in agriculture, forestry, and related undertakings never reached half of the total male emigration but hovered in typical years between 30 percent and 40 percent. These figures are national, but it does not appear that they differ substantially from those for the South. In fact, the more fortunate and skilled ranks of

the working classes appear to have been more prominent in the
early years of migration from the South than they were during
the peak years before World War I. In rural areas reports of the
emigration of small proprietors or their children, intent on
bolstering or advancing family fortunes, were common. The
urban element in this emigration should not be overlooked. As
early as 1875 urban workers and artisans were reported to constitute approximately 20 percent of the movement out of Sicily.
For the last twenty years of the nineteenth century, the absolute
reduction in the size of the population of the capital city of
Potenza due to emigration was three times as great as that for
the whole region of Basilicata.[17]

A survey of U.S. consuls in 1886 yielded the unanimous
opinion that the poorest laborers and peasants were not migra-
ting. The consul at Catania reported that although agricultural
day laborers worked the hardest and longest for the lowest pay,
they migrated less than other workers. Inquiries about emigration had come to one consul from "gardeners, carpenters, bricklayers, blacksmiths, tailors, etc.," as well as from a couple of
bookkeepers. The consul at Palermo, while contemptuous of
all lower-class Sicilians, did admit that the emigrants were "the
more frugal, thrifty and energetic of the class." At Naples the
consul, after "careful investigations and calculations," concluded
that mechanics and artisans made up 21 percent of the emigration from his district. Professionals, businessmen, and "those
ready to take up anything except hard work" made up another
11 percent.[18]

As early as 1912 Francesco Coletti contended that emigrants
were, on the whole, better educated than those who stayed
home. My own comparison of birth and school records for the
commune of Valledolmo, Palermo, offers modest support for
Coletti's view. Of a total of sixty males born in the commune in
the year 1879, twenty-three had emigrated before they had
reached the age of twenty. From incomplete school records, it
is possible to identify thirteen members of this age-cohort who
advanced in their schooling as far as the third class, the highest
grade regularly offered in this commune. Of these thirteen
"well-schooled" individuals, six were among the emigrants. Thus,

at the least, 46 percent of those who went as far in school as
the local system permitted had emigrated, as compared with a
maximum of 38 percent emigration from the whole age group.[19]

In the commune of Laurenzana, Potenza, 44 percent of all
young men born in even years between 1884 and 1894 and listed
as literate in the military draft records were abroad at twenty
years of age. Only 9 percent of those classified as illiterate were
emigrants. The point to be stressed here is not that a majority
of these youthful emigrants were literate, though the figures do
show 78 percent literacy for those listed as being abroad compared with 46 percent literacy among their peers who remained
in the commune. There were sizable numbers of youths each
year who were not in the commune and for whom there was no
information recorded. It is possible that the group about which
the communal officials recorded information was not representative of those about whom the records are silent. Rather, the
significant observation is that nearly one-half of the youth
known to be literate, excluding the small middle class, had emigrated by such an early age.[20]

Emigration in the twentieth century remained, as Table 1.1
illustrates, overwhelmingly a working-class phenomenon. With
a few exceptions, priests for example, professionals found emigration a degrading experience. Opportunities to practice their
vocations were generally limited to Italian colonies in the new
lands, and even there success was not assured. As a result, both
private observers and official Italian government publications
discouraged the professional who might be considering emigration. Professionals never reached 1 percent of the emigration
stream during the peak years of the early twentieth century.

Yet, to say that the emigrants were workers or from the lower
strata of Italian society is not to say that they were a homogeneous group. They were not. Many did, however, occupy
positions which made an ideology of individual mobility attractive to them, and seem to have emigrated in the conviction that
they would either improve their chances of achieving their goals
or prevent their family's loss of such property and status as it
already held. Emigration constituted not so much a search for
an alternative to the old order as a logical extension of it. Thus,

Table 1.1
Occupations of Male Adult Passport Recipients per 100 Emigrants, 1909

Region	Occupation					
	Agriculturalists	Construction Workers	Excavation	Artisans and Manufacturing	Liberal Professions	Other and Unknown
Piedmont	34.37	14.86	22.65	18.30	1.17	8.65
Liguria	37.23	6.59	17.08	9.54	1.50	28.06
Lombardy	27.14	18.89	13.19	10.43	.37	5.98
Veneto	22.08	24.35	39.60	10.32	.16	3.49
Emilia	18.92	8.21	57.49	8.30	.29	6.79
Tuscany	19.97	9.88	55.02	8.97	.56	5.60
Marches	22.34	5.20	58.09	8.42	.15	5.80
Umbria	23.11	4.04	60.17	5.28	.09	7.31
Latium	58.98	2.00	31.33	2.30	1.38	4.01
Abruzzi and Molise	38.85	5.54	47.32	4.92	.19	3.18
Campania	51.04	7.69	22.23	10.74	.22	8.08
Apulia	35.46	14.63	28.35	11.68	.17	9.71
Basilicata	65.56	4.63	14.21	12.11	.18	3.26
Calabria	57.20	7.76	22.29	7.67	.14	4.94
Sicily	41.74	8.72	28.22	12.44	.21	8.67
Sardinia	30.61	7.45	33.91	20.26	.66	7.11
Kingdom	36.18	11.61	35.12	10.26	.37	6.46

Source: Bollettino dell'Emigrazione, no. 18 (1910), Table 7, pp. 20–21.

Note: These categories are based on functional similarities and tend to blur status factors. They include the following subcategories of workers:

1. Agriculturalists, shepherds, gardeners, foresters, and others engaged in rural employment.
2. Masons, hodcarriers, stone cutters, brick makers, and other workers in the construction industry.
3. *Terraiuoli*, unskilled workmen, day laborers, and others employed in excavation, construction of roads, and water works.
4. Workers employed in other industries (mineralogical, metallurgical, glass works, textiles, etc.) and artisans (carpenters, shoemakers, tailors, barbers, etc.).
5. Those who practiced a liberal profession (medical doctors, pharmacists, midwives, lawyers, engineers, teachers).
6. Those who practiced other professions and persons whose occupational status was unknown.

preindustrial men striving to keep from sliding into an undifferentiated proletarian mass, were thrust into industrial America. Two elements in the emigrant's society, associational activity and education, each considered in the following chapters, will further delineate this ideology.[21]

2

WORKERS' MUTUAL BENEFIT SOCIETIES
IN SOUTHERN ITALY

A large part of the literature on Italian immigration to the
United States presents immigrants as isolated individuals handicapped by an Old World social psychology which hindered
collective or cooperative behavior. Thus, lacking what William
Hoglund has called "associative spirit," the Italian newcomers
and their families faced the demanding task of learning to live in
the New World, separated from their non-Italian neighbors by
language and suspicion and, as a result of long cultural condi-
tioning, unable to unite with their fellow Italians in effective
assaults on common problems. Social scientist Edward Banfield
added to the currency of this interpretation when he introduced
the concept of "amoral familism" to explain poverty and back-
wardness of a southern Italian village in the mid 1950s. Amoral
familism in his analysis accounted for "the inability of the
villagers to act together for their common good or indeed for
any end transcending the immediate, material interests of the
nuclear family." A corollary of this position is that, since voluntary association was beyond the capacity of amoral familists,
any organizational activity in America must have been the product of changes fostered by the new environment. When viewed
from this perspective, Italian immigrants have also been represented as generally lacking a spirit of initiative and having
exceedingly limited perspectives on mobility and the role of
education in promoting it.[1]

However, one should be suspicious of the premise supporting
this interpretation, since Sidney Sonnino found a wide variety
of types of associations among Sicilian laborers in the early
1870s. He concluded that among "the Sicilian *contadini*, the

spirit of association" was "very much alive," but that they
lacked the educational resources necessary to take full advantage of their associations. Three decades later Francesco Nitti
discovered widespread organizational activity among the working classes of Basilicata and Calabria.* This chapter will focus
on the level of familiarity with voluntary organizations among
the agricultural and working classes of southern Italy and Sicily
in the period preceding the heavy emigration. Chapter 3 will
investigate the status of schooling in the South and the significance of illiteracy in assessing the character of the emigrants.[2]

Organizations of workers and agriculturalists began to appear
in southern Italy soon after Italian unification. I shall concentrate

---

*An initial comment on the use of *class* in this chapter is in order. E. P.
Thompson has observed that *working classes* "is a descriptive term which
evades as much as it defines." This vagueness inherent in the plural form is
an asset for my purposes. *Class* as a singular category carries a sense of
closure and commonality of values and ways of viewing the world which I
do not wish to impute at the beginning of my analysis. I shall eschew the
singular form *working class* in order to avoid the impression that the
individuals treated here are necessarily representative of all those who
might be included in such a rubric, or that they share a consensus on issues
other than those I will explore below. The persons included in this chapter
represent the same range of middle positions in the social structure of
southern Italian village society which supplied a major portion of the emigrants. They were the small producers, craftsmen, artisans, and agriculturists whose traditional statuses were most affected by modernization and
industrialization which rippled through their rural society. By self-ascription
they were the honest and respectable working classes who were distinguished from those above them by earning their livelihoods from their
own labors, and from those below, the day laborers, by their traditional
status derived from the possession of skills, or the ownership of land or
other agricultural resources. Class terms carry modern meanings which are
not appropriate for the society under consideration. Villages in southern
Italy were affected by changes taking place elsewhere, but even now, seven
decades after the great migrations to the United States, many villages and
towns have not experienced industrialization directly. Thus, the proletarian overtones of *working class* should not be applied to these segments of
the society. They certainly were not part of the capitalistic bourgeoisie,
a class present only in small numbers in the larger cities of the South.
Nor will *middle class* serve to identify these workers. That term is more
accurately assigned to the small contingent of clerks, bureaucrats, teachers,
clerics, and professionals in the villages.

here on a form of association usually referred to as "società
di mutuo soccorso," the mutual benefit society, which proliferated in the last quarter of the nineteenth century. A close
examination of such groups reveals much about the organizational context in which Italian workers struggled to overcome
their problems and fulfill their aspirations as well as the cultural
context in which they defined those aspirations and developed
strategies for achieving them. The evidence will help assess the
validity of my thesis that southern Italians, by the time heavy
emigration was taking place, possessed skills necessary to maintain voluntary associations and recognized the possibilities for
promoting individual goals through associative endeavors. The
central concern will be with attempts among the working classes
to solve shared problems through associational means, not the
ultimate success of these efforts. That the potency of the associations was limited is not surprising given the very limited
resources under their control and the magnitude of the forces
they faced. Indeed, had they been able to hold back unwanted
change, they would have greatly diminished the need for and
popularity of emigration in southern Italy. Finally, I shall
explore the degree to which the emigrants were able to carry
this type of institution with them. [3]

Workers' societies appeared in significant numbers in Sicily
as early as the 1860s. The first mutual benefit society in Trapani,
a city of 31,000 in western Sicily, was founded in 1863 under
the name "Società degli Onesti Operai," Society of the Honest
Workers.* Within a year it had 497 regular members and 49
honorary members, and by the end of its first decade the
membership had exceeded 700. The innovation spread through
the province, as workers in four other communes established
such societies by 1866. The pattern was much the same in the

*This movement began, as many have, in cities and larger towns and
then spread rapidly to smaller outlying communes. While there were important variations between southern provinces in the average size of communes,
very few had less than 1,000 inhabitants and most had over 2,000. The
evidence in this chapter is drawn from a representative selection of
different sized communes ranging from a village of 1,600 to provincial
cities.

province of Palermo, where at least nine societies date from the 1860s, including ones serving fruit vendors, agricultural workers, and master shoemakers. One without trade designation and bearing only the name "Abraham Lincoln" appeared in 1862. By 1870 there were societies in Matera, Genzano, Potenza, Lavello, and Avigliano.[4]

The mutual aid concept grew steadily in popularity, as may be judged by the number of organizations established during the next two decades. There were thirty-five such foundings in the province of Palermo in the 1870s and ninety-two more in the succeeding decade. The ten years ending in 1885 witnessed the most concentrated result, with 106 societies established in the province. In that year Sicily, which contained 10 percent of the Italian population, had nearly 9 percent of the nation's societies. After 1885, the launching of new societies fell off gradually until the early 1890s, when a new wave of organizational interest centered around the "Fasci dei Lavoratori." There was a modest revival of interest in mutual benefit societies after the suppression of the Fasci in the mid-1890s. New societies continued to appear well into the twentieth century, although one observer noted a decline in leagues of contadini, partially because of increased hostility on the part of the signori. As late as 1917 there were 259 active societies in the province of Messina. The pattern in other southern Italian provinces seems to have been essentially the same, except for the lack of the Fasci movement outside of Sicily. Taken as a whole, the southern provinces had 37 percent of the Kingdom's population and accounted for 30 percent of all workers' societies in 1885. The proportion of southern societies in the national total fell back in the next decade, as southern workers increasingly turned to emigration for help in solving their problems. Table 2.1 gives data on the founding dates of societies extant in 1895.[5]

Societies defined their membership eligibility in a variety of ways. The most typical form was a commune-wide organization which allowed persons of local or national note to hold honorary membership while restricting effective membership to the

Table 2.1
Founding Dates of "Società di Mutuo Soccorso." Existing as of 1 January 1895 – Southern Regions

| | Date Unknown | *Numbers Founded* | | | | | | | Societies Existing 1 January 1895 |
		1850-60	1861-70	1871-75	1876-80	1881-85	1886-90	1891-94	
Abruzzi and Molise	1		10	11	31	61	43	36	193
Campania	2	2	27	17	50	175	117	110	500
Apulia	1	3	10	11	30	61	49	45	210
Basilicata			4	3	9	27	13	22	78
Calabria			3	7	12	45	39	52	158
Sicily	2	1	40	32	47	108	58	62	350
Sardinia		3	5	11	2	13	13	21	68

Source: Ministero di Agricoltura, Industria e Commercio, Direzione Generale Della Statistica, *Elenco delle società di mutuo soccorso* (Rome, 1898). Adapted from Table 2, p. 203.

laboring classes. The latter group was usually designated as those who derived their livelihoods from their own labors. Master artisans were eligible as long as they worked alongside their journeymen. Such organizations had a strong entrepreneurial flavor that often led them to exclude agricultural workers, through custom or regulation. The result was that small villages often had two societies, one for the town workers and one for rural ones. In cities and larger towns specialization was more pronounced. Separate societies for the more populous trades were common when the numbers were sufficient to support such exclusiveness. In urban areas middle-class groups such as retail clerks and government employees formed their own societies, as did the small numbers of Protestants.[6]

Sociologist Jack C. Ross draws a distinction between the forms of voluntary associations prevalent in modern industrial societies and those characteristic of primitive ones. Citizens of modern states can select their organizational memberships from a variety of specialized groups, each with a narrow range of goals. Persons in primitive societies are far more likely to belong to a single multiple-purpose association with a plurality of goals. Where choices exist they will be between organizations similar in structure and purpose. If one accepts southern Italian society of the late nineteenth century as on the *Gemeinschaft* side of a *Gemeinschaft-Gesellschaft* continuum, the mutual aid societies conform to this typology. These societies attempted to provide a wide range of services for their memberships. Although the emphasis varied, most groups shared a broad common base of functions. Chief among these were health, life, and unemployment insurance; education for intellectual, moral, and social advancement of the membership and their families; support of the economic and trade interests of members; advancement of local communal interests; maintenance of social centers; and the initiation of producer and consumer cooperatives.[7]

Mutual insurance was a primary concern of the bulk of these voluntary associations. The provisions of the Workers' Society of Villarosa were typical. This society provided a daily subsidy in case of illness, to begin eight days after the onset of illness.

Services of the society's doctor and surgeon were available to ailing members. Other societies also had pharmacists to serve their members. These provisions were void if the malady was due to the abusive use of alcohol or the result of riotous or bad conduct on the part of the member. In case of death, the society as a unit would participate in the funeral and form an honor guard at the church and cemetery. The society would assume the costs of the funeral when a deceased member's family was unable to bear them. After twelve years of continuous membership, a member was entitled to a daily pension if he was unable to work as a result of old age or a disability not of his own making, and if he was adjudged by the society to be in financial

Table 2.2
Average Number of Members per Society
(For Societies Existing on 1 January 1895)

	As of 31 December 1885		As of 31 December 1894	
	Societies	Members per Society	Societies	Members per Society
Abruzzi and Molise	162	144	193	126
Campania	403	163	500	121
Apulia	245	154	210	129
Basilicata	99	133	78	116
Calabria	105	139	158	116
Sicily	433	100	350	115
Sardinia	38	117	68	104
Total for Kingdom	4,900	164	6,725	151

Source: Ministero di Agricoltura, Elenco delle Società, adapted from Table 3, p. 205.

need. Lastly, the society assumed responsibility for the care of minor orphans of deceased members, providing them with general education and the mastery of a trade, as well as overseeing their moral behavior and trade ethics.[8]

These societies never developed the sophisticated actuarial

machinery or the unified national character of the British
provident associations. They remained, like the English Friendly
associations, almost entirely local, face-to-face associations
concerned with the concrete needs of individuals. The provision
of certain kinds of aid only if the victim's family could not fulfill its traditional duties was common. A society at Avigliano
typified this case-by-case approach to assistance by providing
for a council that determined the amount and duration of any
assistance on the basis of individual need and the state of the
society's treasury.[9]

A second and hardly less important objective of these societies
was social and cultural advancement of both the individual
members and the working classes generally. The Villarosa group
announced that their principal aim was "the union and fellowship of all the working classes, in order to unite finally into a
single family, so that they can reciprocally succor each other
materially and morally. It is, also, the purpose to promote the
literacy and cultural education of every worker." A society at
Matera sought the "moral, material, economic and intellectual"
betterment of the working classes. Others were more ambitious
and sought the betterment of the whole human family. To
accomplish its educational goals, the Matera society established
an Educational Commission that had the responsibility of overseeing and assisting the evening schools, in which members
were to learn the duties of citizenship and the important skills
of reading, writing, and arithmetic.[10]

Literacy for members was a vital concern of most societies.
The Matera society's first constitution required the expulsion of
anyone under thirty years of age who, a year after first joining
the society, had not learned to read, write, and master the rudiments of arithmetic. The penalty was later replaced with a rather
substantial ten-lire fine for the same deficiency. Other societies
seem to have maintained the expulsion rule. One such group
expelled illiterates if they obstinately persisted in refusing to
attend evening school. A third stipulated that, starting three
years after the formation of the society, no new member would
be admitted who could not "read, write and keep accounts."
This same society required all illiterate members under thirty-six

Table 2.3
Societies Existing on 1 January 1895 (Classified According to Number of Members)

	100 or Fewer Members	101 to 200	201 to 300	301 to 400	Over 400	Unknown
Abruzzi and Molise	116 (60.1%)	47 (24.3%)	17 (8.8%)	8 (4.1%)	2 (1.0%)	3 (1.5%)
Campania	305 (61.0%)	114 (22.8%)	36 (7.2%)	16 (3.2%)	15 (3.0%)	14 (2.8%)
Apulia	135 (64.2%)	40 (19.0%)	15 (7.1%)	7 (3.3%)	9 (4.2%)	4 (1.9%)
Basilicata	46 (58.9%)	23 (29.4%)	4 (5.1%)	1 (1.2%)	2 (2.5%)	2 (2.5%)
Calabria	88 (55.6%)	47 (29.7%)	15 (9.4%)	2 (1.2%)	3 (1.8%)	3 (1.8%)
Sicily	215 (61.4%)	85 (24.2%)	24 (6.8%)	12 (3.4%)	5 (1.4%)	9 (2.5%)
Sardinia	50 (73.5%)	7 (10.2%)	8 (11.7%)	2 (2.9%)	1 (1.4%)	
Total Kingdom	3,649 (54.2%)	1,779 (26.4%)	620 (9.2%)	249 (3.7%)	290 (4.3%)	138 (2.0%)

Source: Ministero di Agricoltura, *Elenco delle società*, adapted from Table 4, p. 207.

to attend evening school. The latter obligation was prevalent as a minimum requirement of society members. In addition, a literacy requirement for holding office in the societies was common.[11]

The failure to school one's children brought universal condemnation by the societies and usually was ground for expulsion if the member persisted in neglecting this duty. The society at Lavello commanded its members to treat their children "as men and not as beasts." Fulfillment of this duty characteristically involved sending all children to the three years of elementary school required by the state or using an acceptable evening school as a substitute. There was occasional mention of further formal schooling, as in Vaggiano where members' children ages six through twelve were to be kept in school. The society at Migliano made it clear that "no excuse or motive of any kind could justify failure here." Another society made exception only if reasons of trade or livelihood made it necessary to move a great distance from a school. At Matera master craftsmen had the additional responsibility of promoting literacy and education among their apprentices and workers. Beyond this, parents had the charge of preparing sons for a useful trade and raising them as virtuous, hard-working, and patriotic citizens.[12]

In order to achieve their educational objectives, the societies made provision for the establishment of schools, especially evening and holiday schools for members and their families. Statutes often called for hiring a teacher to run the school if no qualified instructor could be found among the membership. Occasionally, acceptable public evening schools existed; in such cases the societies were content to remand their members to these. Children, especially orphans of members, were welcome at these society-sponsored schools. Some societies broadened their approach to the challenge of illiteracy. A society at Brindisi di Montagna required that "all members who can read and write have the obligation of instructing the illiterate members in the society's social rooms." The society was to provide the necessary supplies, including paper, books, pens, lamps, etc. Reading rooms, lecture halls, discussion groups, and libraries became increasingly popular with societies founded in the twentieth century. This may have reflected an improvement in public education and success in their earlier efforts to promote literacy, thus diminishing the need for societies to urge basic education on their membership.[13]

In place of the concern for literacy, the later societies often sought technical education to advance industry and agriculture. In 1908 a society of masons and carpenters proposed to establish a technical institute in Chiusa Sclafani for the advancement of their trades. A few years later an agricultural society in Girgenti (Agrigento) announced an ambitious plan for agricultural education and advancement of the farming arts, which included a school of practical and special agriculture, conferences, publications, a circulation library, and a traveling professorship in agriculture.

This interpretation of rising literacy is further supported by the example of societies with more "middle-class" memberships, such as Palermo's retail clerks, civil service workers, and local members of the Carabinieri (the national police). These societies did not display the degree of concern which laborers' groups manifested for establishing evening schools or for the encouragement of members to educate themselves and their children, probably because they had few members who were not already convinced that education was of great value and therefore needed moral support in maintaining their resolve. Rather, they concentrated on providing cultural resources, such as libraries and lectures, to an already literate and educationally alert membership, and on ensuring that orphans of members had sufficient financial support to complete their educations.[14]

It is difficult to determine the exact degree to which societies fulfilled these educational objectives. A Catholic circle in Lercara Friddi with 160 members was roundly critized by the local mayor eleven years after its founding for being mainly a meeting place for friends while failing in its avowed purposes of the "moral and social education of the village." However, the majority of evidence that remains cautions against the assumption that this circle represented the norm. Table 2.4 presents what is at best an understatement of the percentage of societies engaged in two types of educational activities. Societies in the South, excepting Sardinia, far exceeded the rest of the country in their efforts to provide schooling for members and their families. Scattered minutes for an agricultural society in Alcara Li Fusi indicate that the newly formed group soon turned to the question of education. It appropriated 150 lire to establish an evening school and approved a candidate to begin teaching on the first of October. For the next two years at least, it continued to hire a teacher, purchase lamps for the school and shoulder the additional expense of hiring quarters for the school in a more central location than the society rooms.[15]

Table 2.4
Education in Societies Existing on 1 January 1895

	Percentage of Societies Operating Evening or Holiday Schools for Members and their Families	Percentage of Societies Offering Subsidies for the Education of Members or their Children
Abruzzi and Molise	9.8 (15.2)[a]	9.3 (14.4)[a]
Campania	13.0	5.6
Apulia	11.4	3.3
Basilicata	10.2 (16.6)[a]	6.4 (10.4)[a]
Calabria	15.8 (22.1)[a]	10.7 (15.0)[a]
Sicily	11.4 (18.6)[a]	5.7 (9.3)[a]
Sardinia	4.4	4.4
Kingdom	6.9	6.2

Source: Ministero di Agricoltura, Elenco delle società, adapted from Table 5, p. 209.

[a]Percentage of societies with educational activities among those for which activities were reported. After working in the communal and provincial records from which this national survey was compiled, I am convinced that the smaller figures represent an underreporting of the total educational activities of the societies.

Several societies rewrote their statutes after a few years of operation. Despite major revisions in other areas, they invariably restated the educational and school provisions without substantial modifications. This suggests that these societies found the educational provisions in their first constitutions workable and still worthy goals to pursue. A workers' circle in Catania received a silver medal in a citation from the Italian king for its efforts toward popular education and its aid to deaf-mute children. The society accepted the award at a ceremony attended by a number of prominent citizens and presided over by the prefect and the director of schools for the province. When later societies moved from a concern for basic literacy to the advocacy of more advanced eduation and the provision of resources for higher levels of intellectual life, they signaled the achievement of their earlier goals. Clearly, some of the associations had been successful in transforming the educational pronouncements of their constitutions into action.[16]

A corollary to the educational concerns of the societies was their preoccupation with the good conduct, or *civiltà*, of their members. Without exception, they restricted their membership to persons of good character. The list of types excluded from the Vittorio Emanuele Society included:

> Those with bad reputations; vagabond workers who have abandoned their art or trade leaving their family in misery; those who cause public scandal with their public intoxication; those heads of families that don't see to the moral and intellectual education of their sons or others under their guardianship; those who without reason abandon or cheat on their true wife; those with maladies which make them incapable of earning a living; those who make their living from begging; those in bankruptcy who cannot satisfy their creditors, and those convicted of crimes of blood, theft, battery, fraud, falsehood, and outraging of decency.

This is a fairly complete list of the restrictions imposed on membership by these groups. Many societies ensured the maintenance of their standards through a committee whose job was to investigate the background of candidates.[17]

Once admitted, the societies expected a member to "behave in a sane, controlled and non-ostentatious manner," so as not ruin his "high reputation." The oath taken on admission to the

Giuseppe Mazzini Society in Miglionico required all new members to swear to live as "hard-working and honest citizens." Sobriety, patriotism, abstinence from gambling, friendship or brotherhood toward members, support of those who might come under unjust attack or criticism, honest and ethical behavior in the exercise of one's trade, a determined effort to carry out family obligations—essentially, a life of decorum and propriety—were expected of all members. Even less enlightened groups such as a society at Avigliano, though it did not prohibit physical conflict, did make sneak attacks and use of forbidden weapons causes of expulsion from the society.

The mechanism to enforce these codes of conduct usually included a committee or commission to investigate and report to the society on the misconduct of members. One society provided a three-stage process for dealing with obstinate wrong-doers: a private warning, a public reprimand, and finally, removal from the membership rolls. Another had three *censori* charged "to supervise the conduct of the members and through paternal or more extreme measures to try and correct those who stray and those who live public lives of reprobation and scandal to the embarrassment of the Society." In addition, the officers and leading members were expected to set exalted examples of civilization and virtue for all the membership. Finally, they fostered their goals by sponsoring patriotic celebrations and by adopting mottos such as One for All and All for One and Love your Neighbor as your Self.[18]

The goal of a true brotherhood of right-living members was, of course, always elusive. Alcara Li Fusi's agricultural society suspended a member for two months with an option to reinstatement if his behavior during the suspension warranted it. This action resulted from charges that the member was an embarrassment to himself and the society as a result of his addiction to wine and because of his quarrelsome nature when under its influence. On another occasion it was forced to take similar action against another member for his indecent and provocative insults to a fellow member. Even in societies of which wine merchants were prominent members, the abusive use of alcohol and gambling were strongly condemned.[19]

Although with few exceptions these societies exhibited little sophisticated familiarity with parliamentary procedures or rules of order, they gave evidence of considerable experience in conducting meetings. They recognized the need for rules governing the conduct of members in meetings that were more specific than broad admonitions to brotherly consideration and courteous behavior. Representative rules included "absolute prohibition of talking without the recognition of the president; interruption of a speaker by talking, making noises with one's mouth, leaving one's seat or by moving furniture; a limit of speaking to any one issue three times in one meeting; and a prohibition against fighting, assuming airs or showing contempt or ridicule toward any member." This last prohibition reflected a concern for brotherhood and equality which led one society to define its president as the "first among equals" in an attempt to eliminate sources of envy. Such rules for behavior at meetings indicate at least a rudimentary familiarity with the need for rules of order in conducting the society's business. This is an important step in the development of effective organizational skills.

In addition to their strongly moralistic aspects, the societies often tried to exert a conservative influence in business and economic affairs. Societies of artisans in urban areas sought to control quality standards, master-journeymen relationships, and competition in the trades. Members were admonished to be cautious in contracting debts and to be prompt in the payment of any obligations. They demanded full measure, both in quantity and quality, in all business dealings. The society at Stigliano was attempting to establish such an idealized set of relationships when it required that:

> The members who are of the class of workers must respect their foremen and master craftsmen while the members that are of these high classes must respect, love and protect the good and honest worker, and give them their examples of moderation, of patriotism, of *civiltà* and of virtue and be dedicated in the holy purpose of educating honest and industrious youth for the nation.[20]

Besides the technical education mentioned above, a number of societies sought other means to improve craftsmanship and advance the economic or business careers of their members. The society at Villarosa offered gold or silver medals to those who developed their trade or art to its highest state; to those who invented new, or improved already existing tools, machines, or techniques in their art or trade; and to those who performed courageous and heroic acts in times of public emergency. A society at Avigliano conducted an annual fair for the display of the work and products of the membership. Prizes were to be given on these occasions to workers who distinguished themselves in the exercise of their trades.

Loans and mortgages to members at low rates of interest, often 4 or 5 percent, were an additional way in which the societies sought to advance the business fortunes of their memberships. Among cultivators this was a defense against widespread usury in the lending of agricultural capital. A number of societies assumed the responsibility of finding jobs for unemployed members. The Avigliano group sought out employment opportunities for its members in other cities when the labor market in the home commune was saturated. Cooperatives provided still

Table 2.5
Economic Support of Members by Societies
Existing on 1 January 1895

	Percentage of Societies			
	Making Loans to Members	Instituting a Consumer Cooperative	Organizing a Producer's Cooperative	Providing Employment Placement for Unemployed Members
Abruzzi and Molise	34.7	2.0	1.5	6.7
Campania	25.2	1.0	1.6	16.4
Apulia	32.3	3.8	2.8	10.0
Basilicata	34.6	1.2		8.9
Calabria	30.3	29.4	8.9	29.4
Sicily	11.7	2.5	1.7	9.7
Sardinia	17.6	1.4	1.4	10.2
Total Kingdom	17.1	6.0	2.5	8.1

Source: Ministero di Agricoltura, Elenco delle società, adapted from Table 5, p. 209.

another element in the societies' repertoire. Consumer cooperatives were incorporated in the statutes of one society as early as 1874. In an earlier version of its constitution, the same society seems to have attempted to establish a producers' cooperative. Promotion of thrift through society-sponsored savings banks was also a popular feature of these worker organizations.[21]

Table 2.5 gives a minimal summary of the extent to which societies were engaged in making loans to members, establishing cooperatives, and finding work for unemployed members.

Finally, the societies actively entered into community questions which affected the general economic welfare. The Alcara Li Fusi society, for example, held a special meeting to protest strongly the abandonment of work on the construction of a road between Alcara and the nearest large town of Militello. They contended that the action severed the commune's ties with the civilized world, hindered commerce, made travel to the commune impossible during the winter months, as well as further aggravating a serious unemployment problem in the area. On another occasion the society supported an appeal for the establishment of a notary public in the commune to facilitate and advance legal and commercial life.[22]

Much evidence demonstrates that these societies were not created by the bourgeois, clerical, and propertied classes to divert workers' attention away from more radical programs of social reform. Voting and office-holding memberships were almost universally limited to "workers." Undisguised hostility against those "who make their living from the labor of others" was a persistent theme in the statutes. They bestowed honorary membership on prominent local and national politicians chiefly in order to receive their patronage. Associations often tried to secure the services of doctors, pharmacists, and schoolteachers at bargain rates by electing them honorary officers. The Italian government certainly did not treat the societies lightly. Provincial officials kept a chary and watchful eye on them, demanding annual reports on their activities from local officials and from the Carabinieri. Occasionally the activities of a society would cause concern that reached all the way to the ministerial level in Rome.[23]

Reactions of national leaders ranged from occasional hysteri-
cal excesses to disinterest. Francesco Crispi saw in Sicilian lower-
class organizations the beginnings of a social and political
revolution which had to be crushed completely. A minority of
prominent politicians shared his fears. An indifference, bred of
middle-class myopia which hid from most leaders the fact that
the working classes could act in important ways without leadership from the upper ranks of society, was the norm. Francesco
Nitti made much of the work of an energetic, socially conscious
priest in Calabria, who enjoyed some success in promoting
Catholic leagues among *contadini* after 1905. Nitti was especially impressed by the cooperatives organized by these confessional organizations, but he completely missed the significant
fact that ten years earlier Calabria had been the hotbed of the
nation for worker-initiated cooperatives.[24]

Local officials recognized the political potential of the
societies and reported on any efforts to gain electoral power.
Mayors seem to have been more threatened politically by soci-
etal activity than the local division of the national police. The
latter, not being natives of the locality in which they served,
may have had a broader perspective and less personal involvement in any changes in status or deferential relationships which
organizations might foster. Fears of the local *signori* were well
founded. A sizable number of societies fully recognized the
relationship between literacy and the franchise and sought to
qualify their members to vote. The agricultural society at Alcara
Li Fusi explained that it needed to operate an evening school
partially as a means of putting members on the voting lists.
The same society, once its members were enfranchised, sought
to consolidate its political power by forbidding membership in
any other society with different political views. It further required that, in administrative (local) elections, the society caucus
and instruct all members to vote as a block for the candidate
who received majority support within the society, an interesting
preface to interest-group politics in the United States.

The society in Stigliano was very interested in maintaining
status distinctions within the laboring classes. Yet its very existence so raised the anxiety of one well-placed opponent in the

commune that he wrote to the prefect to warn of the spread of the "principle of international socialism under the guise of a mutual benefit society." He thought the society a threat to the old order, in which "all the proprietors and cultivated gentlemen meet together as only one man with only one thought, dedicated only to the betterment of the town."[25]

The character and activities of Southern Italian mutual benefit societies generally are consistent with Robert Anderson's position in the debate among anthropologists concerning the place and purpose of voluntary associations in times of social change. Anderson views these groups as neutral elements that are not first causes of social change, though they may under certain circumstances sustain it. In other instances they can reinforce traditional ways. Italian societies certainly exemplify this. They had much in common with the Friendly Societies that appeared in England a half-century earlier. Both were rooted in the desire for protection from disabling illness and assured funeral provisions. While both prompted the suspicion of local authorities, they did not develop radical or revolutionary tendencies. Rather, they exuded a general moralistic tone in their self-help ideology, which stressed self-confidence, self-reliance, prudence, thrift, self-improvement, and fellowship. Both movements experienced similar organizational and administrative difficulties and developed similar solutions, as in the case of protecting their treasuries from the claims of intemperate members whose misfortunes were the product of their own follies. They seldom sought to promote profound structural changes but to secure and advance their members' places in the already existing society. While the societies often failed to reconcile their members' traditional statuses to the changing social and economic order, they did provide training in skills and the reinforcement of values and behavior which the emigrants would find useful in their sojourns in the New World.[26]

Lastly, the question remains: to what extent were the members of these societies representative of the masses of Italians who emigrated from their country during the period before World War 1? I have noted above the importance of occupational groups outside of agriculture in the emigrant population,

as well as the wide variety of agricultural types subsumed under
the rubric *contadini*. Certainly the mixtures of rural and urban
workers, of agriculturalists and artisans, varied greatly over time
and from region to region; but those not in agricultural occupations always constituted an important element of those leaving.
Thus, members of both artisan and agricultural societies might
be expected to be among the emigrants. The history of the
association movement suggests a close tie with emigration.
Organizational activity in the South peaked just prior to heavy
out-migration and then slowly fell behind that of the rest of
the kingdom as emigration surged into a mass movement.

A number of societies recognized the possibility of migration
on the part of their members and made provisions for such
eventualities. As early as 1870, a group in Potenza anticipated
that its members might have to migrate to find work and
planned its employment service with this in mind. A number of
organizations followed the example of one in Avigliano, which
allowed migrants to keep their memberships active. When a
"sister society" existed in the new locality, it would be asked to
act as agent for the home association. If none existed, the member remained eligible for insurance benefits, being required only
to have a doctor's certificate confirming the disability and the
member's own willingness to pay all postage costs. Many societies made provision for associate memberships for any members
of other societies who were temporarily immigrants to their
communes. The latter provision, of course, dealt solely with
internal migration, but they all testify to the mobile character
of the membership.

The records give some insight into the size of overseas emigration by members of the societies. The mayor of the commune
of Episcopia reported in 1889 that 38 percent of the membership of one local mutual benefit society was currently abroad.
The membership of a society in Celico dropped from 120 to 80
in a single year due to emigration. A truck farmer and president
of a league of contadini told a visitor to his commune that the
league had almost ceased to exist because so many of the members were in America. The story of artisans like the baker from
Celico who reported that he had been abroad twice, first to

Brazil without success and then to New York where he was able to save 2,000 lire in two years, was repeated over and over again. In 1919 fourteen Italians in Cleveland wrote home asking to be enrolled as members in the agricultural society at Alcara Li Fusi. Six were identified as *massai* (small landowners or farm stewards) and four as *contadini* or peasants. The remainder gave no trade or occupational identification. They indicated their familiarity with the operation of the organization by including in the letter of application, money for payment of dues and fees and a pledge to submit to the *Statuto* and legal orders of the president.[27]

A large landowner in the province of Potenza made a revealing statement concerning the nature of emigration from his commune when he reported that:

> The emigration has created in Lagonegro a little bourgeoisie called "Americana"; they come back from the United States or Argentina, having a little income of three to five lire per day and are content to live on this without working, the same as a pensioner, and with only the ambition of becoming a communal counselor or president of the local workers society. There are about 100 families of this sort.

This passage reveals the frustration of the upper class with changing status and economic patterns. It also suggests the direction of workers' aspirations when they had the financial means necessary to pursue them. The income the *padrone* referred to undoubtedly came from newly acquired landholdings or businesses established with savings built up while overseas. This financial independence freed the returnees from dependence on the sporadic employment offered by the old economic leaders. Equally revealing is the report from Sant' Eufemia d'Aspromonte in Reggio Calabria, where 33 percent of the 543 registered voters were in America in 1907. The voting lists represented the literate and propertied minority in a commune of 6,000 persons. Yet they emigrated in about the same proportions as did the population from the town as a whole. The same source suggests that emigration of from 10 to 30 percent of the

total population of a village was common throughout the
province.[28]

An Italian government survey of Italian societies outside
Italy in 1908 provides a rough measure of the persistence of the
associational tradition among emigrants abroad. It found a total
of 1,403 societies with 224,218 members. In the United States
there were 394 societies with 33,462 members; in Brazil, 277
with 15,890 members; and in Argentina 317 with 125,736
members. A report from 1905 suggests the range of activities
of the societies in Argentina. Two hundred and thirty assumed
funeral expenses for deceased members. One hundred and
twelve offered relief in times of illness and subsidies for chronic
disability. One hundred and four provided aid when a member
was unable to work. Forty-four maintained some form of producers' or consumers' cooperative, while forty-five supported
schools and forty-three kept libraries. The Italian emigrant
was obviously able to take his societies with him, though the
configuration of services varied with the needs of a new environment. For instance, the general availability of elementary
schooling, as well as of public and charity adult education,
freed Italian associations in the United States from responsibility for this form of instruction.[29]

Clearly, an important segment of Italian emigrants carried
with them on their migrations the concept of voluntary associations as a means of achieving mutually desired ends. They also
had experience in the initiation and operation of such organizations. The wide-ranging objectives of their societies suggest
that they also carried with them a complex of aspirations and
expectations that was in many ways similar to a configuration
of values and cultural expectations prevalent in the United
States. The combination of traditional, guildlike functions with
self-help and mutual advancement through education is remi-
niscent of Benjamin Franklin's Leather Apron Society, the
Knights of Labor under Terence Powderly, and the industrial
education programs for blacks as symbolized by Booker T.
Washington's Tuskegee Institute.[30]

3

SCHOOLING IN SOUTHERN ITALY

Students of Italian emigration have placed great emphasis on Italian literacy statistics, on the assumption that the high rates of illiteracy indicated a low level of preparedness for life in an advanced industrial society. They have also used the figures, often by implication, as indications of the Italian immigrant's interest in and willingness to support the education of his children. Illiteracy thus becomes a measure of the power of an inappropriate, even backward, culture to hold immigrants to irrational, self-defeating behavior, preventing them from making rational adjustments to their new environments.[1] Having found evidence to reject the popular notion that a highly individualistic culture gave emigrants from southern Italy no experience or understanding of the importance of voluntary association, I now wish to explore in some depth the relationship between illiteracy and schooling there, and the value the common people attached to education. If formal schooling was largely unavailable in the area, do illiteracy figures measure that value correctly? Or does the evidence documented above, that workers' societies showed widespread concern for establishing schools, offer a more reliable guide?

The fundamental organization of the Italian elementary school system grew out of the Casati Law, passed in 1859 by the parliament of Piedmont. Upon the unification of Italy it became the basic statute for the whole peninsula. The law placed elementary schooling under local administration and financing, just as a parallel statute delegated responsibility for all but main roads to the local communes. A result of this law was to leave large areas without effective transportation or

schools, for large landowners opposed both land taxes and popular education, leaving most communal authorities without
sufficient money or political motivation to provide adequate
schooling.[2] The elementary school system consisted of lower
and upper divisions, each segregated along sex lines wherever
numbers of students were sufficient. Attendance in the lower
course was mandatory for all children ages six through nine.
Age, and not successful completion of the course, defined the
point at which one could legally withdraw. Thus, in southern
communal records I often found individual children listed in the
first class for the whole required three years.

The school records leave one with a general impression of
large and widespread age-grade retardation. National figures for
the school year 1907-08 confirm this impression. Of the 3,002,168
children enrolled in public elementary schools, about 42 percent
were in the first *classe*. Only 50 percent of this class was promoted to the second class, which made up 28 percent of the
total student body. Students in the third class made up only 20
percent of the school population. Although 51 percent of the
third class passed the *compimento* (the *proscioglimento* before
1904), the first big examination in the Italian system, few of
these went on to the higher elementary level for which the test
qualified them. The fourth class represented only 6 percent of
the elementary population. Only .6 percent of all elementary
students enrolled in the sixth class. The high attrition rate
following the compulsory three years and the trend toward
failure to complete the full three-year inferior course stand out
vividly in Table 3.1.[3]

Elementary schooling expanded in the period between Italian
unification and the turn of the century; however, there was no
real improvement in several important indicators of quality in
education. About the only thing Sidney Sonnino could say
about education in Sicily in the mid-1870s was that it was
"utterly lacking" among the rural classes. In 1871 illiteracy was
calculated at 87 percent of the island's whole population, and
he thought it certainly was nearly 100 percent for the contadini
classes. Yet this was the decade of the greatest overall national
growth in schooling prior to the twentieth century. The eleven

Table 3.1
Italian Elementary School Students, 1907–1908

Classes	No. of Students	Percentage of Total Student Population	Percentage of Class Promoted
1st	1,260,317	42	50
2d	856,587	29	55
3d	607,317	20	51
4th	181,323	6	59
5th	77,875	3	68
6th	18,749	.6	70
Total	3,002,168		

Source: Ministero della Pubblica Istruzione Direzione Generale dell'Istruzione Primaria e Popolare, *L'istruzione primaria e popolare in Italia con speciale riguardo all'anno scolastico 1907–08* (Rome, 1910), 1:108.

Table 3.2
Elementary Schools, Students, and Teachers in Italy

Ratio of	1871–72	1882–83	1892–93	1901–02	1915
Schools to teachers	1/1.02	1/1.03	1/1.03	1/1.05	
Schools to students	1/46	1/44	1/46	1/48	
Teachers to students	1/45	1/43	1/45	1/45	1/49

Source: L'istruzione primaria e popolare, p. 106.

years from 1871-72 to 1882-83 witnessed a 26 percent increase
in schools, a 27 percent increase in teachers, and a 21 percent
increase in students. The increases in the next decade dropped
to under 18 percent for schools and teachers, although the
student body maintained the previous decade's growth rate. The
nine-year period 1892-93 to 1901-02 recorded a consistent
slowing of growth, with increases of 7 percent for schools, 10
percent for teachers, and 11 percent for students. Most importantly, there was practically no change in the critical student/
teacher ratio over the thirty-year period. Table 3.2 clearly
shows that Italy remained overwhelmingly a nation of one-
teacher schools. Before the twentieth century it was unable to
do much beyond maintaining the status quo in the ratio between
a growing student body and instructional facilities. The slight
gains made before the early 1880s were soon lost, as the rate of
increase in students remained higher than other growth during
the last years of the decade. In 1901-02 fully 25 percent of the
children aged six through 9 were not enrolled in either public
or private schools. At the same time, 35 percent of the total
enrollment in those grades was of children over the age of nine,
and some even over the age of twelve. Those statistics reflect in
part the lack of upper grades in many communes.[4]

Many of the same patterns were characteristic in private elementary schooling. In 1907-08 enrollment was overwhelmingly
concentrated in the inferior grades, with nearly 70 percent of
all classes being at that level. The student body was largely
female. Over three-quarters of the schools were exclusively for
girls. The school/teacher ratio was 1/1.7, each teacher generally
being responsible for two classes. The teacher/student ratio at
1/24 represented slightly less than half the teaching load found
in the public schools. Children in private schools by 1907 constituted less than 5 percent of the total elementary-school
population. This percentage was fairly constant throughout
Italy's sixteen compartments. Latium, dominated by Rome, was
predictably high, with 13 percent private-school students, while
Basilicata ranked lowest, with 1.4 percent of its students in such
non-public schools.[5]

A study by the Central Committee for Southern Italy suggested

that six factors were primarily responsible for poor school attendance in that region: emigration, *la miseria* (extreme poverty
and the resulting cultural deprivations), the negligence of communal school officials, insufficient and unhealthful school
buildings, ignorance of educational laws among communal
officials, and their persistent refusal to enforce the legal penalties
available for improving attendance. Other observers noted these
same general factors, though often giving differing opinions as
to their relative importance. Emigration, for example, produced
many disputes and will be discussed more extensively below.
Later scholarship gave more emphasis to *la miseria* than did contemporaries.[6]

The availability and quality of elementary schooling in
southern Italy are central factors in understanding the popular
response to them. By any popular measure schooling in the
region was miserable. The number of schools per one hundred
inhabitants in the nation in 1907 was 1.95. The figure for the
southern compartments ranged from a high of 1.70 for Abruzzi
and Molise to a low of 1.47 in Basilicata. The province of
Syracuse (Sicily) had the lowest ratio of 1.21. Only two southern
provinces, Sassari (Sardinia) and L'Aquila (Abruzzi), with 2.03
and 2.27 respectively, exceeded the national average. A calculation was made in the early twentieth century of the number
of additional schoolrooms needed in each provincial capital
to house adequately the children required to attend elementary
schools. Necessary increases ranged from 1 percent for Turin
to 210 percent for Cagliari, Sardinia, and an average for all
cities of 53 percent. The southern cities tended to be at least
50 percent over the national average, five of them needing at
least a 100 percent expansion in facilities to house those who
legally should have been in school. Moreover, the existing
schools were inferior to those in the North. Thirty-one percent
of all Italian schoolrooms were classified as "unfit." Among
southern compartments, Apulia had the most favorable figure
of 38 percent, while Abruzzi and Molise had the poorest record
in this category, with 58 percent described as "unfit." Seventy-
one percent of Sicilian and Calabrian elementary schools had
insufficient instructional materials. Apulia, with only 44 percent

of its schools deficient in didactic materials, came closest to the national average of 42 percent.[7]

In a study of schools in the province of Caserta, Professor Alessandro Lustig, a member of the Superior Council for Instruction, found that only 11 percent of the buildings had been constructed specifically as schools. The rest, containing 71 percent of the classrooms, were structures converted from other purposes, usually at the lowest possible cost. Twenty-seven percent of the schools were housed in rented quarters, many of which were not remodeled. He classified three-fourths of the sites as unsuitable for schools, one-fourth being located too near swamps, pigsties, or other unhealthy places. Eight percent had no latrines and 68 percent of the existing latrines did not meet the most basic hygienic standards. Dirt, dust, bad lighting, and poor ventilation characterized the 65 percent of the schools which the professor called "absolutely wretched." Ninety percent were simply "unclean," while 28 percent lacked water and 90 percent were furnished with desks of poor design or improper size. A similar though more limited study of thirty-three schools in Palermo revealed that 79 percent were in rented buildings, 52 percent had unhealthy or inadequate surroundings, 89 percent lacked latrines, and 56 percent had no water. The schoolrooms typically were small, dirty, unhygienic, poorly illuminated, and inadequately ventilated.[8]

Changes in the composition of the teaching profession compounded a chronic staffing problem in the South. Italian law and tradition called for male teachers in boys' elementary schools. Yet there was a steady decline in the number of men entering teacher-training institutions and a corresponding drop in the proportion teaching at the elementary level. By 1906, while normal schools for men still comprised 22 percent of the total, they enrolled only 8 percent of the students. The trend becomes clearer when one notes that in 1906 the percentage of female teachers was 70 percent, an increase of nearly 5 percent in six years. In 1914 there were only two male applicants for ninety-one positions in the province of Messina.

The reasons for this change are several. Salaries were notoriously low in the elementary schools, and communes generally evaded mandatory increments by not allowing teachers to remain in a position long enough to become eligible for tenure. Many communes were slow in paying even the low wages of their teachers. The problem was serious enough in Nicosia, Sicily, in 1909 to cause an editorial in the new communal newspaper to ask why the town could not meet its obligation to pay its teachers regularly at the end of each month. Some communes failed to pay their teachers at all. In 1905-06, 1,025 teachers from the southern provinces, representing 83 percent of the delinquent communes, appealed to the national government for emergency payments of back salary.[9]

Working conditions also contributed to the declining attractiveness of teaching. In 1885 a report on schooling in Palermo explained the difficulty of attracting young teachers to rural areas. Older teachers, comfortably established in urban areas with their seniority, would not consider the lower-paying positions in rural communes or remote *frazioni* (hamlets). The younger teachers feared that a rural assignment would become a permanent exile in what they considered a culturally barren, socially backward, and physically unattractive hinterland. They were generally reluctant to raise families in such an environment. The report offered few hopes or remedies beyond a supplementary state stipend to offset the financial inequities associated with rural positions. Twenty years later, in a period of oversupply of teachers, rural communes still faced serious recruiting problems. While one attractive commune with thirty openings had 450 applicants, 7.5 percent of the schools in L'Aquila and 6.5 percent in Catanzaro and Potenza had to be closed for lack of teachers.

A commission studying Calabria found that low income and the difficulties of finding adequate lodging had created the rural "teacher crisis," driving teachers away from remote communes. Improving economic conditions, the commission asserted, produced a cost-of-living increase which resulted in an effective decrease in teachers' salaries, since they remained stable while wages in private employment increased. In addition, increasing opportunities in public employment, especially the railroads, postal services, and telegraph and telephone services, drew young men away from elementary-school teaching. The commission, in its travels throughout Calabria, found many smaller communes "where the schools had not been in operation for more or less long periods of time due to lack of teachers." To remedy the situation they proposed four courses of action: instituting normal school scholarships that would require service in a given commune after graduation; construction of suitable housing for teachers in smaller communes; issuing teaching certificates valid only in smaller communes; and finally, establishing career ladders that would require teachers to begin their service in rural areas.[10]

The financing of elementary schooling in the South was a persistent problem. Only six of twenty-five southern provinces exceeded the national average of per capita expenditures for elementary education in 1899. Eighteen of the provinces were at least half a lira below the national average of 2.04, with the low for the kingdom being Girgente (Agrigento), which spent less than one lira per inhabitant. Almost a decade later, a study of thirty-three communes in western Aspromante showed their per capita outlay was 1.15 lire at a time when the national average had increased to 2.46 lire. Despite this comparative inadequacy, these communes were expending about one-third of their total budgets on elementary education, as compared with larger northern communes which supported their elementary and a portion of their secondary schooling with about one-fifth of their communal budgets. Even with this relatively high rate of spending by extremely poor communes, there was recurrent criticism of the local governments for putting circuses ahead of education.

A conference on illiteracy in Abruzzi hit hard at communes that spent large sums on bands and festivals while more basic needs were not being met. The conference cited one commune for spending 700 lire of its unassigned budget for music, while poor relief received 100 lire and financial scholarships to poor students were limited to 35 lire. Pacentro, a commune of 3,958 inhabitants, spend 4000 lire for bands, festivals, and fireworks, while the adult illiteracy problem went unchallenged. The distribution of national support to localities in the form of grants to aid in school construction gives further indication of the problems facing southern towns. The average grant for the ten-year period of 1889–98 to communes in the northern province of Liguria was 1,561 lire per 1,000 inhabitants, whereas in Calabria during the same period the average was 80 lire per 1,000. Over the longer period of 1879–1908, state support to communes averaged 1,810 lire per 1,000 inhabitants. None of the seven southern compartments came within 300 lire of matching this national average, and four of them received less than 750 lire over the thirty-year span.[11]

Numerous factors account for this under-financing of elementary education. Ignorance of opportunities for state support of school construction provides a partial explanation for the sharp inverse relationship between need and support from Rome. The general poverty of the communes also contributed to the problem by leaving them without the resources needed to meet local contributions required in order to receive state aid for construction projects. As was noted above, large numbers of schools were maintained in buildings rented from local proprietors. These individuals had two reasons for opposing the construction of communally owned school buildings: they would be burdened with further tax obligations and they would lose the income from their properties rented to the school authorities. At most they would support the commune that purchased their buildings rather than constructing new ones. In instances where a decision to build was made, competition over the site on the part of landowners, warring political factions, and geographical divisions of a commune could delay construction for long periods.[12]

A natural alliance of various types of property holders worked not only to hold down local taxes, and thus local spending, but also to shift the burden to others. A strongly regressive tax structure left large landed estates comparatively unburdened. Thus the amount of income available to the commune was considerably less than it might have been. The major sources of communal income were those which fell heaviest on the small proprietor and laborer. Peasants' mules and sheep were heavily taxed while the cattle of large landowners remained outside the tax structure. The grain taxes were equally regressive. The

commune of Campobello di Licata in Girgente (Agrigento) provides a particularly pernicious example of this practice of
shifting the tax burden. In response to the Sicilian unrest in
1893–94, the councilors created a rural guard of twenty-one
men to protect property interests, financing it by a per-unit
land tax on holdings up to six units. None of the councilors, of
course, had units so small as to be required to pay the tax.[13]

Hostility toward popular education also contributed to inadequate support. Large landowners, as Lorenzoni's well-known
study documents, had long believed that education was detrimental to their interests, and they often reacted to times of civil
unrest with demands for reduced educational opportunity.
Italian Commissioner of Emigration Aldolfo Rossi learned from
one southern mayor "that the local ruling classes have always
contended and still maintain that the knowledge of reading and
writing among the masses is a disaster." Calabrian communal
officials were even more explicit. One mayor reported that
"the illiterate contadini are docile, the truly dangerous individuals are the semi-literate who believe themselves to be something extraordinary because they can read and write." Another
mayor explained that in his commune the *proscioglimento* (the
exam given at the end of the third elementary class) was administered "with great precaution and with respect for all the
formalities" because the certificate issued to those successfully
completing the exam conferred the franchise. He explained
that the cost of buying votes in an election was already over
300 lire and so the commune proceeded very cautiously in increasing the size of the electorate. The Italian administrative
practice of making elementary-school teachers and the local
school superintendent subordinate to the mayor left the schools
helpless victims of an official whose political power base,
administrative expediencies of office, and frequently class
interests and personal inclinations opposed major advances in
popular education.[14]

Internal organization of the public elementary system limited
the influence these schools could exert in the South. The basic
curriculum was decreed by Rome and was standard throughout
the kingdom. By 1906 the elementary program called for in-

struction in the mother tongue, penmanship, arithmetic, history, geography, civics, nature study, drawing, singing, and gymnastics. Girls were required to study domestic science while boys could elect to study manual training or agriculture. There were repeated complaints that the southern schools, especially those in rural areas, did not offer all parts of this fairly comprehensive program, failing to live up even to the low Italian standards of quality. Inspectors neglected their supervisory duties, overlooking the inadequacies of wretched schools and ignoring teachers who were incompetent, negligent, or both. Large classes demoralized teachers and blunted their effectiveness. As late as 1906 the Lancaster system of mass education, using a small teaching staff for large numbers of students, was utilized in Piazza Armerina, Sicily. Instruction generally was characterized as mechanical and unimaginative, with few attempts being made to relate it to the students' life situations. English Italophile Norman Douglas condemned Italian pedagogues and legislators alike for being theorists. Douglas asserted that the former closed their eyes to the natural exuberance of young people and their need for physical activity. Most of the instruction was reduced to pure memorization. Teachers made no attempts to tie the study of history to political celebrations or historic sites. Special subjects such as nature study, singing, and drawing were often poorly taught or more often simply ignored, since the national curriculum provided no guidelines for what should be included in these subjects or for the length of time to be devoted to them. Manual training generally included paper cutting, pasteboard work, straw braiding and clay modeling. Despite attempts to promote it in normal schools, teachers were generally hostile to manual training.[15]

Opinions on parental responsibility for poor school attendance of children varied. An observer of elementary schooling in western Sicily in the early 1890s felt that only a few parents sent their children to schools out of "pure motives," namely a desire to educate them. His analysis of the schools in his own commune, however, undercut his statement. Arguing that the schools were not meeting the needs of the majority of the population, he said that only those with no need for the labor of

their children could afford to allow them to stay in schools
through the fifth class. Overcrowding, an average of eighty-eight
students in the first classes, made the schools ineffective and
tended to drive students out. The fact that the schools offered
no practical or applied subjects justified the contadini's indifference to extended schooling, according to the author. The schools
simply were not meeting the social, economic, moral, or patriotic needs of the commune. The solution, he felt, was to be
found in manual labor on the model of the *Slojd* and more
flexible scheduling for children who could attend only in the
latter part of the day. He ended his study with a plea for a transformation of the schools, making them a source of true preparation for real and patriotic life.[16]

A Florentine society formed to support popular education in
Calabria found that the problems of poor school attendance lay
not with parents but with the schools. A committee of the
society visited 175 of the 232 communes in the province. One
of their more important findings was that many contadini preferred to pay to have their children study under private teachers
rather than patronize the free public schools. The visitors in-
quired systematically as to why this was so and received responses
that reflected conditions in each locality. The most common
responses were: "because the public school doesn't exist; because the public school is at an inconvenient distance; because
during the harvest the parents prefer to send their children to
evening school, and the public evening school after 1904 was
reserved for adult illiterates only; because in the periods in
which there is no agricultural labor to be done, the private
masters take the children all day, not for just a few hours; because the private schools remain open in the months in which
the *contadini* do not have work, while the public schools have
vacation exactly when the *contadini* is disposed to go to school;
and because the teacher or teachers in the public schools do not
teach well."[17]

Inflexibility and inappropriateness of the public-school
calendar and opportunistic scheduling by private masters
created a situation in many communes where the contadini
"sent their children to the first classes in the communal school

obtaining free the first rudiments that are the most difficult,"
then withdrew them and sent them "to private evening schools."
The public evening school for adult illiterates at Gioiosa Jonica
rigidly adhered to state policy and opened one-half hour before
dark. The private evening schools, however, opened an hour or
two before sunset to accommodate the contadini who went to
the country in the evenings and returned to the city a little
after noon the following day. A private schoolmaster in the
Circondario di Gerace adjusted his calendar to the work-cycle of
his clients. He started in October and taught through March, the
period when most of the children of the contadini and artisans
were free. From April to September many contadini and small
proprietors left the town for the country. Every second year
there was a heavy labor demand for making olive oil. The private
evening classes were geared to this occurrence, and some instructors even moved out of the town to locations more convenient for those engaged in the harvest.

The public school in the village, however, rigidly adhered to
the calendar set by Rome and opened on the third of November.
It thus wasted a month and lost a significant portion of its
potential students. The committee felt that such rigidity was an
important stimulus to the proliferation of private schools.
Aldolfo Rossi found that public-school teachers might contribute directly to the unattractiveness of the public schools, as in
one commune where peasant women complained that teachers
neglected their public instruction in order to earn fees from
private lessons.[18]

The conviction on the part of the working classes that the
public-school offerings were irrelevant to their needs also provided opportunitites for private educators. Private girls' schools
were frequently cited as giving their children the advantage of
learning the tailoress's trade. At Gioiosa Jonica, a very intelligent female teacher observed that, "notwithstanding the requirements and obligations made on teachers to train the students in
modern feminine employment, the natural tendency of the
public school teachers is to cut a fine figure by teaching dainty
and delicate works such as lace and shirt embroidery. With these
works they obtain the praise of the *signori* [gentlemen] while

the children of the people go to private teachers to learn to cut
and sew the more common coarse clothing." In either case,
literacy for girls was a secondary concern. The committee viewed
the situation in Gioiosa Jonica as unusual, since "the domestic
arts in public schools of the minor communes are almost totally
unknown." The popular interest in vocational training in schools
was neither new nor particular to Calabria.[19]

We have already noted the widespread interest among workers' organizations in agricultural and trade education. In 1884 a
conference of workers at Palermo called for Italy, and especially
Sicily, to catch up with the rest of Europe in establishing industrial schools and museums of applied arts. The delegates asserted
that the education of workers and apprentices suffered from the
lack of such schools. Although schools existed at Catania,
Messina, and Trapani, only Catania's received government subsidy. "Museums of the arts and industry," the conference proclaimed, "are the universities of the sons of labor." By 1899 the
Giornale di Sicilia was praising and promoting government
attempts to introduce manual training into the elementary
schools. The newspaper warned that it was necessary to keep a
balance between the theoretical and the practical, but otherwise
exhibited unqualified faith in the moral and intellectual value of
the movement and stressed its liberating potential for the public
school and the general population.[20]

The same newspaper gave wide coverage to the rising interest
in agricultural education throughout the island. It reported
agricultural conferences being held from Catania to Trapani
that were aimed at preparing and encouraging elementary-school
teachers to introduce agricultural studies into their curricula.
These conferences were usually staffed by local health officials
and "traveling professors of horticulture." At one, sponsored by
a local mayor who was also a "doctor of agricultural science,"
the citizens of the commune turned out "en masse," demonstrating solidarity among public officials, elementary schoolmasters, and contadini from the countryside. At San Fratello,
the local boys' school received a grant of seven acres of land on
which elementary-school teachers were reported to be teaching
"practical agriculture with true enthusiasm." The children

showed great interest in their work and there was much competition and heated activity among them. The report stressed that "in the new education teaching has for its aim the love of agriculture and meets with the approval of the fathers of the families who willingly send their sons to get a boost in their economic and social position." The promotion of such practical programs in elementary education was in no way unique to the rural parts of Sicily. Workers' groups in Palermo, Messina, and Catania sponsored evening and Sunday classes in industrial drawing and applied arts. Similar endeavors took place throughout the South.[21]

In spite of the great inadequacies in schools, then, both rural and urban workers manifested much interest in elementary education. The popularity of private masters is one powerful piece of evidence that this was so; the promotion of vocational education by workers' societies was another. The Florentine committee was especially surprised by the desire on the part of the rural population of Calabria to solve its educational problems. A district superintendent of education there reported that 61 percent of the children ages six through twelve subject to the compulsory education law were enrolled—a figure, the committee noted, that was only 2 percent lower than in Florence. From talks with teachers, they calculated that about one-third of the students left during the year, which compared favorably with withdrawals of between 25 and 30 percent in Florence.

Though not official, the committee felt the data indicated that the desire of parents there to send their children to school and "the attractive force the school exerts on them" equalled that of the population of Tuscany. This seemed all the more impressive because in the South the attendance laws were haphazardly enforced. Many teachers testified that children enrolled voluntarily, without the need for parental compulsion. The physical effort which those from remote areas exerted in getting to school also impressed the committee. At Grotteria the children from an outlying settlement had to descend a steep hill, cross the Jonica River and climb another rugged hill to attend the communal school. The little contadini who traveled two-and-a-half kilometers to get to the schoolhouse in Gioiosa Jonica seemed to the committee to be expending energy every morning far greater than anything found in the cities. They found that such hikes by children from remote settlements were fairly common.[22]

Statistics from Castelvetrano in western Sicily gave rare insight into the composition of the elementary school for the year 1891–92.

Table 3.3
Fathers' Occupations of Students in
Elementary School, Castelvetrano, 1892

	First Class		Third Class	
Occupation of Father	Percentage of Total	Total Number	Percentage of Total	Total Number
Contadini	46	161	17	14
Artisans or shopkeepers	38	132	27	22
Clerks and professional	5	18	18	15
Possidenti (landlords)	11	40	38	31
Total	100	351	100	82
Poor children	58	202	23	19
Those of average financial condition	42	149	77	63
Total	100	351	100	82

Source: Giovanni Scaminaci Piccione Dei Frangipane, *Note ed osservazioni sulla scuola primaria di Castelvetrano* (Palermo, 1893), pp. 5–6.

Children of the classes which made up the majority of the emigrant population—contadini, artisans, and small merchants—constituted a large proportion of the lower grade. Whether one classifies it by trade or economic status, a portion of these children enjoyed both continued schooling and promotional success. The two were not necessarily closely correlated, as has been shown above. The first-to-third-class ratio was about half that of the national average of a decade later. This makes the fact that the higher class was made up of 44 percent of the children of workers and small merchants and 23 percent poor children even more significant.

Three years later, on the eve of the fasci uprisings, an incident in Piana dei Greci gave dramatic testimony to the place of the school in the southern Italian social order. The prefect at Palermo reported that subversive ideas had carried so far that the workers and contadini actually boycotted the communal schools by refusing to send their children there for a number of days. Their choice of the schools as a target for the expression of their hostilities toward the bourgeoisie and the government suggests that, although many working families sent their children to school, they recognized what other observers had asserted—namely, that the schools as then constituted best served the interests of the middle classes by supporting the status quo. The same commune, a few years later, had a thriving private school conducted by socialist Luigi Mamola, giving further evidence for the contention that the lower classes recognized both the potentials of schooling and the inadequacies of the contemporary public schools.[23]

I have been unable to find any scholarly work that investigates the complex interplay between schools and social change in southern Italy as Roger Thabault did for the French village of Mazierse. He argues that the school had an indispensible part in preparing, first the artisans and then the peasants, for new roles in an emerging exchange economy. It taught the use of symbols in communication and storage of knowledge. With this they were able to liberate themselves from the concrete, present-oriented world of the closed community and develop a new abstract conception of themselves as men. Thabault's impressive work should caution us against any easy dismissal of either the impact of schools on the working classes or of their recognition of the importance of schools to their future in a changing society.[24]

Certain elements in the upper classes showed much concern for the advancement of schooling and literacy among the working classes. The interest in curriculum reform and vocational training which arose around 1890 and movements such as the

Florentine society to promote popular education illustrate this. In 1910 the *Associazione Nazionale per gli Interessi del Mezzogiorno* (National Association to Promote the Interests of the South) was founded with the goal of applying educational remedies to southern problems. It centered its efforts on the establishment of nursery schools in poor and remote villages and on providing instruction for adult illiterates who, with the society, recognized their illiteracy as a serious handicap. A number of library and cultural societies in the South sought to elevate popular culture. The library association founded at Palermo in 1909 attempted to reach out to the classes of workers and agriculturists and to fight illiteracy and ignorance through the use of "the universal means of communication of human thought, the good book."

This group of middle-class men, lawyers, doctors, university professors, and newspaper editors carried out a two-phase program. In a matter of a year they established thirty-five scholastic libraries, most of which were small collections placed in individual schoolrooms. They also set up three larger collections, under the care of directors, which served broader school populations. Their plan envisioned that these collections would provide access to the family through the children. Popular libraries could be established for adults once working-class families were penetrated in this indirect way. The association looked forward to establishing libraries stocked with technical books in factories and other locations convenient to the laborers' work, as well as in prisons and on military bases. They received books from the Dante Alighieri Society and support from a number of charitable institutions and government agencies.[25]

A similar group in Castelvetrano mounted a more comprehensive program to upgrade the education level of their commune, in the hope of reducing the incidence of adult delinquency and protecting the opportunity for the lower classes to emigrate successfully if they needed to do so. The group drew up a list of the children required to be in school but who were not enrolled, a duty assigned by Italian law to the mayor. That a private group had to do this gives further testimony to the laxity in enforcement of school laws. They also sought to aid poor but

worthy students so they could stay in school and to provide a
school for adult illiterates, "a special need of the community
that doesn't need to be demonstrated." Further, they sought to
realize the long-discussed reestablishment of the communal
library. The library had a long and tortured history. It had existed in some form intermittently since 1845, usually housed in
a church and controlled by religious or private groups. The reformers sought to make it truly public and centrally available,
assuming that it would be a powerful force for general cultural
advancement. Establishment of a socially conscious semimonthly
newspaper also contributed to revitalization of the commune.[26]

Religious support for popular education appeared sporadically
throughout the South during the period before World War I in
spite of deep hostilities between state and church. Catholic
circles and organizations often urged general educational advancement upon their members, in addition to fostering spiritual
growth. A circle in the province of Palermo sought to protect
its membership's opportunity to send their children to the
public schools by maintaining close watch over the schools and
teachers "like leopards of the families," to insure that instruction
was given and that respect for religion and morals was maintained. In cases of dereliction, they were to make legal complaints
to the scholastic commission, the city administration, or higher
educational officials. Occasionally clergymen strongly supported
schooling. A bishop of Piazza Armerina, in his first pastoral
letter, expressed concern for the education of the poor and
their children and admonished teachers "to keep in mind the
noble treasure of youth they have under their charge." More
often, however, the clergy seems to have been chary of the
state schools.[27]

Emigration itself heightened the lower-class interest in schooling and produced educational initiatives by both governmental
and private organizations. A forty-eight year-old truck farmer
and president of a league of contadini in Catanzaro told Aldolfo
Rossi that its members were all in America, where they were
learning the importance of the league and of its role through
the local chamber of labor in operating schools. School inspectors such as Enrico Muzi commented on the increased desire for

schooling in areas of high emigration. Muzi found the sense of
the need to read and write very strong among the common
people. He reported, after living among them for some time in
Abruzzi, that the letters coming back to Italy from emigrants
in America contained sentences like "Send! send the children,
the brothers, the sisters, to school, make whatever sacrifice required to send them there." In response to these directions he
saw "bands of little contadini with coarse pouches over their
shoulders moving toward the school from the most horrid rural
hovels . . . and the delight of the old illiterates in listening to
their little grandchildren read."

Muzi's observations were confirmed by "all his eminent
colleagues," who responded to a questionnaire circulated by the
promotors of a conference on education in Abruzzi. These
school officials agreed that emigration was pushing many more
children into the schools. Camillo Carradini, Director-General for
Primary and Popular Education, saw the same impetus coming
from emigrants who broadened their perceptions by "contact
with more advanced forms of life of other peoples of Europe or
across the ocean." However, emigration also worked at cross-
purposes with this increased desire for education, by creating
labor shortages and increasing the need for the children's labor
in the fields at certain times of year. He suggested that provincial councils be given latitude to adjust the school year, especially
in the spring and in areas where labor demands were heavy.[28]

Salvemini found the same phenomenon in Calabria. Illiterate
emigrants and their families found themselves reliant on others
to communicate the simplest news or the most personal and
intimate messages. Honest and discreet intermediaries were not
always available on either side of the Atlantic, and so the emigrant soon felt "the acute pain and shame of illiteracy" and
enjoined "his wife to send the children to school." When he repatriated himself, he also went to night school and did not
"find any sacrifice necessary to educate himself too great."
Emigrants themselves testified to this intensified educational
sentiment. Antonio Mangano found an increased sense of the
importance of literacy among returned emigrants, who drove
themselves and their families to learn. He visited one village in

which 13 percent of the population was attending evening school.[29]

Recurrent proposals in the United States to restrict the immigration of illiterates sent the Italian government and private agencies into a flurry of activity designed to improve preparation of the Italian lower classes for migration. Starting in 1903, a series of campaigns attempted to upgrade and expand adult education through evening and holiday schools. The first such endeavor received support from both the Emigration Commission and the Ministry of Public Instruction. This joint effort accounted for the opening of more than 3,000 schools for adult illiterates in 1904–05 and numerous training programs to prepare teachers for these schools. Expansion of the effort was temporarily curtailed by a dispute over which agency would have the major responsibility for supporting schools and by diminution of the immediate threat to restrict immigration of illiterates. Nonetheless, many of the schools continued to operate and showed excellent results, which Table 3.4 illustrates.

Table 3.4
Adult Evening and Holiday Schools, 1912–1913

Area of Italy	Number Attending	Number Taking Exam	Number Passing Exam
North	13,255 (9%)	9,813 (74%)	7,980 (60%) (81%)
Central	14,344 (10%)	11,293 (79%)	9,203 (64%) (81%)
South	118,936 (81%)	96,210 (81%)	77,013 (65%) (80%)
Totals	146,535	117,316 (80%)	94,013 (64%)

Source: "Il commissariato generale dell'emigrazione e la lotta contro l'analfabetismo degli emigranti," *Bollettino dell'Emigrazione,* no. 6 (1919), pp. 11–13.

Southerners were the main ones to benefit from these schools. Measured either in terms of persistence in classes or in percentage of successful completions, their performance surpassed that of the rest of the kingdom.[30]

More sweeping proposals for the preparation of potential emigrants appeared from time to time, as many Italians felt shame and discomfort about the low reputation of their country created by illiterate emigrants abroad. One approach, tried on an experimental basis in Abruzzi by the Humanitarian Society of Milan, centered around a brief course aimed at providing basic skills necessary for economic success abroad. The instruction offered a precise knowledge of the immigrants' rights in the countries they were going to; some knowledge of the geography, economy, and potential dangers or pitfalls in those countries; and 200- to 300-word vocabularies in the most appropriate foreign language. The most important duty of this school was to develop a sense of human dignity and of "Italianness," so that the immigrant could "demonstrate the former and conserve the latter." The plan was beyond the resources of the country to implement on a grand scale. After World War I, when the Italian government finally moved into the field with special programs for prospective emigrants, they ignored this rather comprehensive model and concentrated on teaching agricultural skills. As a result, their efforts were of limited benefit to emigrants destined for urban industrial areas.[31]

Finally, military service played a significant part in the southern educational awakening. Many observers noted the tendency for young men to have their horizons broadened and their expectations heightened by service. The process undermined local dialects and the kind of lococentrism which led to suspicion of the motives of people in the next commune. More important here is the clear success of the military in increasing literacy among its personnel. An average literacy rate of 62 percent among those who entered service, and about 73 percent among those released between 1896 and 1903, represented roughly an 11-percentage-point increase in literacy while in service. This advance was the product of vigorous programs which required illiterate soldiers to attend classes in addition to their other duties.

A closer examination of the figures reveals important internal trends. Conscripts entered service at age twenty. An individual's length of service varied from one to three years, depending upon his family obligations. More than 13 percentage points separated the group with one and three years service who were released in the year July 1904–July 1905. The longer term of service produced a full 80 percent literacy. This difference is the result of two factors. First, those with fewer family obligations who were required to do longer service included a larger number of members who were literate when they entered. Secondly, longer service provided the men with greater exposure to the military literacy classes. This story is significant for emigration because migrants tended to be among those lower classes with fewer immediate and pressing obligations at home. It is just this group which was able to take advantage of schooling opportunities and literacy instruction in the army.[32]

By way of summary, Tables 3.5 and 3.6 present correlations between several measures of the quality and quantity of Italian schooling and illiteracy at the turn of the century. The strong relationship found between these measures and illiteracy supports the contention that where schools were inadequate illiteracy was the result. Conversely, in progressive communes which supported elementary education through efficient administration, adequate buildings, and scholarship aid, popular interest in schooling produced higher literacy rates. Evidence presented above suggests that illiterates and the lower classes generally had little or no influence in the decisions which determined the kind and extent of public schooling opportunities available to their children. Table 3.6 gives some indication of the negligence among local officials in enforcing school laws.

Faced with this situation, the lower classes often turned to private and associational means to remedy the deficiencies. I argued earlier that these activities indicate the persistence of popular interest in the face of the wretched state of public schooling. Table 2.4 shows that workers' societies in the South were more interested in the maintenance of private schools than such societies throughout the country as a whole. The nearly negligible relationship between the availability of secondary schools and illiteracy is consistent with the general interpretation presented here. The responsibility for establishing and maintaining secondary schools lay with the state. These schools,

Table 3.5
Relationships between Quality and Quantity of Schooling
and Illiteracy by Province
(Pearson Product Moment Correlation Coefficient)

	Illiteracy (1901)
Expenditure in 1899 on elementary and popular education (lire per inhabitant in 1901)	–.76
Percentage of elementary schools with insufficient fittings, 1906–07	.51
Percentage of elementary schools with insufficient instructional materials, 1906–07	.63
Percentage increase needed in capital city of province to house all children required by law to attend school, 1906–07	.50
Number of elementary schools (1908) per 1,000 population (1901)	–.74
Number of secondary schools (1906–07) per 100,000 population (1901)	–.12

Source: Ministero della Pubblica Istruzione, *L'istruzione primaria e popolare in Italia*, vol. 1, pp. 779–81, 522–27, vol. 2, 12–19, 567–69, 655–56.

removed from the hands of local interest groups, were more uniformly distributed throughout the country.

Secondary education reached only a small portion of southern Italian families in the period before World War I. Nevertheless, a number of emigrants had personal experience at this level of schooling, or had a relative who went beyond elementary education. Individual immigrant life histories often include references to a brother, uncle, or cousin, who used education to move into a clerical position in the expanding state bureaucracy, or even into a profession. Thus it is appropriate to take a brief look at this level of schooling in Italy.

Italian secondary-school education contained the two broad subdivisions of classical and technical studies, as well as an independent and lower-order program for training elementary schoolteachers. The classical program began in the *gymnasium*

Table 3.6
Relationships between Quality and Quantity of Schooling
and Illiteracy for 30 Southern Provinces
(Pearson Product Moment Correlation Coefficient)

	Mean	Standard Deviation	Correlation with Illiteracy (1901)
Percentage of communes not completing lists of children required to be in school	27.0	18.9	.362
Percentage of communes not comparing the lists of children required to attend school against actual attendance roles	76.6	16.9	.441
Percentage of communes giving instruction to illiterates	11.2	11.3	-.226
Average percentage of agreement (by communes) between the obligation to attend school and actual attendance	53.1	8.7	-.567
Percentage of communes totally owning their schools	35.0	19.1	-.337
Percentage of communes renting a part of their school buildings	27.4	14.6	-.008
Percentage of communes in which all school buildings were rented from private owners	37.7	20.3	.327
Percentage of communes whose schools' physical conditions were rated wretched	85.6	9.4	.301
Percentage of rooms lacking in the province to meet legal attendance obligations	39.3	16.1	.462
Percentage of communes where kindergarten or infant schools existed	21.4	14.9	-.491
Percentage of communes lacking evening schools	30.9	21.5	-.107
Percentage of communes with no available scholarship funds	50.9	25.9	.455
Percentage of illiteracy	68.3	8.1	1.000

Source: Ministero della Pubblica Istruzione, *L'istruzione primaria e popolare in Italia,* 2:432–41, 461–1950.

with a five-year course of study. It accepted students at age
eight or nine, most of whom entered after study in private
schools or with private tutors. Only rarely did students from
public elementary schools enter the gymnasium. The course of
study consisted of Latin, Greek, French, Italian language and
literature, mathematics, and a very little drawing and natural
history. Graduates were eligible for minor posts in civil service
and for admission to the three-year course of the *lycèe* which
continued the classical studies in preparation for the university.[33]

Technical studies had a parallel set of institutions. On the
lower level, for children ages ten to fourteen, the technical
school offered a three-year course of Italian language and literature, French, geography, arithmetic and geometry, elements of
science, drawing, and bookkeeping. Graduates were eligible to
apply to the technical institutes which offered specialized subjects such as surveying, agriculture, and commerce, as well as
general instruction in such subjects as math, physics, and drawing. These institutes served as feeders for the science programs
in the universities. Normal schools offered two- and three-year
programs. The latter prepared one to teach at either elementary-
school level, while the shorter course restricted graduates to
teaching in the lower three grades. Male students could enter
the normal schools at sixteen, females at fifteen. This meant
that a gap of two to six years existed between completion of
elementary school and entrance to normal school. This time
could be spent in temporary enrollment in a gymnasium but
usually represented a hiatus in schooling.[34]

The limited availability of secondary schools in the South
presented a serious handicap to poor but ambitious students.
In 1906 there existed nationally less than one boys' normal
school for every two provinces, and 1.7 girls' normal schools
per province. The per-province averages were 4-gymnasia, 2.3
lycèe, 3.8 technical schools, and barely more than one technical institute. Even though the South was more equitably supplied
with secondary schools than elementary ones, such schools
were few and far between. The situation in centers of emigration
such as Melfi, Termini Imerese, and Caltanissetta was representative. In 1892 the communal council of Melfi, a town of

Students Enrolled in Secondary Level Schools, 1911–1912

Region	Students/100,000 Population in Classical Schools (Ginnasi e Licei)			Students/100,000 Population in Technical Schools (Scuole Tecniche, Istituti Tecnici e Nautici)			Students/100,000 Population in Normal Schools		
	Male	Female	Total	Male	Female	Total	Male	Female	Total
Piedmont	157.3	18.3	175.6	295.7	112.6	408.3	6.9	130.3	137.2
Liguria	193.9	18.2	212.1	470.9	122.6	593.5	7.3	146.1	153.4
Lombardy	101.0	14.5	115.5	264.7	108.6	373.5	5.4	117.4	122.8
Veneto	117.3	8.6	125.9	199.9	46.5	246.4	5.5	121.4	126.9
Emilia	120.0	18.0	138.0	280.5	121.4	401.9	2.1	128.7	130.8
Tuscany	142.3	15.7	158.0	248.7	46.7	295.4	4.9	146.6	151.5
Marches	163.6	34.0	197.6	279.0	119.8	398.8	19.3	124.1	143.4
Umbria	108.5	18.4	126.9	307.2	92.0	399.2	19.0	114.5	133.5
Latium	356.4	46.1	402.5	440.8	116.6	557.4	9.8	185.5	195.3
Abruzzi and Molise	113.6	11.4	125.0	124.4	20.6	145.0	8.5	73.8	82.3
Campania	272.2	15.2	287.4	291.2	20.8	312.0	16.6	126.4	143.0
Apulia	171.2	17.1	188.3	257.6	62.3	319.9	14.9	81.9	96.8
Basilicata	104.1	11.0	115.1	122.3	8.6	130.9	22.6	77.7	100.8
Calabria	208.5	13.8	222.3	128.8	4.6	133.6	15.1	73.2	88.3
Sicily	208.2	29.5	237.7	291.4	64.8	356.2	24.6	108.9	133.5
Sardinia	183.2	27.2	210.4	184.0	49.5	233.5	10.0	125.8	135.8
Italy	166.8	18.5	185.3	265.9	73.1	339.0	10.7	119.8	130.5

Source: Ministero di Agricoltura, Industria e Commercio, Direzione Generale della statistica e del Lavoro, *Notizie sommarie sugli istituti per l'istruzione media e normale negli anni scolastici dal 1909–10 al 1911–12* (Rome, 1916), pp. 17, 19, 21.

14,000, voted unanimously to establish a technical school and to assume partial responsibility for its financial support by raising a school tax. The remainder of the financing came from state funds and tuition. Twenty years later, technical studies remained the only secondary education available to children in the commune. Termini Imerese, population 20,000, petitioned unsuccessfully for a *lyceum* in 1901. At the beginning of World War I, students who wished to study at the advanced secondary level still had to make the 30-kilometer trip to Palermo.[35]

The city of Caltanissetta (population ca. 35,000) was the only center in a *circondario* of fifteen communes and 181,242 inhabitants to have any classical schooling in 1891. In addition, since 1862, the city had been the seat of the Royal School of Mining, which prepared the sons of miners for supervisory and engineering positions in the local mines. As late as 1912 there were only two lyceums, four gymnasia, three technical schools, one technical, institute, and one female normal school in the province. The province was well off by southern standards. Eight others had only one lyceum and generally poorer overall provisions for other secondary facilities. Yet, as Table 3.7 illustrates, response to secondary education in several southern regions was well above the national averages. The comparatively high male enrollment in normal schools throughout the South suggests a special educational adjustment in a situation of high mobility aspirations and relatively low availability of white-collar jobs. Men continued to seek positions in this low-paying field, which in more prosperous areas of the country was turned over largely to women.[36]

Literacy, then, was closely associated with the quality and quantity of schooling available in southern Italy. The lower social classes had little control over the provision of public schooling. They took advantage of it where it existed. Illiteracy resulted where it was lacking or was offered only under extremely inconvenient circumstances. Clearly, the prevalence of illiteracy among emigrants is not a good criterion of their attitudes toward education, nor is it an indication of the inappropriateness of their traditional culture for their futures as urbanites. Such evidence is better viewed as a measure of past opportunity than as a prediction of future response to schooling.

4

EPILOGUE AND PROLOGUE:
THE MEANING OF THE OLD WORLD BACKGROUNDS
OF IMMIGRANTS FOR AMERICA

Observers of American immigration in the early twentieth century drew what they held to be significant distinctions between "New" and "Old" immigrants. The former included mostly southern and eastern Europeans who began to arrive in large numbers during the last two decades of the nineteenth century. They were thought to be culturally and often racially inferior to the "Old" arrivals who came from northern and western Europe in the eighteenth and nineteenth centuries. This sentiment ultimately shaped the immigration restriction legislation of the 1920s, which discriminated against the new arrivals. It also provided a popular basis for attributing a multitude of problems associated with America's increasingly urban and industrial society to this new and "inferior" stock of settlers. Successful attacks on the principal research identified with this position after World War II brought it into general scholarly disrepute.[1]

This "Old" versus "New" categorization of immigrants was recently given new life as part of a broad interpretation of urban society in the United States. Edward C. Banfield locates a major source of urban problems in the existence of a lower-class culture. Holders of this culture lack orientation toward the future, which leads to behavior directed toward immediate gratification and to apathy. He identifies the "New" immigrants with this culture in the process of assessing Timothy L. Smith's assertion that immigrants to America tended to be future-oriented and to plan ahead carefully for their enterprise. "Those who looked ahead were most numerous," Banfield suspects, "before the introduction of steamships reduced the duration of the voyage from several weeks to several days, among townsmen rather than peasants, and among those for whom the alternative to immigration was not the prospect of immediate starvation." He continues, "among the Old Stock Americans it was a rare day laborer who could not read, write and cipher; among peasant immigrants it was a rare one who could. The immigrants from present-oriented cultures were slow to see the advantage of education and of self-improvement generally. . . . Unlike the Old Stock Americans and the more future-oriented immigrants from England and Northern Europe, the peasant immigrants seldom patronized the free mechanics libraries. Very few became skilled workers." There may have been other causes for their tendency to remain unskilled laborers, yet he concludes that, in part, "it was probably because their present-oriented outlook and style did not suit the requirements of work and organization." Finally, he suggests that "it was symptomatic of these different attitudes toward self-improvement and 'getting on' that compulsory school attendance laws were adopted only after large-scale peasant immigration got underway. Until then it had been taken for granted that anyone able to go to school would not fail to do so."[2]

The present-oriented peasants Banfield refers to in this passage were the Irish who arrived in the middle of the nineteenth century. It seems clear, however, that he wishes the interpretation to be read more broadly. Smith was referring to eastern Europeans in the later years of the century. At any rate, it is reasonable to subject the proposition to the test of emigrants from the Italian South, a peasant society which supplied great numbers of migrants to urban America in the era after the introduction of the steamship. If the Italians fail to conform to such a culture type, the general application of the concept should be seriously questioned, and its power as a tool for the analysis of immigrant contributions to current urban problems is in doubt.

Perhaps Banfield has agricultural day-laborers in mind when he speaks of present-oriented peasants. It is hard to view agricultural proprietors, planters who rent land, or even sharecroppers as being other than future-oriented.[3] The agricultural enterprise is based on present capital and labor investment for future returns: "deferred gratification." The relevant future is at least a growing season away; for arboreal culture it may be several years distant. His lower-class ideal type, whose apathy and desire for present gratification precluded holding a steady job, would seem far more compatible with urban rather than rural life, with townsmen rather than peasants. (He did articulate the theory in conjunction with an analysis of twentieth-century urban problems.) Since I am considering a culture or world view, not specific skills directly transferable to life in urban America, it would be more consistent with Banfield's overall analysis to reverse the statement and hypothesize that the higher the proportion of peasants to townsmen the larger the number of immigrants who looked ahead.[4]

Steamships may have lessened the physical ordeal of the transatlantic voyage, but it was only a relative difference in a world that quickly adjusted to the new standard of hardship. The older pre-steam-power pace of life quickly faded from memory. Emigration remained a major investment in time, money, and hopes, as well as a sacrifice of the emotional and social comforts of home and community in the hope of future returns. Italian peasants emigrated as readily from remote inland villages where they had to travel many kilometers on foot or pack animals to the railroads as from coastal cities with convenient rail connection to ports of embarcation.

Banfield's reference to emigration as an alternative to starvation is a form of the old "push" versus "pull" analysis of emigration. According to this school, those who are motivated to emigrate by the pull or opportunities in a new land are future-oriented and are therefore superior stock to those who move only as an alternative to remaining in a famine-ravaged homeland. The history of immigration to America seldom reflects such a neat dichotomy that suggests a clear difference between present- and future-oriented motivations. "Push" and "pull" were, in fact, two elements in an equation that measured alternative futures and allowed a choice between different strategies of social mobility based on anticipated returns from staying or going. I have shown how economic conditions at home influenced these decisions. Chapter 5 considers briefly the familial information networks or chains which supplied information and aid from abroad. Even in periods of severe hardship when many left, many others remained behind. Choice continued to be a central feature of the process. The question of who left and who did not still pertains; assertions of simple "push" mechanisms are inadequate to answer it. "Push-pull" distinctions will not bear the inferences Banfield wishes to draw from them.

The overall findings of the previous three chapters run almost directly counter to the Banfield claims. I have shown that those who left, whether agriculturalists or townsmen, were likely to have some stake in the society and to act as if they had confidence in their ability to influence their futures. The thrust of chapter 1 is that there are certain minimal levels of cultural and psychological capital that are as necessary as money for "financing" emigration. The group in southern Italian society who seem to be the most probable nominees for the victims of Banfield's pathological lower-class culture, the rural and town day-laborers, were the very ones who were least likely to leave. Important segments of the working and agricultural classes expressed, through their societies in Italy and abroad, as I will demonstrate below, values that were antithetical to this culture. Their beliefs about the importance of education, their embracing of public schooling when it was available, and their attempts to provide substitutes privately when it was not, call into question the assertion that they were hopelessly mired in such an ethos. Clearly, present-oriented culture and a psychology of apathy and immediate gratification cannot be generally assigned to Italian immigrants as part of the heritage which influenced their lives in the New World. Rather, the immigrants clearly belong among the future-oriented in Banfield's time-horizon theory.[5]

5

IMMIGRATION AND THE GROWTH
OF THREE ITALIAN COLONIES

The rise of what Italians in America usually called a "colony" was dependent on the development of a sizable and semipermanent population in a given city. Systematizing of personal relationships within institutional structures could only take place when a group of Italians had reached a certain minimal level of stability and integration into the local economy of an area. A description of this process of community building is reserved for later chapters. The immediate task is to explore the coming together of Italians in the three cities, their residential distribution, family organization, and place in the economic structure. The intent of this chapter is to suggest what influences these social, economic, and demographic factors had on the growth of colonies.

A Few Words about "Chains"
and the Peopling of the Colonies

Scholars have long been aware of the fact that immigration and resettlement in the New World was not a random process. Both Italian and American observers of the initiation of the process in Italy agreed that personal contacts and communications with fellows who had previously migrated were the most important sources of information and inspiration for prospective emigrants. By comparison, the labor agents and ships' agents often credited by American nativists with flooding the country with unwanted immigrants were of miniscule importance in promoting immigration. "The brother calls the brother, the friend calls the friend

and thus it is the way they all go." Resulting were situations
such as that in the province of Potenza where the Italian pre-
mier Zanardelli was greeted by a local mayor "in the name of
the eight thousand under my administration, of which three
thousand are emigrants in America and five thousand are preparing to join them."[1]

Once in the United States the immigrants reportedly clustered
together in regional groups. One Italian visitor found specific
streets in New York City dominated by eastern or western
Sicilians. Urban sociologists Miller and Park graphically portrayed
the phenomenon in a series of multicolored maps showing the
varying regional compositions of each building in a several-
block area of the city. Post–World War II Australian scholars
have systematized the study of this personalized type of organization of migration under the rubric "chain migration." John S.
MacDonald has pursued this line of investigation in terms of
both American and Australian immigration. His research illuminated the internal dynamics of the chain and its consequences
for residential and occupation configurations in the country
of immigration. Yet the "chain" metaphor has had both productive and counterproductive consequences. As used by Mac-
Donald, it leaves the impression of a single dimension and a
feeling of closure. In part, this is attributable to the superficial
and unsystematic nature of the sources he relies on for his
American research, and in part, to the natural product of his
stated intent of studying the internal structure of particular
chains through participant observation in Australia.[2]

A far richer and more complex picture of the migration
process emerges when one looks at the dynamics of chains as
they operated both in communities of emigration and immigration. Passport application records of Italian communes are good
sources for the study of the variety of destinations chosen by
emigrants from a locality. Termini Imerese has been claimed as
an important, if not primary, source of immigrants for a number
of Italian-American colonies. It was one of the more common
home villages among Italians in Rochester and Kansas City. A
look at the destinations listed for passports in 1901 from this

Sicilian city of 20,000 suggests both the existence of chains and their variety. There were specific destinations listed on 709 of the 724 passport entries in the register. Eighty-six different destinations were recorded in one year from this single commune. Table 5.1 gives the most popular destinations for this year. New York City heads the list, appearing on 30 percent of the applications. Chicago with 17 percent and Pittsburgh with 10 percent of the migration follow. At the other extreme, forty-nine New World cities or towns were listed in the register only once during the year. Similarly, the Sicilian mining commune of Villarosa, population 12,000, included thirty-one separate destinations on a total of 285 passport applications for the year 1911.[3]

Table 5.1
Cities of Destination Prominently Mentioned in
Passport Application Records, Termini Imerese, 1901

City	Percentage of Total Year's Entries	City	Percentage of Total Year's Entries
New York City	30%	Lawrence, Mass.	1%
Chicago	17%	New Haven, Conn.	1%
Pittsburgh	10%	Allegheny, Pa.	1%
Cleveland	4%	New Orleans	1%
St. Louis	3%	Buffalo	1%
Cincinnati	3%	Albany	
Baltimore	2%	Minneapolis-St. Paul	
Boston	2%	Stubenville, Ohio	.5 to .99%
Providence	2%	Syracuse	
Toronto	2%	Portsmouth, N.H.	
Washington, D. C.	2%	Mt. Morris, N.Y.	

Source: "Registro della domanda di nulla osta per ottenere passaporto per l'estero," 1901 Archivio Comunale—Termini Imerese.

The precision of designation and spelling of such minor cities as Oswego, Oneida, Oneonta, Winnipeg, and Akron, all with non-Italian orthography, makes evident the preplanning and prior knowledge involved in the migration. Clearly, chains existed which directed migrants into the two largest Italian-American colonies. At the same time, most of the emigration was spread out over a multitude of smaller Italian colonies in the United States. The more important streams remained fairly constant during the period from 1901 to 1914. Chicago appeared on an average of 15.8 percent of the entries, while Pittsburgh's share of the annual migration varied between 6.96 percent and 13.1 percent. Passports to Toronto ranged between 1.4 percent and 7.3 percent, and those to New Orleans were between 0 and 4.55 percent (see Table 5.2). Rochester, though reputed to be heavily settled by immigrants from Termini, received only .55 percent of the total passport designations during the prewar period. Minneapolis/St. Paul represents an interrupted chain; after receiving nearly 1 percent of the 1901 migration, the Twin Cities virtually disappear from the lists. Yet fragments of a 1907 parish census of the St. Paul colony show several families from Termini still residing in these Minnesota cities. The chain, for one reason or another, ended abruptly. The view from this commune of emigration, then, is one of residents leaving for many destinations to join friends or family already abroad. The majority of emigrants leaving in a given year shared destinations with only a few of their townsmen.[4]

Variety characterized the situation in the cities of immigration as well. A 20 percent sample of Italian surnames beginning with the letter C in the naturalization records for Utica, New York, yielded a total of 362 separate communes of origin out of 1,187 cases. This represented an average of 3.3 persons per commune. A total of 528 persons (44.4 percent) came from communes contributing 11 or more persons to the sample. Eleven persons represent slightly less than 1 percent of the sample. The commune with the largest representation, Alberobello, Bari, contributed less than 5 percent of the total group analyzed. A similar study for Rome, New York, produced 122 communes of origin in a total of 275 cases of naturalization, or an average of 2.25 persons per commune. Fifty-two percent

Table 5.2
Percentage of Passport Applications From Termini Imerese to
Pittsburgh, New Orleans, Chicago, Toronto, and
Canada Excluding Toronto, 1901–1921

	Total Applications	Pittsburgh	New Orleans	Chicago	Toronto	Canada Excluding Toronto
1901	724	9.0	1.2	15.1	1.5	.5
1902	1,010	8.6	.9	18.3	1.4	.1
1903	815	8.5	.6	13.9	2.1	.5
1904	623	6.7	.3	16.6	3.0	.6
1905	513	13.1	1.2	16.7	4.7	.4
1906	570	12.8	1.2	15.9	4.0	.9
1907	596	7.2	.5	16.4	4.4	1.2
1908	351	8.8	4.6	16.2	3.4	1.4
1909	416	8.9	1.0	14.6	6.0	.5
1910	488	8.2	.6	14.7	3.9	.6
1911	302	8.6	.7	19.2	7.3	1.0
1912	390	9.2		16.4	6.4	1.3
1913	479	8.8	.2	14.4	4.6	1.3
1914	445	6.9	.2	11.2	7.2	3.4
1920	253	4.7			4.0	.4
1921	700	5.0			4.7	.7

Source: "Registro ... nulla osta ... ," 1901–21, Termini Imerese.

(144) of the sample came from villages contributing 1 percent
or more (3 or more persons) to the sample. The largest single
group represented 7.2 percent of the sample.[5]

A study of the origins of Italian couples married in Rochester's
Italian parishes suggests the same complexity of patterns.
Marriage records for a total of 3,850 individuals between 1904
and 1917 list the precise place of baptism. Six hundred eighty-
nine separate communes were represented in the sample, indicating an overall average of 5.6 persons per commune. The
actual range was from 1 to 532. Three hundred sixty-seven,

9.5 percent of the sample, came from villages that appear only once in the records. Seven hundred seventy-six people came from 543 villages which contributed less than four people. At the other extreme, twelve villages contributed 1 percent or more. These groups varied in size between 40 and 532, with a mean of 141.2 persons per commune (see Table 5.3). In terms

Table 5.3
Italian Immigrants Married in Rochester (1904–17)
Size of Streams from Italian Communes to Rochester

	Number	Number of Communes Represented	Immigrants Per Commune	Percentage of the Total Sample
Persons coming from communes contributing less than .1% to total (1–3 immigrants)	776	543	1.4	20.2%
Persons coming from communes contributing .1% to .9% to total (4–39 immigrants)	1,380	134	10.3	35.8%
Persons coming from communes contributing 1% or more to total (40 or more immigrants)	1,694	12	141.2	44.0%
Totals	3,850	689	5.6	100 %

Source: Marriage registers, St. Anthony's, Mt. Carmel, and St. Lucy's parishes, Rochester, New York.

of percentage, these village groups ranged from 1 percent to 13.8 percent with only two villages contributing over 5 percent to the total sample. Kansas City's Holy Rosary Parish marriage registers supply Old World origins on 920 persons marrying between 1891 and 1915. They represented a total of 173 villages, or a ratio of 5.3 immigrants per commune. The most productive commune contributed 78 individuals (8.4 percent) to the total. Immigrants from five communes represent 5 percent or more of the total. Interestingly, Termini Imerese is one of these towns, with 50 immigrants (5.4 percent). Yet Kansas City hardly enters into the picture when migration is viewed from Termini. Eighty individuals (8.6 percent) came from communes which contributed no other son or daughter to the sample.

Table 5.4 presents data on the province of origin taken from the same parish sources. The Utica sample represents only a small proportion of the total prewar marriages of Italians in that city. The Cleveland, Ohio, figures are from a single parish in a city with a number of scattered Italian parishes. Records from the earliest Italian parish in the city were not available to this researcher. The figures show differing patterns of origin for the three cities. Cleveland's Mayfield district, at least, was predominantly Sicilian, with almost all the immigrants coming from the province of Messina. The remaining 30 percent of non-Sicilian origin was distributed fairly evenly throughout the southern provinces. Rochester and Kansas City also had large Sicilian populations. Yet in these cities the migration was more evenly distributed through the island. The 52 percent non-Sicilian migration in Rochester was spread widely over the southern and central provinces. Utica displayed the most scattered pattern of origins, with Apulia being the most prolific region, contributing 36 percent, and Bari providing a provincial high of 21 percent. Clearly, there were sizable groups of immigrants from a single commune, province, and especially, a region. Yet they lived side by side with large numbers of individuals who could count relatively few fellow townsmen or *paesani* in the colony. Fifty-six percent of the Rochester sample came from communes contributing less than 1 percent to the colony's population. Parishes, with the exception of Mount Carmel, tended to have cosmopolitan congregations. At the same time, immigrants from most provinces spread themselves over at least two of the three parishes in significant numbers (see Table 5.5).

The variety of origins in the colonies derived from the multitude of small family-based migration chains, raises questions about the presence of and power of the *campanilismo* phenomenon. Vecoli found this spirit of localism, which restricted immigrant loyalties to fellow immigrants from one's

Table 5.4
Province and Region of Origin of Italian Males Married in
Rochester, Utica, and Cleveland by Percentage of Total Sample

	Rochester (1904–17)	Kansas City (1891–1915)	Utica (1912–15)	Cleveland (1906–07, 1912–14)
Agrigento	5.8	7.0	1.1	6.3
Caltanissetta	7.7	.4	1.1	1.4
Catania	.7	.2		2.1
Enna	14.8			2.1
Messina	2.0	1.1	.5	37.9
Palermo	16.7	27.3	4.2	19.8
Ragusa	.3	.1		
Syracuse		1.1		
Trapani	.4	28.5		.4
Total Sicily	48.4	66.1	6.9	70.0
Catanzaro	2.1	2.3	12.2	3.5
Cosenza	1.0	6.0		5.0
Reggio Calabria	3.1	.1	4.2	.4
Total Calabria	6.2	8.5	16.4	8.9
Matera	.9		1.1	.7
Potenza	3.4	5.9	2.6	1.1
Total Basilicata	4.3	5.9	3.7	1.8
Bari	1.8	.1	21.1	2.8
Brindisi			7.4	
Foggia	2.1	.6		2.1
Lecce				
Taranto	.1		7.4	.4
Total Apulia	4.0	.7	36.0	5.3

Table 5.4 (continued)

	Rochester (1904–17)	Kansas City (1891–1915)	Utica (1912–15)	Cleveland (1906–07, 1912–14)
Avellino	1.9	6.8	.5	
Benevento	1.0	.3		
Caserta	8.8	.5	3.7	3.5
Naples	.3	.2	.5	.4
Salerno	2.5	.4	3.7	.7
Total Campania	14.5	8.3	8.4	4.6
Campobasso	2.1	2.3		3.5
Chieti	1.5	1.0		1.1
L'Aquila	9.5	.4		4.3
Pescara	1.6			
Teramo	.7	.3		.4
Total Abruzzi and Molise	15.4	4.2		9.3
Frosinone	1.7		19.6	
Latina	2.6		6.9	
Rieti	.1			
Rome	.5			
Viterbo	.1			
Total Latium	5.0		26.5	
Other	2.2	5.8	2.1	

Source: Marriage registers, St. Anthony's, St. Lucy's, and Mt. Carmel parishes, Rochester; St. Mary of Mt. Carmel and St. Anthony's parishes, Utica; and St. Anthony's parish, Cleveland.

Table 5.5
Italians in Rochester (1904–17)

| | Parish | | | | | | Totals | |
| Province | St. Anthony's (1904–14) | | St. Lucy's (1913–17) | | Mt. Carmel (1906–14) | | | |
	Percentage of Parish from Province	Percentage of Province in Parish	Percentage of Parish from Province	Percentage of Province in Parish	Percentage of Parish from Province	Percentage of Province in Parish	Number	Percent
Agrigento	5.5	51.6	9.6	10.9	3.9	37.5	192	4.9
Caltanissetta	10.5	52.8	3.2	2.0	8.6	45.2	356	9.2
Catania	.6	29.7	1.8	.6	1.4	70.3	37	1.0
Enna	2.7	8.0	.9	2.3	30.2	91.4	616	15.9
Messina	2.1	43.0	4.1	1.3	2.5	54.7	86	2.2
Palermo	13.8	36.5			22.7	62.2	679	17.5
Ragusa	0.0	7.7			.6	92.3	13	.3
Syracuse	.1	66.6			.1	33.3	3	.1
Trapani	.2	26.7			.6	73.3	15	.4
Total Sicily	35.5	32.0	19.7	2.2	70.6	65.8	1,997	51.5
Catanzaro	1.8	42.7	1.8	5.3	2.1	52.0	75	1.9
Cosenza	.5	28.1	.5	3.1	1.2	68.8	32	.8
Reggio Calabria	2.2	47.1	.5	1.2	2.4	51.8	85	2.2
Total Calabria	4.5	42.2	2.8	3.1	5.6	54.7	192	4.9

Matera	1.3	65.7	3.2	20.0	.3	14.3	35	.9
Potenza	5.7	71.0	1.8	2.8	2.0	26.2	145	3.7
Total Basilicata	7.0	70.0	5.0	6.1	2.3	23.9	180	4.6
Bari	.7	26.5	1.4	6.1	1.8	67.3	49	1.3
Brindisi	.1	100.0					1	.1
Foggia	2.4	59.7	.9	2.8	1.5	37.5	72	1.9
Taranto	.1	20.0			.2	80.0	5	.1
Total Apulia	3.2	45.7	2.3	3.9	3.4	50.4	127	3.3
Avellino	2.8	59.5	9.6	25.0	.7	15.5	84	2.2
Benevento	1.2	70.0	1.4	10.0	.3	20.0	30	.8
Caserta	14.3	83.0	12.4	8.7	1.4	8.4	311	8.0
Naples	.8	82.4	.5	5.9	.1	11.8	17	.4
Salerno	2.1	33.6	.9	1.8	3.8	64.5	110	2.8
Total Campania	21.1	68.8	24.8	9.8	6.3	21.4	552	14.2
Campobasso	2.8	60.0	1.8	4.7	1.6	35.3	85	2.2
Chieti	.6	23.8	3.2	16.7	1.3	59.5	42	1.1
L'Aquila	16.5	80.7	15.1	9.0	2.0	10.4	367	9.5
Pescara	1.5	50.0	3.2	13.0	1.1	37.0	54	1.4
Teramo	.9	76.2			.3	23.8	21	.5
Total Abruzzi and Molise	22.2	70.3	23.4	9.0	6.3	20.7	569	14.7

Table 5.5 (continued)

| | St. Anthony's (1904-14) | | St. Lucy's (1913-17) | | Mt. Carmel (1906-14) | | Totals | |
Province	Percentage of Parish from Province	Percentage of Province in Parish	Percentage of Parish from Province	Percentage of Province in Parish	Percentage of Parish from Province	Percentage of Province in Parish	Number	Percent
Frosinone	.4	18.6	5.0	25.6	1.3	55.8	43	1.1
Latina	4.0	71.3	11.5	24.8	.2	4.0	101	2.6
Rieti	.1	50.0			.1	50.0	4	.1
Rome	.3	54.5	.9	18.2	.2	27.3	11	.3
Viterbo	.1	50.0	.5	50.0			2	.1
Total Latium	4.9	55.3	17.9	24.2	1.8	20.5	161	4.2
Other	1.4	25.7	4.1	8.9	3.5	65.3	101	2.6
Total Individuals	1,799	46.4%	218	5.6%	1,862	48.0%	3,879	

Source: Marriage registers, St. Anthony's, St. Lucy's, and Mt. Carmel parishes, Rochester.

own Old World village, to be a powerful force that fragmented the Chicago Italian colony into many small settlements.[6] Townsmen clustered together, "maintained their distinct identities, practiced endogamy, and preserved their traditional folkways." This accounted for "the marked incapacity of the south Italians for organizational activity" and their propensity to allow parochialism to defeat cooperative ventures.

If such a spirit of campanilismo had been prominent in Rochester, the colony would have been hopelessly divided and impotent. Few villages supplied sufficient sons and daughters to constitute a group large enough to support any organizational life beyond the family. The marriage registers present the opportunity to explore one facet of this question. The choice of a marriage partner offers a sensistive measure of the strength of campanilismo on this side of the Atlantic. A decision to marry outside the circle of immigrants from one's Old World village may indicate an intention to settle permanently in America. It also may have been influenced by a restricted number of possible mates from one's own *paese* and greatly expanded contacts with eligible outsiders. Yet, if village loyalty was important in defining eligible partners, we would expect to find a high rate of intramarriage among those from the same Italian communes.

Assuming a more or less equal distribution by age and sex coming from the various communes, immigrants from productive villages would have numerous possible mates and many competitors. Those from communes supplying few immigrants would find a smaller group to select from and proportionately fewer rivals. This was not always true. Young males, as with most immigrant groups, were overrepresented among the Italians. This put marriageable women at a premium and should have given them an advantage in choosing suitors from their own *paesi* if this were a valued criterion. A male had the choice of returning to Italy in search of a wife or arranging to have a potential bride sent to America, where the union would take place. The scholarly and popular literature records both phenomena as common responses. The data to be used here include those who elected the second but not the first option.

Campanilismo might be said to be at work when endogamous

Table 5.6
Percentage of Marriages between Italians from the
Same and Different Communes, Rochester (1903–17),
Utica (1912–15), Cleveland (1906–07, 1912–14)

| | *Marriages Where One or Both Persons Were Born in Italy* | | | | | |
| | *Rochester* | | *Utica* | | *Cleveland* | |
	Male	*Female*	*Male*	*Female*	*Male*	*Female*
Husband from same commune as wife	39.8	42.3	38.0	40.1	38.4	41.0
Husband from different commune than wife	60.2	57.7	62.0	59.9	61.6	59.0
Total marriages	2,005	1,878	187	177	289	271
Percentage of total by sex and city	100	100	100	100	100	100
			More than 5%[a]			
Husband from same commune as wife	70.7	60.6	64.0	47.8	55.3	50.0
Husband from different commune than wife	29.3	39.4	36.0	52.2	44.7	50.0
Total marriages	362[c]	611[c]	50	69	94	104
Percentage of total by sex and city	18.1	32.5	26.7	39.0	32.5	38.4
			Less than 5%[b]			
Husband from same commune as wife	32.9	33.7	28.5	35.2	30.3	35.3
Husband from different commune than wife	67.1	66.3	71.5	64.8	69.7	64.7
Total marriages	1,643	1,267	137	108	195	167
Percentage of total by sex and city	81.9	67.5	73.3	61.0	67.5	61.6

Table 5.6 (continued)

	Marriages Where One or Both Persons Were Born in Italy			
	Rochester			
	1-5%[c]		Less than 1%[d]	
	Male	*Female*	*Male*	*Female*
Husband from same commune as wife	57.6	54.5	23.2	26.5
Husband from different commune than wife	42.4	45.5	76.8	73.5
Total marriages	462	319	1,181	948
Percentage of total by sex and city	23.0	17.0	58.9	50.5

Source: Marriage registers, St. Anthony's, St. Lucy's, and Mt. Carmel parishes, Rochester; St. Mary's of Mt. Carmel and St. Anthony's parishes, Utica; and St. Anthony's Parish, Cleveland.

[a]Marriages with one person from communes supplying 5% or more of the individuals in the marriage registers.
[b]Marriages with one person from communes supplying less than 5% of the individuals in the marriage registers.
[c]Marriages with one person from communes supplying from 1% to 5% of the individuals in the marriage registers.
[d]Marriages with one person from communes supplying less than 1% of the individuals in the marriage registers.
[e]Only two communes are in the +5% category for males, while there are four when calculated for females. This accounts for part of the discrepancy in numbers. Women also outnumbered men in the large commune groups. The difference in the number of large communes for the sexes does not affect the analysis. An analysis for women from the two dominant male communes and for men from the four dominant women's communes did not produce significantly different results.

matings exceeded the rate expected if mating were to occur randomly throughout the colony. However, this standard is entirely too lenient. It would allow small, but statistically significant, deviations among small groups to give a false reading and reduce the phenomenon to a negligible social force. The social significance and potency attributed to campanilismo require a more demanding test of their presence and strength. If it was an important force in shaping adjustments here, it should be demonstrated by greater than chance endogamous marriages among individual village groups. The assumption is that, if the village of origin was an important characteristic of a mate, opportunities existed to allow discrimination on that characteristic, and that with considerable more than chance probability individuals would choose *paesani* to marry. This should be especially true in the period studied here, when many immigrants planned eventual repatriation to Italy, and before World War I and restrictive legislation sharply limited easy migration.

More than 60 percent of the marriages made in Italian parishes in Rochester between 1904 and 1917, in Utica between 1912 and 1915, and in Cleveland during 1906–07 and 1912–14 united persons from different Italian communes.* Table 5.6 presents a summary analysis of this data. There are some differences, depending on whether husbands or wives are used to organize the data for analysis. Overall, endogamy rises to or above chance levels for those from communes with many immigrants in the colony and falls below it for those from less productive villages. If the couples are divided into those who came

---

*The marriage registers in each parish soon after 1900 called for the specification of the place of baptism for each partner. The data for Rochester is very good and complete. It includes almost all marriages made in the three Italian parishes of the city. Priests with few exceptions recorded the commune and province of baptism for each party. This is used here as the commune of origin. In Utica and Cleveland, the data is more sporadic. Only for occasional periods did priests enter something different from "Italia" or "Italy." The Cleveland data is from only one of the several Italian parishes in that city. Thus, the data for these two cities should be viewed as imperfect samples and used with caution. They are presented here to be compared and balanced with the systematic evidence from Rochester.

from villages which supplied over 5 percent of the total individuals in the marriage registers and those whose villages contributed less than 5 percent, the patterns for the two groups are approximately the opposite.

The less than 5 percent group comprised more than 60 percent of the total marriages. Approximately two-thirds of these were exogamous pairings. Those from the productive communes practiced endogamy at rates which ranged from chance to over 70 percent. A more detailed breakdown for Rochester shows that the incidence of intramarriage decreases as the size of the immigration from the Old World village in the city decreases. Less than three-fifths of the group coming from communes contributing between 1 and 5 percent of the marriage partners exercised endogamy. About three-quarters of the marriages of those coming from communes supplying less than 1 percent of the population were exogamous. This group represented a majority of all marriages in the three Italian parishes. There is greater variation associated with sex in the patterns for those from the dominant communes in Utica. In Cleveland this group approaches chance intermarriage. For those from the less productive communes, the patterns in these cities are close to those in Rochester.

This evidence suggests that a preference for a spouse from one's own home commune existed for a minority of the populations in the colonies. If it existed among the majority, it was not strong enough to motivate special efforts and sacrifices to satisfy it. The tendency for this form of campanilismo to appear only among large groups of townsmen raises the possibility that a sense of communal identity or loyalty was initiated or heightened by life abroad in the presence of many fellow townsmen within the context of a more heterogeneous colony. Shared pasts prompted present associations in reponse to new and unusual experiences. Those with family, friends, and acquaintances here naturally turned to them first in coping with new experiences in a colony of strangers. This natural process of forming alliances and friendships increased the awareness of common pasts and promoted higher incidences of interaction and thus greater likelihood of intermarriage. Immigrants with few paesani interacted with other Italians in a context which minimized the importance of communal origins. Other priorities shaped their developing patterns of friendship and association. Immediate and practical influences determined the role of village loyalty for each group. Campanilismo was only one of the many forces influencing association and cooperation in the immigrant colonies.

The greater incidence among males compared to females of intramarriage from the dominant communes suggests a sex difference in which women had less opportunity or motivation to select partners from their own communes. Females probably could not follow the masculine practice of sending back to Italy for a spouse and may have been less able to travel back themselves in search of a partner. If this last option were only available to men, it would explain the different proportions of women in the large and small communal groups. There was a somewhat larger number of women from the two most prominent villages in Rochester (406 versus 363). The males from this group may have gone back to Italy in search of brides in greater numbers than those from the smaller group with weaker communal loyalties. This would account for the greater proportion of males to females in the latter group, the pattern one would expect in an immigrant community. These "small commune" males did not take advantage of their option to bring a bride from the Old World and instead chose from the surplus of women from the dominant communes and from females from the lesser communes, with little regard for their village origins. As a result, they exhibited a pattern much like that of the women from their groups.

The data for Rochester, when analyzed by parish, provides further support for this interpretation of the limited and special nature of campanilismo (see Table 5.7). St. Anthony's, which had more than two-thirds of the individuals from moderately productive communes, those supplying between 1 and 5 percent of the marriage register entries, experienced the greatest proportion of endogamous matings for this category. Mount Carmel included the majority of those from the dominant communes and had the heaviest intramarriage among the parishes

Table 5.7
Percentage of Marriages between Italians from the Same and
Different Italian Communes by Parish, Rochester (1904–17)

	All	*5%*[a]		*1–5%*[b]		*Minus 1%*[c]	
	Male	*Male*	*Female*	*Male*	*Female*	*Male*	*Female*
			St. Anthony's (1904–14)				
Husband from same commune as wife	43.2	66.7	60.2	63.7	65.2	27.5	29.2
Husband from different commune than wife	56.8	33.3	39.8	36.3	34.8	72.5	70.8
Total marriages	929	51	211	347	211	531	442
Percentage of the category in parish	46.3	14.1	34.5	75.1	69.3	45.0	46.6
			St. Lucy's (1913–17)				
Husband from same commune as wife	22.2	0.0	55.6	42.9	38.5	18.1	20.3
Husband from different commune than wife	77.8	100	44.4	57.1	61.5	81.9	79.7
Total marriages	117	2	9	21	13	94	79
Percentage of the category in parish	5.8	.6	1.5	4.5	4.1	8.0	8.3
			Mt. Carmel (1906–14)				
Husband from same commune as wife	38.6	71.8	60.9	38.3	29.4	20.1	24.8
Husband from different commune than wife	61.4	28.2	39.1	61.7	70.6	79.9	75.2
Total marriages	959	309	391	94	85	556	427
Percentage of the category in parish	47.8	85.4	64.0	20.3	26.6	47.1	45.1

Source: Marriage registers, St. Anthony's, St. Lucy's, and Mt. Carmel parishes, Rochester.

[a]Marriages with one person from a commune supplying 5% or more of the individuals in the marriage registers of the three parishes.
[b]Marriages with one person from a commune supplying 1% to 5% of the individuals in the marriage registers of the three parishes.
[c]Marriages with one person from a commune supplying less than 1% of the individuals in the marriage registers of the three parishes.

Table 5.8
Intramarriage by Province, Rochester, 1904–1917

	Percentage Intramarriage	Total Individuals	Total Intramarriages		Percentage Intramarriage	Total Individuals	Total Intramarriages
Agrigento	45.9[a]	111	51	Avellino	33.3	39	13
	63.0[b]	81			28.9	45	
Caltanissetta	65.8	155	102	Benevento	20.0	20	4
	51.0	200			40.0	10	
Catania	35.7	14	5	Caserta	51.4	177	91
	21.7	23			68.9	132	
Enna	78.9	298	235	Naples	28.6	7	2
	73.9	318			22.2	9	
Messina	27.5	40	11	Salerno	40.8	49	20
	23.9	46			32.8	61	
Palermo	65.5	336	220	Campobasso	37.2	43	16
	64.5	341			38.1	42	
Ragusa	42.9	7	3	Chieti	20.0	30	6
	50.0	6			50.0	12	
Syracuse	0.0	1	0	L'Aquila	69.1	191	132
	0.0	2			75.0	176	
Trapani	42.9	7	3	Pescara	28.1	32	9
	37.5	8			42.9	21	
Catanzaro	30.2	43	13	Teramo	26.7	15	4
	40.6	32			66.7	6	

Cosenza	30.0	50.0	20	12	6
Reggio Calabria	25.8	69.6	62	23	16
Matera	35.3	33.3	17	18	6
Potenza	66.7	60.5	69	76	46
Bari	25.7	64.3	35	14	9
Brindisi	0.0	0.0	1	2	0
Foggia	40.5	56.7	42	30	17
Taranto	33.3	50.0	3	2	1
Frosinone	23.5	88.9	34	9	8
Latina	57.7	62.5	52	48	30
Rieti	0.0	0.0	2	2	0
Rome	0.0	0.0	10	1	0
Viterbo	0.0	0.0	2	0	0
Other central and northern provinces and non-Italian-born	41.5	8.5	41	199	17
Totals	54.7		2,005		1,096

[a]Calculated for males.
[b]Calculated for females.

for this group. St. Lucy's, which had only a small percentage of any of the categories, also had the lowest rates of intramarriage. It appears that the effect of numbers on promoting communal loyalties was limited by propinquity. Campanilismo counted most where fellow townspeople lived close together. Others from the same commune in other parts of the colony and in different parishes did not demonstrate as great an interest in communal origin when selecting mates and did not exhibit any great effort to cross parish boundaries in search of someone from the same commune. The division of the colony into three neighborhoods, each with its parish, does not seem to have been the product of any spirit of campanilismo and, in fact, produced patterns of loyalty which cut across communal boundaries.

Campanilismo as an influence in the selection of marriage partners did exist for those with many paesani to reinforce such sentiments. These individuals were a minority in the colonies. For the majority, Old World village loyalties were insufficient to prompt sacrifices of other, more immediate interests and opportunities. Intramarriage by province and region increased substantially over that by communes. Over 54 percent of the marriages in Rochester, 56 percent in Utica, and 61 percent in Cleveland involved partners from the same province. Intramarriage by region was 72 percent for the two New York cities and nearly 86 percent in Cleveland. Both measures follow the communal pattern of greater endogamy in the most populous groups (see Tables 5.8 through 5.11). This may be explained by the importation of Old World provincial and regional prejudices, the reinforcement given to these by life in a colony with a great variety of people from different origins, and the ease with which this much broader form of regionalism could be satisfied when choosing a marriage partner. The social significance of these more general forms of parochialism should not be overemphasized. Geographical distribution in the colonies of Rochester and Utica was not severely limited by such Old World characteristics. Each of the parishes in the colonies had a cosmopolitan composition.

Carla Bianco recently published a study of a colony comprised almost entirely of the descendants of one Italian village, using

Intramarriage by Province, Utica, 1912–1915

	Percentage of Intramarriages	Total Individuals	Total Intramarriages
Agrigento	0.0[a] / 0.0[b]	2 / 9	0
Caltanissetta	0.0	2	0
Messina	0.0 / 0.0	1 / 1	0
Palermo	75.0 / 85.0	8 / 7	6
Syracuse	0.0 / 0.0	0 / 1	0
Catanzaro	73.9 / 77.3	23 / 22	17
Reggio Calabria	62.5 / 83.3	8 / 6	5
Matera	50.0 / 100.0	2 / 1	1
Potenza	20.0 / 14.3	5 / 7	1
Bari	82.5 / 71.7	40 / 46	33
Brindisi	64.3 / 75.0	14 / 12	9
Taranto	42.9 / 66.7	14 / 9	6
Avellino	0.0 / 0.0	1 / 2	0
Benevento	0.0 / 0.0	0 / 1	0
Caserta	28.6 / 28.6	7 / 7	2
Naples	0.0 / 0.0	1 / 0	0
Salerno	28.6 / 50.0	7 / 4	2
Campobasso	0.0 / 0.0	0 / 2	0
Frosinone	62.2 / 63.9	37 / 36	23
Latina	15.4 / 22.2	13 / 9	2
Lucca	0.0 / 0.0	1 / 0	0
Other	0.0 / 0.0	3 / 6	0
Totals	56.5	189	107

Source: Marriage registers, St. Anthony's and Mt. Carmel parishes, Utica.

[a]Calculated for males.
[b]Calculated for females.

Table 5.10
Percentage of Intermarriage of Italians by Region, Rochester (1903–17)

	Sicily	Calabria	Basilicata	Apulia	Campania	Abruzzi and Molise	Italia Centrale	Italia Settentrionale	Non-Italy	Total Males	Percentage of All Males	Percentage of Marriages Outside Region
Sicily	92.4[a]	.4	.4	.1	1.8	.8	.1	.2	3.7	977	48.5	7.6
	85.3[b]	6.0	4.3	2.2	6.9	3.1	1.3	11.1	25.5			
Calabria	36.8	33.6	3.2	2.4	7.2	3.2	4.8	.8	8.0	125	6.2	66.4
	4.3	62.7	4.3	6.5	3.5	1.6	7.9	5.6	7.1			
Basilicata	5.9	2.4	63.5	1.2	12.9	5.9			8.2	85	4.2	36.5
	.5	3.0	57.4	2.2	4.2	2.0			5.0			
Apulia	29.6	3.7	7.4	37.0	11.1	8.6		1.2	1.2	81	4.0	63.0
	2.3	4.5	6.4	65.2	3.5	2.7		5.6	.7			
Campania	11.6	.7	2.7	2.4	55.8	7.9	2.4	.7	15.8	292	14.5	44.2
	3.2	3.0	8.5	15.2	62.7	9.0	9.2	11.1	32.6			
Abruzzi and Molise	8.7	3.2	4.8	1.3	10.6	61.2	1.6		8.7	312	15.5	38.8
	2.6	14.9	16.0	8.7	12.7	74.9	6.6		19.1			
Italia Centrale[c]	13.5	1.8	2.7		11.7	13.5	47.7		9.0	111	5.5	52.3
	1.4	3.0	3.2		5.0	5.9	69.7		7.1			
Italia Settentrionale[d]	4.5	9.1			4.5	4.5	9.1	50.0	18.2	22	1.1	50.0
	.1	3.0			.4	.4	2.6	61.1	2.8			
Non-Italy	30.0				30.0	10.0	20.0	10.0		10	.5	
	.3				1.2	.4	2.6	5.6				

Totals (female)	1,058	67	94	46	260	255	76	18	141	2,015
Percentage of all female	52.5	3.3	4.7	2.3	12.9	12.7	3.8	.9	7.0	
Percentage of marriages outside region	14.6	37.3	42.6	34.8	37.3	25.1	30.3	38.9		

Source: Marriage registers, St. Anthony's, St. Lucy's, and Mt. Carmel parishes, Rochester.

[a] The top figure in each cell equals percentage for husbands.
[b] The second figure in each cell equals percentage for wives.
[c] Tuscany, Marches, Umbria, Latium.
[d] Piedmont, Val D'Aosta, Lombardy, Trentino-Alto Adige, Friuli-Venezia Giulia, Emilia-Romano, Veneto.

folklore in the Italian and American towns of Roseto as a basis
for judging continuities and changes. By her testimony, Roseto,
Pennsylvania, was probably the most homogeneous Italian
community in America. Italians in Rochester, Utica, and Kansas
City faced quite a different situation. Distinctive traditions of
even the largest groups of villagers were shared with only a small
minority of the total Italian immigrant population and faced
uncertain futures in colonies composed of persons from many
different communes. Migration patterns militated against the
maintenance of particularistic cultural features and promoted
an amalgamation of similar or commonly held traditions into a
more general Italian-American culture.[7]

Residential Patterns, Family Structure, and Occupational Opportunities in the Three Cities

The three cities used in this study were composed of large
numbers of immigrants and their children (a characteristic of
most late nineteenth-century American urban areas). The 516
Italians listed in the 1890 census of Rochester, and the thousands more who were to settle more or less permanently in the
city during the next four decades, found an area in which the
immigrant population nearly equaled that of the old Americans,
while the American-born sons and daughters of immigrants
greatly outnumbered either group. By 1930 nearly 24,000
Italians made up 32 percent of the foreign-born, while their
almost 31,000 children represented over 25 percent of the
American-born of foreign or mixed parents in the city. The
figures for Utica were 8,311 (39%) and 12,780 (31%), respectively. Kansas City had a smaller colony of 3,733 Italians and
6,218 members of the second generation representing 15 percent and 10 percent of their total categories in the city. Table
5.12 shows that the period 1890–1930 was one in which the
proportion of foreign-born in the populations of each city
declined modestly. At the same time, the percentage of Italians
in both the total population and especially the foreign-born
population, rose steadily until they reached a high of 39 percent

Table 5.11
Percentage of Intermarriage of Italians by Region, Utica (1912–15)

	Sicily	Calabria	Basilicata	Apulia	Campania	Abruzzi and Molise	Italia Centrale	Non-Italy	Total Males	Percentage of All Males	Percentage of Marriages Outside Region
Sicily	50.0[a] / 46.7[b]	7.1 / 3.6					35.7 / 10.9	7.1 / 8.3	14	7.4	50.0
Calabria		74.2 / 82.1	3.2 / 12.5		3.2 / 7.1		6.5 / 4.3	12.9 / 33.3	31	16.4	25.8
Basilicata			25.0 / 25.0		12.5 / 7.1	12.5 / 50.0	12.5 / 2.2	37.5 / 25.0	8	4.2	75.0
Apulia	4.5 / 20.0		1.5 / 12.5	93.9 / 96.9					66	34.9	6.1
Campania	6.3 / 6.7		6.3 / 12.5		43.8 / 50.0		25.0 / 8.7	18.8 / 25.0	16	8.5	56.2
Italia Centrale[c]	7.7 / 26.7	5.8 / 10.7	3.8 / 25.0	3.8 / 3.1	9.6 / 35.7	1.9 / 50.0	65.4 / 73.9	1.9 / 8.3	52	27.5	34.6
Non-Italy		50.0 / 3.6	50.0 / 12.5						2	1.1	100.0
Totals (female)	15	28	8	64	14	2	46	12	189		
Percentage of total	7.9	14.8	4.2	33.9	7.4	1.1	24.3	6.3			
Percentage of marriages outside region	53.3	17.9	75.0	3.1	50.0	100.0	26.1	100.0			

Source: Marriage registers, St. Mary of Mt. Carmel and St. Anthony's parishes, Utica.

[a] The upper figure in each cell equals percentage for husbands.
[b] The second figure in each cell equals percentage for wives.
[c] Tuscany, Marches, Umbria, Latium.

Table 5.12
Population Statistics—Rochester, Utica, and Kansas City
(1890–1930)

	1890	1900	1910	1920	1930
Rochester					
Total population	133,896	162,608	218,149	295,750	328,132
Foreign-born	39,775	40,748	58,993	71,321	74,696
Foreign-born as % of total	29.7	25.0	18.5	24.1	22.7
Italian	516	1,278	10,638	19,468	23,935
Italian as % of total	.3	.7	3.3	6.5	7.2
Italian as % of foreign-born	1.2	3.1	18.0	27.2	32.0
Utica					
Total population	44,007	52,383	74,419	94,153	101,740
Foreign-born	11,769	13,470	21,308	23,257	21,309
Foreign-born as % of total	26.7	23.8	28.6	24.7	20.9
Italian	325	1,661	6,688	8,435	8,311
Italian as % of total	.7	2.9	8.9	8.9	8.1
Italian as % of foreign-born	2.7	12.3	31.3	36.2	39.0
Kansas City					
Total population	132,716	163,752	248,381	324,410	399,746
Foreign-born	20,858	18,410	25,327	27,320	24,278
Foreign-born as % of total	15.7	11.3	10.1	8.4	6.0
Italian	611	1,034	2,579	3,318	3,723
Italian as % of total	.4	.6	1.0	1.0	.9
Italian as % of foreign-born	2.9	5.6	10.1	12.1	15.3

Source: U. S. Bureau of the Census: Eleventh Census (1890), *Statistics of Population* (Washington, D. C., 1895), 1:466, 472; Twelfth Census (1900), *Statistics of Population* (Washington, D. C., 1900), 1:625, 632–33; Thirteenth Census (1910), *Statistics for New York* (Washington, D. C., 1913), pp. 641, 644–45 and *Supplement for Missouri* (Washington, D. C., 1913), p. 626; Fourteenth Census (1920), *Population—New York,* pp. 718–19, 725–26 and *Population—Missouri,* p. 567; Fifteenth Census (1930), *Population* (Washington, D. C., 1932), 3:300–04, 1316, 1359.

of the foreign-born population in Utica in 1930. By 1910 in
Utica and 1920 in Rochester, Italians had become the largest
foreign-born group in the two cities. In Kansas City they fell
slightly behind the Germans and "Russians" for that honor.
Thus, the Italians were the most numerous of the late-arriving
immigrant groups and by 1920 were statistically more and more
synonymous with "immigrant" in increasingly "American"
cities.[8]

The Italian population in the three cities did not grow in
a lock-step fashion. The rate of growth in Utica hit its peak
between 1890 and 1900, a decade ahead of the other cities
(Table 5.13). This fact helps to account for the seemingly pre-
cocious instutional development in that colony.

Table 5.13
Percentage Increase of Italian-Born
Population by Decade

	1890–1900	1900–10	1910–20	1920–30
Rochester	147.6	732.2	83.0	22.9
Utica	411.0	302.6	26.1	–1.4
Kansas City	69.2	149.4	28.6	12.2

Source: See Table 5.12, p. 96.

The foreign-born of the three cities experienced a decided
shift toward greater residential clustering. In 1890 the index of
dissimilarity for each of the cities was below a modest 11.0.*

*The index of dissimilarity is a measure of the degree to which a group
is over- or underrepresented in a given territorial area. In this study the
geographical unit of measure is the city ward. The index can be roughly
conceived as a measure of the percentage of individuals of the measured
group who would have to change their ward of residence to equalize the
group's distribution throughout the total population. Sam Bass Warner
has designated an index of 25, in a study using ward-size units, as representing a "segregated pattern." ("If All the World Were Philadelphia: A
Scaffolding for Urban History, 1774–1930," *The American Historical
Review*, October 1968, p. 35.)[9]

By 1920 the figures ranged between 16.3 and 26.5. A substantial part of this increase is the result of the high residential congregation of Italians. In 1910 the index figures for Italians of 58.9 for Rochester and 70.4 for Utica were higher than for any other identifiable ethnic group. (Jews, for example, are lost in the census data under categories of Russian, German, Austrian, and Hungarian.) In both cities the small black populations were the only groups rivaling the Italian residential concentration. Rochester's Poles probably surpassed that city's Italians in this dimension, but it is impossible to identify them in the 1910 figures. Ten years later they definitely did. There is no reason to suspect that their settlement pattern changed appreciably during that decade. The figures for 1920 reveal slight drops in the indexes for Rochester and Utica and indicate high concentration in Kansas City. Table 5.14 presents relevant indexes for 1890–1920.

The data also highlight a significant difference between Italian settlement patterns in Rochester, Utica, and Kansas City. Tables 5.15 and 5.16 present evidence on the Italian patterns of settlement in the wards of the three cities. The first, by far the largest colony, tended to be less compact and concentrated. By 1910 it had three cores flanking the center of the city on the northeast (Wards 16 and 18), northwest (Wards 2, 5, and 9), and southwest (Ward 11). Thus, the colony contained three districts, with the central business district and the Genesee River hindering easy communcation between them. In 1910 four wards held nearly 70 percent of the foreign-born Italians, the Sixteenth Ward having slightly over 30 percent. A decade later, after a reorganization of ward boundaries, there remained four chief wards, each with between 10 percent and 19 percent Italian-born and a collective total of 60 percent of the city's Italian immigrants.

A similar picture emerges from random samples of Italian households in Monroe County taken from the New York State censuses for 1893, 1905, 1915, and 1925. Table 5.17 presents the distribution of these families by ward in the city of Rochester and in the remainder of the county. These data differ from those in Table 5.15 for several reasons. They are from different

Table 5.14
Residential Dissimilarity Indexes, 1890–1930

Category	Date				
	1890	1900	1910	1920	1930
Foreign-born					
Rochester	10.8	12.2	20.5	21.5	
Utica	10.9	14.6	29.8	26.5	
Kansas City	10.3	13.0		16.3	
Italians					
Rochester			58.9	55.6	
Utica			70.4	66.9	
Kansas City				67.1	
Philadelphia					50.7
Blacks					
Rochester	42.6	46.3	47.3	47.2	
Utica	67.2	38.1	67.8	70.1	
Kansas City	17.7	18.7		47.6	
Philadelphia					50.7
Poles					
Rochester				66.9	
Utica			52.0[a]	49.9	
Philadelphia					44.0
Irish					
Rochester			25.8	24.4	
Utica			14.2	15.9	
Philadelphia					21.5
Germans					
Rochester			34.0	29.6	
Utica			32.1	33.9	
Philadelphia					32.4
Welsh					
Utica			41.3	46.7	

Source: See Table 5.12, p. 96; the Philadelphia figures are from Sam Bass Warner, Jr., "If All the World Were Philadelphia: A Scaffolding for Urban History, 1774–1930," *The American Historical Review* 74, no. 1 (October 1968):36–37.

[a]This figure represents all Austrian, Hungarian, and Russian born and is thus only a very general approximation.

Table 5.15
Percentage of Italian-Born Residents in Wards, 1910–1920

Wards	Rochester 1910	Rochester 1920	Utica 1910	Utica 1920	Kansas City 1920
1	1.7	.4	4.3	1.9	1.1
2	12.6	5.9	3.9	2.0	2.2
3	1.3	.7	0.0	.2	.6
4	.9	.2	.1	.2	.2
5	7.5	7.0	25.5	10.9	66.7
6	.2	.2	.5	.4	1.6
7	2.9	3.8	.1	.2	11.1
8	1.2	4.6	59.0	69.9	1.1
9	15.4	14.6	.3	.3	1.7
10	.4	.7	5.4	7.5	1.4
11	11.7	10.3	.2	.5	.5
12	.3	.4	0.0	.2	.6
13	.2	.3	.3	4.3	2.2
14	.6	.7	.4	.6	3.5
15	2.9	6.6	0.0	.1	.9
16	30.2	18.7	0.0	0.0	3.9
17	1.8	.6			
18	8.6	16.7			
19	.8	.9			
20	.5	1.3			
21	0.0	.2			
22	.1	2.3			
23	0.0	.9			
24	0.0	.7			

Source: U. S. Bureau of the Census: Thirteenth Census (1910), *Statistics for New York* (Washington, D. C., 1913), pp. 641, 644–45 and *Supplement for Missouri* (Washington, D. C., 1913), p. 626; Fourteenth Census (1920), *Population–New York*, pp. 718–19, 725–26; and *Population–Missouri*, p. 567.

Table 5.16
Italian-Born in Key Wards, 1920

	Wards			
	9th	*11th*	*16th*	*18th*
Rochester				
Italian-born as % of total ward population	33.7	16.4	29.5	11.0
Italian-born as % of total foreign-born ward population	80.5	60.9	78.7	45.8
Utica	*5th*	*8th*		
Italian-born as % of total ward population	33.1	29.4		
Italian born as % of total foreign-born ward population	71.8	73.1		
Kansas City	*5th*			
Italian-born as % of total ward population	13.4			
Italian-born as % of total foreign-born ward population	66.0			

Source: U. S. Bureau of the Census: Fourteenth Census (1920), *Population— New York,* pp. 718–19, 725–26; *Population—Missouri,* p. 567.

censuses collected by different organizations and were taken five years apart. The units of measurement are similar but not the same. The federal census data report Italian-born individuals, while I have coded the state schedules by families. This may explain the trend in the state data to deflate the Italian influence in the wards that the federal counts report as most heavily Italian, and to inflate it for the outlying districts. The latter were areas of second settlement by newly established families and successful older ones; they might be expected to have smaller families and fewer Italian-born members. The older, central wards had higher individual-to-family ratios and contained a preponderance of boardinghouses and families who took in boarders. Nuclear families were more common in outlying wards.

The overall effect was to exaggerate somewhat the number of

Table 5.17
Percentage of Italian Households in Rochester and
Monroe County by Wards, 1893–1925

Ward	1893	1905	1915	1925
1	1.6	3.5	.5	
2	14.8	7.5	3.8	2.1
3	3.1	4.0	.8	.8
4	1.6	2.7	.5	.5
5	7.0	6.2	7.0	4.2
6	7.0	.9	.8	1.0
7	.8	9.3	5.7	2.9
8	9.4	2.7	4.6	6.0
9	10.9	10.6	9.2	7.6
10	3.9	1.3	2.2	4.4
11	3.9	11.5	7.6	9.1
12	.8	1.8	1.1	.3
13	3.1	2.2	1.4	1.3
14	10.2	1.8	.8	.8
15	3.1	.9	6.2	6.0
16	5.5	15.5	13.8	6.3
17		1.3	1.6	3.7
18		3.5	13.0	13.1
19		.4	1.6	3.7
20		.4	1.4	4.2
21			.5	.5
22			4.1	8.6
23				.8
24				2.3
Totals in city	88.3	88.1	88.1	90.1
Totals outside city	11.7	11.9	11.9	9.9

Italians in outer wards at the expense of the central wards in the
data from the state enumerations. Approximately 10 percent
of the Italian households in each census were outside the city.
This also changed the composition of the population on which
the percentages were calculated. Finally, several changes in ward
boundaries render it impossible to make direct comparisons between the census years. Still, the picture by either measure is
one of a colony which never enjoyed close residential propinquity and experienced ever greater dispersion as new wards
opened to Italian settlement. Interestingly, there is no sign of
significant urban-suburban migration during the period. A slight
decline in the nonurban population for 1925 is probably the
result of closing labor camps for canal and railroad workers,
which housed part of the "rural" Italians recorded in earlier
years, and the extension of city boundaries to incorporate
Italians who initially lived outside Rochester.

By contrast with Rochester, both Utica and Kansas City had
large single clusters of Italians. The colony in Utica concentrated in the contiguous Fifth and Eighth Wards, which together
represented over 80 percent of all Italian-born in both census
years. In Kansas City over 77 percent of the Italian immigrants
congregated in the Fifth and Seventh Wards.

Finally, it is important to note that, even in the instances
where there were heavy concentrations in a single ward, Italian
immigrants never contributed more than one-third of a ward's
total population. The Eighth ward in Utica, which contained
almost 70 percent of all Italian-born in the city in 1920, still
had 17 percent of its population made up of native-born of
American parents and another 11 percent of foreign-born non-
Italians. The largest single group, 43 percent of the ward's
population, was composed of American-born children of immigrants. Perhaps three-fourths of these were "Italian," if the proportion of Italians in the total foreign-born population can
provide a rough guide. Thus, about two-thirds of the population
of the ward was "Italian." Kansas City's Fifth Ward had over
one-half of its population that was neither Italian-born nor
American born of foreign parents. First- and second-generation
Italians probably represented no more than 25 percent of the

total population of the ward. This inability to gain numerical superiority among adults in a ward at an early date had important implications for the development of political life in the colonies. It is significant that the Utica Italians, with their greater domination of a ward, were the first effectively to break into American politics.

In all three cases the Italians found themselves in cities with single-family residences (see Table 5.18). The ratio of families per residence in Rochester was 1.20 to 1. Utica's was 1.55 to 1, while Kansas City had a ratio of 1.33 to 1. Within each city there was considerable variation, the higher ratios being in the older sections with their subdivided buildings and boarding-houses, while the newer sections were closer to a 1 to 1 status. In both Utica and Kansas City the Italians settled in wards with the highest proportions of families per residence. Kansas City's Fifth Ward had a ratio of 2.07 to 1 in 1920, while the Eighth Ward in Utica was the city's most crowded, with 2.13 families to a residence.

The story in Rochester is somewhat less clear. Italians moved into areas with higher family/residence ratios. However, the disparity between those wards and the city as a whole was never as great as in the other cities and, in fact, there were three other wards in 1920 with higher ratios than the heavily Italian wards. It is impossible to determine with certainty from these sources if this represents a real difference of residential patterns in the cities' Italian populations. Yet, the movement of two of the three clusters of Italian settlements in Rochester displayed centrifugal tendencies as the colony expanded outward toward newer areas of single-family homes. Both the Eighteenth Ward in the northeast and the Fifteenth in the west, which were the main recipients of this influx, remained below the city-wide ratios in 1910 and 1920. The third population center, in the Eleventh Ward, remained stable, as did the family-to-residence ratio, which was close to the overall Rochester average.[10]

Again, the state census samples give interesting data which, while not directly comparable, are generally in accord with those used above. Table 5.19 shows a steady increase over the early decades of the century in the proportion of single-family

Table 5.18
Families Per Residence by Ward, 1910–1920
(Heavily Italian Wards Underlined)

Rochester			Utica			Kansas City	
Ward	1920	1920	Ward	1910	1920	Ward	1920
1	1.79	2.25	1	1.64	1.52	1	1.69
2	1.77	1.89	2	1.83	1.82	2	1.57
3	1.36	1.53	3	1.48	1.60	3	1.35
4	1.40	1.69	4	1.34	1.62	4	1.13
5	1.21	1.34	5	2.52	1.20	5	2.07
6	1.27	1.38	6	1.44	1.51	6	1.83
7	1.48	1.79	7	1.43	1.27	7	1.45
8	1.26	1.43	8	1.85	2.13	8	1.87
9	1.25	1.43	9	1.51	1.58	9	1.41
10	1.07	1.09	10	1.40	1.71	10	1.26
11	1.23	1.27	11	1.40	1.43	11	1.50
12	1.19	1.26	12	1.45	1.44	12	1.46
13	1.19	1.18	13	1.39	1.37	13	1.10
14	1.08	1.08	14	1.48	1.33	14	1.13
15	1.13	1.14	15	1.37	1.53	15	1.09
16	1.52	1.58	16		1.13	16	1.09
17	1.11	1.10					
18	1.15	1.14					
19	1.08	1.05					
20	1.08	1.06					
21	1.06	1.04					
22	1.09	1.09					
23		1.02					
24		1.05					
City average	1.20	1.20		1.55	1.55		1.33

Source: See Table 5.12, p. 96.

Table 5.19
Percentage of Italian Families Living in
Different Types of Residences, Monroe County, 1905–1925

Type of Residence

Year	One- Family	One- Family with Boarders	Two- Family	Three- Family	Four- Family	Five- or More Family	Boarding- house
1905	31.0	18.5	25.5	7.9	7.9	3.7	5.6
1915	41.7	7.5	25.8	11.7	5.3	6.1	1.7
1925	58.6	6.2	22.6	6.2	3.2	2.4	.8

housing at the expense of families with boarders and residences
with four or more families. The duplex, a common Rochester
housing arrangement, remained a stable choice for the Italians.
These residential patterns suggest increasing stability and
prosperity in the colony.

    A number of other indexes point to increasing prosperity and
family stability among Italians in Monroe County. The proportion of families with intact husband and wife teams increased
between 1905 and 1925. An increase in the number of units
headed by females suggests more widows, but is small in comparison with the decline in households headed by single males
and boardinghouses. There was a decline in the number of
Italians living alone. The average age of heads of Italian households and their spouses increased steadily over the period. The
figures suggest a tendency toward greater ethnic solidarity with
a decline in the number of families in which one member of the
couple was of another nationality. Children became increasingly
prominent in Italian families. The children-per-family ratio rose
from 2.8 to 3.5 between 1893 and 1925. The number of years
lived in the United States at the time censuses were taken increased constantly, indicating a decline in the proportion of
newcomers to older residents in the colony. For male heads of
households, years in the United States went from 11.7 years in
1905 to 18.6 years two decades later. The figures for wives and
female heads of families increased from 9.1 to 16.1 years.

Data on citizenship of the heads of households have a puzzling seesaw quality. About two-thirds were aliens in 1893 and 1915. In 1905 the figure dropped to less than half. Perhaps the answer lies in the irregular growth pattern of the colony. The 1905 figure may have been an artifact of the relatively slow growth of the Italian colony in the late nineteenth century. The great increase in immigration to Rochester in the prewar years of the twentieth century wiped out the earlier gains in naturalization reflected by the 1905 figures. The modest increase in years in the United States during 1905–15 and the much larger increase in 1925 are consistent with this speculation. In 1925 nearly 60

Table 5.20
Percentage of Various Household Organizations
among Italian Families, Monroe County,
1905–1925

	1905	1915	1925
Husband and wife	85.8	88.9	92.2
Female head (no husband)	3.1	4.3	5.0
Male head (no wife)	9.7	6.8	2.6
Boardinghouse	1.3		.3

Table 5.21
Average Age of Male Heads, Wives, and Female Heads of
Italian Households, Monroe County, 1893–1925

	1893		1905		1915		1925	
	Male	Female	Male	Female	Male	Female	Male	Female
Mean	36	32.1	36.9	32.3	37.9	33.9	40.9	35.8
Median	34.4	31.7	36.5	30.6	35.7	30.6	39.1	34.2
Standard deviation	9.3	8.7	10.3	10.3	10.9	11.0	10.5	10.5

Table 5.22
Ethnic Composition of Household Heads and Spouses
(Percentage of Total Household Heads),
Monroe County, 1893–1925

	1893	1905	1915	1925
Husband and wife Italian-born	68.8	73.9	77.6	76.8
Husband Italian-born, Wife American-born	10.9	9.2	8.3	12.2
Husband American-born, Wife Italian-born	.8	.4	.8	.8
Husband Italian-born, Wife other immigrant	6.3	2.2	2.2	1.6
Husband other immigrant, Wife Italian-born	1.6	.4		.5
Single Italian	11.7	13.7	11.1	8.1

Table 5.23
Percentage of Italian Families with Children,
Monroe County, 1893–1925

Number of Children	1893		1905		1915		1925	
	%	Cum. %	%	Cum. %	%	Cum. %	%	Cum. %
0	29.7	29.7	24.8	24.8	19.5	19.5	14.4	14.4
1	15.6	45.3	15.5	40.3	15.1	34.6	17.0	31.4
2	17.2	62.5	17.3	57.6	17.8	52.4	14.4	45.8
3	19.5	82.0	14.6	72.2	18.1	70.5	17.2	63.0
4	7.0	89.0	11.9	84.1	13.0	83.5	12.5	75.5
5	5.5	94.5	7.1	91.2	8.4	91.9	10.7	86.2
6	3.1	97.6	5.8	97.0	4.6	96.5	6.8	93.0
7	2.3	100.0	2.2	99.2	2.4	98.9	4.4	97.4
8			.9	100.0	.8	99.7	1.3	98.7
9							.8	99.5
10							.5	100.0
11					.3	100.0		
Mean	1.99		2.34		2.53		2.96	

Table 5.24
Average Number of Years Lived in the United States for
Male Heads, Wives, and Female Heads of Italian Families,
Monroe County, 1905–1925

	1905		1915		1925	
	Male	*Female*	*Male*	*Female*	*Male*	*Female*
Mean	11.7	9.1	13.0	10.5	18.6	16.1
Median	10.3	7.3	11.0	8.9	18.7	15.6
Standard deviation	9.0	7.4	8.2	7.6	8.8	8.4

Table 5.25
Percentage of Male Heads of Italian
Households with United States Citizenship,
Monroe County, 1893–1925

	1893	*1905*	*1915*	*1925*
U. S. citizen	35.9	53.1	37.0	59.3
Alien	64.1	46.9	63.0	40.7

percent of the heads of households held U.S. citizenship. We can
be more confident of this figure because the enumerators for
this census were required for the first time to record the place,
date, and agency responsible for granting citizenship. Tables
5.20–25 summarize data supporting this picture of increasing
prosperity and stability.

Finally, there is the question of the number of non-nuclear
family members and nonfamily members in the households. The
presence of boarders is sometime taken as a sign of disorganization and as an opportunity for pernicious influences on children.
Families without boarders increased from just under 60 percent
of the total to slightly over 81 percent in 1925 (see Table 5.26).

The proportion of boarders per household dropped from 1.6*
and .5* to .15 over three censuses. For those families which had
boarders, the average number dropped from something over 4.1*
and 2.7* to 1.6 per family in the three census years. Boarders
were a rapidly diminishing phenomenon as the colony matured
and settled into life in Rochester.

Table 5.26
Percentage of Italian Families with
Non-Family Members in Their Households,
Monroe County, 1905–1925

Number of Non-Family Members	1905	1915	1925
0	59.7	81.1	90.3
1	11.1	6.8	6.0
2	7.1	3.5	2.1
3	2.2	4.1	.8
4	4.4	1.9	.8
5	3.5	1.1	
6	2.2	.5	
7	1.3	.3	
8	1.8	.3	
9 or more	6.6	.5	
Mean	1.6[a]	.511[a]	.157

[a]These are minimum estimates.

The data on family structure suggest a more complex pattern
but one that is consistent with the previous interpretations.
Tables 5.27 and 5.28 present the basic data on family types.
Nuclear families contributed about 80 percent of the samples in

*This is the lowest approximation. The real figure could be higher.
Coding limitations prevent a more exact figure. All families with nine or
more boarders were recorded as having nine. The 1925 figure is not
affected by this limitation.

Table 5.27
Percentage of Italian Households with
Non-Nuclear Family Members,
Monroe County, 1905–1925

Number of Non-Nuclear Family Members	1905	1915	1925
0	79.6	73.5	80.7
1	10.2	16.2	8.8
2	6.2	6.2	6.5
3	.4	1.1	2.1
4	1.8	.5	1.0
5	1.3	.5	
6		.8	.3
7		.5	
8		.3	
9		.3	.3
10			.3
11			
12	.4		

1905 and 1925.* The figure dropped below 74 percent in 1915.
The average number of relatives per extended family varied
little over the decades. The figures were 2.13, 1.88, and 2.04
for the three censuses. The significant changes came in the types
of relatives in these households. There was an increase in
married children and elderly parents or in-laws over the years,

*The terms used in describing family structure have a variety of defini-
tions. "Nuclear family" here refers to a single couple and their unmarried
children, if any, or to a widow or widower and other single Italians listed
in the census as heads of households, provided the household does not
meet the criteria for extended units. "Extended family" designates a
household with one or more persons related to the head or spouse other
than unmarried children. "Vertically extended families" include one or
more persons from the categories of parent or head or spouse and married
children and their spouses. Families with other types of relatives are
"horizontally extended."

Table 5.28
Percentage of Italian Households of Various Family Types,
Monroe County, 1905–1925

Family Type	1905	1915	1925
1. Nuclear	79.6	73.5	80.7
2. Extended vertically to include parents and in-laws	2.2	4.9	4.2
3. Extended vertically to include married children and their families	1.8	3.8	4.4
4. Extended horizontally (includes relatives other than in numbers 2 and 3)	11.9	14.1	8.6
5. Numbers 2 and 3		.3	
6. Numbers 2 and 4	4.4	3.2	2.1
7. Numbers 3 and 4		.3	

with a corresponding decrease in other varieties of relatives.

The increase in vertically extended families is characteristic of an aging and increasingly stable colony. The percentage of families with relatives other than parents or married children among all extended families declined from 78 percent to 67 percent and 56 percent across the decades. This high early incidence of horizontally extended families suggests the importance of the familial dimension in chain migration. The decline in this variety of family organization closely parallels the reduction in immigration caused by World War I and the immigration restriction legislation of the immediate postwar period. While the proportion of extended families did not change greatly, their character varied in response to changing demographic conditions.

The range of occupational opportunities available to immigrants in the two New York State cities was similar. Construction, including laying and maintenance of railroad track and utilities excavation, provided important sources of employment for early Italians in both cities. Rochester witnessed the consolidation of several competing gas and electric corporations into a single utility in the 1890s. The first major project of the new Rochester Gas and Electric was to bury all the electric service in the downtown area. The construction of this conduit complex, as well as a separate one for the telephone company,

provided many jobs for unskilled laborers. The newly consol-
idated Rochester Railway Company extended its trolley lines to
most outlying areas of the city, with the active encouragement
of the city. This, too, provided temporary work opportunities.
The boom of suburban electric railways to connect Rochester
with outlying resort areas, and the construction of electric
trolley lines to compete with the major steam routes, especially
the New York Central, provided continuing demand for construction labor after the turn of the century.

   This troublesome competition for the Central eventually
ended when Vanderbilt bought the Rochester Railway Company
with its valuable, exclusive franchises within the Central empire.
The elimination of competition left the city to suffer under
heavy fares and rates, but construction continued at a rapid
pace. The Erie Canal lost the active interest and support of the
Rochester business and commercial establishment. The Press
protested the expenditure of nine million dollars of state
funds on "useless" improvements and opposed the construction
of a new canal when proposed in 1902. Nevertheless, canal
construction and maintenance provided another important
source of employment. The Italian colony recognized this and
viewed both enterprises in a different light. In Utica over
twenty prominent Italians joined American businessmen and
labor leaders in a banquet to boost the proposed new canal.[11]

   More important for the long run, and a factor which distinguished Rochester and Utica from Kansas City, was the relatively heavy concentration of light industry in the former
cities. Mens' clothing was an important industry in both cities.
In addition, Rochester had a large ladies' shoe industry, while
knitting mills supplied Utica with her number one source of
employment. Kansas City had nothing to compare with these
enterprises. Her fledgling men's clothing manufacturing went
into decline after the turn of the century. Rochester and
Utica thus provided opportunities for both skilled and semiskilled industrial employment that was lacking in Kansas City.
This was reflected in different occupational profiles for the
various Italian colonies. Utica, for example, had a prominent
contingent of tailors who provided important leadership in the
early organization of the colony.[12]

   The Monroe County census sample records a gradual improve-

ment in the occupation positions of Italian immigrants as they
moved from construction to industrial jobs (see Tables 5.29 and
5.30). In 1893, 60 percent of the male heads of households
were simple laborers. In succeeding censuses the figure drops to
55.5 percent, 36.8 percent, and 28.1 percent. This change can
be interpreted as a result of the greater stability of the population in the colony. Early laborers on canal and railroad construction projects either moved on at the end of such jobs or
settled in the colony and sought out more permanent

Table 5.29
Occupations of Male Italian Heads of Households
and of Their Eldest Sons, Monroe County, 1893–1925

	Percentage of Total						
	1893	1905		1915		1925	
Occupations	Fathers	Fathers	Eldest Sons	Fathers	Eldest Sons	Fathers	Eldest Sons
Professional, clerical, & salesmen	7.2	3.2	16.2	4.3	13.7	5.3	15.7
Proprietors & managers	19.2	14.3	2.3	13.8	6.8	13.9	2.6
Craftsmen & other skilled laborers	4.8	15.7	16.2	28.5	13.7	30.6	28.9
Operatives & other semiskilled laborers	8.0	8.7	27.9	14.1	36.2	19.3	26.3
Service trades	.8	2.3	4.6	2.3	5.1	2.5	2.6
Unskilled laborers	60.0	55.5	32.5	36.8	24.1	28.1	23.6

and better-paying employment. Eldest sons never experienced
this heavy concentration in unskilled labor classifications: no
more than one-third of them ever held such jobs.

In all likelihood, these young men were largely from more
settled families and gave consideration to the long-range stability
of a position when making occupational choices. As more and
more immigrants faced the same commitment to a future in
Rochester, their retreat from the unskilled positions brought
them ever closer to the pattern of the second generation. Escape
from unskilled labor for the immigrant heads of families came
through finding skilled or semiskilled jobs. The proportions of

Italians at the top in white-collar jobs, as proprietors and managers and in the service industries, remained quite stable. Eldest sons found more opportunities in the white-collar area and significantly fewer as proprietors. The latter category, which included saloon keepers and merchants, had been an important source of community leadership for the first generation. The sons were also more heavily represented in the semiskilled occupations than their fathers' generation.

Table 5.30
Percentage of Wives and Female Heads of
Italian Households in Various Occupations,
Monroe County, 1893–1925

Occupations	1893	1905	1915	1925
Professional, clerical, and saleswomen			1.5	.5
Proprietors & managers			1.2	.3
Skilled trades & craftswomen		1.0	2.0	10.3
Operatives & semiskilled laborers		1.5	1.8	1.9
Service trades	.9	.5	.3	
Unskilled laborers	1.8	1.0	.3	.3
Housewives	97.3	96.0	93.0	86.7

This apparent occupational advantage of the sons should not be overemphasized, however. The sons considered here are those who were still living at home. Most were unmarried and in the early stages of their careers. We do not have a measure of fathers and sons at comparable stages in their lives. Insensitivity to important status gradations in the crude white-collar category makes the sons' progress look somewhat better than it was. Their predominance in the semiskilled areas is a better indication of the degree of advantage they held over their fathers. Even in the early years of their careers relatively few sons were laborers. After extensive longitudinal cohort analyses of immigrant groups in Cleveland, Josef Barton reports a similar pattern of modest gains for both fathers and sons. Each generation experienced distinctive patterns of employment.[13]

Very few Italian wives and female heads of households were initially in the labor force. Between 1893 and 1925 the nonwage earners (housewives) in the group declined slowly from over 97 percent to slightly under 87 percent. The clothing industry provided employment as tailoresses and operatives for most of those who worked outside the home. Wives' contributions to most families did not include a pay envelope. Unrecorded are the contributions of those who took in laundry or helped their mates run small businesses or boardinghouses.

The pattern of employment among married Italian women, while not conclusive, is consistent with Virginia Yans-McLaughlin's contention that Italian women were slow to move out of the home into work situations which conflicted with traditional family values. When they did seek employment in Rochester, they turned to the clothing industry where they found positions as tailoresses. Early twentieth-century studies of working women reported similar choices by Italians elsewhere. Deficiencies in language and social skills might explain the low levels of entrance into clerical and sales jobs. It is also true that these positions exposed workers to wider social contacts in relatively unsupervised settings which, according to McLaughlin's thesis, was antithetical to roles considered proper for Italian women. The social organization of labor in the clothing industry was more acceptable. Women often worked in all-female groups or on piece-work at home. Outside contacts were minimal. The evidence here does not permit a closer judgment on the relative merits of the two explanations. The almost total avoidance of domestic service by Italian wives is consonant with the argument for the primacy of family mores in determining employment patterns, though again it is not conclusive.[14]

Louise A. Tilly has questioned the prevalence of cultural prohibitions against domestic service in southern Italy with census data that reveal this work as an important source of nonagricultural employment for women. She speculates that periods of such employment were common in the lives of young women before marriage. This should be especially true in rural areas where there were few opportunities for industrial employment. Manuscript census returns for Villa Vallelonga in L'Aquila, a major center for migration to Rochester, suggest that domestic service in this village of five hundred families and 3,400 souls was an uncommon experience. Four women were live-in domestics in 1901. One "servant girl" was the sixty-six-year-old housekeeper for an aged priest. (Three other priests lived in the village without such household help.) Another woman aged sixty-eight, worked in the home of a contadino. The remaining two, a mother and daughter of contadino origins (ages sixty and twenty-nine), were "maid servants" in the house of a blacksmith. No large landowner, prosperous peasant, merchant, artisan (except the blacksmith), or member of the small middle class (exempting the priest) had live-in help. There is no record that married or unmarried women worked regularly as domestics on a day basis.

It is possible that there was widespread nonresidential domestic service which women failed to report or the enumerators neglected to record in the census. I cannot be absolutely certain that such circumstances did not pertain, although internal evidence on the ways the recorders treated the request in the census for *"Professione or Condizione"* makes such an occurrence seem highly unlikely. Even if such a condition did exist, it could not be the source of Tilly's domestics. Her regional data are aggregates of local counts. If it wasn't recorded at the local level it couldn't be summarized at higher levels. Perhaps the regional figures reflect a greater incidence of domestic service in urban and more industrialized areas. Could domestic service have been carried on unnoticed by the census within kin networks? That is, could girls have lived in the homes of relatives as domestics but be listed as kin in the census? Probably not. The number of families with females of likely age, marital status, and kinship (niece, cousin, sister-in-law, etc.) were few. In those which did exist, the presence of other adult and minor kin usually suggests classical extended families rather than hidden instances of temporary domestic service.

Unfortunately, the evidence does not yield a definitive judgment. Villa Vallelonga is only one village, albeit a very important one. It was a center of emigration and, as an agricultural community with few wage-earning alternatives to domestic work, it is precisely the setting which Tilly felt would show the primacy of economics over values and mores. Those who stand with McLaughlin in asserting the continuing importance of traditional family values in shaping the lives of Italian women in America will undoubtedly welcome this evidence. Those who prefer a more parsimonious view, which locates the origin of behavior patterns in the immediate economic structure, are not likely to concede the question. The former interpretation is supported here but is not fully vindicated.[15]

By way of summary, the material presented in this chapter can be related to the interesting and important debate over the viability of the ghetto hypothesis. The ghetto as an explanatory force has been central to much historical and contemporary analysis of urban life. Best known in this tradition is probably Oscar Handlin's influential summary of the position with respect to immigrants in *The Uprooted*. This ecological theory posits immigrants and their descendants huddled together in homogeneous, distinct, and separate residential areas of a city as the core of an argument linking persistently unwelcome social, economic, and psychological characteristics to entrapment in these narrow, closed urban environments. Sam Bass Warner, Jr. and Colin B. Burke initiated a rethinking of the validity and power of the ghetto concept as the central organizing concept in the study of immigrants in cities. They identified two fatal flaws in the interpretation. "First, most immigrants never lived in ghettos; second, such ghettos as did exist were probably not the uniform environments that the interpretation implies."

Warner and Burke are willing to concede the appropriateness of a limited ghetto model in the case of Italians and some other eastern European immigrants. Howard P. Chudacoff is less willing to concede even this after a study of Omaha. While he finds Italians more concentrated residentially than other groups, he is reluctant to apply the term *ghetto* to their neighborhoods. Italians were few in number, and even in the most concentrated pockets they shared their streets and blocks with many individuals of different origins. Far from being entrapped, they were nearly as mobile geographically as native Americans. (Chudacoff reports dissimilarity indexes for Italians of 69.4 in 1910 and

53.1 in 1920. Since these measures compare Italians to the native white population, fine contrasts with my indexes, which use the total non-Italian population as the standard, are not justified.)

Still, the similarities between Omaha and the cities considered here are striking. The Italian-born population in each of the cities registered among the highest dissimilarity indexes yet they never approached numerical domination of a ward. Utica, which comes closest to the population prerequisites for a ghetto, falls quite short. Rochester, with its lower dissimilarity index and three separate concentrations, least fits the requirements. The federal and state censuses' shifting patterns of residential dispersion in the New York cities are akin to those in Omaha. Campanilismo, a force which, if stronger, might have promoted a kind of mini-ghetto, proves to be of limited importance. Trends in housing patterns, family organization, and occupation all suggest changes which are not consistent with the centrality of disorganization, debilitation, and maladjustment in the ghetto hypothesis. Italians in Utica, Rochester, and Kansas City did cluster together to a greater degree than most other groups, but their colonies were far from the "air-tight cages" of the ghetto hypothesis. Without a reasonable amount of residential propinquity, it is unlikely that the institutional development described below would have taken place as it did. Perhaps the Italian colonies approached the ghetto ideal type in the largest cities, though Nelli argues against this for Chicago. But the Italians in these more modest cities escaped the most pernicious features attributed to that variety of urban life.[16]

Italians coming to the three cities from homes throughout southern Italy increasingly appear to have settled into a life built on the expectation of long stays in the cities. They faced the problems of defining their relationships with each other and with the broader American society. In this effort the task of balancing immediate interests and realities against considerations motivated by Old World influences appears as a central theme. The next chapter follows the intellectual movement to define the Italo-American. Later chapters will consider the problem as it became operationalized through the community-building process.

6

FROM ITALIAN TO ITALIAN-AMERICAN

Upon committing themselves to more or less permanent residence in the New World, Italians turned their intellectual
energies to the formulation of an acceptable Italo-American
identity. Irving Child built a study of the assimilation of Italians
in America around the question "Italian or American?" His
formulation would have been rejected by most Italians who
wrote on the problem in the three cities. For them the question
was never an either/or proposition. Without exception they
agreed that the circumstances of life in the New World prevented
the simple maintenance of the old unmodified ways, and that
Old World provincialism would perforce give way to a new
identity. Nor did any of the early commentators believe that
Italians should surrender the essentials of their "Italianness."
In broadest terms, these writers agreed that they should, and
inevitably would, remain Italian while becoming Americans as
well. Over time, the view of what should constitute the Italian
and American elements of the formula changed as longer residence and new local circumstances altered the perceptions of
colonial leaders. Within the broad conception there were
certain concerns and topics, such as defending the good name of
Italians, which recurred throughout the period; while others,
like the preservation of the Italian language among the second
generation, were associated more with one or another period
in the growth and development of the colonies.[1]

Before going on, it is necessary to note the looseness in the
use of several terms used in the discussions of this issue. Most
writers on the subject, and the newspapers which printed or
reprinted their words, tended to use words such as *race,
nationality, blood, peoplehood*, etc., in inexact ways. Often

they were used interchangeably and with no clear indication as to whether the traits attributed to them were inherited or acquired attributes. A Kansas City paper quoted favorably the contention of an Italian businessman touring the country that Italians had contributed much to America, "because we have in our blood the tradition of the classic culture that reflects itself in all our ideas." He went on to explain that "there is a law which dominates everybody and is ignorant of both diplomacy and demography, it is the law of heredity and of adaptation which neither psychology nor biology can ignore. The innate characteristics do not disappear for one's whole life but they can be modified, articulated or improved according to the environmental circumstances. Large populations, races and nationalities are subject to the same rules that govern the development of the individual's personal psyche, that is, like a collective personality. This ferment does not happen at home but must follow the law. As a result of this law Italians in America have a notable and decisive influence to play in the development of American civilization." Even with all this, Professor Ottolenghi felt that the Italians here had "much to acquire" from the American environment which includes "such different civilizations." He felt that the intensity of both work and sport among Americans made the country an "antidote for those who bring a neurasthenic disposition with them." Other important Italian acquisitions here were a sense of discipline, voluntary compliance with laws, and a sense of religious toleration.[2]

Editors did not have to rely solely on Italians for flattering assessments of potential Italian contributions to American culture. George McLean Harper, professor of English literature at Princeton University, hoped that in the struggle to make their livelihoods and learn American ways immigrants would not give up those good qualities which are particularly Italian—such as the habit of clear, logical, and skeptical thinking, a fine natural perception of beauty, and a gentleness of manner. He was unclear as to how the immigrants had acquired these virtues; however, he was confident that their children could retain them if they would only learn Italian and read Dante. He predicted

that it would be 10,000 years before America could produce
such a poet and philosopher. The Italian readers, like the editor,
were undoubtedly delighted by this recognition of their poet.
They had long ago learned to invoke the name of the illustrious
Florentine in support of their claim to being the heirs and
carriers of a great civilization.[3]

A corollary to the assumption that Italian immigrants could—
or in fact were—destined by heredity to remain Italian while
becoming American, was the insistence on a definition of
America as a pluralist society. Spokesmen for this view of
Americanization pointed out that the United States was made
up of the sons and daughters of many nations, a true nation of
immigrants. Their conception of the melting pot more closely
resembled the popular description of Canada as a mosaic of
different cultures than the aggressive American notion of purging
the immigrants of their "foreign ways" and replacing them with
American values and practices. Perhaps a better metaphor for
the Italian conception of the Americanization process would be
the lapidary drum, in which various kinds of stones rubbing
against each other are all polished and refined in appearance
and value while not losing their essences.

Confident that their cultural essence was hard and durable,
Italians were not at all reluctant to subject it to the refining
process. Both Rev. J. B. Bisceglia of Kansas City and editor-
businessman Clement Lanni repeatedly referred to the creation
of America and Americans in the present and future tenses.
Bisceglia spoke of the formation of a new civilization, while
Lanni took pride in being part of the process that is responsible
for "the great world citizen, the American, who is now in the
making." He was overjoyed when Professor Bruno Roselli of
Vassar College gave a two-hour address at the prestigious
Women's City Club on Duse, Pirandello, and Papini. Such
American interest in contemporary Italian culture, he felt,
would bring a new American awareness of the potential of
Italian-Americans. Italian leaders were fond of lecturing over-
zealous "Americanizers" on the true meaning of Americanism.
In the heat of the debate over the exclusion of "undesirable
and unassimilable" immigrants, one editor took exception to

Secretary of Labor James J. Davis's aspersion cast upon Italian immigrants. Davis's behavior, the leader felt, indicated that he had not been "truly Americanized." Davis, he pointed out, had been born in Wales.[4]

The first task of early leaders and especially of the ethnic press in creating the new identity was to defend the good name of Italians and their colonies here. The American press at first tended to treat the colonies as exotic enclaves that provided material for special-interest stories. However, they soon took critical stances, stressing crime, social disorganization, and radicalism. Italian editors reacted both with rage and embarrassment when an American newspaper highlighted these aspects of the colony, leaving the direct or indirect impression that they applied to all Italians. A bloody incident in Rome, New York, that resulted in the arrest of forty-eight Italians of which twelve were charged with homicide, provided the kind of situation that Italians, already sensitive about their reputations among Americans, dreaded. Both Italian papers in Utica alternated between condemning the American press for using such sensational incidents to reinforce their negative stereotypes of all Italians, and denouncing their conationals for allowing such "drunken bloodbaths" to occur, thus blackening the name of the whole colony. *L'Avvenire* felt that the practices of carrying handguns and knives unnecessarily and the use of them without full and real cause were doing irreparable harm to the Italian image in America.

The papers had repeated opportunities to lament "always the knife" and warn their readers against such violent acts. One typical incident involved the near-fatal assault by two young Sicilian brothers, aged sixteen and seventeen, on a labor contractor in a dispute over a one-dollar board fee. A psychoanalyst might find it interesting that the same issue of that paper carried a large piece on an exhibition given by an itinerant fencing master at the local theater. Occasionally an Italian paper would support the exposures of American journalists, as when *La Luce* commented that all the repulsive titles for the knife user, such as "bloodthirsty, filthy and stupid should not be spared."[5]

In this same vein, the press continually reminded the colony

that they lived in a sort of fish-bowl in which all their actions
contributed to the reputation of Italians in America. An event
as innocuous as a forthcoming band concert was reason to remind the participants that their efforts would not only reflect
on themselves but on the honor of the Italian name. A lacka-
daisical showing by Italian worker societies at a Columbus Day
parade moved the editor of *La Luce* to launch into a strong
reprimand stressing the obligations of such groups to contribute
to the advancement of the respect and honor of the colony.
"Our Societies," he asserted, "do not in any way have as their
mission to make people laugh but rather they must make themselves respected." Through repeated appeals of this type,
editors stressed the importance of collective action to advance
the reputation of Italians. Lanni went so far as to lecture newly
elected Italian politicians. He reminded them of the extra responsibility they had shouldered, because their actions would
reflect not only on themselves but also on the great mass of
Italians in the city, who would rise or fall in honor as did their
leaders.[6]

While Italian leaders and their press continued to remind
their fellows of the importance of discreet behavior, they
seldom dampened their criticism of American journalists for
the adverse publicity Italians received. The latter were accused
of limiting themselves to narrating the bare facts of a "black
chronicle when Americans or other groups were involved,"
but would "cry out against the Italians as the shepherd at the
sight of the wolf every time an Italian was accused of a crime."
Responsibility for most of the negative Italian image was laid at
the door of the American press. Occasionally the outrage was
so great that it produced a colony-wide uproar. A raid by 150
policemen on gangsters and their cigar stores in Kansas City's
"Little Italy" provided such a reaction that a mass meeting was
held at the neighborhood school to protest the insult, police
brutality, and the tendency of the police, city officials, and the
Kansas City Star to lump all Italians together as criminal types.
One enraged letter writer referring to the incident contended
that the gangsters were American-born and had been rejected by
the colony. In 1911, fourteen Italian societies in Utica announced

that they were banding together to join a national campaign against the American press, which was harming the good Italian name.[7]

Occasionally Italians found themselves portrayed in other than the "Dago" image. In 1905 the *Utica Daily Press* printed a very favorable article which lavishly praised the Italian colony for making much progress in a short time. It pointed to their rapid increase in numbers, their large savings in local banks, and the import duties in excess of $30,000 paid by their merchants, who had the reputation for prompt payment of their debts. The paper also noted the ample number of Italian-American professionals—doctors, dentists, and midwives; their two energetic newspapers; provision for intellectual development; active construction of buildings in the colony; increasing political and civic participation; and the prosperity of its numerous societies. In the face of such an assessment, the editor of *L'Avvenire*, in the name of the whole colony, enthusiastically pled guilty on all counts. Unremitting pride and glorification of Italian achievements, whether they were the successes of a merchant, reports of large numbers of Italians naturalized, or a successful tour of an Italian opera star, formed other elements in the program to create a positive Italian-American identity. Even such simple events as the purchase (by a successful merchant) of the grand home of a prominent, old American family was of great symbolic importance and a source of obvious pride for one Utica editor.[8]

The legend of Columbus proved to be a fortuitous element in this process of building respect for the colony. He was a popular hero in both lands. Schoolchildren in Rochester held special activities on Columbus Day as early as 1890. In Palermo, Sicily, in spite of the recency of the glories of the Italian unification, the major part of the history curriculum for the first elementary grade was devoted to Columbus's exploits. Invoking his name was sufficient in any defense of Italians; there was no need for long explanations. Occasionally, an Italian would feel the need to challenge claims to Columbus's origins which were apparently being made by the Spanish. The appearance of this "false history" inevitably produced a stinging rebuttal in English, defending the Genoese claim to the great navigator as their most distinguished son.

The importance and significance of Col021us to Italian self-definition are symbolized in the masthead of *La Luce*. It featured two scenes. The first depicted the arrival of Columbus with nude Indians onshore to greet him. The second featured a steamship halfway between America (represented as the Statue of Liberty waving a flag) and Italy (presented as a similarly draped woman with an Italian flag). In the background were cities with characteristic American and Italian architecture. The masthead was designed by Carlo Milanese, an engineer and architect who was then enjoying prominence in the colony as a cultural and professional leader. In Milanese's mind, "the upper represents the new light of civilization being brought to the primitive natives, the new light in the New World. In the second, progress is portrayed. Two flags, two people so distant from each other, America with her wonderful mechanical and engineering products and Italy, mother and cultivator of civilization and the fine arts." Clearly, Italians were being told to think of themselves as modern-day Columbuses. Columbus Day celebrations, Columbus parks and streets, all became ways of reinforcing this contention and exacting sometimes grudging recognition from Americans. Politicians soon learned that to address Italian audiences as "sons of Columbus" was a sure-fire opener.[9]

While Columbus offered Italians a unique opportunity to bask in the glory of an Italian and American hero and to obscure any contradictions in their dual commitment to being of both nationalities, the status of Italy in Americans' eyes was a consistent concern of the colonies. The commemoration of 20 September (the day on which Garabaldi seized Rome from papal control) acquired here a significance beyond the celebration of an Old World national holiday: it had to be tied to their New World existence. Editorials proclaimed it as the celebration of a great world victory for freedom and the end of the threat of theocracy through papal claims to temporal power. In like manner, Marconi was often invoked to demonstrate that Italian science had much to offer even to technologically advanced countries like the United States. Technological and

engineering achievements such as the construction of the
electric railroad through the Alps received prominent treatment
in the Italian-American press. The discovery that an Italian
immigrant, Antonio Meucci, filed an application for a patent on
a telephone five years before Alexander Graham Bell but lacked
the money to complete the processing, led to a widely reprinted
article, "Was an Italian Immigrant the Inventor of the Telephone?"[10]

Pride in Italy and things Italian suffered in a period of strain
and discomfiture during World War I. An example of how
sensitive a nerve Italy's reputation was, can be seen in the
reaction of the chairman of the Federation of Italo-American
Irredentists Associations to two sentences in the New York City
history curriculum. The Utica paper endorsed the protest
completely and printed the refutation in the hope that the
heretical history would not spread. The points in question were:
"Italy before the war was under treaty obligation to support
Germany and Austria but she remained neutral"; and "Italy
later entered the war on the side of the Allies because she feared
for her territory." The first assertion, Professor Oldrini stated,
implied that Italy was a traitor to her former allies, ignoring
the fact that she was entitled to withdraw from the alliance
when her allies initiated a war of aggression. The second statement distorts the truth "that Italy denounced the Triple Alliance
to urgently protect France's east and south without which she
could not have withdrawn all her troops to the Marne and
would thus have been unmistakably crushed by Germany; and
the world, including America, would have been under military
command of triumphant pan Germanism." Once warmed up,
he went on to tell it as he saw it:

> You teach the childhood of New York that Italy declared
> war on the Central Powers in 1915, although she was barely
> prepared for such a war, in fear of losing her territory. When
> the whole civilized world proclaimed in speech and printed
> public documents, that Italy rightfully fought for her
> national aspirations, but above all in defense of civilization,
> losing 507,000 men on the battlefields, nearly half a million

more dead of wounds and diseases contracted in her hard
war; and fighting with such valor that she destroyed single
handed Austria's army and autocratic empire, thereby
freeing many subject peoples and unmistakably determining
the collapse of the German Empire itself.

We of New York, one hundred percent loyal to this Republic,
indignantly protest in the name of all Italo-American citizens
and residents, and of the 300,000 soldiers of Italian blood
enlisted under the Stars and Stripes in this war . . . against
. . . such history.[11]

The negative effects of Italy's participation in the war did
not disappear as quickly as immigrants here might have wished.
In 1926 Missouri senator James Reed cast aspersions on the
bravery and fighting quality of the Italian army in a speech on
the Senate floor, when he asserted that the Allies had to save
Italy at the cost of American blood after her soldiers had de-
serted. Reed, who had previously been praised by the Kansas
City Italian press for his isolationist stand, now received the
full impact of its wrath. One piece, an open letter by the
president of the council of Italian societies, presented a "true"
history of the Italians' important contributions to Allied success
and asserted that the only American casualty in connection
with the Italian phase of the war was the result of a bathing
accident. The point at issue, the Italian war debt, was ultimately
turned to advantage when the colony started a drive to raise
money to help pay it off. In all, they collected $873 from
4,430 subscribers in less than three months. This ingenious
campaign allowed the colony to merge patriotic support for
both mother and adopted countries into one activity.[12]
   There was general agreement in the colonies that it was
desirable, perhaps inevitable, that Italians should learn the ways
of Americans without completely surrendering their Italian
culture as they learned to be "Americans." There was difference
of opinion, however, on what constituted this new man and the
means necessary to produce him. Knowledge of English was
generally agreed upon in the Americanization portion of the

formula. In many different conscious and less conscious ways, the Italian-American papers pushed the message that mastering English would bring economic, social, and political rewards. The more militant "Americanizers," such as Clement Lanni, persistently and pointedly argued for it. Most simply reported favorably on the advances made by those who had mastered English and announced the opportunities offered by societies, churches, and night schools for learning the language. Only very occasionally did any reservations against learning English appear. In 1903 the editor of *La Luce*, writing on the preoccupation with English, stressed that while he did not want his readers to abandon the study of that language, which could be more or less useful to them at the moment, he felt that "in the civilization of the Italian langugage . . . [were] thousands of secrets for our future in America."[13]

The second generation presented the language problem in reverse. Shortly after taking up his work among Italians in St. Paul, Minnesota, Roman Catholic priest Rev. Simon Nicolas Odone wrote to a colleague in Baltimore seeking counsel on the best Italian catechism to use with Italian children. The advice returned by the Baltimore priest, a veteran of many years' service in America, was to abandon the idea of an Italian-language catechism for all but adults. "They [the children] speak English in the school and the streets, this *is* and *will be* their language" (Odone's italics). The Baltimore priest made it clear that to insist on instruction in Italian would entail the added burden of teaching the children the language before they could be taught their catechism. This lesson was to be learned and relearned by a succession of parents and colony leaders. Parents often spoke only a dialect, but even if they spoke Italian, their children were far more likely to become literate in English than Italian.[14]

Although English did not carry any emotional ties to "Americanism" (see n. 13), Italian was viewed by some as an indispensable cornerstone of Italianness. The realization that their children were not learning it produced recurrent demands for action to correct this deficiency in the second generation. A Utica editor recognized the problems, and felt that both the deficiency and

its remedy lay within the family. In an editorial, "A Duty of the
Heads of Families," he maintained that it is the most sacred
duty of the parents to the homeland to see that their children
learn Italian, because "although born here they are Italians
and have, thus, the right to know the language of their homeland."

At this point it seems that the author was expressing a clear
commitment to the Old World. However, he went on to cloud
the issue and express the common dual commitment to both
nations. Knowing his audience, he felt he had to convince them
that nothing would be lost if the father insisted on the exclusive use of Italian in the home. The children, after all, learned
English from the first day they went to school. He next dis-
paraged the mixed use of Italian and English as a"horrible and
barbaric blend." He then appealed to the vanity and self-esteem
of the immigrants by pointing to those who, knowing a little
English, try to "use it like professors with their children . . .
[with] pernicious effects for the children." It is well known, he
asserted, that after a certain age one never truly masters the
form and pronunciation of English. Since parents could remain
masters of their native tongue, it was futile to rack their brains
in an effort to speak imperfect English to children who would
quickly surpass their elders in its usage. Finally, the appeal
called for the emulation of the French, Russians, Germans, and
Jews who competed to keep their idioms alive. Clearly this
editor felt his readers would not respond to an appeal based
solely on a call of duty to Italy.[15]

His argument, however, ignores a salient fact—namely, that
many heads of families were only imperfect masters of Italian as
well. A combination of regional dialects, corruptions of English,
and Italian quickly became the vernacular of the colonies.
Jerre Mangione, in remembrances of his youth in Rochester,
records that two Sicilians would only use proper Italian when
they met for the first time, to prove that they were schooled
and not peasants. His experience with the absorption of Amer-
icanisms reflects the subtle transitions which can rapidly take
place in an informal vernacular. As long as Mangione could
remember, the word *baccauso*, signifying toilet, was part of the

local vocabulary. It was only as an adult on his first visit to Italy
that he realized that the true derivation of the word came from
an earlier period in America when the backhouse flourished! It
may well have been a remnant of the migrant-camp era for
Rochester immigrants.

In the Mangione home only Italian was spoken, at the insistence of his parents. Jerre's mother and many of the immigrant
generation of relatives had very little facility with English. Mrs.
Mangione would not allow her children to speak a language
which the entire family could not use. "I might as well not have
my children if I can't talk with them" was her attitude. The
only exception allowed to this policy was the instance of a
sister who used English when she talked in her sleep. An uncle
who had allowed his children to grow up knowing so little
Sicilian that he was virtually unable to converse with them,
suffered barbs from the family as well as the anguish of the
actual generation gap. Outside the home the children were
expected to use English and their mother took pride in their
proficiency. They spoke it so well, in fact, that almost none of
their relatives could understand it. In each instance the reasons
for the choice of one or the other language were eminently
practical and had little to do with nationalistic sentiments or
loyalties.[16]

Mangione seldom heard proper Italian except when a univer-
sity-educated uncle made speeches. Probably few other second-
generation Italians had a more intensive exposure. In 1927
Rochesterian and cultural conservative G. Oberdan Rizzo
scolded the colony's business and professional men, only 10
percent of whom he claimed could speak, much less write,
proper Italian. For largely second-generation leaders "Italian
was nothing but 'Siciliano' or worse," in spite of their education.
He chided them for being unable to communicate to or through
the Italian press and for being outdone in the Italian lodge
meetings by mere laborers. This appeal was mainly to pride and
only incidentally to recall an obligation to Italy. Significantly,
Rizzo ended his letter by admonishing all Italian high-school
students and professionals to learn Italian, "of all the *foreign*
languages, the one most useful to you" (my italics).

For those advocating the language of Dante as an essential element of the Italian-American identity, another means had to be found for teaching it to children. This concern was part of the early appeal for support of Italian parochial schools. Another popular action was to request that Italian be offered in the public-school curriculum along with German and French. Success in such proposals also placated Italian sensitivities by symbolically placing their language on a par with other modern languages. Also, Americans studying Italian would come to understand Italy's heritage and appreciate her contributions to Western civilization. A corollary set of motives lay behind the early concern by a Utica paper over the paucity of Italian materials in the public library. There were a great many German-language books and works of German authors in the library because, the paper asserted, the Germans sent many readers to the library to ask for them. Italians must do the same for "only with the diffusion of our own language and of the homeland traditions can they enjoy the esteem and affection which they do not now enjoy."[17]

Although there were occasional introductions of Italian into public-school curricula before World War I, the campaign for its inclusion received the greatest impetus in the 1920s, when it became clear that other measures to teach the language to the second generation had failed. In Utica a 1914 editorial stated that if it wasn't practical to have Italian taught in the elementary and middle schools, at least it should be introduced into the high schools without delay. The paper reasoned that increasing numbers of Italians attending the Utica Free Academy could profit from such an opportunity. Nothing came of this or, at a later date, of more concerted efforts supported by the state officers of the Sons of Italy Society. Throughout the period the academy regularly offered Latin, French, and Spanish and intermittently taught Greek and German. Italian was not offered. The first Italian-language course to be taught in a Kansas City public school was in the city junior college's night school and was introduced at the instigation of a group of American students. After announcing the course, a correspondent of *La Stampa* hoped for a large enrollment of Italian "adults as well as students."

Three weeks prior to this announcement and approximately two weeks before the opening of the 1923 fall semester, the same correspondent reported on his investigation into the status of Italian in the public schools. In a talk with the principal of the high school, he was told that Italian was not offered because no one had requested it. "Is such possible in a city with a population of 20,000 Italians?" he asked. There was "a curious circle" here. The school board had not instituted Italian because it was not requested, and it was not in demand because it was not offered. To break this cycle, he requested all children entering high school and their parents to demand that Italian be taught rather than French or English. The principal assured him that when twenty-five enrolled, a class in the language would be opened. If many asked, the board would open more classes. The correspondent showed a certain skepticism, for he asked his readers to help compile a list of those who requested Italian in order to destroy the "no request, so not offered" pattern of excuses. The matter then disappeared from the paper, suggesting that the demand did not materialize as Italian leaders had insisted it would. Three years later a letter decried the lack of Italian language taught in secondary schools, with the observation that in the Midwest Italian-Americans could only study "their beautiful language in college."[18]

The Italian-American press generally viewed American citizenship as a good thing. Editorials pointed to the political and economic advantages accruing to the individual and the colony from citizenship. These columns also assured readers that in becoming American citizens they were not surrendering their Italianness or performing an act disloyal to their native country. The papers periodically published various kinds of ads and encouragements toward naturalization. One popular item was a page with parallel columns giving representative questions from naturalization exams in both English and Italian. Readers learned of classes and other opportunities to prepare for the exams and received basic instructions on how to apply for citizenship. In addition, the press often published the names of the latest group of new citizens and showed undisguised pride when

Italians were well represented. Ardent "Americanizers" distinguished themselves from their fellow journalists only by the frequency and the lengths to which they would go in promoting naturalization. Lanni even advocated a hitch in the military. Immigrant soldiers first went to Camp Upton near New York City, where they prepared for naturalization by learning to read and write English and mastered other useful skills such as arithmetic. Recruits could study there for up to six months, though this was seldom necessary. To Lanni, the most attractive feature of this program was the opportunity to obtain citizenship in three rather than the usual five years.[19]

Even the Italian government expressed no open hostility to the trend toward naturalization. In 1922 the Italian ambassador to the United States, Vittorio Ricci, urged immigrants here to take up citizenship. He told a San Francisco audience that "the Italians who neglect to become American citizens are without a country. Here you labor, here you construct your houses and raise your families. Make yourselves, then, completely united with the adopted land." In 1912 the Italian parliament revised its citizenship law and, while it did not go so far as some advocated in making provision for double citizenship, it did partially recognize such a position. Although Italians lost their Italian citizenship when they acquired foreign citizenship, this did not eliminate the obligations of military service incumbent on all Italian-born males. This provision became a real threat to naturalized Italo-Americans, who during the Mussolini years were sometimes impressed into the Italian military while on visits to Italy. Most important, however, was the ease with which Italian citizenship could be reacquired under the 1912 revisions. Rendering military service or entering government employment, renouncing foreign citizenship and taking up residence in Italy, or residency for two years in Italy or with special permission in a foreign country other than the one where one held citizenship all were ways for Italians to recover their citizenship.[20]

In summary, the generally accepted definition of an Italian-American was an individual who carried two countries in his

heart, who was the product of the best of two civilizations and
two peoples. His foremost heroes were those who had significance for both nations. For a short period in the wake of World
War I the balance swung strongly toward emphasis on the
American side of the equation, with the Sons of Italy temporarily ignoring their Italian programs in an all-out effort to teach
English. The frenzy did not last long. By 1921 ethnic pride had
reasserted itself, as illustrated by the publication of the following poem of Rose Russo, the ten-year-old daughter of a prominent Missouri musician:

It Took a Dago

It took a Dago to find our Land,
It took a Dago to lead that Band
Which has traveled like a toy,
O'er the world to give joy!
It took a Dago to make Spaghetti
Perhaps his name was Capuletti;
It took a Dago to make the vino,
It took a Dago to find cassino.
It took a Dago to pull harp strings,
It took a Dago to do all things!
So if you are from Sardinia,
Or if you're from Catania
You're all right, the whole world tell,
If you're a Dago, all is well![21]

The elements on both sides of the Italian-American equation
were not fixed or static. Between 1900 and 1930 subtle transitions took place in Italian-Americans' self-perceptions, symbolized in the sports reporting of the local press. In 1903 a
prominent and long-time resident of Utica, Elia Pellettieri,
sponsored the colony championships in *bocce* with a box of
cigars. The leading teams were composed of men from the
towns of Lucca and Laurenzana. The Laurenzanesi carried the
day. In self-concept they were Italian. Patriotism in their
speeches referred to obligations to Italy. Respect and obligations due America were like those of guests for their host. By

the 1920s the papers reported on Italian baseball and basketball
teams competing in industrial, city, and church leagues. Bocce
continued to be played by the older immigrants, of course, but
the recreational interests of Italians now closely paralleled those
of Americans, as the "pool hall" became a center where the
young men of the colony could meet, and poker even replaced
briscola as the favorite card game. Patriotism was now associated
with America. Italy and things Italian remained important, but
in the nature of a cherished and romanticized past that had
emotional significance and served as a determinant of group
status in the new home to which they were now committed.[22]

The Italian intellectuals and professionals whose opinions provided the material for the major part of this chapter were atypi-
cal. Although they sought to speak for, and of course to, the
whole colony, the credibility of their assertions must be scruti-
nized independently of their own testimony, as far as this is
possible. Yet for certain kinds of information they provided the
only sources in the colony. Among their biases, perhaps the
most dangerous for the historian is associated with their paternal
attitude toward the masses in the colonies. When an Italian
editor lectured what he condescendingly called "our working
men's societies" on what their appropriate activities and duties
should be, or announced that an alliance had been formed to
foster the educational redemption of the working classes, he
contributed to a prejudicial stereotype.

Yet this very material indicates the fact that the workers'
organizations had indigenous leadership and direction. The same
is true of the colony as a whole. Whether they were interested
in instilling Italian high culture or pushing "Americanization,"
these leaders were part of a small vocal minority in a community
overwhelmingly composed of persons of working-class origins.
The degree to which appeals to language maintenance as a
national obligation were reflected in the actual sentiments of
the majority of people in the colonies is questionable. The
leaders recognized this themselves and in their admonitions included arguments based on utility and pride. A closer examina-

tion of the social, business, and educational life of Italians in
the three cities will test the congruence between the intellectual
ideal and the everyday reality of the Italian-American experience.

ORGANIZATIONAL GROWTH IN "ITALIAN COLONIES"

Description of the process of community building is complicated by several factors. First, the creation of a colony involved
both the definition of a variety of relationships among Italians
themselves, and between Italians and Americans. The energetic
pursuit of competence in English and an enthusiastic embracing
of American education by a young immigrant (detailed below)
represented only one of several popular responses to living in
American society. A second occurrence that complicated the
picture was the steady arrival of new immigrants. It is a challenge
to describe a fluid population which became increasingly complex as older settlers making their adjustments were joined by
new immigrants. This steady supply of newcomers led contemporary observers and some scholars to view immigrants and
their problems as static, when in fact these colonies were undergoing important changes. While older residents were moving
toward one or more of several types of accommodation with
life in these cities, far more visible newcomers were going through
the most trying early stages of settlement, giving the appearance
to outsiders of a persistent and unchanging "Italian problem."[1]
The overall pattern, then, was increasing complexity and
variety as the colonies matured. The first immigrants attempted
to re-create what was already familiar to them and then proceeded with modifications as changing perceptions, needs, and
desires dictated. Later arrivals had the example of those already
in the colony, but they lacked the experience necessary to
understand and appreciate the views of the earlier migrants. The
popular term "greenhorn" sums up the distance that existed between old-timers and newcomers. So the more recent immigrants
began approximately where earlier settlers had begun before

138

them, and followed in a fashion similar to the colony's pioneers,
thus producing social and cultural layering in the colonies. With
a selected use of evidence, one could argue that by the 1920s
the Italians had been fairly quickly and thoroughly Americanized,
or that they stubbornly persisted in their traditional ways.
Either portrayal alone is an unacceptable distortion. A cross-
sectional slice through the colony would reveal numerous semi-
stable strata. Time of arrival and length of residence are
important factors for understanding the location of individuals
in the layers. Other significant variables include occupation,
family obligations, educational level, and intentions concerning
repatriation. Old World origins are also relevant. Groups with
many fellow townsmen or relatives had more options when planning their organizational life. The colonies at their most advanced stage in the 1920s, far from being homogeneous, were
mosaics of social and cultural forms. Increasing dominance of
the second generation and the termination of mass immigration
slowly reversed this, but that story is largely beyond the scope
of the present investigation.

Early Italian immigration to each of the three cities under
consideration here was sporadic and generally temporary in
nature. Canal, railroad, and public utilities construction attracted roving bands of men specializing in excavation and other
unskilled outdoor work. Such temporary settlement remained
one important characteristic of Italian migration to the cities
during the early twentieth century. Day laborers often lived
in camps or in boarding enclaves outside the city, run by a few
more permanent residents of the area. Most stayed only as long
as the construction project offered employment. They had
little impact on the American community and usually considered themselves transients. These early migrations always
involved single males. Passport records, New York State census
schedules, and the St. Paul, Minnesota, parish censuses all give
evidence of families experiencing the same migratory patterns.
It is possible to find examples of families with children born in
three or four different communities on this side of the Atlantic
as well as one or more born in Italy.[2]

Some years after his arrival, a Rochester resident described

his early experience in this migratory way of life. He arrived in
New York City in May 1902, not yet sixteen years of age. His
uncle immediately took him to Fairhaven, Vermont, to work on
the construction of a trolley line. In September there was a strike
against a tyrannical boss and a number of men set out for Sara-
toga Springs, New York, where they found work on a sewer
excavation project. The uncle, dissatisfied with his failure to replace the Italian foreman already there, moved on alone to
Pennsylvania. His nephew caught up with him again in Ralston,
Pennsylvania, where the latter found him a job on a railroad
construction project. They lived in a shanty camp under very
harsh conditions throughout the winter. When this job ended,
the young man changed jobs but not location. He spent two
years working in a tannery and was just beginning to feel a
sense of permanence when a change of foreman necessitated
another move.

Planning to meet a friend, he came to Rochester in the spring
of 1905, where he hoped to find a job plying his trade of shoe-
making in one of the numerous shoe factories there. Pay for
such work was poor, so he went back to construction while he
looked for a better-paying and more permanent job, which he
eventually found in a woodworking factory. By now showing
signs of growing tired of the transient life, he expanded his ties
with Italians in Rochester, becoming involved in a play given
by Italians at the Labor Lyceum and Concordia Hall. He
launched an active campaign to learn English, first by reviewing
his Italian grammar thoroughly and then by attending school.
He also pushed forward with a self-improvement program that
included regular reading of "the instructive kind" of literature
and three years of mandolin lessons. The young man developed
a real commitment to the evening school. Once married, he
brought his wife to the classes and promoted them among his
fellow Italians. He had been in Rochester for eight years at the
time he wrote of his experiences. During that period he made
one visit back to Italy. His experience of early mobility in following day-laboring jobs, succeeded by more permanent residence and greater involvement in both Italian and American
communities, was part of the biography of many Italians in the

Ecce Homo Society, Rochester, at the home of one of its leaders about
1928. A clothing manufacturer sponsored their band. The immigrants
drew on familiar Old World forms in establishing their associational life
and also participated in broader American organizations. (Courtesy of
Margaret Zaccone.)

An Italian leads organized labor's symbol of a strike breaker in Rochester's
1910 Labor Day Parade. (From the Stone Negative Collection of the
Rochester Museum and Science Center.)

The Red Band, Utica, 1921. (Courtesy of Sam Puleo.)

Hucksters loading their wagons in preparation for their daily rounds, 1911. The close proximity of the Rochester public market and the East Side Italian colony made the continuation of traditional patterns of shopping possible and provided the wholesale produce for numerous Italian merchants and peddlers. (From the Stone Negative Collection of the Rochester Museum and Science Center.)

Women shopping at the Rochester public market, 1913. (From the Stone Negative Collection of the Rochester Museum and Science Center.)

A wading pool in an immigrant area of Rochester, 1913. (From the Stone Negative Collection of the Rochester Museum and Science Center.)

Children at the Rochester Truant School about 1900. The problem of truancy touched all lower-class groups. (Courtesy of the Rochester Public Library.)

A typical residence on Frank Street, Rochester, between Smith Street and Lyell Avenue. Italians were well integrated into this block before World War I. The prevalence of single houses and free-standing duplexes in the three colonies provided small plots of land for gardens, which were the source of much competition among the immigrants. (Courtesy of the Rochester Public Library.)

A business district in the Italian colony, North and Ontario streets, Rochester, 1911. An Italian druggist, real estate broker, photographer, tailor, shoemaker, confectioner, and several barbers, grocers, and fruit dealers shared these business blocks with a number of non-Italian merchants. It is important to recognize that the urban environment of Rochester, Utica, and Kansas City differed significantly in scale and spatial features from the tenement sections of New York City. (Courtesy of the Rochester Public Library.)

The first block of Frank Street, Rochester, 1915. In the center are the Roman Catholic cathedral, the Eastman Kodak factory, and Gioia & Bellanca Company, one of four Italian macaroni manufacturers in the city. Italians succeeded Irish residents in this block after 1905. (From the Stone Negative Collection of the Rochester Museum and Science Center.)

Old School No. 6, corner of Lyell Avenue and Frank Street. It became the first Italian parish and parochial school in Rochester. (Courtesy of the Rochester Historical Society.)

Old School No. 5 in the Italian colony of Rochester, 1926. During the period covered in this study, this school changed from one of the most modern to one of the more antiquated buildings in the city system, making impossible any simple characterization of the physical resources provided for the education of Italian children. This building was replaced in 1927, starting the cycle once again.

three cities. At any given time there were a number of these
highly mobile individuals only briefly resident in a city. Others
were in the process of making the city their last stop.[3]

The first cores around which an Italian colony solidified
were the boardinghouse and the saloon. In Utica these two
indispensable early institutions were united in a single family's
hands. Elia Pellettieri came to Utica in 1865 at the age of seventeen after spending several years in Cuba as a musician. He apparently worked for Alessandro Lucca, a plaster statuary maker
and saloon keeper. He later married Lucca's daughter and inherited the saloon in the early 1870s. This establishment and
the adjacent boardinghouse became the first stopping-off places
for increasing numbers of Italians who drifted into the city to
work on railroad construction and in the city's many brickyards.
The boardinghouse provided temporary shelter until more permanent arrangements could be made, while the saloon served as
social and recreational center, union hall, and general focal
point for the colony. It was there that men learned of job opportunities, and on rainy days and Sundays, or when there was
no work, they passed the time at the Italian bowling game of
bocce, and card games such as *briscola* and *tresette.* Indicative
of the prominence of the saloon keeper, the first society was
founded at Elia's house, with his brother Salvatore as its first
president.[4]

It should not be surprising, after seeing the importance of
associational activities to Italian workers, to find the same Italians as immigrants turning to similar activities. In fact, the
first institutional activities of Italians took place in this area.
In 1889 they incorporated a society "to aid and assist each other
when in distress, to aid and succor the family, widows, and
orphans of members when needed, and to produce benevolence
and charity toward all" under the title Società Italiana di Pro-
gresso ed Aiuto. Among the leaders of this first society were
individuals who had spent a number of years in the city.

President Pellettieri first came to Utica as a traveling musician
at the age of nine. He settled there permanently in 1881. Five
years later he opened a grocery store, the first of a series of
successful business enterprises. Pietro Cavallo, another who

came to Utica in the capacity of a traveling musician, settled there with his family in 1874 and became foreman of the Weaver Brickyards. Other leaders were residents for a least five years prior to the founding of the society. Their initial employments were as laborers in a brickyard, a stove foundry, and a shoe factory. Two of them went on to entrepreneurial activities. Later-arriving immigrants did not have to wait so long for fortuitous conditions to found societies.[5]

Six years later a second society appeared in the growing colony. The Società Capi dei Famigli Italo-Americana di Mutuo Soccorso sought "to unite and combine the efforts of all its members to improve the condition of its membership socially, morally, intellectually, and materially by wise and timely counsel, instructive lessons and lectures on moral and social subjects; to promote benevolence and charity by visiting, aiding and caring for the sick and destitute members; to encourage each other in business, and give assistance in obtaining employment." The early leadership of this society closely resembled that of Progress and Aid. Salvatore Pellettieri was again the president. (He gave up his post in the earlier group a year after its founding.) Others included a stone mason, a coal-yard worker, and several laborers. One went on to found an important packing company, while another was later to serve as founder and longtime business agent of The Italian Construction Workers Union.

In all of these early societies, the leadership was composed of men with a number of years residency; yet, as it turned out, only one of these leaders spent the major part of the rest of his life in the city. Societies arose at a point in which the Italian population had grown so that it could support such institutions, when a feeling of semipermanence made organization practical, and when an increasing sense of community interest and growing family obligations made it necessary. It is significant that one society was called Heads of Families and the other made specific mention of widows and orphans in its incorporation statement.[6]

Such early societies closely resemble in structure and scope their contemporary namesakes in Italy. They are clearly worker

initiated and led. Their leaders tended to have some skill and to
be upwardly mobile. The Utica papers repeatedly identified
the societies generally as "our worker societies," making explicit
the heavy working-class composition of these organizations.
There were important differences between the Italian and American forms that may have reflected new circumstances associated
with immigration. No elaborate benefit schedules or regulations
and constitutions usually associated with the societies in Italy
have survived in the three cities. The incorporation papers commonly carried an explicit provision that the support or benefit
function of the society would be extended solely at the discre-
tion of the society. The Società Marsicana De Muto (*sic*) Soccorso of Rochester proposed "to give such mutual aid and assistance to its members as it may be able, . . . and to pay such
benefits in case of sickness or death as may be warranted by the
funds of the organization on hand from time to time, but, however, all contributions by the Corporation are to be voluntarily
given."

This desire on the part of the early societies to avoid binding
commitments and remain free to make separate decisions on
the worthiness of individual members perhaps reflects the short
time the immigrants had had to get to know each other. The
highly dynamic nature of the colony meant that societies had
to make quick evaluations of the characters of prospective members, while a man's reputation in Italy was either well-known or
fairly easy to check up on. Also there are numerous indications
that most Italians still considered their sojourn in the United
States to be temporary. As a result, long-term and fixed commitments made less sense and carried higher risks than they did
in the homeland. Retirement plans were less necessary.

Still, the societies did provide significant aid to members.
The Progress and Aid Society announced in 1904 that, on the
average, it was paying out between $700 and $800 a year in
subsidies. The largest single recipient was a member who received a total of over $200 after losing a leg in an accident. The
societies often engaged doctors to serve their members. Not the
least among the benefits offered were funerals. The sight of
Michele Tufolo, a young, unmarried immigrant who drowned

while working on a construction project, being accompanied to his last resting place by the combined memberships of the Progress and Aid and the Bersaglieri societies, must have given some secret comfort to his fellow immigrants. If the ultimate misfortune should befall them, they would not be buried anonymously and unmourned.[7]

Although the benefits at times of sickness or death were important to the immigrants, the societies' services to the living and healthy were far more numerous. The societies generally expressed a concern for the moral and intellectual advancement of their members. Yet there was no attempt to establish schools or hire teachers for the exclusive benefit of a given membership. Members of a Rome, New York, society sought "to attain proficiency in art, literature and music." A Rochester group proposed to maintain a reading room, while another expected "to encourage literary research." I have already noted that the Heads of Families Society contemplated offering lessons and lectures to its members. Those intellectual concerns found occasional manifestation in the activities of the societies.[8]

Also important, if reporting in the Italian press is representative of the doings of the societies, were their social functions. Societies typically had at least two major social gatherings a year. In the winter there would be an annual ball or dance held at a local hall. The eleventh annual dance of the Progress and Aid Society attracted more than five hundred. Another traditional event for these groups was the summer outing. These were grand, day-long affairs held in local parks. The picnickers usually met at a central spot in the colony and paraded with a marching band to the park. Early in the twentieth century, the Progress and Aid Society made this affair into an excursion. A large part of the colony marched to Central Station where they took a train to Trenton Falls and held their outing at the foot of the park's cascade. Activities included races, bocce, music, fireworks, and speeches. Polish bands and marching units occasionally participated in these festivities. Banquets were also popular.

These activities were generally considered as fund-raising functions and, as such, were open to the whole colony.

However, occasionally a society would play on its exclusiveness and close its affairs to nonmembers. The societies also provided a means for making intercolony contacts. Visits by a whole society or by a delegation from one community to the festivities of a society in a different community were common. In 1902 both of the early Utica societies, along with ones from Canastota and Oneida, traveled to nearby Rome to participate in a parade and gala picnic (complete with bicycle and horse races) held under the auspices of the Società Stella d'Italia.

A steady stream of greenhorns arriving each year prompted concern in the societies for helping fellow immigrants to live more effective and successful lives in the United States. Utica's Giuseppe Garibaldi Society exhibited this "Americanization Italian style" when it proposed "to materially improve the condition of its members morally and mentally by instructive lessons in American Citizenship." A Rochester group sought "to familiarize its members with the laws of the State of New York [and] to promote interest in public affairs." By the early twentieth century the societies were active participants in American national holidays and other patriotic celebrations. In 1905 the Fourth of July parade in Utica had contingents from seven Italian societies, including equestrian and "military" units.[9]

The societies also provided a mechanism by which the immigrants could deal collectively with the broader community and promote their interests. In 1902 master tailor Francesco Brindisi, as president of the Progress and Aid Society, circulated a protest to the American press on their reporting of Italian news. The society felt it was enough to cite the facts concerning an individual event without throwing the responsibility for it onto all Italians. A year later they petitioned the governor of the state to declare 12 October (Columbus Day) a legal holiday. The societies also provided the organizational mechanism for a local subscription drive in support of a hospital for tubercular children in Italy.[10]

By the turn of the century the colony at Utica was larger and more diverse than it had been five or ten years earlier. One result of this continual growth was increasing specialization and variety in new associations. The appearance of more specialized

organizations suggests, following a popular theory in voluntary
association research, a drift toward modernism. Yet the general
societies with broad-based, working-class leadership and membership and multiple goals flourished, and new ones continued to
form. Judged by numbers of members, this older type of society
remained strongest in all of the three cities as late as 1910. Kansas City's Società Italo-America far surpassed any other group
in size. Utica's Progress and Aid Society remained the dominant
organization, while the Heads of Families Society slipped badly.

Second place in the latter city went to the very vigorous
Società Calabria, founded in 1903 under the principles of "con-
cord, brotherhood, education, instruction, work [and] honesty."
This new variant on the mutual benefit society stressed common
origins from a specific region, province, or city in the kingdom.
Sicilians and Calabrians formed the first such society in Utica
(Magna Grecia) in 1901. The Società Laurenzana followed in
1902, with Salvatore Pellettieri as a leader, this time among his
fellow townsmen. The Missanellesi formed a society in 1904,
followed by the Italo-Albanians in 1905. The same period witnessed the founding of the Società degli Artigiani, Società
Guglielmo Marconi, Società Bersaglieri, Società Militare Ufficiali
di Artigieria, Società Giuseppe Garibaldi, and Società Vittorio
Emanuele III, illustrating the continuing importance and popularity of the general and nonterritorially exclusive society.[11]

The territorial exclusiveness of the new societies was often
muted and other Italians were welcome to join. Competition
for members and the limited pool of candidates if eligibility
was narrowly defined both worked against campanilismo. Society building expanded so rapidly in Utica that by 1904 many
were overextended and most, including the oldest, offered
amnesty periods on dues and lowered entrance fees to lure
back wayward members and to attract new ones. In Rochester
supposedly exclusive societies solved the problem of limited
potential membership by interpreting territorial origins very
loosely. A Sicilian founded the San Bartolo di Geraci Society
for his fellow townsmen from Geraci Siculo, Palermo. Fortunately he welcomed others into the group, for it was a man from
Santo Stefano di Camastra, Messina, who soon became its

leader and a dynamic force in maintaining the society for many years.[12]

Religiously based mutual benefit societies were another variant on the theme. These groups were associated with a Roman Catholic parish or Protestant mission. Bishop McQuaid, first and longtime leader of the Rochester diocese, was more suspicious of such societies than American churchmen generally were. He supported specifically Catholic and ritually unobjectionable organizations. The Catholic Mutual Benefit Association, founded in Buffalo in 1878, rapidly spread through the Rochester diocese under McQuaid's encouragement. Our Lady of Mount Carmel, branch no. 279, established in 1914, was the first Italian chapter of this society. Other dioceses were less cautious in this regard. Thus, there were early societies in both Kansas City and Utica that were confessional and closely associated with the Italian parishes, although not officially sanctioned parish organizations.[13]

Occupationally exclusive societies were common in Italy, where members in a given trade were sufficiently numerous to warrant such specialization. In larger Italo-American colonies similar groups appeared before 1900. Barbers and masons incorporated mutual benefit societies in 1886 in New York City. In 1894 and 1898 bakers organized two societies. Such trade-centered groups formed more slowly in the provincial cities I have studied. The first of these in Utica was a society for the "brave and honest artisans," established in 1902. The association dissolved in less than a year because of financial problems. During its short life it successfully completed a fund-raising project to benefit Sicilian hurricane victims. In the same year, grocers and wine and liquor dealers founded a commercial alliance. Some years later the Italian saloon keepers established an association "to aid and assist its members in their moral, intellectual, physical and social welfare, and in a proper case, if it sees fit, afford them protection in a material or financial manner." Merchants formed the Italian-American Progressive Commercial Association to help members avoid contracting bad accounts and to assist in systematizing the collection of claims. They also sought "to mutually enlighten one another regarding correct

business methods and generally to inculcate progressive commercial enterprise and mutual business advancement."

Italian day-laborers moved organizationally into the main-
stream of American labor with the founding of the "Italian
Street and Building Laborers Union" in 1901, which soon became Local 35 of the International Hod Carriers' Union. They
stressed unity and protection to the point of clapping a $10
fine on members who supported or sustained nonunionists.
Their first big victory came in 1913, when the contractors agreed
under pressure to provide tools, thus ending the necessity for
the laborers to carry a pick and shovel all over the city as they
looked for work. By 1905 the Italian masons also organized
along trade-union lines.[14]

The great varieties of clubs, circles, and other types of associations formed in the colonies are further examples of the trend
toward specialization in function. In Utica, Circolo Filodrama-
tico was founded in 1900 and by 1901 was offering "good family entertainment" in the form of recitals and plays. Social life
and recreational activities came under the aegis of clubs. An
East Side Social Club held dances in 1901. The Gold Star
Pleasure Club did the same, while the Young Men's Social Club
put on a combination concert and ball in the summer of 1902.
The Imperial Social Club soon followed suit. The Columbia
Club, with a saloon keeper as leader, held a clambake at which
they reportedly bested a similar Irish group 47 to 15 at baseball.
(The paper did not print the Irish club's version of the score.)
The Italian Club and the Hot Air Social Club also sought to
meet the needs of the immigrants for an organized social life.
Gymnastic and fencing groups such as the Italian Empire Ath-
letic Club provided organized outlets for exercise and sport.[15]

Music held a special place in the Italian colony and the Italians of Utica moved early to support it organizationally. An
evening of choral singing and mandolin and guitar music held
at a private home in 1902 provided the inspiration for a guitar
and mandolin players' club, which soon held its first annual ball.
Societies supporting Italian choral and band music appeared in
1901. Failure of an early concert to raise sufficient funds to
purchase expensive instruments and uniforms needed by the

band did not end the concern. The colony continued to support
the Italian Band through the Musical Society, which held picnics, concerts, and balls for the benefit of the band. Lastly,
there was a commission of fathers established in 1902 to support an Italian boys' band for youths aged ten to sixteen.[16]

Longer residence brought immigrants into the American
political arena. In the early days of the colony the few Italian
voters were of little consequence in city politics except under
unusual circumstances, such as in 1887, when the total Italian
vote of 15 held the balance of power between two warring Irish
factions in a Utica ward. By the turn of the twentieth century,
the activities of societies promoting citizenship and other similar efforts produced an increasingly important bloc of Italian-
American voters. Predictably, Italian political clubs arose to
attempt to rally these new voters toward one or the other major
party.

The Circolo Elettorale, formed in 1905, is of particular interest. Its spokesmen styled it a movement above party partisan-
ship. In fact, it was an attempt to form an Italian caucus that
would direct and control the Italian vote as a bloc in the interest of the colony. Italian socialists had their own organization
independent of the broader, German-dominated party in Utica.
They held theater parties, balls, and picnics that were both
recreational and educational in nature, with prizes as part of
their programs. At a 1904 "Grand Ball" given jointly with the
Germans, they gave out prizes to the best dressed, most elegant,
and most beautiful girls.[17]

The first organizations of professionals, intellectuals, and
large merchants emerged in the years after 1900. Until 1905,
recognition of professionals in the Italian press of Utica appeared
primarily in the form of advertisements or announcements of
their establishment in the colony. They remained almost completely outside the associational life reported in the newspapers.
Then, in the spring of that year, *L'Avvenire* published a letter
lamenting the fact that the colony lagged behind others in the
upstate area in promoting cultural and artistic interests. The
letter cited organizations in Buffalo, Rochester, and Amsterdam
which were doing much for the growth of high culture in their

colonies. A Rochester circle, the writer reported, was presenting shows and plays as well as supporting a fencing academy and vocal and instrumental concerts. The young author then asked why Utica did not have similar activities. It was not the lack of resources, he asserted, but failure to comprehend the moral advantages for youth to be derived from such a circle. This interest in an organization primarily geared to promote culture in the colony was not new. An ephemeral "Educational Club" appeared in 1900, and in 1904 at the tenth-anniversary banquet of the Heads of Families Society the editor of *La Luce* made a strong appeal for an association under the name Dante Alighieri to promote education and culture. This time, however, the idea, supported actively by *L'Avvenire,* took hold.[18]

Within a week a meeting was held to plan for the establishment of the Circolo Educativo e Ricreativo, which was to promote "recitation, dance, music, fencing, boxing, wrestling, etc." The leadership at this meeting differed very little from the artisan–small merchant contingent which dominated the workers' societies. One Francesco Brindisi, a tailor and foreman of a large shop, served in leadership positions in a number of societies, at one time holding the presidency of two large groups simultaneously. A half-dozen professionals and several prominent business men of the colony attended a follow-up meeting. The press symbolically indicated the changed order of things by placing Brindisi and others prominent at the earlier meeting halfway down the list of those in attendance at this meeting. Election of officers at a subsequent meeting finalized the upper-middle-class takeover. The highest offices (president, vice-president, secretary, and treasurer) went to professionals, the major merchant banker, and the Italian who then held the highest position in the city's textile industry. Brindisi and the proprietor of a barbershop won positions on the board of directors. Otherwise, a new class of organizational leaders enjoyed a clean sweep.[19]

Despite *L'Avvenire's* brave predictions of great advances for the Italians of Utica, the "Circle" failed to fulfill its early promise. There is little evidence that it had much influence on the broader colony beyond what might have come from descriptions

of the genteel and refined living of the middle class as portrayed
in society-page-style reports of their gatherings. Most activities
of the circle remained within the membership, despite earlier
talk of reaching into every family in the colony. The exception
was a public show at the Star Theater in honor of Dr. Aliberti,
who was to leave for Montreal "to better his condition pro-
fessionally." More typically, they held dinners and dances at
which the members and their children displayed their musical
talents and other cultural refinements. The president, Dr.
Palmieri, used the birthday of his daughter Amelia as an occasion
for one such dinner, at which "nothing was lacking in the pro-
fusion of sweets, liquors, wines, cigars, fruits of every type and
coffee." Entertainment included Amelia on the mandolin accompanied by Maestro Benincasa, in a repertory including pieces
from *Il Trovatore, La Traviata, Cavalleria Rusticana,* and *Tosca.*[20]

With the onset of World War I further new dimensions in
organizational life emerged in the colonies. While more recent
arrivals and relatively stable older settlers continued to turn to
traditional forms of association, the aggressively mobile members
of the immigrant generation, the increasingly numerous second
generation, and the assertive middle class came to realize that
the depth and permanence of their commitment to the New
World called for new organizations and greater unity within the
colony.

A permanent commitment to America by immigrants heightened the importance of specifically Italian-American associations.
The Italo-American Progress Club of Rochester and the Italy-
America Club of Kansas City prospered. Membership in both
groups consisted largely of young second-generation Italian-
Americans. Many of the members sought pluralistic self-
identities that were at once both faithful to their Italian heritage
and sufficiently in accord with American expectations to enable
acceptance and a reasonable opportunity for economic success.
Their ideal was to be bilingual gentlemen or ladies conversant
with the high cultures of both countries. To this end the Rochester group maintained an active educational program, which included classes in Italian, English, and dance, a dramatic group
that staged plays, an orchestra, and cultural and moral lectures

in both languages. In Kansas City the largely American-born members of the Italy-American Club added a concern for charitable work in the land of their fathers. In 1922 this group raised a fund for Italian war veterans afflicted with tuberculosis.[21]

The newly active middle-class segment of the colony spearheaded a movement shortly before World War I to unite all Italians in the United States into a single organization. Attempts to create a nationwide federation of Italian organizations date back to at least 1873. The Sons of Italy, however, sought to create a totally new structure from the local lodges on up. The movement started in New York City, and the structure of the hierarchy left the control of the entire organization in the hands of the downstate city. The New York Supreme Grand Lodge served as the national directorate. The order sought to establish unity and pride among Italians and respect for Italians and Italy on the part of Americans. In ideology and programs to implement it, The Sons of Italy closely paralleled the view of an ideal conception of Italian-Americans as set out in chapter 6. They promoted a dual set of loyalties by calling for continued faith in and love for the mother country while simultaneously instilling loyalty and respect for the adopted country. And to achieve these ends, they used predominantly educational means. Teaching Italian language and culture in the public schools was central to their program. In 1922 they established the Dante Medal for high-school students who distinguished themselves in the study of Italian and gave out scholarships to Italian-Americans for college study. A year later they instituted youth-study tours of Italy for children born in the United States. Finally, they printed a bulletin in English for students, and in Italian for parents, publicizing the opportunities for Italian-language study. The organization encouraged members to attend adult education classes, learn English and civics, become citizens, and take an active part in American political life. They had early pretensions of fostering a national mutual benefit provision, but these soon disappeared, leaving the order to concentrate on the promotion of "Italian-Americanism" and defense of the Italian name. All Italians in America were eligible for membership. Professionals and academicians, who dominated the New York leadership, shaped the society narrowly to fit their own cultural interests while ignoring other matters of interest to the masses of Italian immigrants, and this limited the potential impact of the new organization. Italian culture turned out to be an inadequate basis on which to build a lasting mass national organization.[22]

The Sons arrived in Utica in 1914 when three lodges were organized in less than a year. One of these was a women's unit made up of the "cultured and intelligent element . . . among our women" and brought together "the genteel Italian energies to mutual relief, and to the elevation of education and idealism that are our national patrimony." The gala ceremonies at the installation of this society, Adelaide Cairoli, were typical of the showmanship with which the society publicized its activities. Its flair and exploitation of the media for public relations and propaganda purposes reflect a middle-class style, in contrast to the less imaginative, more staid manner of the worker-led groups. The festivities were graced by several New York City representatives of the hierarchy, including the "Grand Venerable" of the State of New York, who journeyed from his New York City law office for the occasion. The whole affair evoked high praise and nearly two front-page columns from *La Luce,* sparking a year-long preoccupation with the new order on the part of the city's Italian press.[23]

The inauguration of another lodge in 1915 gave the editor of *La Luce,* "Professor" Spina, an opportunity to spell out for Uticans the cultural goals of the order. His speech to the assembled throng of over four hundred Sons of Italy was a full and complete extolling of education as a means of individual and group advancement. After a brief nod to the mutual benefit and group protection features of the order, he focused on his primary concern, *istruzione* and *educazione.* The former, he explained, was theoretical: it illuminated the mind and thinned out the darkness of the intellect. *Educazione* was practical: it moved the will toward good and accustomed it to healthy habits and virtuous acts; it routed corruption from the soul and gave a noble direction to the human passions. There was a delicate balance between the two that put one on the middle way of the

avenue to progress. Many have istruzione while few have the
purity of the soul that comes from educazione. Then, in a
eulogy to education, Spina wrote:

> Istruzione, oh brothers, istruzione and educazione and our
> masses will render themselves always more worthy of esteem,
> ever more ready for the needs of new times and of increas-
> ing progress.
>
> The obligation to perfect ourselves weighs on all, that is,
> making ourselves better. The light of truth illuminates our
> duties for us, rendering useful virtues to us, to our fellows
> and to the honor and glory of our fatherland. Ignorance and
> vulgar prejudices plunder the virtues of their most beautiful
> merits and generate misery and pain.[24]

An important goal of this education was to prepare the Italian
masses for citizenship and, where possible, for assimilation into
the broader society. Spina spoke of the grand advantages to be
derived from citizenship, including the opportunity to take an
active part in public life, which would bring with it added respect and increased benefits for the whole colony. Finally, he
reassured his listeners that this did not mean they loved Italy
any less; rather, it was a very practical type of behavior for
people far from their native land. One could never forget the
place of one's birth, especially as Italy's recent glorious feats on
the field of battle against the barbarians in Libya and against
the despotic Germans stirred every Italian soul.[25]
    Later in the same year (1915), La Luce, with the help of the
state organization, launched a campaign to advance the second
of the tandem goals of the order, the introduction of Italy to
Americans and to the American-born children of immigrants.
The "Grand Venerable" of the state of New York, after a visit
to Utica, appealed formally to the mayor of the city to introduce
Italian into the public school foreign-language program. He
pointed to New York City where the language was being taught
in both junior and senior high schools. Obviously Italians wished
their children to have such opportunities and, he asserted,

Americans would derive benefit from such study too. The mayor diplomatically responded that, although he was in favor of such an addition to the curriculum, the decision was completely the province of the school board He forwarded the request to that body, where the proposal quietly died.[26]

While the style and structure of The Sons was novel, sentiment in favor of unity within the colony was not new. Unified action by some or all of the organizations in a colony to carry out specific projects appeared in these cities at fairly early dates. In 1904 three Rochester societies formed a joint committee to establish an Italian school. The project came to naught. However, the colony was soon united in an effort to finance the construction of the first of three combination church-school buildings to be built before the war. The construction of churches in Utica and Kansas City likewise provided the basis for temporary unity among the various societies. Important colonial festivities also produced concerted action. The most vigorous workers' societies in Utica came together annually to promote, manage, and finance the celebration of Columbus Day. In 1910 the joint committee collected and spent over $500 on the weekend of festivities, which included six bands, dinners, bicycle and horse races, fireworks, a grand ball, a picnic, childrens' theater programs, a spectacle of electric lights, and speeches by outsiders, including a state senator and an Italian newspaper publisher from Philadelphia.

The following year the editor of *La Luce* launched a vigorous campaign to establish a permanent federation of the various societies which would weld the colony into a single large family. He argued that the traditional American political division held no benefit for Italians and, in fact, dissipated the colony's energy and power. He calculated that there were fourteen societies with 1,120 members whom he felt should enter into American life and politics on a "one for all and all for one" basis. The paper urged this action for five weeks, with no success. A similar plea for unity in 1914, which sought to rally the societies around the task of raising and dispensing funds for charity among the needy of the colony, proved no more persuasive. The societies did not share *La Luce's* embarrassment over the fact that the "associated Charities of Utica" received no financial support from Italian groups sufficient to move them to take collective responsibility for the relief of needy Italians in the colony.[27]

The problem of relief of conationals in need, however, provided part of the impetus for a successful effort to unite various societies in Kansas City after World War I. Press reports of meetings held in the summer and fall of 1920 give insight into the tortured process. The first gathering came at the instigation of the pastor of the Italian Catholic parish. He hoped to marshal the colony in support of the parish school and to form a society that would operate as the St. Vincent De Paul Society for the assistance of widows, shut-ins, and the poor. In a speech, he also pointed to the great number of religious and secular societies, which hindered the organization of colony-wide projects. To accomplish his two goals there would have to be coordination and unification of these groups under a single "Colonial Committee." This first meeting produced a decision to have a mass meeting of the heads of all families in the colony. An interim committee met to prepare for the gathering. The goal of founding an Italian hospital found supporters; yet it seems to have been the priest's school that was the heart of the debate. Most members defended the idea of a nontuition "Italian School" as necessary to ensure that children did not "leave the ways of our fathers and ourselves." Proposals called for comprehensive programs that would provide the children with instruction in Italian by a teacher trained in Italy, as well as evening classes for adults in "English, civics, bookkeeping and other material useful in this country.[28]

Conflict over who would control the school surfaced immediately. The Reverend Prospero Angeli's insistence that the committee limit its activities to finding financial support for the school appears to have been at odds with the role envisioned for it by other leaders. Sessions of this committee grew increasingly heated. In an early meeting Angeli pointedly told the assembly that the proposed committee should not presume to have any say over the administration of the school, the selection of teachers, the curriculum, the time schedule, or instructional materials. On 10 September the press announced the founding of the society Educazione, Intelletto, Amore, with a broad educational program. The unified endeavor was short-lived, however. By December *La Stampa* had turned against Angeli, whom it had highly praised only a few months earlier. The paper published a letter which contained a scathing attack depicting the priest as a boastful, power-hungry individual who shamelessly employed Machiavellian methods to undermine the committee. The letter ended with the promise not to "permit the German baton to regain its strength over the spirit of a single signore." No more was heard of the elaborate educational project.[29]

The idea of a federation of the colonial organizations was not abandoned, however, and a committee continued to function through 1920. It staged the celebration of Columbus Day and General Badoglio Day (Sept. 10), protested the harsh and excessive nature of a police raid in the colony, and continued to search for support for the parochial school. (In January 1921 a new priest became pastor at the parish and tensions over the school lessened.) Ties between the various organizations in the colony became permanent with the creation of the "Intersocial Supreme Council." The majority of representatives to the council from each of the mutual benefit societies in the city were business and professional men. The council's initial six-point program of strength through unity, care of the poor in the community, betterment of the colony, better understanding between Italians and Americans, raising moral standards, fostering education among the colony's children, and defending Italian interests in the city and state, represents a decidedly middle-class view of the needs of the colony. At the end of the first year, leaders proudly surveyed achievements which included formal incorporation, organization of the Columbus Day festival, sponsorship of a concert as part of a joint celebration of Armistice Day with the American community, provision of legal counsel for a conational, financing the last leg of a stranded conational's journey to San Antonio, Texas, and most significantly, cooperation with American charities to dispense relief among Italians.[30]

Involvement in distributing charity gave the council both a guaranteed existence and great influence in the colony. In their first eleven months of operation they had available funds of over $3,000 and actually disbursed $2,333.99 to a weekly average of fourteen needy Italian families. At this point the city's Provident Association provided the bulk of the financing. As perceived by the council, the outside agency maintained excessively tight supervision over the operation. The Italians argued that only they knew best the real needs and resources of Italian applicants for aid; to prevent overlapping relief and injustice they should be given complete control over aid to their conationals. They pointed to their success in eliminating undeserving families from the rolls.

Apparently this argument, in addition to the proven ability of the council to raise supporting funds, impressed the Provident Association, for the council soon had complete control over the disbursement of charity monies in the colony. The 1925 budget provided nearly $7,000 in welfare payments. Income included $4,125 from the Provident Association, $941 from the individual societies, and $1,488 derived from the Columbus Day celebration. By 1928 the council was averaging charity disbursements of over $800 a month from a total operating budget for the year of over $10,000. Hard times were already evident in the decline in funds raised by the Columbus Festival and the demise of a number of supporting societies. The Provident Association's contribution of $7,800 took up much of the slack.[31]

The council continued its activities in support of Italian interests and their good name, as well as promoting Italian culture in Kansas City. It was quick to protest slurs on conationals here or in Italy and was especially vehement in its protests against the Johnson Act, which included discriminatory quotas for Italian immigrants. It sponsored numerous lectures and conferences dealing with contemporary Italy and her past glories. In 1924 a Professor Valentini gave a lecture with illustrated slides on Italy's new military stature and modern technology. The same year saw a lecture by another Italian authority, a dinner in honor of the Italian consul, and a debate held on

Defense Day to prove Italian loyalty to the United States. The following year the council joined in an effort to raise money to defray the Italian war debt to the United States "that undoubtedly aided Italy but gave more in our benefit in friendly relations of the two countries dear to our hearts." It also raised $500 for the Salesian Institute for Sicilian war orphans in Palermo and sponsored a three-lecture series on recent archeological discoveries and on actual contemporary conditions in Italy by a professor from the Royal University in Rome.[32]

Parallel organizations existed prior to the war. The Italian Republican, Democratic, and Socialist clubs are conspicuous examples of groups which expanded their activities in the 1920s. Many other groups had features that replicated broader organizational structures and functions found in the American community. New conditions growing out of the war and a maturing second generation fostered the proliferation of such organizations.

Service in the American armed forces made sizable numbers of Italian-Americans eligible for membership in American veterans' organizations. In Rochester this prompted the establishment of the Flower City Post No. 180 of the American Legion as an explicitly Italian-American unit. The new post grew rapidly, spurred on in part by enlistment bonuses. Two hundred and sixty-two dues-paying members were on the rolls in less than five months. The organization held dances, masquerade parties, and monthly luncheons, as well as participating as a unit in the county Legion activities. In 1924 they led the Legion delegates in the Memorial Day parade, an honor that was somewhat lessened when the post was not allowed to carry the Italian Tricolor beside the Stars and Stripes. Their bowling team was a source of special pride. In its first year of competition, the team swept the field and received the Monroe County Championship Trophy at the 1924 County Convention. The post, perhaps more than other parallel organizations, allowed its largely middle-class and professional membership to participate in a broader American organization without having to surrender Italian control and leadership at the local level.[33]

Increases in numbers of business and professional men caused the establishment of the Italian Business Men's Association in Rochester in 1925. It was an association "purely American in ideals with positive and profound respect for its Italian heritage coming through its members." They sought "to promulgate . . . constructive, cooperative and progressive ideas for the ameliora- tion of the conditions of Italians here." American citizenship, civic pride, and the elimination of petty jealousies were key features of their program. Businessmen and professional Italians in Utica, led by a young lawyer, George Schiro, founded the Comity Club to serve the same ends as the city's Business and Civic Association, which they had not been invited to join. In Rochester the Chamber of Commerce welcomed Italians, and newspaper editor Lanni urged active participation in both the ethnic and the broader business associations. In Kansas City the Italo-American Woodmen of the World and The Young Men's Progressive Club were just two of a number of fraternal orders founded on the American model. Veterans established an Italian-American American Legion Post in the same city in 1929. The Immortale Martire di Firenze Girolamo Savonarola Lodge 367 of the International Order of Odd Fellows flourished in Rochester. In the Catholic churches, altar and Holy Name societies and numerous new sodalities increased the similarities between the Italian parishes and the American ones. Italian Protestant churches, strongly influenced by American sponsors and supporters, provided even more striking examples of this phenomenon.[34]

On the distaff side, the Italian-Women's Civic Club carried on many activities similar to American civic and social women's groups. It promoted women's participation in the political life of the city, raised money to support a kindergarten, and sup- ported a variety of cultural and educational programs. For ex- ample, in 1924 it cosponsored with the Women's City Club and the Kindergarten Association a speech by noted Italo-American educator Angelo Patri, at a local high-school auditorium, on "Some Aspects of the Growth of the Child." However, the activity that brought it most notice was its support of higher education. After 1921, it regularly provided a scholarship for a student of Italian extraction at the University of Rochester. It raised funds for this Dante scholarship in a number of ways, including staging theatrical presentations. By the end of the decade the College Men's Club prepared to follow the women's example by supporting higher education through scholarships.[35]

By the late 1920s the original Italian pattern of association was greatly expanded and transformed as the colonies in America grew and offered new class dimensions. The original mutual benefit societies remained popular at the same time that new demands from the American experience in the areas of economic, social, and political adjustments fostered various new forms of associations. As the decade opened, *La Stampa Unita* listed twenty-three societies. By mid-decade the number had increased to forty-four. The city's *Rochester Italian Directory*, itself a product of the increasing complexity of the colony, listed fifty-two organizations in 1931.[36]

The Italians were slow, as this chapter shows, to form nation-wide organizations. They never created institutions comparable to the great Polish and Slovak societies, which united immigrants of these groups across the country into one or two organizations. Even when The Sons of Italy did appear, it failed to develop a truly national superstructure. The multitude of locally based organizations dominated the associational life of the Italian colonies throughout the years before 1930. One popular explanation for this difference between Italians and other ethnic groups suggests that a spirit of regionalism brought from Italy hindered the creation of a broader Italian unity in America. But this alone is an insufficient interpretation. As I have previously explained, local societies based on regional exclusiveness were rather late arrivals in the colonies and were never the dominant form of Italian associational activity. Also, the active participation of such groups in city-wide federations indicates that they were not averse to unity on a higher level in pursuit of common interests. In Rochester immigrants from Valguarnera founded a local lodge of The Sons of Italy exclusively for their fellow townsmen. Italian unity was not necessarily incompatible with local loyalties.

Part of the answer may lie in the comparative importance of

nationalism for the various immigrant groups arriving in the late nineteenth and early twentieth centuries.[37] Nationalism in Polish and Slovak communities had a dimension that was entirely missing in the Italian colonies. Poles and Slovaks, as well as other East Europeans, sensed a real and continuing threat to their national cultures in the Old World. They felt an obligation to keep their cultures safely alive here and to work for the liberation and reestablishment of their homelands as independent states. Italians felt none of this. Their concern for Italy and "Italianness" was of a different nature. As with other groups, their awareness of what was distinctive about being Italian was heightened by living in a foreign country. Their newly created sense of ethnicity had real personal meaning. It did not, however, carry any broader obligation to keep alive a national culture that was being threatened with suppression or outright extinction in the Old World. Italy really existed; Poland or Slovakia did so only in the minds of a nationally conscious people.

Preservation of the national culture in America for Poles and their children before the creation of an independent Poland had a very different meaning than it did for Italians. Italy was , of course, a real source of interest and concern for her sons and daughters here. However, even in peak periods of interest, such as during the postwar Irredentist movement, their concerns were not with the survival of a people but with the relative status and honor of a state. Thus they felt much less urgency. Italians, from the beginning unburdened by the heavy responsibility of a people without a state, were free to concern themselves with their own personal advancement and their colony's place in an American city. National organizations with strongly Old World patriotic goals were a luxury to be indulged in after settling more immediate local concerns.

8

BUSINESS, POLITICS, AND THE PRESS:
NEW OPPORTUNITIES AND NEW LEADERS

The development of a growing and geographically stable colony created opportunities for those with ambition and intelligence. Communication between the colony and the broader community required intermediaries capable of understanding and being understood in both communities. There was a demand for many products and services which the American market did not or could not provide. In addition, a number of immigrants brought with them skills and a willingness to work at tasks that had market value among Americans. The result was the early development of commercial and professional strata in the colonies which reinforced the world view of the immigrants and encouraged them to seek advancement in more traditional leadership roles rather than in the new industrial system. The individuals who rushed in to take advantage of these opportunities were seldom those who had held them in the Old World. This fact also served initially to strengthen the premodern ways. Ambitious and talented men of modest backgrounds, who in the Old World would have been blocked from entry to these positions by gentry and middle-class domination, found the way open to them in the American colonies. Thus, there was no early stimulus to overthrow old ideas of success and cast a future in the modern industrial society.

The growing colonies created a surprising number and variety of opportunities for individuals to enter business for themselves. At the end of 1902, after a little over a year of publication, the Italian newspapers in Utica had carried advertisements or announcements of the openings of eighty-seven business or professional enterprises operated by Italians, representing activities

163

in more than forty different categories. Over five years the
variety of such establishments increased to more than fifty,
while the total number reached 166. These figures are doubt-
lessly understated. Peddlers, part-time entrepreneurs, and professionals, who often did not advertise in the press, are
undercounted. Some idea of the size of the missing element may
be gained from an advertisement for a locally produced macaroni. The ad listed thirteen Utica establishments where the product could be purchased. Of the thirteen, four firms did not
appear in the source used to compile the list.

Even well-established merchants did not always advertise.
Tommaso Bove, long a successful merchant, returned to Italy
in 1904 after twenty-one years in Utica. His departure occasioned
the first newspaper acknowledgment of his presence in the city.
In addition, two engineers served in various capacities in the
colony during this period, as did several "Doctors" who, due
to the loose usage of the term, may have been pharmacists,
medical doctors, dentists, or practitioners in some allied area. A
final caution should be stated. The list does not indicate firms
that went out of business soon after opening. It records initiative, not success.[1]

The single most prominent enterprise was saloon keeping.
Over 17 percent of all advertisements and announcements involved such establishments. I have already suggested the importance of Elia Pellettieri's saloon in the stabilization of the Utica
Colony (see chap. 7). It provided a center for social and recreational contacts among Italians in a largely "single male" phase
of the development of the colony. The proprietors of saloons
often served as labor agents or contractors, ensuring that their
establishments became necessary stops in any search for employment. Saloon keeping was not a business one could enter
easily or quickly. Supplies had to be purchased in an American
market; legal formalities had to be observed; and most importantly, one had to procure the $750 fee for a beer and liquor
vendor's license from the city.

Saloon keepers, therefore, tended to be men who had relatively greater sophistication and experience in getting along in
the United States and were often the ones with longest residence

in a colony. The power and influence of a saloon keeper can be seen in an 1893 lawsuit in Rochester. A labor contractor, Raffaele Falo, had a contract to supply 1,000 men for a job in Pennsylvania but was having trouble recruiting candidates. He sued Angelo Ferranto for slander, charging that Ferranto was dissuading prospective employees by means of false statements in order to keep them as customers of his saloon.[2]

Opportunities in wholesaling and retailing emerged as the growing colony created a demand for specialized products and a familiar style of merchandizing. Twenty-seven Italian groceries and meat markets accounted for over 16 percent of the 1900–05 list of businesses. These ranged from smaller corner groceries and butcher shops attached to the proprietor's home to sizable firms in the heart of the Italian business district. Nine fruit dealers, three fishmarkets, four bakeries, and a milk company completed the list of foodstuff merchants. The larger firms often included import and wholesale operations. One fruit enterprise and several grocery businesses gradually grew into large establishments with regional wholesale trades.

Largest and most active in the early Utica firms was V. Marrone & R. Lofaro and Co., founded in 1893. In 1901 it established a newspaper, partly as a medium to advertise its business activities. The firm had strong commercial ties with other upstate Italian colonies. Vincenzo Marrone occasionally made trips into the nearby states of Ohio, Pennsylvania, Michigan, and Massachusetts to promote business. At home in Utica the firm purchased $6,000-worth of choice property to house its newspaper operation adjacent to the business block already occupied by the import firm. This gave it a commanding presence on Bleecker Street in the heart of the colony. The firm had important contacts in the ports of New York and Boston, where Marrone had cousins in business. The establishment in 1904 of a customs house in Utica allowed the merchants to bypass the New York City middlemen. An announcement in the *Utica Daily Press* that Marrone & Lofaro paid $853 duty at the new customs house on a single consignment of merchandise from Italy gives some idea of the scale of their business. Two months later the firm recorded a payment of $1,031 in import duties.

In addition to importing foodstuffs and running a newspaper, Marrone & Lofaro operated an "agency," a term used to designate a wide range of services important to a colony of newcomers. In this instance the agency acted as a travel agent, securing tickets and necessary documents for travel to and from Italy. They held a notary public commission and provided banking services such as currency exchange, money orders, and the transfer of funds between the United States and Italy. They also acted as real-estate brokers for the expanding colony and purchased residential property for rentals and investment. In 1911, after almost twenty years of operation, the partnership dissolved, when Marrone opened a real estate, banking, and insurance agency, while Lofaro continued in the importing business.

Banking, insurance, real estate, travel, and labor contracting services were typical activities of nine other "agencies" on the 1900–05 list. Antonio Sisti advertised that his "bank," could guarantee payment in eleven days of monies sent to Italy because its affiliation with the Bank of Naples eliminated intermediaries. He also dabbled in labor contracting, advertising in 1902 for "carpenters who know their trade well." The Bank of Naples was by Italian law the official organization for the transfer of immigrant monies back to Italy. In Utica, both Marrone & Lofaro and A. Sisti and Co. were official agents of the bank. In 1904 another agent announced a new and unique function for himself: the Italian Institute of Heraldry appointed him to be its American representative. Thus, he was prepared to aid all those Italians who wished to learn about the origins of their families.[3]

Other important commercial activities in Utica's colony during the early years included ten shoemakers and/or retail shoe shops, ten cafes and restaurants, a laundry, six barbershops, several tobacco and candy stands and stores, a jeweler-watchmaker, new and used furniture stores, a musical instrument store, and a monument firm. Combination artisan-merchants included seven custom tailor shops, three photographers, a cigarmaker, and a cabinetmaker.

The prominence of the textile and clothing industries in Utica attracted skilled Italian tailors, some of whom moved

into entrepreneurial roles. These independent shops ranged
from one-person operations which served a neighborhood
clientele, to the sizable establishment of Vito Pietrafessa in the
central business district of the city. Pietrafessa came to Utica
in 1899 to serve as a superintendent in a large American firm,
which by 1902 employed more than 300 Italian tailors. A year
later he opened his own shop, employing about fifty workers,
an act suggesting the attraction of private enterprise over
positions of responsibility in industry. In announcing the new
venture, the paper took obvious pride in the fact that he had
both Italians and Americans in his employ. The editor asserted
that the same love of work which made this nation rich and
prosperous animated Pietrafessa, who was an outstanding example of the work ethic that was advancing the local colony.[4]
Energetic artisans in the construction trades advanced into contracting. The list includes nine contractors, ranging from small
operators who specialized in carpentry or masonry to larger
ones who accepted full residential and commercial assignments.
N. D. Peters and Co. came to dominate the construction of
sidewalks in the city, and in 1904 two Italians were given the
contract to build a new firehouse. Painting, papering, and "interior decorating" provided another outlet for Italian talent.

Macaroni manufacture provided still another opportunity
created from the special needs of the colony. Each city had at
least one, and often several, of these establishments before
growth, regional marketing, and consolidation limited their
number. Kansas City's Macaroni and Import Company, for
instance, merged with the American Beauty Macaroni Company
of Denver to serve a market that extended from St. Louis to
Los Angeles. Such unions eventually destroyed the local nature
of these firms.[5]

Both the owners of flourishing pasta firms and the successful
merchants constructed buildings that were monuments to their
success. In this way they symbolized in brick and stone a recognition that the colonies had moved from a transitory mentality to
a more permanent status and that individual enterprise was the
preferred avenue to success. In Utica two events symbolized
this phenomenon. In 1903 Guiseppe Nicotera, a meat-market

operator, baker, and ice dealer, invested $41,000 in the con-
struction of a five-story building on Bleecker Street in the center
of the Italian colony. Engineer-architect Carlo Milanese designed
the grand structure and brought two master craftsmen directly
from Italy especially for this project. The building housed two
commercial establishments on the ground floor and apartments
on the others. While this was more grandiose than most of the
construction taking place in the Italian colonies, it was representative of an early twentieth-century type.'It is still possible to
walk down Bleecker Street in Utica or through the streets of
Kansas City's "Little Italy" and find a dozen commercial structures, each housing several stores with second and perhaps third
floors of apartments built by Italians, who proudly inscribed
their names on the stone plaques adorning their new *palazzi.*
Urban renewal has eliminated most of this type of building in
the Rochester colony.

   The second major construction event in the Utica colony
was the completion of the 850-seat New Lyric Theater. This
entirely Italian project was financed by C. Gremaldi, a cabinetmaker–office furniture purveyor; Vito Pietrafessa, a tailor and
factory owner, and G. Patriarca. It was designed by Milanese
and constructed by Devito and Hopple. Both the Italian and
American presses recognized its construction as a major advance
in the colony, signifying confidence, permanence, and success.[6]

   Professionals, who made up a small segment of the Utica
colony, faced a variety of impediments to the profitable practice of their callings. A dentist, two medical doctors, a lawyer,
two pharmacists, two engineer-architects, four undertakers,
five midwives, and a number of musicians appear on the list.
Initially these individuals were largely European-trained. Certain
of these professions, such as those of musician and architect,
could be easily transferred to another culture. Language difficulties presented only slight impediments to their practice in
America. For others, such as the medical sciences, facility in
English and knowledge of the American style of practice were
necessary unless one confined one's practice to the Italian
colony. Even then, there was the hurdle of state and local licensing requirements, which could be a substantial obstacle for

doctors. At least one physician, when forced to go to Albany
to take a licensing exam, never returned to practice medicine.

For those who did obtain licenses, preference for Italian
doctors in the colony ensured a steady clientele. This demand
fostered the development in the 1920s of a parallel institution,
the Italian hospital. Early in the decade the Columbus Hospital
of Buffalo regularly advertised in Rochester as the closest
Italian hospital. In 1927 a Rochester physician bought and
opened the 94-bed Lake Avenue Hospital for his conationals.
Kansas City Italians welcomed the Columbus Hospital in 1924.
These institutions apparently did a lively business, judging by
their large and frequent ads in the Italian press. Licensing
midwives seems to have been less exacting. The wife of a prominent tailor advertised that she was a licensee of a school in
Albany; another received a diploma from the University of
Palermo; while a third midwife stressed that her license was
from the city of Utica. The sole dentist was American-trained.[7]

Lawyers were under even a greater handicap, for to be
effective they had to learn a whole new legal system. While a
doctor could continue to practice among his immigrant conationals according to European standards a lawyer had to be able
to function efficiently in the American system. The only Italian-
trained lawyer who made a pretense of maintaining a practice
could not do so. As a result he lost considerable status when he
went to work for Marrone & Lofaro as an editor for *La Luce*.
His opponents in the colony ridiculed him for his deficiencies
in English and as being nothing more than a notary, in spite of
his university degree. Within a few years the medical and legal
professions became almost the exclusive province of the second-
generation and American-trained immigrants. By the end of the
period (1932) there were thirty-two Italian doctors, lawyers,
dentists, and pharmacists in Utica. Only three of these, all
physicians, had received their professional educations abroad.
Seven were Italian-born but received a substantial portion of
their schooling, including all their professional training, here.
This group included one physician, four lawyers, and a pharmacist. The remaining twenty-two were American-born and trained.
Mangione remembers from his youth in Rochester that it was

every Italian parent's dream to have a son become a professional.
If not a doctor or lawyer, a pharmacist would do.[8] The need
for American training to practice successfully here weakened
the Old World upper-class monopoly on the professions and
made that dream possible for a number of parents of modest
origins.

The growing size and stability of the colony created conditions which made possible the rise of an Italian commercial
and professional class. Yet, the professional, commercial, and
artisan populations of each colony comprised, not a stable, but
a geographically mobile group. This mobility promoted education through exposure to development in other colonies, built
important links between colonies, and permitted a flexible
matching of individual talents to opportunities and needs in
the colonies. Announcements that one or another individual
was leaving to advance his career elsewhere were common in
the Italian press. If it was a professional, such as Milanese going
back to Sao Paulo, Brazil, where he had been a city engineer,
Dr. Palmieri going to Schenectady, Dr. Grana leaving for Tampa,
Florida, or Dr. Aliberti taking his leave for Montreal, there would
be a round of farewell banquets and ceremonies. More humble
folk, such as the tailors, led by master craftsman Pasqualino
Pincitore, who left for Chicago in 1903, merely received the
best wishes of the Italian press.

A mobile period was common in the careers of merchants
and manufacturers. Rocco Sarli arrived in the United States
from Anzi, Basilicata, at age nineteen. He first tested his fortunes in Peoria, Illinois, and then found employment as a travel
agent in a large Chicago agency and import house. After this
schooling in commercial life, he moved on to Kansas City,
where in 1912 he founded the Kansas City Macaroni and Importing Company. Domenico Lanni arrived in Scranton,
Pennsylvania, in the 1880s from his native Benevento Province.
By 1891 he was operating a grocery and labor contracting
business in Rochester. In 1896 he supplied labor for the Erie
Canal renovation. He then spent some time in Syracuse, and
in 1900 took over the directorship of the Central Macaroni
Company in Utica. Three years later, much to the regret of the

editor of *L'Avvenire,* he left for Detroit, where he superintended
the "Uncle Sam United States Macaroni Factory." Soon there-
after he returned to Rochester, where Domenico, his wife and
seven children, four of whom were American-born, settled
permanently. Predictably, he opened a macaroni factory. Finally, the papers also recorded the departures of men like Pietro
Ungano, who returned to Italy after operating a bakery in Utica
for six years.[9]

One additional observation must be made about the men who
moved in to fill the room at the top of the economic structure
created by the growth of colonies. In 1904 Antonio Marcolina,
a "rich proprietor" from Italy, arrived in Utica intending to
establish a grand and large commercial establishment. He represented an exception in the colonies. The overwhelming number
of commercial men for whom any background information
exists were from what were euphemistically called "good and
honest families." Given the enthusiasm with which the press
reported on prestigious Old World family backgrounds, the
paucity of leaders identified as coming from other than humble
backgrounds is significant. Rocco Lofaro's father was a "self-
made man" in the silk industry. His partner Vincenzo Marrone
was the son of an "honest tradesman." Marrone's family appears
to have been socially mobile on both sides of the Atlantic. In
addition to cousins who were prospering in Boston and New
York City, he took special pride in advancements made by
relatives in the civil service of Potenza.

In 1904 *La Luce* even reported the promotion of a female
relative to the second class in an Italian normal school, which
was hardly the reaction of a long-established bourgeois family.
(As mentioned in chapter 3, elementary school teaching had
declined greatly in prestige by the turn of the century.) There
is evidence that even the professionals who emigrated were
often from families of very limited circumstances. The Roberta-
ccio brothers were orphaned at a young age. They received
their educations while they moved around Italy in the care of
their uncle, a priest. Their early schooling was apparently in
their native town of Laurenzana. They also attended the gymnasium in Potenza and the University of Naples, where one

became a doctor and the other an engineer. Their uncle then
led them on to Chicago before the doctor and the aged priest
ultimately settled in Utica.[10]

The period before World War I was one of opportunity for
a wide range of individuals who in the Old World could not
have expected to disrupt the traditional social and economic
orders of their villages. The men who competed to fill the
positions of economic power and advantage were for the most
part not those who filled them in Italy, nor their sons. The
old system of deference could not survive in the New World
colonies, where new persons enjoyed power and influence as
a consequence of their own efforts and talents. Professionals
accustomed to ready acceptance of their paternalistic leadership
found themselves under aggressive challenges from these new
quarters. "Upstart" merchants could challenge an ambitious
lawyer and cast aspersions on his background and qualifications
merely by asking why he had left Italy where his university
degree would have assured him gentlemanly status, and then
administer the coup de grace by winning a libel judgment against
the lawyer in the American courts. And a "shoe peddler" and
a tailor successfully challenged a physician, driving him out of
the colony despite the backing of Vincenzo Marrone and "all
the better people of the colony," as *La Luce* chose to phrase
it. In 1902 the same tailor received a gold medal from the
Italian Council in Albany at a special banquet held in his honor,
a symbolic recognition of the altered power relationship which
middle-class Italians visiting American colonies failed to comprehend. Blind to the new order and wedded to an identification
of leadership with middle-class status and culture, accounts by
these observers often portrayed the colonies as being devoid of
leadership.[11]

The political arena traditionally has offered opportunities
for power and influence to those who could mediate between
the immigrants and the broader political community. The Italian
colonies were slow in developing an Italian-American power
base that would undergird such opportunities. Many Italians
understood at least one important aspect of American politics.
In 1902 *L'Avvenire* lectured the Utica colony on the benefits

of unity. Italians, the editor asserted, were squandering their political potential. There were many more naturalized Italians than most other nationalities, yet because of their lack of cohesion and unified purpose they could not put together a voting bloc that would bring rewards commensurate with the size of the Italian vote. He noted that the American party system met the demands of those who made their voices heard; those who remained silent got nothing. When they sold their votes for a few dollars they were selling the broader interests of the colony as well as their "most sacred and holy right." This editorial was one of a recurring number of attempts on the part of business and professional leaders of the colony to unite the Italian vote behind the Republican party. After the election, the paper congratulated Carmine Scala, a Democrat, on his election as a city constable. This was the first recognition by either Utica paper that he had even been running for office.[12]

In 1903 the Republicans nominated Dr. Frank Cavallo, an American-educated dentist, for Fifth Ward supervisor. The papers supported him with lavish prose, along with their usual elaborate and extended coverage of the whole Republican ticket. Cavallo ran an active campaign, and the paper, recognizing the qualities essential for a mediator, protrayed him as a man who understood both Italians and Americans and who could, therefore, best represent the colony. Nevertheless, the paper was defensive about the fact that he had to make his formal speeches in English. Cavallo lost the election. *L'Avvenire* bitterly lectured the colony that they had failed in their duties of citizenship by allowing themselves to be deceived by the Socialists and Democrats into voting the straight Democratic ticket—which, incidentally, included two Italian candidates. Only the American friends of the Italians had voted for Cavallo, according to the editor.[13]

After this "disaster," the Italian Republicans started preparing in earnest for the election of the following year, 1904. They formed a Republican Club and affiliated themselves with the League of Republican Clubs. They also promoted such developments in other colonies, sending a delegation of speakers to the inaugural meeting of a similar club in Amsterdam, New

York. Between full front-page presentations of the Republican candidates, *La Luce* did mention the Democratic standard-bearer Bryan, labeling him a buffoon while they ridiculed his running mate, Judge Parker, as a man without ideas. The paper even announced that the Democratic party was dying. After the balloting they celebrated the Republican victory but could not claim any local Italian contribution to the triumph.[14]

The following year concern shifted back to local candidates. The Republicans nominated a slate that included Italians in seven of the eleven positions in the Fifth Ward. Salvatore Pellettieri, as candidate for alderman from the ward, headed the "Italian" ticket. He ran the most energetic campaign reported in the Italian press up to that time. He wrote long letters in the papers urging Italians to do as the Irish and Germans had done and unite behind their conationals. The press dedicated an unprecedented amount of space to his campaign and held back no flattering words in describing Pellettieri's character and qualifications. In an unusual gesture, they did take note of Frank Pepe, who was running for collector on the Democratic ticket against an Italian on the Republican slate. The paper conceded that in   · his thirteen years in Utica he had always been honest and hardworking. Pepe won, as did Pellettieri's Irish opponent. The upshot of still another disaster was the formation of an "electoral circle" to educate the Italian masses to their civic and ethnic responsibilities as seen by these frustrated would-be leaders.[15]

In Rochester the situation was somewhat different. The Italians were more widely distributed throughout the wards and lacked the political potential that existed in Utica's Fifth Ward. Powerful longtime Republican city boss George Aldridge recognized this and was slow to offer party nominations to Italians. In 1904 the Democrats ran an Italian in a futile campaign for coroner. In 1911 they tried again at a more realistic level, running Agostino Martino for constable of the Sixteenth Ward, where many Italians lived. Nevertheless he lost. The Republicans finally ran an Italian in the Ninth Ward race for constable. It was a period when Republicans usually won Rochester elections. Not surprisingly, he won. In 1917 both parties ran Italians for constable and the Republicans were again victorious. After the

war the Democrats ran young University of Rochester graduate
and ex naval officer Clement Lanni three times for sheriff,
unsuccessfully. Recognizing changes in the Ninth and Second
Wards' populations, Republicans shifted from the Irish to the
Italians and backed men like macaroni manufacturer Alfonso
Gioia. Finally, in 1924, the Republicans sent Cosmo Cilano to
the State House in Albany. From then on Italians appeared
prominently on both tickets.

In 1926 Lanni summarized the performance of the two
parties up to that date. He found that "since 1904 there have
been twenty-six Democratic candidates of Italian descent for
public office, of whom two have been elected, a supervisor and
a constable. There have been twenty-two Republican candidates
. . . of whom twenty have been elected to office." It is not
surprising that Lanni took the title of his second book on
Rochester politics, *Beat'em or Join'em,* to heart and in the mid-
1920s made *La Stampa Unita* a thoroughly committed and
partisan Republican organ. In Kansas City the most prominently
Italian Fifth Ward remained under the control of an Irish
Democratic boss, although by the end of the 1920s he and his
Italian supporters were under heavy assault by an Italian Democratic club. The bitterness and personal invective in this fight
reached an intensity unmatched in the other colonies, demonstrating the frustration of Italian leaders, who with a small
potential constituency failed to win respect from American
political leaders.[16]

The socialists continued to lead a marginal existence in
Utica. Their activities received respectful, though not overly
lavish, coverage in the Italian press. At one point *La Luce* reported on the well-received socialist conference held by the
editor of the paper *Proletario,* and in the next editorial breath
it urged election of the straight Republican ticket in the coming
election. The paper so completely ignored the Democrats that
its readers would not have known from reading it that any such
organization existed. Perhaps this benevolent toleration of the
socilaists by the press can be explained by the fact that the
socialists never entered the electoral lists in any consistent and
effective way. As long as they remained a propagandizing group,

holding meetings for itinerant lecturers, and concentrated their energies on organizing and reorganizing their local Socialist Circle, the papers could afford to be courteous. The Democrats, on the other hand, were successfully competing for Italian votes. That presented an entirely different situation.

The Republican party remained for the Italian press the party of prosperity and progress. No evidence has appeared to show that the Grand Old Party actively subsidized or owned a part of the Italian papers. Yet they may well have paid handsome fees for the full-page advertising the papers carried before elections. Like the Swedish editors studied by Fritiof Ander, their Italian counterparts held strong predilections toward Republicans. The Republican campaign coffers, advertising money, and the likelihood that most of the local advertisers, as businessmen, were apt to be Republicans undoubtedly reinforced those propensities. The fact that the papers themselves were commercial operations and often owned by Italian businessmen is also noteworthy. Also, like those of the Swedes, Italian political views and voting behavior were influenced by both local and broader factors bearing on the working classes generally. While the Utica press trumpeted its Republicanism and its merchant establishment, the bulk of the colony voted for Democratic slates that included more modest Italian candidates, such as tailor Francesco Brindisi or Rocco Pellettieri.[17]

The success of Italian political leaders depended ultimately on the support of both Italian voters and American political leaders. This agreement was not easily obtained. Many who sought to serve as mediators failed to win the endorsement of one, and sometimes both, groups. The relative positions of the two major parties locally and the size of the potential Italian electorate set limits for the aspirants to political influence in the colonies. Neither major party expressed great interest in the Italians until there were signs that they could be important in gaining or maintaining power. Then it was the minority party, which had less to lose, that was most generous in offering endorsements to Italians. Their offers were not the most advantageous base on which to rally the colony.

While out of power, Utica Republicans welcomed the help of

Italian professionls who, because of their social and political
views, found the alliance compatible. The Italian voters ignored
the advice of the *pezzi grossi* (bigwigs) and supported the
dominant Democratic party. Their actions, whether motivated
by recognition of the returns to be gained by supporting the
likely winners or by identification with the ideology of the party,
resulted in reducing the potential influence of individual Italian
leaders in the broader political community. In Rochester the
local situation was reversed. The Democrats first opened their
tickets to Italians though the honor involved small chance of
success; the far more valuable Republican nominations were
given out grudgingly. Lanni's *La Stampa Unita* began in the
camp of the Democrats and shifted loyalty only when the
Italians' situation had improved to the point where they could
exact concessions from the Republican machine.

Journalistic enterprises appeared in response to the need for
formal means of communication between various segments of
the maturing colonies. In time they also provided important
service to those from the outside who wished to communicate
with the colony. The Italian press throughout the country was
overwhelmingly commercial in nature, relying on advertising
and subscriptions to pay the bills and to turn a little profit if
possible. The papers in the three colonies under consideration
here were, with one exception, of this type. The exception is
Il Messaggero of Kansas City which, although it was the organ
of a Protestant missionary enterprise, was in much of its content, format, and other features similar to the commercial
press. It sought a wide audience in the colony. Thus it has been
included here as part of the ethnic press of the colonies.
    Utica was the first of the three colonies to found a paper. At
the turn of the century, the merchant-agent team of Marrone
& Lofaro capitalized *L'Avvenire* Publishing Company, at
$5,000. It soon passed into the hands of a board of directors
including restaurateur–furniture merchant Salvatore Pellettieri;
Alfred J. Purvis and Anthony Dehm, operators of a typographic
shop; and Vincenzo Capasso. In 1901 Marrone, Lofaro, and
Teresi founded *La Luce*. Thus, within a year after the U.S.

Census counted 1,661 Italians in Utica, the city had two vigorous Italian weekly newspapers. *L'Avvenire* had a life of ten years, while *La Luce* was published for over twice as long. Less than a dozen colonies, all larger and older, had papers earlier, and only the very largest were fortunate enough to have more than a single successful publication at this early date.[18]

Both papers sought to extend their readership by establishing correspondents in various upstate colonies between Albany and Syracuse. *L'Avvenire* even made an attempt to attract subscribers in Rochester, 135 miles from Utica. Eventually the larger colonies established papers of their own. Albany had its own paper in 1908, Auburn in 1914, Amsterdam in 1909, Schenectady in 1903, and Syracuse in 1906. Nearby Rome established two long-lived papers in 1911. Still, towns like Watertown, Little Falls, Canastota, Gloversville, and Oswego remained open markets in which the papers competed. Information on the circulation of these two early journals is limited to the self-reports in *Ayer's American Newspaper Annual Directory*. Neither probably had a circulation of over 2,000 during the first decade of their operation. In 1913 the Italian Socialist Club introduced a weekly, *Lotta Operaia,* which expired after World War I. *Il Pensiero Italiano* appeared in 1914 as another Republican weekly. It remained in business through 1929. The spring of 1921 witnessed the establishment of *L'Ordine* (later *Il Messaggiero dell'Ordine* and then *The Messenger*) which survived World War II. In the same year *Il Pagliaccio,* a weekly specializing in humor and comment, began. It struggled through the decade with a circulation of less than a thousand.[19]

The chronicle of Italian publishing efforts in Rochester reveals many more false starts and short-lived enterprises in the early years of the century. At least seven papers were introduced in the city before 1920. In that year Clement Lanni, fresh from a career as a local star athlete in high school and college and a hitch as a navy officer, brought together the two surviving papers (*La Tribuna,* founded in 1912 and *La Domenica,* founded in 1904) as *La Stampa Unita,* which he published until World War II. At the end of the decade a second weekly, *Il Settimanale Italiano,* appeared. Kansas City, with its smaller and

slower-growing Italian population, did not establish an Italian
newspaper until 1919 when an Omaha paper, *La Stampa,* transferred its operations to that city. By the mid-1920s it claimed
a circulation almost double the size of the Italian-born population of the city. In 1926, the Reverend J. B. Bisceglia transformed his small monthly, which had for several years enjoyed
limited circulation, into a full-fledged weekly paper under the
title *Il Messaggero.*[20]

Several students of the foreign-language press have contended
that, rather than promoting the maintenance of the Old World
ways and a mentality of exclusiveness, the papers actually were
agents of assimilation and "Americanization." This generalization is valid for the Italian press of these three colonies only if
assimilation and *Americanization* are given meanings consistent
with the views detailed in chapter 6. What frequently appeared
from the outside to be efforts to preserve an exclusive culture
were, in fact, pleas for change, adjustment, and the creation of
new forms rather than an obstinate clinging to the old. The
paper articulated the idealized concept of an Italian-American
identity described in chapter 6 which, in the promoters' minds
at least, would be compatible with the best of both the Italian
and American cultures. The very existence of a press signified
recognition of change and acceptance of a more extended stay
in America. If the newspapers were to serve the interests of
their readers, they had to help Italians understand, adjust to,
and exploit their American environment as best they could.
Without exception the editors seem to have implicitly accepted
this assignment.[21]

From the very beginning the papers took an active interest
in the civic life of their respective cities and sought to interpret
various situations to their readers. Many, if not most, of the
public issues of the day, whether local or national, had an impact on the colonies. The papers regularly discussed local issues,
such as paving streets and increasing the police and fire forces,
as well as national issues, such as protection of the public from
the "coal trust," in terms that had meaning for their readers.

Very early in its life *L'Avvenire* used a third of its front page
to urge Italians to support a public library bond issue in the

upcoming election. Local philanthropists F. T. and T. R. Proctor offered the city a matching funds arrangement for the construction of a grand new building, and the paper urged that the necessary financial commitment be approved. After relating some of the history and present status of the library, the editor got down to his real reasons for favoring the proposal. First, some of the money would come into Italian pockets through the jobs they would find on the project; secondly, it would be a fine palce for Italians to spend their leisure hours in instructive activity, reading the best Italian books. The present fine collection of Italian literature could be expanded if new space were available for it. Three weeks later the paper rejoiced over the positive voter response. But *La Luce* was not so sure that it approved of the priorities of American philanthropists. Its editor suggested that "those unfortunates who go to bed without any supper and those who even lack a bed to go to" should come before the libraries and universities that men like Andrew Carnegie endowed. Still, *L'Avvenire* persisted in its stand and expressed civic pride in the great new educational institution when it opened in 1904.[22]

In 1914 *La Luce* gave its readers a lesson on the impact of war on trade and the possible financial consequences for them. Among measures recently passed by the House of Representatives to make up for declining revenues from import duties, the paper pointed out, were increased taxes on beer and wine, on theaters, and on billiard and bocce establishments. In the same year the paper introduced a column, "The American Viewpoint," in which prominent Utican Chester W. Davis sought to explain Americans and their ways to Italian readers. The entrance of the United States into World War I and the resulting mobilization produced a whole range of new topics to dominate news coverage, locally and nationally. Certain American organizations and institutions, such as the Chamber of Commerce, needed explanation. *La Luce* turned its attention to this organization in 1905 in an article on the nature, purposes, and services offered to the community by the chamber. It was also a favorite with Clement Lanni, who promoted it a number of times in the 1920s. The papers apparently saw no need to explain other American

institutions, such as labor unions or mutual benefit and fraternal
societies, to Italians already familiar with such organizations in
their homeland.

American laws and regulations were other subjects on which
the papers frequently instructed their readers. Whether it was
explaining state game laws on shooting birds, child labor statutes, changes in naturalization and immigration legislation,
requirements and procedures for obtaining licenses to practice
the trades of chauffeur, plumber, barber, electrician, peddler,
or beautician, or the comparison of workmen's compensation
statutes in various states, the newspapers served both the immediate needs of their readers and the broader interests of the
community. When no explanation seemed adequate for the
misfortunes and problems in the news, the editor of *La Luce*
put his tongue in cheek and blamed a long catalogue of miseries,
anguish, and tribulation on the interminable upstate New York
winters. Clement Lanni found he could introduce his readers to
some of the nuances of business and industrial life in Rochester
and at the same time promote his advertisers by running a full-
page write-up on a single type of enterprise. In one issue he
featured the Rochester Business Institute and its new president.
His readers learned of the background of the new head man,
the history of the institution, and the many course offerings,
which he praised as excellent means of getting started in business.[23]

Undoubtedly of more immediate importance for many
workers was the concern that most of the papers displayed for
keeping their readers informed on the state of the labor market
throughout the country. Reports of strikes, industrial closings
or expansions, and wages paid in various states were regular
features of the papers. Uticans, for example, learned in the fall
of 1914 that the recent period of unemployment in the coal-
mines was over and that a period of high employment created
by heavy foreign orders was expected. Any miners or others
who were in need of jobs knew where they could find them. On
the local level, the papers were more specific and individualized.
From its inception, *L'Avvenire* pointedly took up the role
of employment intermediary. The editor announced that he

would run free of charge the ad of any unemployed person
looking for work. There is no record of whether a young Italian
skilled in carpentry and fluent in Italian and English found employment as a result of his ad; however, he and others in the
same position did find a medium for publishing any special
qualifications they might have. Advertisements of labor contractors in search of workers were an omnipresent feature of the
papers. The request for laborers followed seasonal patterns.
Winter brought requests for snow shoveling by both the munici-
palities and the railroads. In the spring the construction season
commenced and contractors sought their complements of men.
Fall produced calls for men, women, and children to help in the
harvesting of fruit and vegetable crops.[24]

Finally, there were general-information articles on a variety
of subjects, ranging from suggestions on how to save coal in
home heating to health tips. The papers supported public health
by frequent announcements of locations of TB clinics, advice
on how to defend oneself and family against epidemics, and
information on childhood diseases such as infantile paralysis.
In the early years, the Borden Company aided this effort by
providing regular columns on infant care and health as part of
their advertisements for evaporated milk. Individuals in the
colonies also provided material of this type.

La Stampa carried an informative series of five articles on
narcotics by a prominent Missouri Italo-American physician who
founded the Narcotics Education Committee. The author ranged
in some detail over the physical and moral consequences of
drug use, causes of the present problem, ways to prevent potential users from taking up drugs, and a program for the re-
habilitation of those already addicted. In general, he felt that a
breakdown in family discipline and moral supervision created
the problem. Therefore, greater family responsibility would prevent children from innocently drifting into situations where
they could be corrupted. Those who were already users should
be the objects of special concern of medical men and the church.
He felt that the church was not doing what it should to reclaim
these lost souls. In general, this was not an area for legislation
but for an educational program carried on in the home, school,

colony, and peer groups. Only in the area of stiffer penalties
for pushers and dealers did he think legislation was a viable
approach to drug problems. In the 1920s the Foreign Language
Information Service greatly simplified the papers' task by providing already translated articles on a wide variety of subjects.
Most editors printed large amounts of this "boilerplate."[25]

For international news the editors were frequent users of the
scissors and paste-pot technique. They lifted most of their
stories from the New York City Italian dailies or papers from
Italy. In the early years, the papers carried a fairly full account
of world events. The Russo-Japanese War greatly interested
both Utica papers as, of course, did Italy's later exploits in
Libya. As a rule the papers covered any major event of world
import, though they showed special interest in those stories
that involved Italy and the United States. Coverage of Italian
news lacked any immediate ties to the colonies. Although they
ran columns which carried news from the Italian provinces,
only rarely was the content of these anything more than clip-
pings from major Italian journals.

Very occasionally a paper would carry a piece of news that
was derived directly from a source in a local area. These were
usually items relating to the fortunes of the Italian branches of
families prominent in the Italian colonies. Once a Utica paper
attempted to establish closer ties through a "correspondent" on
the Italian scene, an Italian immigrant who was visiting Sicily.
After several stiff, stuffy, and not very newsy columns, the
feature quietly disappeared from the paper.

In their coverage of Italy and other Italian colonies in America,
the papers tended to prefer stories of crime, sensation, and
personal tragedy to politics. One rarely finds the results of communal elections reported. An extended report of the suicide of
a young sulfur-miner from Castrogiovanni in neighboring Villarosa, without a note to explain his motives, represented the
standard fare offered to the readers of the Italian-American
press. A full page might be devoted to the brigand Varsaone—
his family, his loves, and his band. When the press did break
this pattern, it is interesting to note that it often chose stories
with educational themes. The establishment of an agricultural

school in Potenza, a commercial college in Rome, advancement
of women through education into the professions, discontent of
a federation of schoolteachers, proposed reforms in elementary
education, and the spreading of schools for domestic education
from Switzerland to Italy all were considered newsworthy.[26]

Other than their special interest in Italy and things Italian,
the papers seldom deviated from popular American stances on
national and international questions. Despite his perspective as
a transplanted European, the editor of *La Stampa* strongly
supported the prevailing isolationist sentiment of the Midwest
in the postwar era. In 1922 he supported the reelection of
Missouri senator Reed because of the senator's clear vision,
which concentrated on "minding our own business rather than
fighting the battles of the other fellow." Two years earlier a
correspondent had placed Reed in the same heroic category as
the signers of the Declaration of Independence and commended
his "almost superhuman efforts," which had saved the country
from "that political monstrosity known as the League of Nations." Thereby, Reed and his handful of senate colleagues
"stood the acid test of Americanism and saved the free institutions of the country." The author considered his support
a major concession since Reed was a Democrat and he was a
Republican. He ended with a plea not to submit U.S. economic
and political institutions to risks in the less civilized or barbaric
world.[27]

The papers introduced readers to a wide variety of goods and
services available, and in some cases necessary, for life in urban
America. Advertising usually consumed at least half, and often
much more, of a newspaper's space. The Italian papers considered here did not differ appreciably from the pattern observed by Park in the foreign-language press as a whole. The
majority of the advertising was local, both in terms of space
purchased and in number of ads. Not all of the copy had salubrious results. National ads tended to be from patent medicines
making extravagant claims. Every week readers of most of the
papers learned how LI LOZOGO of Doctor Pietro Fahrney of
Chicago cured some horrible and long-standing affliction which
had obstinately resisted the best efforts of other medical men.

Steamship companies and political parties (usually Republican) at election time were other big purchasers of space. Local advertisers were both from within the colony and from American firms which sought Italian patronage. If the products advertised are any indication, the Italians either arrived with a taste for American consumer goods or developed it rapidly once they got here. American furniture, automobiles, radios, player pianos, the latest household appliances, and jewelry—especially gold watches—were popular items.[28]

Other features included the serialized fiction so common in most of the ethnic press. Such material tended to be short stories or novelettes of little or no literary merit. Occasionally the papers also published poetry, short stories, or songs written by local readers. Bisceglia's *Il Messaggero* did more of this, since these writings served in part as vehicles to publicize the Protestant mission. It also represented his greater concern for higher forms of literary work. His paper seldom carried the sensationalist reporting common in the others. He chose a wide variety of material, including works of prominent Italians and Americans, in addition to the specifically religious and particularly Protestant copy. Whenever possible he sought to link English-American culture and Italy; thus Robert Browning was one of his recurring subjects. Browning also served to stimulate the interest of Bisceglia's American middle-class female supporters in his work and gave the objectives of his mission added luster. One might easily suspect that the Browning Memorial Garden at his mission was more symbolic to the American women who contributed to it than to the Italian children who tended it.

English slowly began to appear in the press. At first it was only when the editors wanted to speak to the American community, when they scolded daily papers for unfair coverage of events in the Italian colony, or when they wished to impress potential advertisers with the influence their journal had among Italians. By the eve of World War I, the editors occasionally used English when they spoke to the colony's youth. This became common in the 1920s as the papers generally became bilingual, including English pages or columns and, in the case of *La Stampa Unita*, parallel editorials printed in each language.

Italian remained the dominant language throughout the decade, though the future of an "Italian Section" in an otherwise English publication was clearly on the way.

I have written more extensively on the Italian press elsewhere and will summarize here that portion of the argument which bears on the topic of opportunities for leadership. Editors were of a different stripe from the immigrants who rose from more humble backgrounds to assume direction of commercial and associational activities in the colonies. The literary skills requisite for editors limited this opportunity to a very few in a colony. At first, intellectuals and displaced professionals filled these positions. The petulance which they expressed when the colony rejected much of their paternalistic leadership revealed their incomplete understanding or acceptance of the new social order that was developing in the colonies. As the colonies matured and grew more pluralistic, educated members of the second generation assumed editorial posts. They profited from a greater understanding of their second-generational peers and from their own familiarity with the outside communtiy. At the same time, they were unsympathetic toward the conservatism of their fathers' generation when it retarded their efforts to shape the colony in more "American" ways.[29]

The editors were not wholly free agents, but as managers of commercial enterprises they had to consider the advertisers and others who sought to communicate through their journals, as well as the interests and needs of the readers where patronage made it possible to sell advertising. They often faced local competition from rival papers. Dailies or large weeklies from New York or Chicago circulated in the colonies, offering further competition for readers' attention. Finally, as facility in English increased in the colonies, the American press threatened the position of the Italian papers. The influence of the editors was greatest when their concerns coincided with those of others in the colony. Then, their control of an important communications resource gave them a central prominence. When they stood largely alone, as in their support of the Republican party (or the Democratic party in Rochester), the limits of their influence became apparent. For influence in the colonies, they were the rivals of many persons with bases in religion, social and associational life, education, business and commerce, labor, the professions, or politics. The very same personal characteristics which gave some men access to editorial positions also limited in important ways their ability to lead the colonies. Aside from idiosyncratic characteristics, aspirants to influence from other sectors of the colony enjoyed advantages particular to the positions they held. The colonies refused to confer supremacy upon any single category of leader during the period covered in this study.

Throughout the years 1890–1930 the leadership of the colonies changed considerably in response to new levels of awareness, rising expectations, and changing orientation. A settlement of largely male laborers, a colony of families with young children, and a mature community in which second-generation adults increasingly assumed leadership each offered different opportunities and demanded different things of their leaders. Yet one characteristic of men in leadership positions in the colony remained consistent throughout the period. Irrespective of the level on which or capacity in which a leader functioned, with few exceptions he had to be able to act as an intermediary between the Italians and the broader community. The ability to identify with, work in, and exert influence upon the immigrant society, and at the same time serve important interests of the "American" society, placed an individual on an upwardly spiraling staircase of prestige, influence, and power. The immigrant who acted as court interpreter and guide to newspaper men and politicians interested in gaining access to the immigrant community, gained a certain recognition and importance in Rochester police, political, and press circles for the services he could perform. This, in turn, brought him status and influence among his conationals, who recognized the usefulness of his contacts with the "authorities." The more his status advanced in the immigrant community, the greater his value to the "outside" community.[30]

The career of Nick Camelo provides an illustration of such a leader in the early phase of the growth of the colony in Utica. Camelo first appeared as a saloon keeper and proprietor of a

hall used for Socialist and Republican meetings. Soon he advertised for a hundred men for long employment. He continued
to function as a labor agent throughout his stay in the city and
quickly moved into other activities. These included founding
the East Utica Land Company and the Utica Construction
Company, offering notary and banking services, and serving as
agent for such companies as the Pacific and Gulf Coast Oil
Company of Palo Alto, California, and the Marconi Wireless
Telegraph Company. In addition, Camelo sought to advance
his position in the colony by becoming an intermediary between Italians and the courts. He took every opportunity to
publicize his influence with the courts.[31]

In 1902 *L'Avvenire* praised Camelo for his efforts to help
and protect the workingman and noted with pride his special
relationship with the city police. In January 1903, the paper
pronounced "Another Victory for Nick Camelo" in conjunction
with his winning the release of an Italian convicted of assault
on his young wife. The paper reported that Camelo, convinced
of the young Italian's innocence, succeeded in getting a county
court to set aside the verdict of a village justice and free the
prisoner. *La Luce* gave a more modest account of the incident,
noting only that Camelo arranged for the release of the prisoner
on $200 bail. A month later he received credit for being an able
defender of conationals involved with the courts. Because of
his hard work, familiarity with civil and criminal procedures,
intelligence, and the respect he held among American authorities, Camelo was able to obtain victories where others had
failed. The occasion for this praise was his successful intervention on behalf of an Italian worker involved in a lawsuit with
another Italian.

In September Camelo returned to Utica after serving for a
number of months as labor agent on a job setting up telephone
lines in Watertown. The press immediately credited him with
the release of another conational from jail, thus reinforcing his
reputation as having great influence in the courts. By 1904
Camelo seems to have overreached himself. *L'Avvenire* announced two more triumphs, one of which involved an Italian
victim of an unprovoked assault on the street by an American,

who then added to the injustice by having the poor immigrant
jailed for 59 days on a charge of disorderly conduct. The paper
reported that Camelo instituted a $5,000 suit against the pug-
nacious American, which resulted in a $400 judgment for the
victim of the assault and false arrest. Two weeks later *L'Avvenire*
admitted that both cases had been tried by American lawyers
and that Antonio Daniele, another prominent agent-notary had
served as interpreter and as the major assistant to the American
counselors in each case. This revelation seems to have ended
Camelo's claims to special influence in the American legal system.
He continued to receive press recognition for other activities
for several years, but he was no longer credited with special
powers as an intermediary between the colony and city government.[32]

The importance of this story lies in Camelo's own recognition
of the potential rewards of serving as a mediator between two
societies. In all likelihood, he greatly exaggerated his interventions
with the courts in an attempt to build his position in the colony
from which he could command the influence in the American
community to which he had already laid claim. He recognized
the possibilities for reward and the advantage to be gained
through service to both the colony and the broader community.
Ultimately he lacked the resources to deliver on his promises
and ended up claiming credit for other men's work. In choosing
legal services as a specialty, he had selected an area with great
potential that required close familiarity with American politics—
if not an American law degree—for fully successful exploitation.
Camelo had a position as interpreter-agent for an American law
firm for a short time. When this relationship dissolved, he lost
an opportunity to provide legal aid to his conationals. His refusal—or perhaps failure—to enter politics in 1905 eliminated
another possible basis for influence outside the colony. But
Camelo continued to function as a man of influence because of
his services to both the colony and the broader community
associated with his other activities. His failure was only relative
to the larger role he sought to play.[33]

Leaders in other areas also found their success dependent on
being able to serve the two communities. Continued success as

business and professional men, and especially as politicians and newspaper editors, depended upon the ability to function in and communicate with both the ethnic colony and the broader society. The same was true for most of the leaders of organizations discussed in chapter 7. It was equally the case for the clergy and educators, as the succeeding chapter will show. In a colony increasingly committed to long-term residence in America and concerned with successful accommodation to the broader society, anyone who could not bridge the two societies and advance these goals had limited value as a leader. Rewarding financial, mercantile, political, intellectual, and social opportunities opened up for those who had the ability to provide such spans. Few existed for those who could not.[34]

The nature of the tasks facing those who assumed positions of leadership in the colonies, the skills they possessed, the social, economic, and political contexts in which solutions had to be worked out, and the conservative individualistic ethos of the immigrants all worked together to reinforce a traditional definition of success. Mobility came most easily, naturally, and soonest to the entrepreneurs. To be sure, Italians served as foremen and in similar supervisory positions in the textile and construction industries, but they much preferred to be independent shop owners or contractors. Striving for success through moving up in the emerging corporate and bureaucratic organizations of modern industrial society was delayed for Italians by this early reinforcement of more traditional routes to status and power.

This may not be a complete explanation for the slower rate of Italian entrance into the upper levels of corporate leadership, however. The question of whether Italians in the three cities found places in this new opportunity structure at a different pace from other comparable groups remains to be investigated. Italians in Rochester widely believe that prejudice and resultant discrimination by American business leaders has kept them out of upper-management levels of several Rochester industries. This sentiment probably has merit. My point is that forces rooted in the background of the immigrants, in conjunction with the pattern of opportunities created by the growing colonies, worked toward the same ends.

9

EDUCATION IN THE ITALIAN COLONIES:
THE SCHOOLS

A revisionist school of historians has recently gained prominence in the area of American educational history. They reject
an older interpretation which included the enlightened working
class in the coalition of forces responsible for the reforms that
created modern mass public schooling. In its place they stress
the heavy-handed use of schools by a ruling elite to impose values acceptable to themselves and supportive of their interests on
the reluctant and, at times, defiant masses. Immigrants are one
important group who were "victims" of this cultural aggression.
The Italian experience with schooling in America can stand as a
partial test of this thesis. Were the Italians unwilling or even
passive participants in the schooling process, or were they to
some degree independent and active agents in shaping their own
educational experience? In light of the importance of alleged
inequalities in educational resources and teaching personnel in
inner-city public schools and elsewhere, it is important to ask
whether Italian children found such discrimination in resources
and curriculum when they first confronted American urban
education. Put differently, were Italian children offered something like the common schooling called for in the ideology of
the public school or did they receive less because of prejudice in
the system? An examination of schools in the colonies and of
the relationships of Italians to them and to possible alternatives
provides at least partial answers to these questions.[1]

Italians did not have to learn the gospel of education in
America. They left Italy with a well-developed faith in the instrumental and cultural power of the schoolhouse and a commitment to literacy and self-improvement. From the time of

their first appearance, Italian newspapers exhibited a continuation of this deep concern for education in each of the colonies. In 1901, Bishop Scalabrini, the founder of the Pius Order of St. Charles, a missionary order that supplied priests for Italian immigrant congregations, visited the order's parish in Utica. In an address to the congregation, he pointed to church, family, and school as the only means for obtaining a good education. Utica's Italian family-life was well established and the colony now had a church. Although the latter was still struggling financially, the bishop urged the congregation to push on and direct its attention to establishing a school. This would mean sacrifices and a diversion of money then being spent on less important things. Still, he urged that these sacrifices be made, for "only the youth can recover the past and only through them can we give praise to our generation and our beautiful Italy who, full of confidence, waits for days of prosperity and greatness for all of her children." A local Italian editor felt that any father dedicated to the education of his sons could not see it otherwise. The prelate's charge to the colony represents a basic perception of the nature and importance of education that was widely held in the three colonies.[2]

The bishop's remarks provided the opening call for an editorial campaign to promote an Italian school in Utica. *La Luce* picked up the theme in 1902 in a series of three editorials that made impassioned pleas for a school in the colony. They started by invoking "the holy name of the school, this grand fountain of civilization," and moved on to reminiscing about happy days spent as schoolboys. The nostalgia included students' flights of fancy in which Garibaldi and a bloodstained Christ were prominent and made indelible impressions that stamped their souls as Italian. A new generation was growing up distant from this blessed institution, and the obligation on the part of the colony to make up this deficiency was imperative. The third installment dealt with what the editor felt was one of the obstacles facing successful establishment of a school, those who "in search of their own economic betterment, in America, pay little heed to their fellow brothers." Then he restated his earlier argument, calling the school indispensable to the education of

the American-born generation of Italians. He ended the series
with a dramatic appeal to the mothers of the colony to inspire
their husbands and children to plant their feet firmly and allow
fate to guide them rather than abandoning themselves to continual drifting. Later the same year, the report of an effort in New
York City to establish an Italian school provided *L'Avvenire*
with a vehicle for promoting one in Utica. The school was described as being the true cradle of *civiltà* and the greatness of a
people, and thus the faith, the holy ambition, of every Italian
colony abroad.[3]

Financial commitments assumed by the parish in the construction of its church and the declining energies of their aged
pastor prevented an immediate realization of the hope for a
school. The Reverend Antonio Castelli guided the incorporation
of Utica's first Italian parish after a number of years during
which local priests ministered to the colony on an informal
basis. Father Castelli, already advanced in years, had served as
an assistant pastor in several Utica churches since 1886. He also
acted as chaplain for a Catholic orphanage. With their part-time
pastor, the parish launched an ambitious building program which
fell far short of its hopes. Excavations started in the spring of
1896. Mismanagement and poor cost estimates brought the project to a quick halt, as the basement alone cost $7,000 while
the whole project was slated for only $11,000. Refinancing al-
lowed the congregation to seal off the basement and prepare it
for use as a church. The parish devoted the next seven years to
raising additional funds for the completion of the structure. At
his blessing of the church, the bishop of Syracuse jestingly reflected on the role outsiders played in supporting this early
activity. After reading the names of the donors of various windows, he quipped, "It seems as though this were a church erected
by the Italians of Cork."[4]

The two papers, refusing to allow the idea to die, continued
to appeal for an Italian school until it came into being. In an
article printed a year before his death, Father Castelli bemoaned
the declining status of Italians in Utica, where they had "lost the
simpatico [respect] of other people and found themselves called
uncivilized." This situation only heightened the importance of

providing means for the education of all children. He referred
here to both instruction and a "sane moral and civil education."[5]

The subject reappeared in an extremely flowery article cele-
brating the founding of a Saturday school at Utica. Starting with
a metaphor, the editor compared the appearance of the school
to a beautiful sunrise whose rays brighten the summits of moun-
tains, melt the pure white snows, and usher in the flowering of
spring—so would the school awaken and nurture the Italian soul
in the children of the colony, provide for the "rising of the
sweet, beautiful and luxuriant spring" of life. The editor stressed
that until this time the colony had built and maintained institutions such as the "diverse Italian societies well organized and of
highest utility and advantage for our workers." Now the rapidly
growing number of children required attention. The Saturday
school at the Italian parish gave partial consideration to this
need. The paper hoped that the seed would soon grow into a
full-fledged plant but conceded that "Rome was not built in a
day." Finally, it admonished fathers not to allow their children
to miss a single Saturday of instruction.[6]

The arrival of a young Scalabrini missionary priest to assist
in the parish finally brought the project to fruition. He immediately directed his attention to the school and by early 1904 had
martialed the support of the leaders of the principal workers'
societies. Through the winter and spring he operated the Saturday school and initiated construction of a school building. A
campaign in the community produced several hundred dollars
from contributions—all under ten dollars and most under one
dollar. The new school opened on a five-day-a-week basis the
following September even though there were windows missing
and doors unhung. The staff of three nuns from the Sisters of
St. Francis met a total of 175 children in the four lower grades
and separate boys' and girls' advanced classes (covering grades
five through eight) of about 45 students each. Two of the three
second-floor classrooms served as quarters for the nuns. By 1909,
an enrollment increase to nearly 300 pupils required that the
whole school be used for classrooms.[7]

Kansas City had the honor of being the first colony to initiate such schooling. As in the other colonies, early Kansas City

Italians became the responsibility of a nearby Roman Catholic parish. In 1890 Rev. Ferdinando Santipolo, a Scalabrini missionary priest, arrived to take charge of the fledgling Holy Rosary Italian congregation. He soon opened a Sunday school staffed by Sisters of Mercy from the local St. Agnes Academy. After moving through several "store front" locations, they built their first church building and a combination rectory-school. The new school opened in 1896 under the tutelage of the Sisters of Mercy, with an enrollment of about twenty-five children. Soon they received a legacy of $7,500 which allowed them to build a separate school building costing $10,000. The new structure opened, with seventy-five students and the Sisters of St. Joseph succeeding the earlier order.[8]

In Rochester parish schools opened concurrently with each church. Bishop McQuaid, however, was slow to encourage the growth of Italian national parishes. He first sought to employ regular diocesan priests in work with the Italians. Unlike most other Catholic groups arriving at this time, Italians spoke a language familiar to a number of American priests. Many dioceses sent promising young seminarians to study at the American College in Rome, where they learned the basics of the language. On their return they held positions in the chancellery administration or in the local seminary. These individuals in Rochester were also assigned to work with Italian immigrants. The result was that Italians were served by some of the better-educated and more competent priests in the American church. In Rochester they included a future bishop and an archbishop. Still, their sympathies and perceptions were those of the American Roman Catholic church. Italian ethnic and national sensitivities did not receive the same support that Polish feeling did, for example. With no Polish-speaking priest in a diocese, the bishop had to import a Polish priest to initiate work among these immigrants.[9]

The German-American Reverend Emil J. Gefell, first pastor of Rochester's earliest Italian parish, spent seven years studying at the American College before being ordained in Rome in 1896. Ten years later he opened the first Italian parochial school, about two months before the completion of St. Anthony's

Church. Its combination church and school was in an abandoned
public school building purchased at auction by Bishop McQuaid.
In 1909 Our Lady of Mount Carmel opened to serve Italians
east of the Genesee River, followed three years later by St.
Lucy's, southwest of downtown. In each instance the parishioners immediately began construction of a building to serve as
both church and school. Such combination buildings, with the
sanctuary on one floor and the school on the other, were common structures in the Rochester diocese before World War I.[10]

It is difficult to assess the comparative contributions of various groups to the origins of the several parochial schools. In
Rochester the diocesan historian assigns a major role to the
leadership of the American hierarchy, especially Bishop McQuaid.
There is important circumstantial evidence for this position.
The bishop's strong national advocacy of parochial schools is
widely known. Within his diocese practice closely followed his
advocacy. By 1896 all but one of the city parishes had schools.
The exception was St. Stanislaus's Polish parish, which was in
the process of erecting its school building. In Utica the historian
of Mount Carmel parish mentioned the interest of the Syracuse
bishop in a school for the Italians. Yet even a casual reading of
the early Italian press in Utica makes it clear that there were important lay initiatives from at least 1901 and that both Italian
priests, especially the recently arrived Father Formia, played
leading roles in promoting the project. Repeated references to
Bishop Scalabrini's charge to the colony to look to the schooling of its children suggest that he contributed to the local impetus. In Kansas City the arrival of an Italian priest prompted the
creation of a school there. Certainly if Utica is a viable example,
the local interest in a school from within the colony at least
equaled that of the American church hierarchy. Whether both
groups envisioned the same results from the establishment of
schools is less certain.[11]

The early financing of these schools provides evidence of
the colonies' interest in them. An important element in Bishop
McQuaid's conception of his "Christian Free School" was that
it, in fact, be free to the student. All three of the Italian parish
schools in Rochester followed this no-tuition policy initially.

The purchase of an old public school building which served as St. Anthony's first church and school established the parish financial commitment at $12,915 in 1906. Six years later the parish reported back-salary due to the Sisters of St. Joseph, who staffed the school. At this point seven teachers were "costing" the parish $1,750 per year in accumulating debt. In 1914, after reaching a total of $5,820, this item disappeared completely from the annual budget.

In its first year of operation, St. Lucy's debt of $38,000 represented construction and outfitting costs on their combination church and school building and $300 due the teaching nuns. The latter item increased to $1,050 in 1914 before being dropped from the 1915 report. These "floating debts" effectively represented contributions by the Sisters of St. Joseph to the operation of the schools. Their disappearance from the budgets resulted from the order abandoning any pretense of charging for their services rather than payment of the debts by the parishes. The Sisters of Mercy who served Mount Carmel parish did not charge for their services. Thus, the parish's early budgets carry only the $38,000 debt incurred from their building program.[12]

While an exact determination of the cost to the parishes of operating their schools is impossible, certain revealing figures are available. Clearly, they received the majority of their teaching services free. However, there were seldom enough sisters available and each budget indicates salaries for lay teachers. The figures for this category were erratic. At Mount Carmel they ranged from $29 to $667 between 1909 and 1918. St. Lucy's paid out between $270 and $475, while St. Anthony's spent $100 to $500 for extra instructors before 1918. By way of comparison, the highest salary of a full-time elementary teacher in Utica at the turn of the century was $500 per year. At the start of World War I, the average teacher received $650. The school system paid $100 a year to permanent substitutes and $1.50 a night to evening-school instructors. If lay teachers in the parochial system received appreciably less than public school teachers then, as they have more recently, it would appear that the parish schools hired the equivalent of at least one, or often two, full-time lay instructors. In addition, by this date Mount Carmel was contributing $480 to the support of a convent for their sisters.

In each parish the operation of a school required sizable expenditure for building space and equipment beyond that necessary had the parishes been satisfied simply with churches. The financial records of the parishes do not allow a precise determination of this additional cost, since the combination school-church-building pattern produced a single budget entry for mortgage and outfitting debts. The same is true of other costs such as fuel, utilities, insurance, janitor, structural maintenance, and the like, which appear as single items under "church," "school," or "church and school" expenditures. School supplies, books, etc., ran from $40 to $340, though these items at times were not in the budget. A $74 piano rental fee appeared in 1918 in the Mount Carmel statement. Income came from four regular sources—pew rental, plate collections, special collections, and fund-raising events such as bazaars, dinners, raffles, and fairs. In addition there were occasional bequests.[13]

The financial situation in Utica is much clearer. The school building cost a total of $7,346, of which over $6,800 remained as debt at the end of the first year of operation. The parish charged tuition from the beginning. In 1905 this amounted to $418. This, plus other miscellaneous income equaling $601, paid for the sisters' maintenance. The next year tuition income was up to $525, but the sisters' support increased to $820. Throughout the rest of the decade, the school had to rely on outside contributions and several hundred dollars annually from the church. By 1911 the cost of supporting the sisters was nearly $1,400, of which tuition covered about one-half. The capital and maintenance costs remained hidden in the overall church budget. Throughout the early 1920s, tuition revenue remained well below half of the salary of the teachers. In 1922 tuition equaled about 29 percent of the outlay for salaries, school supplies, and rent for the sisters' quarters. The following year they acquired their own convent at a cost of $4,500. In 1928 the parish built a new combination school and gymnasium at a cost of $55,000. The annual budgets began to separate many of the operating costs and reveal that over 29 percent of the total expenditure, nearly $18,000, went to the operation of the school. This is still an understatement of the total cost, for some part of the more than $3,500 in principal and interest included under church expense was due on the school and convent. Because tuition was no longer collected, the whole financial burden of the school fell upon the congregation.[14]

While the exact cost of operating schools cannot be determined, it is clear that the Italian parishes assumed major burdens that added from 30 to 50 percent to the total cost of operating a parish. The Utica colony seems to have shouldered the greatest part of this burden itself. From the beginning it gave its sisters "support" or salaries and provided them with a residence. In its fund-raising activities it sought contributions from outside the colony. Early lists of contributors to subscription campaigns include a few non-Italians. Yet these extracolonial contributions were seldom for more than five dollars, which was typical of individual Italians. Non-Italians undoubtedly bought raffle tickets and attended bazaars. Still, the parish does not appear to have had any substantial financial support from outside the colony. Most of the revenue came from internal sources, including collections, pew rental, bazaars, tuition, and funds raised by church societies. In Rochester the sources were much the same, except for tuition. That city's three parishes also enjoyed a partly disguised contribution of the perhaps involuntary "donation" of teaching services. The nuns who lived at their motherhouse or in nearby convents spared each parish the burden of providing residences during the early years. Although the Utica colony immediately assumed responsibility for a greater proportion of the true "cost" of its school, each colony made substantial financial commitments in order to establish and maintain parish schools.[15]

Once established, the parish schools undoubtedly proved a disappointment to a number of their lay promoters. Those who had anticipated that the schools would be true Italian schools where the Italian language and national culture would be taught were quickly disabused of that notion. A local teaching order supplied the religious teaching staff of each school. In

Rochester the Sisters of St. Joseph had no Italian-American
member in the order when the three parish schools were founded.
A young student, soon to become Sister Eligia, was in training
at Nazareth Academy in 1912 when she contributed her language skills in the door-to-door survey which recruited children
for the new St. Lucy's school. She returned to St. Lucy's as a
teacher in 1918 for eight years, and again in 1950 to complete
her career. A second Italian-American joined the order in the
early 1920s. The Sisters of Mercy did not have a single Italian-
speaking nun at Mount Carmel school during the prewar period.
Bishop McQuaid insisted from the beginning that his parish
schools "give as good a secular education as can be obtained in
the public schools, and a Christian education besides." He required that the Josephites' Nazareth Academy meet state norms
in teacher training. By the 1890s it was generally accepted practice for parochial students in Rochester to take the New York
State regents examinations. This insistence on excellence resulted
in a pronounced upgrading of diocesan schools. It also locked
the teaching orders and the schools into "American" curricula
and standards.[16]

Bishop Hickey was explicit about what he expected the parish school to achieve among the Italians when he spoke at the
cornerstone ceremony for St. Lucy's:

> You are people who have come from Italy, a country where
> the very air you breathed was the air of the Catholic Church,
> you are given this building in the hope that it will enable
> you to continue your fidelity to your religion . . . . You are in
> this country to become Americans and you must do what
> you can to advocate and better this glorious land. We want
> you, the Italian-Americans of this city, to show the native
> citizens what general Italian Catholicism is and means, and
> the way that you may best do this is to be unfailing in your
> fidelity to your church.
>
> In this institution there is a school where your sons and
> daughters may be taught the ways of America and how to
> read and write English. You must allow them to avail them-
> selves of these opportunities. By keeping predominant in

your minds and hearts the doctrines of the Catholic Church
you will make citizens of which this city and country will
soon be proud.[17]

Sister Eligia and her fellow Josephites understood perfectly
that the bishop expected them to bring their charges to full participation in the American church. They carefully proceeded to
use the children as "Ambassadors of English" to the adult colony. Teachers instructed students to go home and rehearse lessons with their parents. Bishop Hickey backed a movement to
encourage Americans to attend St. Lucy's Church and to send
their children to the school in order to set examples of true
American behavior for the Italians. A 1908 diocesan visitation
to Utica's Mount Carmel School revealed that it, too, functioned
very much in an American manner in the education of its 292
children. The books employed at the school gave no evidence of
interest in Italian culture or language. From the catechism, Bible
history, history and geography, to the readers, spellers, and gram-
mars, there was nothing that distinguished the school from
others in territorial parishes of the diocese.[18]
    When the schools did not meet the expectations of those
who wished a truly Italian education for their children, the call
for a "strictly and purely Italian school" was periodically re-
issued. A decade after the establishment of the Mount Carmel
School, an articulate tailor's wife chastised the Utica colony for
"naivete in thinking that lacking a school, a few lectures by
traveling professors were sufficient to kindle the spirit of Italian-
ism." "While the French and Germans everywhere had their own
schools," she charged that Italians "slept tranquilly and lulled
themselves in the futile hope of a better future." In the early
1920s the parochial school in Kansas City began teaching Italian
as a foreign language, thus tacitly admitting that the situation
had shifted from one of cultural maintenance to one of cultural
retrieval. Beyond this, parish schooling in the three colonies
provided little direct support for the maintenance of Italian
culture.[19]
    Considerably fewer than half the children in the colonies
attended these Italian parochial schools. Prior to their

establishment, Italian parents could and did send their children
to schools operated by territorial parishes. This practice continued even after the Italian schools were in operation. In 1920
St. Lucy's graduated eight girls and one boy from the eighth
grade. The nonethnic Cathedral School listed seven Italians in
its graduation roster for the same year. Most Italian children,
however, attended public schools. It is impossible to reconstruct
the exact proportion of who chose one or the other type of
school, but an approximation is possible. Rochester's school
census of 1913 attempted to list all children in the city between
the ages of four and eighteen years. The figures are enigmatic
and frustrating, as the separate categories do not add up to equal
the totals reported. Nor are they completely representative of
the ratio of public to parochial school students at the elementary level since they also include high school students. Taking
these shortcomings into account, the figures suggest that approximately 70 percent of the children in school between the ages
given were in public schools.[20]

In Kansas City the 1921 confirmation class at the Italian
parish provides evidence of the proportions of children attending public and parochial schools. Here the bias is apt to be in
favor of the parochial school, since the city had active Protestant missions whose children attended public school and would
not be included in this calculation. In a class of 119, 31 percent
of the children ages ten through fourteen attended parochial
schools. The remainder were in public schools. In Utica Father
Formia made varying estimates of 15, 26, and 23 percent for
the proportion of Italian children in his parochial school for the
years 1916–18. In 1920, 33 percent of Italian eighth-grade graduates were from Mount Carmel School and 67 percent from the
public schools.

Thus, it appears that a figure of one-third is a reasonable
upper limit on the proportion of Italian children who attended
Italian parochial schools. The public and parochial school student
bodies were not fixed and rigid. A small but regular movement
of students occurred between the schools in any given year. In
1910–11 and 1916–17, 4.9 percent and 2.2 percent respectively,
of the student body left Mount Carmel for the public schools.

Since the parochial schools did not normally offer kindergarten, children destined for a parochial education often spent their first school year in a public institution.[21]

The appearance of parochial schools was a significant event in the development of each colony. While the spirit behind their initiation was to a degree the product of a concern with the preservation of Italian culture, they were far more important as manifestations of the immigrants' commitment to a long-term future in America and to the building of a viable Italian-American colony. The schools had little precedent in the Italians' background. For more than forty years, schooling in Italy had been almost totally the province of the state. The Italian parochial school here was most of all a parallel institution "as American" as a school in a territorial parish, or a public school which continued to account for the schooling of the majority of the colonies' children. The significance of the parochial schools lies in the fact that they appeared in the first place, and that they continued to be supported by the colonies in the form they took.

The public schools which enrolled the majority of Italian youth varied significantly in the closeness of the ties they developed with the colonies. Two of the three colonies had, for a time, a single public elementary school that served the majority of the colonies' children and was often referred to by the press in a possessive way as "our school." In Utica this was the Bleecker Street School. Originally the city's academy building, the structure was remodeled and opened by school officials in 1900. At that point, it was the largest elementary school in the system, with a faculty equal in numbers only to those of primary schools which included advanced departments (grades seven and eight). Physically, it seems to have been well above average for the city's school plants. It had continuously flowing drinking fountains on each floor and electric lighting, both novelties for Utica elementary schools at that time, as well as a favorable window-area to floor-space ratio. Alterations included the installation of showers and a recreational area in the basement. Only its heating system seems to have been deficient; several years elapsed before the district engineer remedied

the problem. In spite of its size and the expectation that it
would adequately supplant two congested and inadequate buildings, Bleecker Street School was overcrowded almost from its
opening day. By 1903 public pressure was so great that Utica
installed its first portable schoolrooms on the Bleecker Street
premises to house the overflow. These two-room frame structures became semipermanent "temporary expediencies" as the
Italian colony continued to grow. The 1904 opening of Mount
Carmel School averted a major school population crisis but did
not relieve the overcrowding at Bleecker Street.[22]

As the colony rapidly expanded eastward, the system made
further adjustments. A new building, Wetmore School, opened
in the winter of 1900 in the east end of the city. Along with the
older Mary Street School, it enrolled increasing numbers of
Italians. Even this did not fill the need, and in 1908 school officials transferred a large number of Italians from Bleecker
Street to another school which previously only a few Italians
had attended. The result was to limit Bleecker Street to kindergarten through fourth grade, shifting the fifth and sixth grades
to Union Street, which was formerly used only as an advanced
school (seventh and eighth grades). The pressure continued, and
in 1910 the city started construction on what became the largest elementary school building in the city, with a capacity double that of the Bleecker Street School. Originally, educational
planners had expected to be able to assign two rooms in the new
structure for use as a branch of public library, leaving four or
five rooms available for future growth. The John E. Brandegee
School opened in 1911, with all of its twenty-one rooms filled
beyond capacity. Designed for 900 students, it had an enrollment of over 1,400 and an average daily attendance of 986.
Part of the unexpected wave of students came as transfers from
the parochial school. The remainder appears to have resulted
from the continuing growth of the colony. The crush continued
and the school board added a twenty-one-room annex to the
Wetmore School in 1913. In addition, it converted the attic
and basement of that school for academic use.[23]

With the opening of Brandegee School the dominance of
Bleecker Street School as the colony's chief school ended. In

1900 the Bleecker Street building was close to the geographic heart of the colony. During the next decade the colony expanded eastward along Bleecker Street. By 1911 the Brandegee School location was central in the colony. The Bleecker Street building then served the western end of the colony, Wetmore and Mary Street schools enrolled the children in the east, while Lansing did the same for the south side. Thus, by 1911 no school enrolled a majority of the Italian children in the city, nor was any school, except for Mount Carmel, close to being exclusively Italian in student body. In spite of its location Brandegee had a sizable enrollment of non-Italians, most of whom were of East European immigrant backgrounds. These schools were not "ghetto schools" in the sense that they contained homogeneous student populations. Nor were they inferior physical plants. Several were new and the most up-to-date buildings in the city. The others had undergone extensive renovation and expansion, which placed them among the best of the older buildings in the system.

In Kansas City, Karnes School served as the dominant public elementary school throughout the period under study. First opened in 1880, it was situated in the center of the Italian settlement and naturally carried the responsibility for the education of the colony's children. In 1914 the school moved from its original seven-room building to a larger thirteen-room structure a few blocks away. While Italian children attended other schools on the periphery of the colony, through 1930 Karnes was "the Italian School" in a way unlike the schools in the other colonies. In 1926, for instance, slightly over 90 percent of graduates were of Italian origin. Rochester's geographically scattered colony spread over many elementary school zones. School Five came as close as any to representing to Italians there what the Karnes and Bleecker-Brandegee schools meant to their colonies. However, most of the city's Italians found themselves to be minorities in a number of ethnically heterogeneous schools.[24]

The ability to identify a specific school as the "Italian School" had important consequences for the school program and the colony's acceptance of it. Karnes School identified more closely with its Italian colony than any other school in

the three cities. By the 1920s its physical plant served as a
social and recreational, as well as educational, center of the colony. Its rooms were available in the evenings for meetings of
clubs and societies, and it provided an auditorium for colony
gatherings, such as those held to protest police actions in the
colony or to organize a federation of all Italian societies. The
building housed a branch library with reading facilities open in
the evenings. The librarians pointedly collected popular and
classical works in Italian and subscribed to the major Italian
newspapers. The Italian press publicized these holdings. An
Italian was in charge of the branch library during the hours when
non-English-speaking adults were most likely to use it. At least
once, the colony successfully mobilized to prevent the demise
of this library.

The school staff worked to attract and hold the interests of
the colony. There was an active PTA, which included many
prominent Italians in its leadership. Men from this group often
spoke at the school's graduation ceremonies. The association
held social functions, evening programs, and generally worked to
interest colony parents in the school activities and work of
their children. An active alumni association initiated by graduates served to strengthen further the ties between the colony and
the school. In the field of adult education the school offered an
evening session with a staff that included Italians. In addition
to the usual classes in English and Americanization, the school
offered "sewing by machine." General evening programs and
lectures were frequent occurrences. The number of these that
were musical, stressed Italian themes, or gave special emphasis
to holidays such as Columbus Day, showed a sensitivity to the
interests of prospective audiences.[25]

In Utica and Rochester the schools serving the colonies, re-
flecting the more cosmopolitan nature of their student bodies,
never developed the kind of exclusive ties with the Italian colony evidenced by the Karnes School. The schools' concerns
were more for immigrants and their children generally than for
any one ethnic group in particular. The Utica Public Library,
like the Kansas City Library, maintained a collection of Italian
works. However, this was never housed in a public school

building. Both Bleecker Street School (later Brandegee School) and School Number Five in Rochester conducted evening classes. Their major goals were English and citizenship instruction. Class rolls reveal the presence of many national groups. Citing this multiplicity of backgrounds, evening school administrators officially discouraged the introduction of Old World culture or traditions into the numerous social, academic, and recreational activities of the schools, for fear of producing jealousy or reviving old European animosities.

The Evening School, a paper published by the combined evening schools of Utica, published essays by students that dealt with their native lands. These tended to be descriptive and to eschew anything that might produce controversy. They did not, however, give any evidence of pressure on immigrants to reject or denigrate their pasts. As early as 1907 Rochester offered Italian as well as Spanish in evening school. Since these were taught in a high school as foreign languages, they required prior literacy in English. Despite relatively few potential students, Italian was offered well into the 1920s. Schoolmen in Rochester also made an early attempt to turn schools into social centers serving the broader needs of their neighborhoods. Centers serving heterogenous immigrant goups opened in two locations in 1907. They offered educational and musical programs, recreation, and independently governed civic clubs. Italian music and lectures on Italian topics were a part of the program, as was an "Italian Civic Club." However, the colony shared the centers with Poles, Germans, Russians, Scots, etc., all of whom had comparable programs.[26]

The influx of children who came from non-English-speaking homes presented an ever-mounting challenge to school systems unaccustomed to having large numbers of working-class and non-English-speaking children enrolled. Marvin Lazerson has suggested that one of the consequences of this pressure in Massachusetts schools was a transformation of the kindergarten from a distinctive movement concerned with play, freed)m, and social reform, to an instrument for control and discipline designed to prepare unruly immigrant children for structured elementary schooling. Utica school officials perceived the possibilities of using the kindergartens in this manner before the turn of the century. These classes operated quietly but with increasing popularity, as measured by enrollments for a number of years before 1899. In that year the superintendent announced a new policy which, in effect, made the kindergartens "Head Start" operations charged with preparing children under seven years of age for regular grade work if they were judged unready when they entered school. Fitness for grade work, not age or time spent in kindergarten, was to be the standard for promotion. He predicted that many would need to spend two years in this class, although some might be ready in only half a year. His two-year prediction proved to be the rule for most children.[27]

In 1906 a teacher explained the program in her classroom as follows:

> The manual training in our kindergarden produces as good results as in any other school in the city. To follow dictation with close attention is exceedingly difficult and to memorize is also hard for the children.
>
> The parents of these children work with the hands rather than the head; therefore, the children whose experience is much more limited than that of average children must have the latent power within them developed almost entirely in the schoolroom. They have very little idea of law or obedience, some of them are half fed and most of them are very dirty. About one-half do not speak English.
>
> Under these conditions it is not possible for them to advance as rapidly as some other children. No one can be very good, very happy at work and very dirty at the same time.
>
> A part of the time which is spent by other kindergartens in the mental development of those in their care we are obligated to use in the ethical culture of the little ones. To feed and bathe them and to encourage the spirit of love, courtesy, and cleanliness is essential.

In spite of the obvious emphasis on the preparation for elementary schooling, the teacher also displayed loyalty for the traditional kindergarteners' creed. She worked actively in two areas of cardinal importance to the early movement. She held four mothers' meetings during the year and, with her assistant, made 206 home visits. The official curriculum published in 1912 reflects a strict adherence to traditional kindergarten principles of handwork and rhythmic and dramatic play. However, a succession of annual reports of the school system reveals continuing tension between superintendents who viewed the kindergartens as means of preparing immigrant children for primary school, and the professional kindergarteners. While accepting the necessity of preparing children for school, the kindergarteners also insisted on continuing their traditional interest in social reform and easing the burdens of children who "have very few of the joys of childhood."[28]

Rochester approached the problem of preparing immigrant children for grade school in a different way. In 1906 the city school opened "foreign classes" to prepare children of immigrants who they judged unready for regular grade work because of deficiencies in English or other skills. The program in these classes as it evolved by 1912 stressed beginning with concrete activities, allowing the "universal language of action" to introduce simple, then more complex, English usage. The lessons indirectly taught basic American (i.e. middle-class) values in hygiene, manners, diet, dress, housekeeping, and family relations. Small classes made it possible for teachers to provide individual attention and permitted them to take into account their pupils' abilities and previous educational preparation and experience. Proponents of the foreign class cited the combination of specially trained teachers, determination to keep the rooms bright, happy places filled with flowers and pictures, and individualization as important elements which brought a sense of self-confidence to the students.

Attendance records suggest that the children enjoyed these classes. In the academic year 1911–12, attendance for all foreign classes ran well above 80 percent of registration and displayed none of the irregularity found in the normal elementary classes. Individual registers for classes including large numbers of Italians, who made up 63 percent of all students in these classes, confirm the pattern of regular attendance for this group. Statements by school officials and news stories in the press always represented

the typical stay in these classes as being only a few months,
after which the child moved into a regular classroom commensurate with his level of readiness. However, the actual attendance
records suggest that only in special cases was the stay less than
two terms, and that the typical student remained in one or another level of the foreign class for one-and-a-half or two years.[29]

The quality of the faculty in these classes indicates that the
school system took seriously the task of introducing immigrant
children to American schooling. Teachers of the foreign classes
were somewhat better prepared than the average teacher in the
elementary grades. All of them had at least the equivalent of a
city training-school course, the typical preparation for being
an elementary schoolteacher at the turn of the century. About
a third were graduates of the newly popular two-year state normal schools. Several had more specialized training in immigrant
or early childhood education. Only one teacher entered foreign-
class work directly from her teacher training program. Most of the
rest were in their middle to late thirties and had seven or more
years of elementary teaching experience when they were first
assigned to the classes. None, however, was even close to retirement.

Only one teacher had problems in the system later. Her career
commenced in 1886 when, after completing high school and local
training class, she started teaching in the elementary schools. She
taught for periods in three schools which had largely immigrant student bodies. In 1916, after earning a state license in immigrant education, she began foreign-class work. The foreign classes at her schoc
were dropped in 1923 and she returned to regular primary school
teaching, where she experienced considerable difficulties with the
elementary supervisor over methods. She retired the following year.[3]

At the opposite extreme in terms of success in the school
system was a woman who began teaching in 1897 after earning
a Scientific and Latin Diploma from the Free Academy and a
certificate from the Rochester Training School. Fourteen years
later she moved into foreign-class work at School Nine. In 1917
she became acting principal of the school and from there she
moved into the middle echelons of the city school administration. She continued her education, earning a B.A. from the

University of Rochester and an M.A. from Teachers College, Columbia, in the early 1920s.

A third, and perhaps intermediate example, is that of a teacher who started teaching foreign classes at School Nine in 1913 at age forty. Her education included degrees from two high schools, the Cook County Normal School, and the Chicago Kindergarten College. Her prior teaching experience included service in regular and special elementary grades, as well as three years as an instructor at a Wilmington normal school. The pattern, then, was to appoint mature, experienced teachers who had above-average preparation for teaching and prior success in the classroom. There is no evidence of any concern that these teachers be familiar with a foreign language, and none of the records indicate that they knew the mother tongues of their students.

Throughout the first years of the twentieth century, the curricula and teachers assigned to heavily immigrant schools offer no evidence that school leaders believed the needs of immigrant children were any different from those of their other students. Utica, for instance, had a single program of study and a single set of textbooks and materials in use throughout the city. They did not seek out persons of Italian extraction to serve as teachers in the schools. In 1911, Rosina Pellettieri joined her sister Laura, a first-grade teacher at Bleecker Street, as the only Italians teaching in the city school system. Adelina Teti taught at Bleecker Street between 1906 and 1908 and her sister Angelina appeared as a permanent substitute in 1916. They represented the total Italian membership on the public school teaching staff before 1917.

After this date more Italians gained teaching positions in Utica. The appointment of Rocco Lopardo to the post of mathematics teacher at the Utica Free Academy in 1923 represented a milestone. "Professor" Lopardo quickly became a prominent figure in the colony. By 1930 there were at least ten elementary school and two high school teachers of Italian extraction in Utica's public schools. With the exception of the "individual work specialist" position, the increase in the numbers of teachers with Italian backgrounds does not appear to have been the

product of a concern for special needs or problems which Italian
children might have had that could best be handled by Italian
teachers. However, Italian elementary teachers were almost
always assigned to schools with sizable Italian student bodies.[31]

If city subject-matter supervisors and the state curriculum
makers did not see any need for special consideration in dealing
with immigrant children, by 1916 teachers and principals of the
schools in Utica with large numbers of immigrant children came
to realize that modifications in material and methodology
might be necessary to give these children an "American education". In that year they met and worked out a proposal for modifications to be made in the course of study appropriate for
their students. Although represented as involving major changes
in the traditional course of study, these were actually alterations
in timing and shifts of emphasis which left the basic elementary
curriculum, its ends, materials, and methods, intact. The new
program divided the first half of first-grade work into two parts,
allowing the "children a longer time for foundation work so
that, when promoted, their progress may be easier and more
steady than it now is." Thus, students spent a full school-year
on what was normally half a year's first-grade work.

Other changes reflected greater concern for "Ethical Instruction." The intent here was to increase the emphasis on
teaching the "American virtues" of honesty, truthfulness, and
fair play and American standards of manners, hygiene, and diet,
as well as a "sympathetic interest in flowers, birds and animals."
Suggested and mandated materials lacked any significant representation of Italian items, though the cultural traditions of the
English, French, Spanish, Persian, Norse, Japanese, Celtic, Slav,
and Indian were to be represented through "ethnic dances."
Perhaps the planners felt that the children of Italian immigrants
would learn about their own cultural heritage through other
means and that therefore concern for it in the school was super-
fluous.[32]

In 1916 a fairly intensive study of the Utica public school
system by the New York State Department of Education included the responses of principals of heavily immigrant-attended
schools to queries concerning what they believed to be the chief

functions of their schools and the means they were using to meet their responsibilities. Their answers give important insights into the views that school leaders had of their immigrant student populations and the ways they adjusted curricula to meet those conceptions. One principal wrote:

> As our school is located in the heart of the Italian district, it has been our problem to study the social as well as the educational needs of these people, and as far as possible, adapt our teaching to meet existing conditions.
>
> Most of the Italian people are not interested in higher education but wish their children to go to work as soon as the law will permit. We aim, therefore, to include in the work of the first six grades such knowledge and information as will be of most use in the kind of life they are planning to lead. It is also true that we are equally anxious that they secure an appreciation of music, drawing and poetry.
>
> The home life of our children is bare, and from an American stand-point, unattractive. The children receive little or no ethical instruction, there is no real social family intercourse and very little proper instruction in common household duties. Because of these conditions we try to have our school work meet the needs as far as we can possibly do so . . . . We should like to have our older boys and girls give more time to manual training and domestic science, as they are now getting only one lesson a week.
>
> As the element of play is so seriously lacking in the home life, we should like to give our children more real play during school hours but there is not sufficient time . . . .

He went on to appeal for an extension of the schools' influence over these children by increasing the length of the school day and year. He praised the results of a summer-school program that had slowed the serious erosion of achievement which normally took place over the summer. Then he continued:

> We have tried to make the people of our district feel free to come to us with their problems and they do come very

often. As a result we have their confidence and can depend
on their support and cooperation in all school matters.

Our greatest problem and responsibility is making Italians
over into real Americans; not only in language and dress but
also in spirit. This work is not something that can be classified by itself as it must pervade every bit of our teaching.
Directly and indirectly we try to teach our pupils the true
meaning of liberty, the principles on which our government
is based and the rights, duties and obligations of its citizens.

This school drew praise from the study for its concern for the
community and social needs of the people.[33]

The second school, described as "literally a melting pot," included Jewish, French, Greek, Lithuanian, Polish, Austrian,
American Negro, as well as approximately one-third Italian students. Organized as a "school-city," it had its own mayor, board
of aldermen, and other city officials. After a series of ward
meetings and primaries, students elected these "officials" in
balloting which they organized and ran themselves. Students
had a role in the care of buildings and grounds, dispensing school
supplies, and governing their own general conduct. All this helped
the child learn "to live and work with others, to adjust himself
to his neighbor and his job, to appreciate the rights of others,
to gauge his own capacities," and "to submit to restrictions
and conventions of society."

The school also featured a dramatic club, a humane club, an
orchestra, and glee clubs. Assemblies provided forums where
prominent men and women from city government, commerce,
and society spoke to the school. The principal stressed "positive
discipline," by which he meant keeping "so busy doing the
worthwhile things that we have not much time to do anything
else." Home and school conferences, frequent exhibits of the
childrens' work, and occasional open houses for mothers drew
parents into the school's orbit. To provide time and space for
study that was often lacking at home, school opened early in
the morning, stayed open at noon, and remained open after
classes were over. Reading tables and a magazine library offered
interested students an opportunity to do their homework at

school. This also avoided trouble that might be caused by idle students waiting outside before school started—a bit of the principal's "positive discipline." As with other "immigrant schools," this one sought every opportunity to convince both children and parents of the advantages of more education.[34]

In sum, after 1900 the schools slowly made adjustments which enabled them to work more effectively with their immigrant populations. These gradual changes represented modifications in methods or materials rather than fundamental alterations in the values and assumptions underlying the school programs. The same period witnessed the sharpening of ideas about what constituted "Americanization" of immigrants and their children. This, in turn, allowed the schools to alter the balance of various elements of the traditional program to meet their popularly assigned and self-defined responsibilities of making all their students good American citizens.

The gradual discovery and adoption of more effective and diversified means of transforming children into the middle-class conception of good citizens had its parallel in the parochial schools, which became increasingly "American" in the structure and content of their curricula. This development had its origins in at least three factors. First, American church leaders shared with those who set goals for the public schools a number of values and assumptions about what was best for America. Secondly, the parochial schools, especially in the Rochester diocese, were attuned to the latest developments in pedagogy in an effort to keep their schools at least equal to their public counterparts. Lay activities pushed, prodded, and challenged both systems to solve the "immigrant problem." Finally, there was the basic appeal to many parents of a curriculum intended to aid social and economic mobility. Failure of the parochial schools to offer real alternatives in the area of secular culture suggests that parents and congregations which supported these schools found their offerings popular.[35]

Far from being negative or even neutral on the question of schools, the Italian press and the colonial leaders who spoke through its pages energetically promoted them among their conationals. From the

very first, the press encouraged school attendance and urged compliance with the compulsory education laws. Every fall brought articles which explained the wheres and whens of school openings and
usually included appeals that parents make sure their children observed the attendance laws and took advantage of the schooling
available in this country. The paper explained the specific requirements of the attendance laws and included in some detail definitions
of what constituted legal absence. They warned parents that they
sinned twice in violating these laws. First, when dragged into court,
they brought humiliation on themselves and the colony. More important, however, they failed to fulfill the sacred parental obligation
to educate their children. Editors also sought to explain the structure
of American schooling. Articles on industrial and trade schools, engineering schools, commercial programs in high schools, and the
like, introduced parents to the various specialized schools and
what each prepared its students to do.[36]

As the colonies matured and parents became more accustomed to American schooling patterns, the papers promoted
enrollment at higher levels of school. By 1920 all the newspapers
were urging parents to keep their children in high school and
whenever possible to consider sending them to college. In 1921
Lanni pointed out that ten years before it had been unusual to
find an Italian boy in a Rochester secondary school. Now, large
numbers of both boys and girls from the colony were doing well
at this level. He repeated the message of "do as other progressive
members of the colony are doing" at every opportunity. *Il
Messaggero* proclaimed that "to deny the benefits of higher education to boys and girls is to rob them of youth's greatest heritage and maturity's greatest asset." In another article, *La Stampa
Unita* stressed the "sacred duty to educate children to their intellectual limits" and pointed out the increasing opportunities
for educated people in industry, commerce, and the professions.
The article portrayed good vocational positions as requiring
more and more education at the same time that there was parallel expansion in the opportunities to get more schooling.
"Education is not a privilege for the favored few but a necessity
for all" summarized both the article and the Italian press's attitude toward schooling. In 1930 *La Stampa Unita* urged several

groups of middle-class Italians to unite in a campaign to raise a
$20,000 scholarship fund to ensure that more of the colony
children would be able to attend college. Lanni did not advocate
strictly academic and higher education. He stressed the occupational opportunities open to those who attended trade or technical schools as compared to those available for individuals who
completed only grammar school.[37]

January and June graduation ceremonies gave the papers
opportunities to repeat their message with added emphasis. The
papers carried long lists of Italian children who were successful
in their year's schooling. Honors such as being selected flag
bearer, conferred in each Rochester elementary school on the
boy with the best record for the semester, were cause for special
journalistic celebrations. In 1902 Adelina Teti graduated from
Catholic Academy with a gold medal for taking first place in
French and a second-place silver medal for calligraphy. Two
years later Laura Pellettieri graduated from the same school
sharing highest honors with four non-Italians. On such occasions
the Utica editors felt that the whole colony should bask in the
glory of the students' achievements. A young Sardinian girl won
a city-wide essay contest at her grade school after only twenty
months in the United States, thereby gaining notice in the American press and a letter from the mayor of Utica. The Italian press
accepted accolades for the girl in the names of her parents, Sardinia, and the colony. In the 1920s Bisceglia regularly reported
on the scholastic careers of local youths as they progressed
through institutions of higher education. The graduation of a
son of the colony from the University of Minnesota with a Ph.D.
in sociology was the culmination of the whole colony's forward
push in education.

The colonies in general and the editors in particular found a
powerful technique for fostering extended schooling by suggesting that children's educational successes conferred honor on
their parents as well as on the children themselves. Such success
was a direct gauge of a parent's merit. Reports on the advancement of a student through the educational levels almost inevitably emphasized the enlightened good judgment and sacrifices
of the parents. A laborer's status in the colony could be

appreciably and permanently enhanced by the educational successes of his children. Even his obituary would make prominent
note of the fact that "he was never careless with the education
of his children." Parents did not simply share vicariously in the
mobility of their children through schooling. They experienced
advancement of their own social, if not economic, status. Constant restatement of this theme must have strengthened the
resolves of those who were making sacrifices for their children's
education and encouraged others to take this avenue to mobility.[38]

Even with such a concern for schooling, the Italian editors
and those who wrote in the papers never sought to make education synonymous with schooling. They recognized the vital importance of other institutions in raising children in America and
the need for education for adults as well as for children. The
importance of family and religion in the character-building and
moral aspects of a child's education was a theme that appeared
in many different guises. The distinction made in Italian between *educazione* and *istruzione* (see above, p. 153) prevented
the development among immigrants of the schooling myopia
that has lately afflicted Americans. In Kansas City, Dr. G. M.
Pellettieri used the most spectacular crime of the 1920s to make
this very point. In a 1923 article, he hypothesized that family
neglect of the "educations" of Leopold and Loeb explained
their brutal crime. The best schools were not able to compensate
for this failure of the familial factor by building spiritual character into the education of these two biologically and intellectually healthy individuals.

The press regularly admonished parents about their educational obligations in even more direct fashion. In 1910 *La Luce*
sounded the alarm for Italian mothers, urging them not to
misread or misunderstand American liberty and freedom. This
editorial encouraged parents to keep a cautious and sharp eye
on their children, always to know where they were, and—with
daughters especially—to learn why it took them overly long to
return from errands. "Too much freedom, too little interest
and too little care toward children and the results are those that
can be found in the press of any language everyday." The concern here, as elsewhere, was not traditionalist in that it rejected

American ways indiscriminately. Rather, it was a plea not to be overwhelmed by the blandishments of the city, to go too "American" or let the new get out of hand. Parents should act selectively to censor dangers such as the cinema and the pool hall from their children's environments. Citing Victor Hugo on the importance of infancy, *La Luce* urged its readers to look to the education of their children from time of birth. By four years of age it was too late, the paper warned. A mother's concern for the education of a child's spirit should commence at his birth, just as her milk nourishes him physically. By the late 1920s Lanni was offering regular advice for mothers in the form of a column, "Our Children," written in Italian by New York City educator Angelo Patri.[39]

Italians' concern for the education of their children did not end with the school and the family. Several writers pointed to the potential of the theater as a powerful force in teaching music, culture, language, and morality to the youth of the colony. Despite their reproach of Americans for ignoring the didactic potential of this institution, there is no evidence that the managers of the local theaters ever presented programs significantly different from the regular fare of American-style burlesque for any length of time. One theater manager asserted that, although he very much wanted to offer all Italian programs regularly, his box office receipts indicated that the colony was not ready to appreciate and support such programming. Music schools and teachers also received strong support in the press as necessary complements to a complete education. Nor was education something to be reserved for children. Editors frequently turned their attentions to advancing the educational level of the adults of the colony. Often these efforts were little more than announcements of correspondence or other courses coupled with admonishments to exploit such opportunities fully.[40]

Occasionally the papers pleaded their case with more urgency and greater persuasion. In 1914 *La Luce* used a quote from Diderot, "Ignorance is the beginning of every blunder," as the text for a strong appeal to the colony. "It is not enough to educate the children," the editor urged, "we must educate

ourselves." He raised the specters of crime and delinquency,
blaming them on a deficiency of education. Yet many Italians
remained refractory and he urged these "loved conationals" to
make themselves better fit for modern life through education.
"Frequent adult evening school, diligently attend illustrated
and educational lectures which are often offered free or for a
small fee. Subscribe to and read magazines, pamphlets, and newspapers, for there rests a germ of culture and instruction in every
page that one reads . . . . Pay no attention to the ignorant; they
should not be valued because they do not understand."[41]

A Kansas City paper also argued that it was not enough to
send one's children to school. One had to set an example by
showing concern for the development of one's own intellectual
and moral capacities. The shame of illiteracy and ignorance
should not be endured. Adult evening schools existed and should
be exploited by all. Diligence in such a school would lift curtains
of ignorance from one's eyes and reveal previously closed secrets on the printed page. By the 1920s, self-educated Americans, especially Abraham Lincoln, became inspirational object
lessons. The papers stressed the opportunities and rewards that
resulted from a continuing concern for personal advancement.

A lawyer and correspondent for *La Stampa Unita* summed
up most of the concern in an appeal entitled "Winter Leisure."
He pointed out that thousands of workers would be either
entirely without work or with greatly reduced working hours
during the coming winter. The Rochester climate limited the
possibility of games and diversions which consumed energy and
promoted domestic peace. Winter, then, could be for the worker
a period of preparation for a more advanced and civilized level
of life. It was the most propitious season for study, offering a
minimum of distractions. He urged illiterates to use the opportunity to tear away the mask of ignorance that kept them from
even writing their names. Those workers who were fortunate
enough to have attended elementary school in Italy should turn
to the study of English. The city's evening schools were free
and ready to advance this end.[42]

Then he considered the often repeated proposal to transform
the workers' societies into schools to teach the Italian language.

The difficulty with this plan, he felt, was the failure of most literacy instructors to adapt to the special needs of adults. Adult illiterates needed a confidential environment to protect them from humiliation when they had to make an extended effort to master that which children learned quickly. Classes held in homes, religious congregations, or mutual benefit societies would provide sympathetic and supportive environments necessary for the "mature man to uncover the mysteries of the simple reading book and write with meek hand deformed letters and not always decipherable words . . . . The arrival of winter each year, especially for the *braccianti* must signal the beginning of a different labor, not immediately productive and valuable in money, but also necessary—study, the noble ambition of breaking, or at least slackening, the claim of ignorance." He strongly chastised the workers' societies, which boasted of their concern for contributions to the moral betterment of their membership and yet showed no regard for education (istruzione and educazione) appropriate to the age, social condition, and psychology of their particular memberships. "What," he asked, "do they mean by moral betterment? "

An example of a class that could provide a model was already in existence and Teresi praised it as a sane approach. "The Union of Italian Laborers has opened a practical English language school, a school in which the teacher is not a *literatus*, his mind stuffed with methods and theories, but an authentic workingman, a profound knower of our simple and coarse laborers." He reported that this self-taught and inventive teacher and the others associated with the school were indifferent to fanciful programs and disdainful of elaborate verbiage. Instead they preferred to stress the practical ends of the union, "to vindicate and defend the elementary rights of laborers." For example, classes for bricklayers taught vocabulary, phrases, and other skills relevant to their job and daily life in Rochester. Such instruction provided the first steps leading the workers from the shame of illiteracy toward support of a more complete school that would offer higher forms of instruction, preparation for citizenship, and Italian language lessons for children. With better use of the winter, "every spring we can offer to America the

unexpected flowering of new virtue, of new capacity, of new
affirmation of acts to acquire a more beneficent and more
worthy justice for us."[43]

The Italian press reflected complete concurrence with
Clement Lanni's statement to a 1928 high-school graduating
class: "Education is bound with progress; education is progress."
Editors repeatedly offered education as the remedy for personal
degeneracy. It was at once the antidote for crime and the best
avenue for individual and group advancement. One paper in the
1920s portrayed the school, as well as the settlement house and
social worker, as the cutting edges of civilization in poor areas
of the great metropolises. The author had in mind the slums of
New York City and Chicago, not intending to imply that his
local colony merited such a designation. The boundless faith in
and expectations for education were translated into editorial
support of expanded educational facilities and higher school
budgets. Bond issues for new buildings and state or local proposals for change in monies allotted to schooling received close
and careful attention. The resulting editorial endorsements were
always in support of expanded schooling. Lanni, an astute pol-
itician, even went to some lengths to warn his readers of the
dangers to quality education inherent in Rochester's system of
electing a school board while leaving the power over school tax-
ation and the final determination of the budget to the city council.
This latter body could and did gain political advantage by cutting
taxes while shifting the blame for results to the school board.[44]

Not all Italians found their educational needs met by the institutions already described. The independent Italian "professor," with
his private school, a common phenomenon of the pre–World War I
colonies, was an early beneficiary of this intense interest in education. These educational entrepreneurs moved in and out of the Italian colonies across the country as their fortunes in developing a
clientele for their schools dictated. Their offerings were in the areas
of language and "elementary education," music, and occasionally
fencing. Typically, a teacher would offer instruction in only one of
these three areas, though sometimes a music master would also offer to teach Italian to children. Of the three varieties of masters, the

music teachers proved to be the least ephemeral. They attracted a sizable non-Italian clientele. Many also found other employment for their musical talent, insuring alternative sources of income. Professor De Roberts held both administrative and teaching positions at the Kansas City Conservatory of Music. In 1903 Professor Antonio Daniele accepted a position on the staff of Utica's counterpart to the Kansas City Conservatory. In later years he headed the conservatory. Others conducted their own orchestras and bands or served as musical directors for theaters.[45]

In September 1901, Professor Napalitano announced that he was reopening his Italian school for the academic year. He offered Italian and English language instruction and "all else needed by Italians for a good elementary education." He employed an Italian woman to teach the "feminine arts." Fees were reasonable and he offered both day and evening classes to meet all students' scheduling needs. Two years later, Professor Raffaele De Petruccellis opened his Italian-language school in Utica. The press described him as an experienced, cultured, intelligent, and diligent teacher with many years of service in the communal schools at Missanello, Potenza, where he had earned the respect of the communal and provincial school officials. Another schoolmaster advertised himself as an 1898 graduate of the Royal Normal School at Bari. In addition to his daily elementary school offerings, he provided private lessons in Italian, French, and Latin. In the course of two years, he moved his "school" to four different locations. A Maestro Colucci offered an even more ambitious curriculum, adding Greek, design, calligraphy, and piano to the three languages above. A schoolmistress served for fifteen years as *maestra* in schools operated by religious orders in Rome before she opened a girls' school in Utica. Her courses included Italian, oratory, educational gymnastics, singing, and domestic tailoring. The tuition for her school was a dollar per month.

Such private initiatives in education relied on the intense educational interest of the colony. They built their curricula on Old World models and appealed most strongly to those who intended to repatriate. Yet, they remained marginal operations unable to compete effectively with the better-financed public and church schools that prepared students for life in America. For those who were planning a future in America, the latter education was a necessity, the former a luxury.[46]

EDUCATION IN THE ITALIAN COLONIES:
STUDENT PERFORMANCE

Evidence on the performance of groups of children in American educational systems is difficult to unearth. When one does find pockets of data it is difficult to tease meaning from them because there are few norms against which to compare a group's performance. We simply do not know, for instance, how many lower-class urban children went to school, how long they stayed, or how successful they were while they were there. There are some crude figures which suggest a low level of schooling among the general population. Most immigrant groups found themselves at a disadvantage in comparison with even this low standard.

In 1914 only 39 percent of the boys and 52 percent of the girls in Springfield, Ohio, reached the eighth grade out of their peers who started elementary school together. Twenty-nine percent of the boys and 41 percent of the girls actually graduated from that grade. The same city lost 32 percent of its males and 18 percent of its females from school before their fourteenth birthdays. Seventy-seven percent of the boys and 62 percent of the girls quit before they became sixteen. A study of Boston in 1918 illustrates a relative disadvantage for immigrants and children of foreign-born parents in the older age ranges. Of children ages fifteen to twenty, over 41 percent of the native-born of native-born parents attended school. Only 31 percent of the native-born of foreign parents and 19 percent of the foreign-born youths in the same age range were in school.[1]

A study based on the 1900 U.S. Census found the pattern reversed for children ages five to fourteen. Sixty-five percent of the children of native-born parents were in school. The foreign-born children attended at a rate of 69 percent, and 72 percent of the children born here of immigrant parents were enrolled. In New York City the 1910 census reported that 91 percent of the children ages six through fourteen attended school. A breakdown of this figure reveals that foreign-born children were slightly less diligent in attendance and the American-born children of immigrants were slightly more so. Among children of native-born parents, 90 percent were in school, while 91 percent of the children of foreign-born or mixed parents and 89 percent of foreign-born children were enrolled in school.

The crucial period for all groups of students was the fourteen-to sixteen-year period when most states' compulsory schooling laws allowed children to terminate their formal education under certain conditions. New York law required that all children ages eight through fourteen attend school. Those who were between fourteen and sixteen could apply for work certificates. Any in this latter group who had not successfully completed the required elementary course of study, or did not possess one of several equivalency certificates issued by the state, attended required evening schools established for this purpose in urban areas. Any in this age group who could not pass a simple literacy test administered by the Health Department were not issued working papers.[2]

The Rochester and Monroe County sample from the New York censuses reveals a pattern of school enrollment among children from Italian households which closely approximates the census and survey data cited above. Table 10.1 presents this data along with federal census data on Rochester and New York State for 1900–30. The age divisions reported in various enumerations seldom coincided. I have reorganized the data where possible, to make it more comparable, but significant discrepancies remain. In general, the more children below the age of seven or above thirteen in any grouping, the lower school attendance is. One must keep this fact in mind when comparing groups with different age boundaries.

Italian families with elementary-school-aged children reported them to be in school in about the same proportions as did other families. Between 1905 and 1925 the reported enrollment in

Table 10.1
Percentage of School Attendance by Age Groups in
New York State, 1900 and 1910; Monroe County, 1905,
1915, and 1925; Rochester, 1910 and 1920

	Native-born			Foreign-born	Italian[a]
	Native Parents	Foreign-born Parents	Mixed Parents		
1900– New York State					
5–20	54.5	55.8		31.1	
5–14	65.3	71.6		68.2	
5–9	48.6	59.1		58.2	
10–14	83.8	86.0		73.0	
15–20	33.6	22.8		7.9	
1905 Monroe County					
6–18					82.8
6–14					86.6
15–16					38.1
17–18					27.8
19+[b]					2.1
1910 New York State					
5–20	63.2	62.0		38.7	
5–14	76.0	81.2		77.9	
5–9	62.6	70.0		68.2	
10–14	90.7	92.9		86.1	
15–20	39.5	22.8		11.0	
1910 Rochester					
6–14	92.4	92.0		89.5	
7–13	95.3	95.7		92.1	
7–20	66.3	60.6		41.9	

Table 10.1 (continued)

	Native-born			Foreign-born	Italian[a]
	Native Parents	Foreign-born Parents	Mixed Parents		
1915					
Monroe County					
6–18					85.3
6–14					95.5
15–16					41.7
17–18					21.7
19+[b]					4.4
1920					
Rochester					
7–20	69.1		69.4	49.0	
6–14	92.8	92.2	92.5	89.0	
7–13	95.0		94.8	90.8	
15–16	59.3	46.8	52.4	48.2	
17–18	26.5	15.7	20.0	13.2	
19–20	13.8	7.3	9.3	7.0	
1925					
Monroe County					
6–18					88.1
6–14					96.4
15–16					65.6
17–18					29.2
19+[b]					4.2
1930					
Rochester					
7–20	80.4		78.3	57.4	
7–13	97.5		96.8	96.4	
14–15	97.4		97.1	98.0	
16–17	75.9		67.6	63.2	
18–20	29.5		19.2	16.1	

Table 10.1 (continued)

Sources: Thirteenth Census of the United States: 1910, *Abstract of the Census,* pp. 232, 237, 243; Fourteenth Census of the United States: 1920, *Population,* pp. 1083, 1084, 1136; Fifteenth Census of the United States: 1930, *Population,* vol. 2, p. 1161; vol. 3, pt. 2, p. 263; New York State Manuscript Census Returns: 1905, 1915, and 1925.

[a]Children of Italian heads of households.
[b]All unmarried children of Italian heads of households nineteen years or older and living at home.

the six to fourteen age category increased from 86 to 96 percent. The favorable picture presented by this group must be judged cautiously, however. Both Italian and American parents were strongly motivated, because of the school laws, to report their children as being "at school" even if they were not attending classes. The censuses cannot reveal absolutely whether Italians were more or less likely to lie to enumerators than other immigrants or Americans. Nevertheless, it is striking that the Monroe County data, spaced between the federal counts, show the same pattern of improved performance and fit nicely into the decennial changes recorded by the Bureau of the Census.[3]

The need to conceal nonattendance disappeared after a child passed beyond compulsory school age. Therefore, the figures for older children are especially important. Among Rochester Italians who were fifteen to eighteen, the proportion attending school increased from 25 percent in 1905 to 32 percent in 1915 and 51 percent in 1925. One would expect lower enrollment in the fifteen to twenty age group reported for Boston, Rochester, and New York State. Still, the record of older Italian youths is impressive. The nineteen and over category includes individuals from a wide age-range, most of whom were beyond normal school age. The data do indicate a small number of Italians pursuing higher education. Taken as a whole, Italian school attendance in Rochester does not appear to have been lower than that of immigrant children generally, or in most cases, that of

the children of American-born parents. The measures used above
indicate only that a child attended school during the year in
question. They do not assess daily attendance or academic progress. Other records provide such information.

Surviving classroom records for the public schools of the
three cities are very spotty for the period before 1920, especially for children who did not enter high school. Rochester,
which has the best preserved records, no longer has any registers
for the schools most closely associated with the colony. Parochial records are even more incomplete, with practically nothing
extant in the case of three of the five parish schools under study
here. However, it is possible to reconstruct something of the
patterns of attendance and promotions in several Rochester
schools where Italians, although a minority, represented sizable
proportions of the student bodies. I will compare Italian children to their classmates in order to avoid the problem of
possible differences between schools arising from varying grading and promotion standards (see n. 2).

Attendance registers for three elementary schools, Numbers
Six, Nine, and Ten, for the years between 1910 and 1924 provide the evidence. Each Italian child identified by surname was
paired with the nearest child in the alphabetical registers with
a non-Italian name. This procedure yielded a non-Italian peer
group to use as an alternative to city-wide norms, which are in-
flated by middle-class children in assessing Italian performance.
Assuming that the student bodies of these neighborhood schools
were fairly homogeneous, this technique provides a crude control for the students' social class in the analysis of their schooling. The data for students indicate whether or not they were
repeating the grade, their age, attendance, and promotion or
failure at the end of the year. Each pair was analyzed separately
for similarities or differences in the four data categories. Table
10.2 presents the summarized results. The categories dealing
with basic success in schooling, "Origin" and "Promotion,"
suggest that Italian children were not very different from their
non-Italian classmates. In fact, Italians had a slight advantage
in the direction of greater success when there were differences
within pairs of children. I must stress here that these measures

Table 10.2
Matched Pairs of Italian and Non-Italian Elementary School
Students, Rochester Public Schools, 1910–1924

	Percentage	Number
Age Difference		
1. Both children the same age	40.0	361
2. Italian 1 year older	21.3	193
3. Italian 2 or more years older	21.0	190
4. Non-Italian 1 year older	10.7	97
5. Non-Italian 2 or more years older	6.7	61
Totals	99.7	902
Origin		
1. Both children came from the same grade the previous year	83.8	653
2. Non-Italian repeating the grade, Italian advancing	9.6	75
3. Italian repeating the grade, Non-Italian advancing	6.4	50
Totals	99.8	778
Attendance		
1. Same (5 or fewer days' difference in total attendance)	29.7	186
2. Italian had the more favorable record	43.9	275
3. Non-Italian had the more favorable record	26.3	165
Totals	99.9	626
Promotion		
1. Same (both promoted or not promoted)	83.3	579
2. Italian promoted, partner not promoted	10.3	72
3. Non-Italian promoted, partner not promoted	6.3	44
Totals	99.9	695

Source: Attendance registers, Rochester Public Schools.

do not record real "success" or "failure" in the schools, but only the extent to which Italian students' careers paralleled those of their non-Italian classmates.

One may view attendance as a rough indicator of the level of parental acceptance of schooling and student satisfaction with school. Less than one-third of the pairs had similar attendance records. (Similar attendance records are defined here as a difference of five days or less in total attendance for one school year.) Among the unlike pairs, the Italian members were more likely to have the superior record. This is somewhat surprising since much of the literary evidence suggests that truancy was a major problem among Italians. There were at least two factors at work here. First, Italians became attendance problems most often at a special point in their school careers. Although attendance problems were real, truancy was not representative of most of their school lives. I will explore this point further presently. Secondly, the non-Italian group used here represented a special population. I did not attempt to make a precise "ethnic" identification of each member of the non-Italian control group. However, they can generally be characterized as a combination of East European immigrants' children and the children of less affluent Americans who could not martial the necessary resources to move out of the poorer sections of the city as new immigrants moved in. A portion of the Italian children, living in stable families and a self-conscious and proud colony, may have been "advantaged" in comparison to the older Americans "condemned" to live among them.[4]

A most important comparison is that of the ages of the pairs. Here the Italian child is at a serious disadvantage. Where there was a difference between the pairs, the Italian was likely to be the older by a year and often by two or more years. In fact, while the Italians in 8 percent of the cases were at least three years older than the non-Italian, the reverse pattern seldom reached this extreme age difference. In Utica the same tendency toward overage students appears in the schools with large Italian student bodies. Table 10.3 lists the percentage of children in each of these schools who can be defined as overage. Each school had the full range of elementary grades, one through six.

Table 10.3
Percentage of Students in Utica Elementary
Schools 14 Years of Age or Over, 1904–1905

School	Percentage
Mandeville	3.8
Hamilton	3.0
Albany	2.3
Court	4.7
South	.3
Francis	1.6
Miller	2.3
No. 18	4.6
Lansing	5.3
Union	5.8
Wetmore	7.9
Bleecker	9.5
Average for above schools	4.6

Source: Adapted from *Annual Report of the Superintendent of the Public Schools, City of Utica, 1904–05,*
p. 16.

With normal progress, students entering first grade at age six
would not be over thirteen years old when they finished the
elementary program. Yet the two most heavily Italian schools
had larger numbers of overage students. Bleecker Street School
had more than twice the city average of such students. Of the
two other schools with above average percentages of older students, Union Street School was in a poor section of the city and
had a number of Italians as well as other immigrant children,
and the Lansing School picked up some of the overflow of Italians on the eastern edge of the colony. By contrast, the schools
with fewest older students, South, Francis, and Miller, served
a stable middle-class area of the city south of downtown. Table
10.4 shows that the pattern of significantly greater numbers of

overage children persisted in the two schools most associated
with the Italian colony in 1917.[5]

Table 10.4
Percentage of Young, Normal Age, and Overage
Students, Utica, September 1917

	Young	Normal Age	Overage
Bleecker Street School	.6	20.8	78.6
Brandegee School	.3	16.2	83.3
Total for all city elementary schools	4.3	35.7	59.9

Source: Adapted from *Annual Report of the Superintendent of the Public
Schools, Utica, New York, 1917–18*, pp. 33–37.

Colin Greer uses similar age retardation figures from studies
of large-city school systems done in the early twentieth century
to argue that Italian children experienced unusually high rates
of failure in school and that the public schools failed miserably
in their task of educating the poor and immigrant children of
the era. This evidence is the foundation of his critique of what
he calls "The Great School Legend," which holds that the
schools did provide a major social remedy for those at the bottom of the ladder. Will the Rochester data support such an interpretation? While some of the tendency among Italians to be
older than other children in the same grade may be the result
of slow progress through the grades, the Rochester data rule
this out as a major explanation. Even if Italian children were
more likely to repeat grades than students in schools with pre-
dominately middle-class populations, they did not fail grades
any more often than non-Italians in their own class. Yet they
were older than their class peers.

Other factors, then, were at work here. Children in southern
Italy customarily started school at age seven or older. The three
years of schooling available to most students created no pressure to take children out of the family earlier. They could easily
complete their required instruction before they were ready to

assume the economic and social responsibilities that would conflict with schooling. A contemporary superintendent of schools
in Rochester identified this as part of an explanation. He pointed
to the tendency for certain groups, such as the Italians, to
start formal schooling for their children as late as the law would
allow. The foreign classes themselves provide another piece of
the explanation. Italians starting school late, then spending a
year or more in these classes before moving into the regular
elementary program, as a matter of course became "overage"
or "retarded" students. Finally, heavy immigration before World
War I produced a steady arrival of children of all ages with many
levels of the skills necessary for success in American schools.
Many irregularities in the conventional age/grade placements
resulted.[6]

A sample of attendance records for foreign classes in the
years 1910–12 and 1916–20, which had large numbers of Italian
students, reveals a marked tendency for the students to be over
the usual age for elementary students entering school for the
first time. In 1910–12 the average age of students in these classes
was just over ten years for both sexes. The age range for the
classes was from six to sixteen, with almost every class having
children from six to fifteen enrolled. By 1916–20 the average
age of students dropped to just under seven-and-a-half years for
both sexes. This represented neither a significant shift down-
ward in age of entrance nor a greater number of enrollments
among six-year-olds. Rather, it was the result of greater concentration around the ages of seven and eight and a reduction in
the number of students over ten years of age. After 1914, war in
Europe cut down the immigration of older young people,
leaving only occasional fourteen- to sixteen-year-olds who had
to begin their schooling with basic English-language training.
A typical student's career started in the foreign class at age seven.
After spending between one and two years there, the student
transferred to one of the regular first or second grades.[7]

The major consequences of this sequence of events surfaced
only when the student reached fourteen years of age. Those
students who entered first grade as six-year-olds and who progressed through the grades without interruption, completed the

required elementary program at about the point when they became eligible to withdraw from school to take jobs. Italian
students, however, might well be two grades away from meeting
these requirements and thus would fall under the legal provision
that obligated them to attend continuation school as a condition
for being allowed to work until their sixteenth birthdays or until they earned elementary school equivalency certificates. It
was this group, both among Italian and non-Italian children,
who provided the overwhelming bulk of attendance problems
in the 1920s. Extant attendance records for both public and
parochial schools reveal a sizable exodus from the schools of
Italians aged fourteen to sixteen.

Parochial schools, such as Mount Carmel in Rochester, found
it necessary to run double sessions of the first four or five grades,
but only a combined sixth, seventh, and eighth grade to accommo
date the few students who remained after reaching leaving age.
This school started a class of seventy-five first-graders in 1921.
By the time they had reached eighth grade, the group was only
56 percent of its original size. The records reveal that most students who dropped out of school because of age or to go to
work left from the sixth or seventh grades. In a single year,
1909–10, eleven children, 18 percent of the enrollment, quit
the school's combination seventh and eighth grade. All but two
of these were in the fourteen- to sixteen-year age range.[8]

A study of 1,551 boys ages sixteen to eighteen, who registered according to law in 1918 for military training, gives some
indication of the school careers for males in Utica at that time.
The figures are not completely representative, since numerous
job opportunities resulting from the labor shortage created by
the war produced lively competition between the labor force
and continuing education. Still, they show that less than 3 percent of the boys surveyed dropped out of school before their
fourteenth birthdays. By the end of their fifteenth year, however, two-thirds were out of school. When figures for the sixteenth year are included, those who had terminated their schooling rises to over 92 percent of the whole sample. The figures
for the highest grade completed add to the story of truncated
schooling. While nearly 53 percent of the boys completed

eighth grade, only 27 percent of the total group went on to any secondary education, and only 1.5 percent graduated from the academic high school. An additional 3.5 percent graduated from the secondary level business course (see Tables 10.5 and 10.6).[9]

Table 10.5
Age of Leaving School for Boys 16–18
Years of Age, Utica, 1918

Age	Number	Cumulative Percentage
11	1	
12	13	.9
13	28	2.7
14	445	31.3
15	546	66.6
16	399	92.3
17	96	98.5
18	13	99.3
19	2	99.4
not given	8	100.0
Total	1,551	

Source: Report of the General Survey Committee of the Industrial Education Survey of the City of Utica (Utica, N.Y., 1919).

The law required those children who left school before age sixteen who had not completed the normal elementary program to obtain a work permit and regularly attend a continuation or part-time school. These two provisions, out of the whole of the

Table 10.6
Last Grade Completed by Boys 16–18
Years of Age, Utica, 1918

Grade	Number	Percentage	Percentage of Total Completing Grade
4	12	.7	100.0
5	94	6.0	99.2
6	316	20.3	93.1
7	310	19.9	72.7
8	393	25.2	52.8
9	193	12.4	27.4
10	113	7.2	15.0
11	40	2.5	7.7
12	24	1.5	5.1
Business school	56	3.6	3.6
Total	1,551		

Source: See Table 10.5.

attendance and child-labor legislation, provided the bulk of the case-load for school attendance officers and court actions in the area of children's schooling. Weekly reports of the attendance officer serving schools in the Italian section of Utica for the late 1920s, plus court records for the same period in Rochester, suggest the extent and range of this problem among Italian children. The records indicate as the chief cause of truancy the hardships of poverty and parent-child hostilities rather than a calculating desire to profit from the children's labor. Disorganized families, rebellious children, ignorant and powerless parents, and bad health frequently appear as themes in this record. The most common occurrence was one in which the parent and the school had both lost control of the child.

Anthony A. had court appearances in 1927 and 1928 before a wayward minor petition was filed by his parents. Anthony failed to answer the court warrant and was arrested a month

later in Cleveland, Ohio. The authorities returned him to Rochester and, although he was then sixteen years old, the court or-
dered that he register in continuation school to make up the
time he was obliged to put in prior to his sixteenth birthday.
Lucio B., age thirteen, proved an even greater trial to his parents. By 1928 he had accumulated seven offenses dating back to
1925, for which his father paid a total of forty dollars in fines.
He had been locked up in the children's shelter five times for
petty larceny and had most recently stolen a Ford touring car.
The school officials described him as a very difficult boy who
had a poor attitude toward school. His parents were "interested
in cooperating with the school but have little control over Lucio."
A brother, Tony, cost his father twenty dollars in fines. In 1925
court records show that he was working on a huckster's wagon
and not coming home nights. The father paid fifteen dollars
more in fines for the action of a third son. The court had sympathy for Dominic C., father of a boy who entered the public
school in 1925 after being expelled from St. Lucy's. School
officials reported that the boy was "vicious, sullen, disagreeable,
untruthful and deceitful, clever at covering his own actions and
shifting the blame and a bad influence on other boys." Dominic
was cooperative, interested in the schooling of his son, but unable to handle the boy.[10]

In Utica the pattern was much the same. Attendance officers
filed a petition of truancy against Frank D., age fifteen, at the
request of the boy's mother. Though on parole from the state
industrial reform school, Frank refused even to register at Brandegee Elementary School. Joe E., age fifteen, was a serious attendance problem in his earlier school career. After September 1929,
he simply refused to attend school and did not apply for the
requisite working papers. His widowed mother was a helpless
paralytic. Despite threats to recommit him to reform school,
Joe continued to ignore all efforts to make him comply with
the child labor and school attendance laws. In a full year he appeared for a single session at part-time school. Otherwise he
successfully eluded both the attendance officers and the county
sheriff. Finally the pressure became so great that he left the city
and was reported to be living in Buffalo.

Not all cases resulted in the effective victory of the child over the wishes of the parents and the courts, however. Samuel F. complained to the court that his daughter Filomena, age fourteen, would not stay in school though he did his best to make her attend. The judge lectured both father and daughter and threatened to commit her to a home for wayward girls. Filomena attended Brandegee School regularly after the court appearance.[11]

Nor were all parents sympathetic to the schools' attempts to keep their children enrolled in school. Mr. Anthony G. appeared in a Rochester court with a defiant attitude. He had a daughter who was having problems in junior high school. Anthony, father of ten, asserted that the girl had had enough schooling and should be home doing housework. He refused, therefore, to pay her book rent. Book rent was a long-standing issue with him. He had refused to pay it for older children in the family. School officials reported with chagrin that in these earlier instances they had exempted the family from the rental, only to discover that they bought a new house and fine furnishings soon after. Among the rest of the family, a fifteen-year-old boy was skipping junior high school though the father apparently paid his book rental fees. Five younger children were regularly attending an elementary school. This court appearance cost Anthony twenty dollars in fines.

Parental apathy was another minor theme apparent in these records. In 1929, Mr. Sam H., owner of a macaroni factory, made his sixth trip to court because his sixteen-year-old son Frank was skipping continuation school and not appearing for work at the macaroni factory. The father testified that Frank was "little better than nothing around the factory" and he was already being paid a couple of dollars a week more than he was worth. Mr. Sam H. further testified that his son could not now and would never get a real job, for no one else would hire him. Frank, described by school officials as slow mentally and lacking in moral responsibility, up to this point was responsible for fifty dollars in fines paid by his father. Fortunately, none of the other children in this family had any such problems with their schooling.[12]

Parental opposition to school attendance could have a

specific rationale behind it. In Utica the school filed a court
warrant in 1930 to force the parents of Andrew I., a twelve-
year-old, to send him back to school. The school officials had
assigned Andrew to the "Opportunity Class" (a euphemism for
a class for mentally retarded children) at the Wetmore School,
and according to school authorities, his mother "positively re-
fuses to send the boy to this class." She would not accept the
school's classification of her son as slow or retarded. In another
case, the parents of thirteen-year-old Nancy L. kept her out of
Brandegee's seventh grade in the winter of 1929. The problem
here confounded both school officials and the court. As the
father testified and the court clerk, an Italian, confirmed, the
mother was bedridden with heart trouble. The family had a boy
in his second year at the academy and the father did not want
to have to take him out of high school. That left only Nancy to
care for her mother, get the meals, and keep house. The record
ends with the superintendent of schools promising to investigate
fully and "see what is best to do in this case."

Finally, there were families who worked as migratory laborers in the fields or in canning factories and followed the harvests
of fruit and vegetables. Such families often returned to the city
from their rural labors late in the fall weeks or even months
after school had begun. Or, like Lucine C., whose whole family
left to pick strawberries in the spring, they never completed the
school year. The sheriff entered the case but could not locate
the family. Thus, while parental complicity in violation of school
attendance and child labor laws was not absent, it was not a
part of the majority of such cases. Rather, the records reveal
a dominant pattern of disorganized families, rebellious and alien-
ated children, and powerless, confused parents caught between
the demands of the schools and courts and the independence of
their adolescent children in a new land. Clearly, a number of
parents were bewildered by a system in which school officials,
when they could not make children behave, turned the responsibility over to the parents and then fined them if they could
not do what the school itself had failed to do.[13]

Not all Italians who left school for work were reluctant
scholars at continuation school and evening classes. Italian names

appear frequently in elementary and vocational classes at these
schools. Alfred N., a sixteen-year-old tailor, completed his grade
school education at Rochester's School Number Nine, compil-
ing an unequaled 100 percent attendance record. Salvatore, also
sixteen and an office boy, attended an impressive 93 percent of
all classes in a bookkeeping course. He was concurrently taking
the evening school junior high programs as well. Among the
girls, sixteen-year-old Rose O. had an attendance record of 88
percent, the best in her sewing class. During the day she worked
in a candy factory. People taking specialized courses included a
seventeen-year-old Sicilian who appeared at 96 percent of his
stenography sessions.[14]

High school attendance is not considered at any length
here because of the extremely small proportion of both Italian
and other working-class families who sent their children to such
institutions before 1920. After the turn of the century there
were scattered Italian high school graduates. Utica Free Academy
included Italians, usually one or two but never more than six, in
almost every graduating class for a decade after 1904. Catholic
institutions occasionally contributed a few more graduates.
After World War I, the number of Italians completing secondary education programs increased slowly to the point where, in
1938, a systematic count of all high school graduates for that
June revealed that Italians made up nearly 26 percent of the
total. The pattern was similar in Rochester, where the first
Italian graduate from a public high school appeared in 1902.
From then on, it was increasingly common to find Italians on
secondary school graduation rolls.[15]

There is a popular tradition in the study of Italians in America
which holds that the immigrant was basically indifferent and
even hostile to the schooling and education of his children. One
explanation for this view reasons that the immigrants were
peasants who were unable to see how education would make
their crops grow better. Such a simplistic view is an untenable
libel against the complex working-class culture of southern
Italy. A more plausible view is that most immigrants' initial interest was to accumulate as much capital in the United States as

possible in order to advance or stabilize their position in Italy. As long as the immigrant thought in terms of imminent return to his homeland, American schooling had no relevance, and rejection of it can hardly be interpreted as a general disinterest in education. In fact, the early appearance of private Italian schoolmasters and tutors probably indicated a wish on the part of parents that their children not be deprived of a relevant education during their temporary sojourn abroad.

Recognition of the probability of a future in America completely changed the place American schooling took in the immigrants' lives. American observers seldom perceived the importance of the locus of this future orientation in determining the relevance of, and thus the response to, schooling. A steady stream of new arrivals possessing a commitment to the Old World could, and undoubtedly did, provide a continuing source of individual examples of parents "disinterested" or "hostile" to schooling. An immigrant's plea that his son or daughter would only be here a short time and could better serve his or her own and the family's future by earning money was incomprehensible to the American schoolman. Similarly, the immigrant found unconvincing the reasons given for the necessity of sending his child to an American school.

Another source of support for the stereotype of Italian indifference or hostility to schooling was the preponderance of Italians among school attendance cases. However, this was a result of a special set of circumstances. The reasons for Italian children starting school a year or two later than other children remain unclear, although I have suggested that this phenomenon follows custom in Italy. The consequences of a late start and a language handicap which further delayed entrance into the regular grades appeared only at the end of a school career. At age fourteen, if an immigrant child had not been behind his age peers in grades completed, he, like they, could have quietly withdrawn from school. This short period of conflict over the demands of schooling came at the end of the typical child's academic career and has provided the statistical justification for singling out Italians as attendance problems. Nevertheless, the vast majority of overage Italians completed the required schooling without becoming truancy problems. Taken as a whole, the evidence does not support the popular view that Italians were generally uninterested in schooling.

One of the surprising things to emerge from this study is the absence of any evidence for a sizable amount of conflict in the second generation between the culture and values of the home and colony, and those of the broader community, especially as articulated by both the public and parochial schools. In a study of the effects of the dominant American culture on children of Italian immigrants, Joseph Tait found that most children were not "experiencing 'mental agonies' or passing through a 'harrowing struggle'" due to a rejection of their backgrounds by the public schools. My study suggests an explanation for this lack of conflict. The Italian immigrants were future-oriented and sympathetic to certain kinds of change. Once they made a commitment to staying in America, schooling became a resource to be exploited for individual advancement. The schools professed to be doing exactly what immigrant parents expected them to do—namely, giving their children the skills necessary to function well in the broader community. Immigrants didn't expect that they would, should, or could be involved in teaching the child the parental culture.

As long as the school officially ignored the backgrounds of its students and in a nondiscriminatory way concentrated on teaching an identical curriculum to all children, the implicit aspersions cast on the culture of the immigrant and his colony, although painful, could be tolerated. The valuable service that the schools offered, which parents could not duplicate, made this tolerance necessary. On the personal level, teachers and administrators could be sympathetic or hostile, heavy-handed or subtle, patronizing or respectful, cruel or kind in the ways they presented middle-class American culture to the Italian child. As long as the system did not overtly condemn the immigrants' heritage, they could point to the committed and empathetic staff members and to the professed goals of providing equal educational opportunity, thus viewing the school in its broadest sense as compatible with their own purpose of preparing their children to be successful Italian-Americans.[16]

11

AMERICANS DISCOVER THE SONS OF COLUMBUS

The arrival of large numbers of immigrants in the four decades before World War I was one element in a constellation of urban phenomena which prompted many Americans to seek remedial measures for newly perceived problems in their society. Historical scholarship on this movement is divided in its assessment of the motives of the reformers. Initially, those concerned with the state of the urban social order received good marks for a high-minded effort to help the unfortunate lift themselves out of the wretched situations which entrapped them in the slums. More recent investigators have questioned the authenticity of this claim of altruism, stressing the desire for social control, efficiency, and the imposition of values supportive of the reformers' class interests as the motivating forces behind their activities.

Both sides of this controversy will find some support in the evidence reviewed in this chapter. Thus, it corroborates Don S. Kirschner's contention that there is merit in both interpretations. He argues that their seemingly antithetical nature is the product of examining one or another facet of complicated and often philosophically inconsistent individuals. Interesting as the question of the motivations of the reformers is, it is not the principal purpose of this chapter. Rather, my central concern is with the range of activities and programs of the agencies and their impact on the colonies.[1]

The first acknowledgment of Italian immigrants in the cities tended to be in the form of "color" articles in the American press stressing their quaint and foreign ways. American newspapers treated the newcomers as curiosities who had little relationship to, or impact on, the life of the community. They

were poor and transitory people who might be quick to use a
knife, but only on their fellows. They were not armed robbers
or burglars, and the police were capable of handling their repulsive habit of begging so they did not seem to threaten the
American community. Occasionally, a reporter portrayed them
as contributors to a richer and more varied American nation.
They even had a small group of defenders, among whom was
Bernard Lynch who argued that the southern Italians were victims of several libels. He asserted that on the contrary, they
were robust, energetic, abhorred poverty, begging, and living in
crowded, filthy conditions, and that their children were bright,
talented, and fond of study. All these characteristics, Lynch
contended, were in direct contrast to the popular myths concerning these immigrants as a potential threat to American
society. The immigrants' increasing presence in crowded, crime-
ridden tenement areas, such as Rochester's "Sleepy Hollow" and
"Poison Row," the *padrone* exploitation of women and children,
the appearance of the Black Hand, their failure to take up
American ways and values quickly, and the realization, according to one reporter, that "each Roman carried a Knife," motivated Americans to take positive remedial action.[2]

The first responses to this new awareness of an "Italian
Problem" were almost entirely private, and usually religious,
initiatives. As early as 1889, a group of Protestant women, several of whom were familiar with the Italian language, organized
an Italian mission in Rochester to provide English instruction
for men who had been turned away from the public evening
schools because of their inability to understand English. The
evening schools concentrated narrowly on instruction in the
basic elementary school subjects for individuals who were unable
to attend, or had not completed, a regular elementary school
program. Specific courses in English for immigrants were still
a decade away. Throughout the 1890s the mission carried on
its self-assigned task of teaching English, arithmetic, and American manners to Italians while, according to the city's historian,
it also awakened a sense of community responsibility. More
sectarian programs followed, as the various denominational
missionary organizations turned their attentions toward the

Italian immigrants. Rochester Methodists assumed the work of the Italian Mission in 1902 and hired an Italian Protestant, Rev. Joseph Vitale, to head the work. By 1906 they had a chapel in the Italian colony.[3]

The early missions had a great deal of difficulty finding Italian-speaking ministers. The use of non-Italians seldom proved to be very effective. A Waldensian, trained in Switzerland and recently returned with his wife from a missionary assignment in China, established Rochester's Baptist mission. The Presbyterians likewise found a Waldensian, who worked in Rochester among his fellow Sicilian Waldensians from the towns of Grotte and Agrigento. The Baptists solved the problem of supplying ministers in 1907, with the opening of the Italian department of Colgate Seminary. From this date all Baptist ministers for Italian missions in the two New York cities were supplied from this source.[4]

Similar combinations of religious evangelical efforts and broader education and Americanization programs appeared early in the new century in both Utica and Kansas City. These missions enjoyed periods of modest success as well as of stagnation or decline. Utica's Baptist mission opened under the part-time guidance of Colgate seminary student Cesidio Simboli in 1909. The Women's Home Missionary Society of the city supported it financially and with volunteer workers. Initially the mission had no members, but the workers professed a faith that their industry and labors, especially through an active Sunday school, would soon yield results. Support for the work grew slowly and erratically. The city's Baptist pastors called for help from the American Baptist Home Mission Society as early as 1905. The following year one of their number presented a very favorable report on the character and needs of these immigrants in America, entitled "Our Italian Brothers." A meeting of pastors favorably received the paper.

A 1910 report shifted emphasis somewhat, as is reflected in its title, "Our Foreign Peoples—A Peril and a Responsibility." The thrust here was toward gaining support for broader state-wide efforts in this field. Despite their early interest, the local Baptist pastors did not sustain an active support of the

missionary work among Italians. Antonio Perrotta, pastor at the
mission for many years, was a member of the Utica Pastors'
Conference between 1912 and 1914 but withdrew, perhaps in
disgust over the failure of this group to provide greater support
for his work. Antonio Mangano, professor at Colgate and head
of the Italian department there, attempted to spark the pastors'
interest by a speech made to them in 1919. He spoke on the
need for missions to the immigrants, and a representative of the
local Italian mission reported on its needs. The conference
founded a committee to look into the city mission work but
the results were negligible. The burden for the support of the
work continued to fall on the Women's Missionary Society, and
later, on the lay-dominated Baptist Mission Board of Utica.[5]

The enterprise itself started slowly with English classes and
"girls' work" proving most popular. By 1911 the Sunday school
had six teachers, fifty-five scholars and an average attendance of
thirty. The gains of one year often disappeared in the next, as a
highly mobile population depleted the small congregation by as
many as nine families in a two-year span. Hostile attitudes of
Roman Catholics, and the falling away of "delinquent members
who persistently refused to walk according to their convenant,"
further vexed the group. Still, the congregation was able to
organize as the Albany Street Baptist Church in 1914. By the
end of World War I, the church had a small but stable adult
membership and, more to the point here, was able to expand
its youth and educational programs. It established a day nursery,
a Boy Scout troop, sewing classes for girls, a Bible school, basketball leagues for both men and boys, and various clubs. In 1919
it hosted the annual convention of the Italian Baptist Convention of America. The membership proved stable enough to survive two troubled periods when its popular pastor Rev. Perrotta
left his post. In 1922 the congregation presented a strong case
to the Utica Mission Board for its need for new and greatly expanded facilities. Finally, in 1930, after much struggle and some
friction at the local and denominational levels over financing, the
church, now with ninety-five active members, moved into a new
fireproof brick and tile addition to a remodeled church building.[6]

Kansas City's Italian colony had the most active, far-reaching, and successful of the Protestant missionary endeavors. Central Presbyterian Church of that city established the Italian Institute and Central Chapel in 1908. It was the outgrowth of an earlier effort to operate a Sunday school for both Americans and Italians in the area. As the former moved out of the neighborhood, work concentrated on the Italian immigrants. The staff regularly included an Italian clergyman and women volunteer workers from the sponsoring church. Work started with the establishment of an "underage kindergarten" for preschool children of the neighborhood, who were "left pretty much to the dangers of the street." After opening with eight students, within a few months the enrollment was up to thirty-five. By the 1920s it was normally above fifty. The teacher was a recent graduate of a kindergarten training program. Junior girls from the local Froebel Kindergarten Training School frequently assisted there.

The early program included a combination of kindergarten and Montessori early childhood theory and methods. The school hoped to foster the children's physical development and to provide an environment where freedom of expression would lead to self-development, with each child developing his own personality. It also sought to prepare the children for elementary school by teaching them English, basic knowledge, and work skills necessary for success at school. In good kindergarten style, the program included home visits with an Italian interpreter and an attempt to involve the mothers in the work of the school. When the public schools established kindergartens, an event for which the institute took at least partial credit, the school became more explicitly a nursery school dealing with children under five.[7]

The arrival of Rev. J. B. Bisceglia in 1918, direct from his ministerial training, initiated a rapid expansion of the institute's activities. Familiar with the general development of social settlement programs, he combined a traditional Protestant evangelicalism with the most current developments in social welfare work, which made the institute unusual in the scope of its programs during the 1920s. Boys' work gained a full-time worker who organized a Boy Scout troop, Cub Scouts, and age-graded clubs that promoted activities such as hikes, games, visits to points of interest in the city, and talks by prominent Kansas City men. The institute was the official agent for the local Rotary organization, selecting forty-two boys who would be given the opportunity to spend two free weeks at the Rotary summer camp. It also fielded a full complement of youth and adult teams in the city settlement house track, baseball, and basketball leagues. Classes in manual training and vocational areas, including such things as watch repairs, attracted children of many ages. Girls' work included various kinds of domestic art classes as well as Camp Fire Girls organizations.

In the health area, the institute operated a clinic that specialized in the medical needs of mothers and children, including concentration on obstetrics, gynecology, and otolaryngology. The clinic, staffed by doctors from the city, was open two days a week. Interpreters aided those who were deficient in English. Institute workers followed up the work of the clinic with home visits and educational sessions for the mothers. An Italian physician examined the nursery school children. Teachers monitored the growth and development of each child and instructed mothers in nutrition and general child care. Other activities and services included a Mothers' Club, a music school specializing in piano, violin, and voice instruction, a Young Italian Music Club, a reading room, the Evangelical Mutual Benefit Society, and a weekly newspaper. In the specifically religious area there were Sunday school classes, Christian Endeavor Societies, and Daily Vacation Bible Schools. The latter included religious instruction along with recreational activities and sewing, music, and manual-training classes.[8]

In each instance an Italian or an Italo-American directed the mission work. Local non-Italian religious groups initiated and sponsored each enterprise. Financial support came from outside mission agencies. The structure of the governing boards of directors varied, but in all cases final authority lay with a body predominantly or wholly consisting of non-Italians. In Kansas City the board of directors for the Italian Institute and Central Chapel included only representatives of the various Presbyterian churches supporting the work. As late as 1926 there were no

Italians on this board. Among the officers and teachers of the Sunday school, only six out of twenty-one were of Italian background. During the same year, there were nine full- or part-time workers at the institute. Of these, five were non-Italians. Three of these were professionals especially trained in religious and social work or in early childhood education.

At no time during the period did the congregations associated with these missionary efforts assume full responsibility for financing the operations. In Utica, where the financial picture is clearest, the Italian church contributed between 18 and 30 percent of the total budget of the Baptist Mission. Both the Presbyterian and the Methodist missions in Kansas City received sizable grants from the city-wide united charities fund for the maintenance of social and educational aspects of their programs. When the volunteer workers, medical, food, clothing, and other contributions are added to the actual budget, it is clear that these operations were very largely dependent on non-Italian support.[9]

It is difficult to assess the impact of these missions on the Italian colonies. The sizes of the church memberships were never very large in comparison with the Roman Catholic parishes. The active congregation in the Utica Italian Baptist Church probably did not exceed a hundred at any time before 1930, and at times during the 1920s it was only about half that figure. The Central Chapel in Kansas City admitted a total of 238 persons to communion from 1910 to 1931; 169 of these were in the decade 1921–30. Between 1918 and 1930, the chapel celebrated forty-nine baptisms and twenty marriages. These small figures should not be interpreted as evidence for a small, stable religious community. In fact, there was considerable in-and-out migration of families associated with these missions. A number were "won" back to Catholicism. Others simply moved to other cities or back to Italy, while a third group moved out of the colony and joined American Protestant churches. A number of Italian ministers soon followed this latter group and took posts in American churches. In short, the missions served at least one group as way stations and training grounds for fairly complete assimilation into broader American life.[10]

The impact of the missions, of course, cannot be measured simply in terms of the numbers of converts to the various Protestant faiths. Many individuals, especially children, came in contact with middle-class American ideals and values through participation in the various, at least overtly nonproselytizing, activities promoted by the missions. The lists of children who participated in Boy Scouts, athletic leagues, nursery schools, etc., as well as adults in English classes, reveal many family names that do not appear on the membership roles of the churches. Indeed, if the families of church members had provided the sole source of participants for their activities, attendance would have been reduced several-fold.

Rev. Bisceglia's newspaper served as another medium for the dissemination of "American" ideas. He also held a position of some power and influence in the Kansas City colony. Along with the priest of the Italian Catholic parish, he usually served as an honorary marshal of the annual Columbus Day parade. He was a founder of the first Italian-owned savings and loan association in the city. An early Protestant minister in Rochester was prominent among the founders of several mutual benefit societies, as well as serving as a spokesman for the colony on a number of occasions. Finally, the presence and modest success which these missionary efforts enjoyed provided an impetus for Roman Catholics to take a more active interest in the religious and social welfare of the Italians in their midst. The cumulative result of these Catholic activities was to produce church-related programs that differed little in their "Americanizing" thrust from those of the Protestant, private nonsectarian and governmental agencies.[11]

The first response of the Catholic church to the Italian immigrants centered largely around a concern that they have a church and a pastor. Beyond this, the church was slow to respond to other needs identified and attacked by Protestant workers. In 1904 Bishop McQuaid proudly showed his school system to an admiring foreign visitor. The visitor later recorded his impression that the bishop and his teaching nuns viewed English-language instruction as their basic task in Americanization. The diocesan historian presents McQuaid as a moderate on the "Americanization" issue, holding that "the acclimatization of the immigrant should be neither impeded nor pressured, but allowed to work out naturally." He could not accept either Archbishop John Ireland's advocacy of a quick and enforced "Americanization" or "Cahenslyism," an ultranationalistic program designed to preserve Germanism among German immigrants here.

When the bishop did take public note of the Italian immigrants, it was an embarrassing experience for the Rochester colony. A group of Italians had tried to extort $5,000 from him under threat of death. McQuaid used the incident as an opportunity to lecture them, as well as other immigrant groups, on learning and respecting American law. As late as 1915, an Italian traveler observed that in the Midwest Roman Catholic priests had little social influence on the masses of immigrants because they limited themselves strictly to ordinary weekly religious functions.[12]

In the latter part of the decade, Catholic programs for the Italian immigrants began to assume contours similar to those already well established in the Protestant missions. In 1916 Rochester's Bishop Hickey opened vacation schools for Italian children at the Cathedral and at Mount Carmel Parish. The following year a third opened at St. Lucy's. These schools featured catechism, reading, writing, singing, sewing, cooking, and some manual training in their six-week programs. In 1917 a group of young Catholic women opened a settlement house, Charles House. They chose a site in the Italian colony on the west side of the city, in part because Protestants had recently established a new mission in the area. Miss Harriet Barry, member of a prominent Rochester Catholic family and granddaughter of an early Catholic philanthropist, led the work. Before returning to Rochester to head the Charles House, she worked in Washington, D.C., with Mary Virginia Merrick, pioneer Catholic settlement-house advocate and founder of the Christ Child Society. Her program included a typical settlement offering of classes and supervised recreation for youth and for working girls, mothers' meetings, health classes, and clinical work. No Italian surnames appear on the original list of officers.

In 1924 the Rochester Catholic Charities Board took over the Big Brothers Club, which the Knights of Columbus had started for Italians under the leadership of Adam Kreag. They converted it into a second settlement, the Genesee Institute, with Fr. Walter Foery as priest-in-charge. Foery was already an experienced worker among Italians as pastor of Mount Carmel. In 1937 he became the fifth bishop of Syracuse. By the end of the period, children born to families of Mount Carmel parish made up one-tenth of all Catholics born in the city, and the Italians had in Bishop O'Hern a religious leader who felt a special fondness for them. The Italians reciprocated the sentiment. In 1932 they presented the bishop with a life-sized portrait of himself to hang in Columbus Civic Center.[13]

Likewise, the Italian-Catholic parishes in both Kansas City and Utica undertook programs which stressed individual social change through education and Americanization. In the former, as in Rochester, much of this activity had non-Italian support and was explicitly directed toward countering Protestant efforts in the colony. A series of articles published in the *Catholic Register* at the end of the decade gives some sense of the intensity of feeling of Catholics toward the proselytizing efforts made by Protestants among Italians. The paper started by heaping ridicule on two pentecostal storefront congregations. The groups were identified as Holy Roller types who went through grotesque and wierd actions during their worship, and even kissed each other. The author portrayed the ministers, both Italians, as charletans who, though once in collusion, were by then bitter competitors for a scattering of poor, misguided Italian workers. Both were scorned for their background as common laborers. The paper reported that the younger one worked summers as a house painter. The paper was more restrained in its description of the Methodists' Institutional Church, only accusing it of hypocrisy in ignoring the increasing number of·blacks who were moving into the neighborhood served by the church, even though "their religious life was practically nil."

This concentration of effort on the Italian Catholics, the paper argued, put the lie to denials of being specifically anti-Catholic made by workers at the institution. The *Register* saved its most vitriolic style for Bisceglia and the Italian Institute and Central Chapel. This report, in the form of a mock interview, protrayed him as a satanically clever and cynical stealer of souls, who coyly reveled in his ability to deceive both the simple Italians who innocently fell under his influence and the Community Chest, which expected him to use the funds they gave him for social work rather than proselytizing. The bitterness and hostility reflected in the article is especially significant because it comes after a full decade of counter-measures on the part of Catholic laymen.[14]

In 1920 the Agnes Ward Amberg Club, a Catholic Women's group, opened a summer school for Italian children at Holy Rosary Church. The first year the school enrolled about 300 Italians and 70 Mexicans. The girls learned both hand and machine sewing, embroidery, and other tasks useful to good housewifery. Boys received manual training in woodwork. Exercises in dance and music permeated the program. Three of the fourteen women identified with the project had Italian surnames. Other social and health activities, such as picnics, ice cream socials, and medical clinics, appeared increasingly during the early 1920s. In 1925 Holy Rosary Parish held the first of a series of revivals. A Roman Catholic missionary, Father DeFilippi, held forth for fifteen days, urging the parishioners "to renew their faith and get away from lethargy." Later missions included a series of services in English to interest youth who might be attracted into the Protestant meetings.

The founding of the Rosary Club the following year marked the opening of a counterattack on the Protestants. The club sponsored and financed activities for children at Holy Rosary Parish in explicit competition with the non- and anti-catholic agencies. The president, the woman the press most often associated with the club's activities, was an Italian-American who had grown up in the Italian colony but no longer lived there. She was the wife of a monument merchant. Half of the ten officers and directors of the club had non-Italian names. Throughout the remainder of the decade, the new club worked closely with and received the aid and guidance of the older

Agnes Ward Amberg Club. By 1930 the Holy Rosary Club assumed responsibility for the operation of the parish summer
school, as well as sponsoring a series of clubs and activities similar to those offered by the non-Catholic missions. The school's
budget alone was over a thousand dollars. In that year the
sense of competition was symbolically played out on the basketball court, where the Rosary Club's quintet defeated the team
from the Italian mission 22 to 10, thereby winning the North
Side championship. The Catholic Intersocial Council of St.
Francis of Assisi was a second group organized, partly at least,
as a foil against the Protestants. In spite of hostility between the
religious groups, the competition produced increasing agreement
on the social and cultural directions which the colony should
be taking and resulted in a single approach to Americanization.[15]

Many nonreligious organizations turned their attentions to the
condition of the immigrants in their cities and sought ways of helping them adjust to life in a new land. Although the services offered
by these groups often overlapped considerably with the religious
endeavors described above, the two are treated separately here because of the explicitly nonsectarian nature of one approach.

An early manifestation of this social and reform movement in
Rochester's Italian colony was the establishment by the Association for Practical Housekeeping Centers of what became the
Lewis Street Settlement House. Started in 1907 as the "Italian
Housekeeping Center," it was to remedy what in the founders'
view constituted one of America's major failings in helping immigrants adjust to their new homes. To quote an early member
of the executive board of the center, "one of the grave problems
in the assimilation of immigrants in our cities is found in the
fact that when the foreigner comes, the American leaves . . . . If only
fifty percent of our citizens were to remain in these immigrant
sections, they would not only be performing an heroic patriotric
duty, but they would largely prevent the formation of colonies
which never help the civic democracy of a people." The author
went on to point to a hypothetical Italian woman who, after
arriving by train in the city, disappeared into the local colony
and for years had no experience of the America which lay

beyond its bounds. The obvious solution was "linking the real Americans of our city, by personal gift and service, to the would-be American who wishes to be of the quality that is 'Rochester made.'"[16]

The center's founders based the organization on the residential principle,* making it "simply the home of the real American women." From it the workers sought by example and through instruction to provide necessary domestic education to Italian mothers and children. Womens' classes in sewing soon produced displays of laces, embroideries, and clothing. While the older girls made underwear and aprons, the younger ones proudly displayed their iron holders, dusters, and dishcloths. Cooking classes in 1911 included lessons in how to boil and mash potatoes, make toast, cook cereals, make bread and rice pudding. They also planned for future projects such as "fried cakes, real black chocolate cake, strawberry shortcake and real American pie." Youthful visitors to the center learned to sweep, scrub, make beds, wash windows, dust, build fires, blacken stoves, and care for ashes and garbage; or, as one sympathetic observer put it, the center taught "the drudgery of housekeeping along with the fun things."

Boys' and men's activities included chair caning and gardening. The center's baths were an exceedingly popular attraction during the summer months in an area where few homes had bathtubs. From this beginning the program expanded to include classes in music, child care, English, and citizenship, as well as an active dispensary with clinics and a full-time nurse, boys' and girls' clubs, game rooms, and an athletic program and branch of the public library housing a sizable collection of Italian and and English volumes. In 1926 the name was changed to the Lewis Street Center to reflect the expanded scope of the work, and as one worker remarked, "How would you like to be a

*Early settlement-house philosophy held that workers should live in the neighborhood they sought to serve. This would provide firsthand experience and invaluable insights into the problems they hoped to address, thus giving them credibility as neighbors of those who were the objects of their charity.

young basketball star who had to say he represented the Housekeeping Center? "[17]

Workers at the center operated out of a largely conservative
view which sought social reform through the uplifting of individuals. They generally expressed sympathy and respect for
the immigrants they worked with. Florence Cross, an early
worker, gave a qualified endorsement when she allowed that
Italians "have many desirable traits. They probably are as promising as were our ancestors who settled from other lands." A
doctor who served at the center dispensary picked up this theme
of a nation of immigrants and asserted that the pioneer spirit
of earlier generations of immigrants animated the recent arrivals too. The immigrant, he asserted, "is one who has become
dissatisfied with life in an unfavorable environment and who has
had the vision and courage to uproot himself and his family and
to brave the perils and difficulties of a far journey to an alien
land . . . . where he can build a better life for himself and his
descendents." He commended the Italians he worked among for
"their splendid historical heritage of culture, their habits of industry, their devotion to the family and their Latin exuberance."
Reports of head workers and the dispensary nurses reveal that
this was not cant. The center programs and contacts with its
neighbors demonstrated a confidence in the latters' ability if
only they were offered some help in adjusting to the strange
surroundings and new conditions they faced. Aid in extraordinary circumstances, homemaking instruction, and education,
broadly defined, were at the heart of the center's program in
the years before 1920.[18]

The Social Center movement was a second prewar progressive reform endeavor which had the immigrant as a part of its
concern. The social centers in Rochester were the products of
an attempt by diverse reform-minded elements in the city to
apply the currently popular idea of extending the range of
activities taking place in schools to make them a focal point for
civic regeneration and reform. The effort in Rochester got
underway in 1906, when representatives of eleven organizations
joined together as the School Extension Committee and

petitioned the Board of Education for a grant to operate a public vacation school, a social center, and several playgrounds.* The board, under the leadership of Professor George M. Forbes, a man committed to utilization of the school in the progressive assault on urban problems, provided the committee with $5,000 for 1907. The social centers quickly became the locus of the committee's and the board's interest.

A recent seminary graduate, Edward J. Ward, came to Rochester to develop the centers. The first center opened in School Fourteen, followed rapidly by ones at West High School, School Nine, and School Twenty-Six. The centers provided programs including physical education, gymnastics, table games, library reading rooms, music programs, lectures, and entertainment for adults and youth who could not take advantage of regular daytime school offerings. Ward soon added an innovation, the self-governing civic club for adults, which brought the movement considerable national notice among educational and reform circles and pushed the centers into the middle of the city's intense political battles. These clubs became forums for the open discussion of subjects as varied as the duties of city officers, gardening, the trusts, the immigrant, the Italian Question, Rochester Pure Milk Campaign, child labor, the fine arts, Prohibition, women's suffrage, and capital punishment. At election time candidates of the various parties presented their platforms. The close ties between the good government reformers and the centers, which provided the former a vehicle for their antiboss campaign, determined local Republican boss George Aldridge to do away with the centers at the first opportunity. Aldridge's political victories over the reformers and the almost inevitable political indiscretions that arose out of an atmosphere of totally free and open discussion of controversial issues soon gave him his opportunity.[19]

*The organizations were: The Central Trades and Labor Council, The Children's Playground League, the College Woman's Club, The Daughters of the American Revolution, The Humane Society, The Labor Lyceum, The Local Council of Women, The Officer's Association of Mother's Clubs, the Political Equality Club, The Social Settlement Association, and the Woman's Educational and Industrial Union.

The significance of the Social Center movement for this analysis lies not in the fact that there were two Italian civic clubs which sought to protect and promote Italian interests, or that the centers stressed the potential contributions of the Italians to the common store of American culture at least as much as the advantages America offered to the immigrant. The clubs pointedly avoided approaching the immigrant with the attitude of "Come, I will help you be like me." Rather, they presented an explicit statement of the rural and small-town bias that was shaping much of the American response to "urban problems," including those of the immigrants. A persistent theme in this progressive reform centered around the attempt to introduce into urban life those elements of rural life which the reformers presumed to have been critical to the development of the American character and civilization. The Social Center movement sought to return the schoolhouse to a primacy it was assumed to have held in the rural cradle of American democracy. Ward paraphrased a contemporary magazine article which he thought captured the intent of the centers:

> In that article the kindly neighborhood spirit which was developed in these school house meetings, social and political, was described. In connection with this description the author asserted that there is no such spirit as the village had in any American city, and that there never can be such a spirit of community interest, such a neighborly spirit, such democracy, until some institution is developed in the midst of our complex city life in which people of all races, classes and parties shall find a common gathering place, a common means of acquaintance, and opportunity to learn to think in terms of the city as a whole—until there is developed an institution which shall serve the people in the city as the Little Red School House served the folks back home.[20]

The superintendent of schools referred to the civic club in similar terms:

> It resembles the neighborhood life in the New England rural

community of former days. There every man knew his neighbor. These individual communities were powerful units in a great democracy. An open forum, the absence of political jealousy, the cooperative spirit that prevails here, all give an opportunity for careful deliberation and help to the formation of right judgements. Recommendations from such are valued and are sure to be more and more sought by all those who are working for the public good.

Center programs manifested this exaltation of the redeeming qualities of the little red schoolhouse. Lectures and discussions often centered around the dangers of "Gesellschaft" and the need to find a way to restore an organic unity rapidly being lost in contemporary urbanized and industrial America. One of the civic clubs chose as its motto From the Corners to the Center. They illustrated their meaning in a banner on which a rural schoolhouse, complete with a flag on a pole and a pine tree, was placed at the crossroads. Arrows on the roads pointed in toward the schoolhouse from each of the corners of the square banner. Even the vocabulary used to describe the clubs reflected a bucolic nostalgia. The opening session of the second year was reportedly "anxiously awaited and so welcome that it took on the cordiality of a great family reunion, a sort of 'Old Home Day.'"[21]

The influence of this popularized version of Frederic Jackson Turner's frontier thesis is evident in attempts to introduce the virtue-building qualities of rural living into the lives of immigrants, and especially their children, which were an important part in a number of the programs discussed above. One popular tactic was to transport the city-bound immigrant, if only for a short period, into a country environment, in the expectation that even a brief exposure would help. By the 1920s Holy Rosary Church in Kansas City was taking children on outings into the country, while Bisceglia's mission sent boys off to Rotary summer camp where, after their rustic experiences, they returned "showing improvement in morale, physical appearance and etiquette."

For all those who couldn't flee the city even temporarily,

the reformers sought ways of bringing remedial rural nostrums
into their urban-centered lives. These efforts often focused
around nature study and gardens. Rochester reformers fought
George Eastman's attempt to build model tenements for his
workers with the argument that "a cottage with its bit of garden
was the right model for the working man." A visitor in 1912
to the Lewis Street Center found a group of boys learning such
skills as spading effectively with the least amount of physical
exertion, making straight and uniform furrows, evenly distributing seeds, cultivating, thinning, transplanting, etc. He declared
the program to be a twofold success, in that it produced a vegetabl
crop as well as gains in health, character, and citizenship among
the boys. *The Common Good* magazine borrowed words from
a national proponent of the nature-study movement to explain
the importance of gardens in Rochester's mission work to anyone who missed the connection between straight furrows and
citizenship.

> Cultivation of plants indicates and develops elements of
> character fundamental to civilized life. Willingness to work
> for daily bread, provision for the future, courage to fight
> for home, and love of country are a few of the virtues at-
> tained. When we consider its universal and fundamental
> character in relation to civilization and human advancement,
> the omission of Soil Lore from a system of education of the
> young is suggestive of a relapse into barbarism. To allow a
> child to grow up without planting a seed or rearing a plant is
> a crime against civilized society; and our armies of tramps
> and our hordes of hoodlums are among the first fruits of a
> system of education which slights this important matter.[22]

The garden was an important element in Bisceglia's Kansas
City mission. As in Rochester, the impetus seems to have come
almost exclusively from Americans. The leader in the introduction of nature study and gardens was Mrs. Charles Nisbet, wife
of the pastor of the Presbyterian congregation that chiefly supported the mission. Fond memories of her rural Georgia childhood, "when people in the South had still the antebellum ideas

of comfort and luxury, a town lot was made to produce the luxuries of a farm, and our residence was surrounded by a five-acre lot with a branch running through it," provided part of the reason for her interests. In this environment Nature's teachers, the birds, the ants, the bees, and even the orchard, taught her life's secrets and irreversibly set the directions for the development of her character.

The second element was her deep interest in Robert Browning's poetry, which led her to the study of Italian language and culture. The result of this combination produced a woman with a strong interest in the Italians in her city and who taught both the Bible and Browning's poetry in her Sunday school classes at the mission. In addition, she led her Browning Society to establish and maintain a Browning Memorial Garden at the Italian mission to perpetuate the spirit of the poet's teachings. Each spring the "Woman's Board of Managers," of which Mrs. Nisbet was a member, distributed seeds among and offered prizes to the children with the best flower gardens. Even the playground at the mission was closely associated with nature study through its influences in "showing the little children how to play and training them to love the sunshine and fresh air, the birds and flowers and to drink plenty of water at the new drinking fountain recently given for the playground by the W.C.T.U."[23]

In 1927 Mrs. Nisbet elaborated upon her conception of the importance of nature study to the development of a child:

> Bringing a child in contact with nature uplifts his soul and thereby develops character. From nature he learns two fundamental lessons. First, that he must work. Second, that he must obey. He soon learns that what he plants he will reap. If he plants weeds, he reaps weeds. If he plants roses, he plucks roses. He learns also if he is lazy after he plants flowers they will be choked out by the weeds. Therefore, he must work.

> Nature teaches him that honesty is the best policy, thus correcting the impression that he receives when he observes dishonesty prospering in the transactions about him.

> It is the duty of the state as well as of social institutions to
> provide the best playgrounds and the most beautiful parks
> and gardens for the children who have no beauty in their
> homes. Let us never forget that beauty and beautiful inter-
> esting play are essential to any child's development in
> character and that an environment which is clean and bright
> and beautiful makes an indelible impression upon his soul.

Many of the activities, not only of Bisceglia's mission but those
resulting from other American responses to immigrants, reflected
this philosophy. The virtues of hard work, honesty, and faith in
a fair return on an honest investment were compatible with the
conservative philosophy expressed by the Italian mutual benefit
societies in the Old Word. Concern for active participation in public life expressed through the "Civic Clubs" also continued an interest of the same worker societies. However, Italians concerned with
achievement and acquisition, and sufficiently confident about the
future to strike out on the bold adventure of migration, undoubtedly had less sympathy for a general retreat from urbanism and an
escape into the softer virtues centering around love and apprecia-
tion of beauty.[24]

During the period under study here, views on the immigrant
and citizenship shifted from what can be characterized as a
move from naturalization to "Americanization." Americans in
the period before World War I gave little attention to the naturalization process. They left it in the hands of the courts, the
federal bureaucracy, and the public schools. The last institution,
along with a few fledgling missions, slowly developed a systematic approach to the preparation of immigrants for citizenship.
The first response was simply to add English for foreigners to
the courses offered by the public evening schools. In these
classes there was a covert curriculum from the outset which un-
systematically exposed the student to American values and institutions through the materials, subjects, and illustrations a
teacher chose to utilize in the process of language instruction.
By 1916 this random instruction was undergoing a rationalization
and systematization to ensure its more consistent and effective

presentation to the immigrant. Soon an administrative structure appeared to oversee and expand these areas of education.

Rochester led the way in this by developing evening school programs specifically for immigrants. In 1900 the superintendent reported to the school board on the increasing number of illiterate immigrants coming to American cities. Some of these people wanted to learn to read and write English, thus constituting a new clientele and challenge for the evening schools. Throughout the decade the Rochester evening schools worked on developing materials, methods, and a philosophical approach appropriate for this new area of responsibility for the public schools. After establishing a "department of immigrant education" with a director devoting his total evening responsibility to this work, the program developers proceeded to systematize the grouping of students according to categories of nationality, level of Old World education, and degree of familiarity with English. Then followed special training programs for teachers working with immigrants, a new three-year curriculum designed to ensure consistency, full coverage by elimination of needless overlap, duplication, and wasted energies, and the development of teaching materials and methods appropriate for adults with immigrant backgrounds.

An example of the increasing conscious manipulation of the covert curriculum was the introduction of a playlet as a substitute for the usual displays of English lessons to mark the closing of the evening-school term. The presentation's theme was "How the Foreigner in Rochester Becomes an American Citizen." Students acted out the whole process in five scenes, demonstrating their mastery of English as well as disseminating familiarity with the naturalization procedures among their families and friends who attended the closing program.[25]

In 1915 the logical separation of the English language and citizenship-preparation functions finally took place with the establishment of classes in citizenship under a teacher with special training in history and government. One of the first two teachers appointed to this post was of Italian background. Monroe County courts exempted those successfully completing the course from the customary naturalization examination.

Actively recruiting students and moving the classes out of the schools and into the immigrant colonies constituted the final steps in building the program. By 1922 the department had classes in eighteen factories and sixteen homes (for women), and fifteen additional classes in hotels, churches, labor organizations, lodges, etc. This program, under Charles E. Finch, Director of Immigrant Education, received state-wide notice as the "Rochester Plan" and provided an influential model for the emerging state interest in this area of schooling. As Finch explained the program in 1916, it sought to:

1. Teach prospective Americans to { speak, read English, write
2. To give practical information and safety suggestions.
3. To prepare for intelligent and patriotic American Citizenship.
4. To make the foreign-born familiar with our laws, customs and home ideals, with our great Americans, and with the fundamental facts of our history . . . .

> We seek to make the school the civic agency that appeals to the immigrant, that inspires his confidence, that effectually accomplishes his assimilation and makes him an integral part of the community in which he lives.[26]

By 1910 Americans were moving to promote the Americanization of immigrants outside the schoolhouse. *The Common Good* published a series of articles praising immigrants for their desire to learn to become good citizens. One major innovation in Rochester was the new citizens' banquet held in an attempt to give added dignity and community approval to the naturalization act. Started in 1910 by the Women's City Club, these gatherings at a downtown hotel became a major annual undertaking, with prominent citizens and politicians welcoming as many as one thousand new citizens. By 1916 the Chamber of Commerce was actively involved in promoting these celebrations. Their efforts in the 1920s received repeated praise from the editor of *La Stampa Unita*. He pointed to the great change that had taken place since the turn of the century, when newspaper reporters attended naturalization court proceedings to collect humorous anecdotes of immigrants' incorrect answers to the judge's examination. "Today," he wrote, "the receiving of citizenship papers is attended with almost as much ceremony and dignity as the receiving of a college diploma."[27]

The Chamber, through its committee on Americanization, stated its aims as follows:

> As Americans we should place higher values on our Citizenship, we should take a deeper and more intelligent interest in the affairs of the nation, and we should seek to realize the larger meaning of the institutions which we have inherited from our forefathers.
>
> The immigrants within our borders should be taught to speak and read our common tongue, they should be led to see the value of American citizenship, and encouraged to adopt American standards of living.
>
> We should treat the foreigner as an asset to be developed rather than another demand upon our time, money or sympathy. We should work with the immigrant not for him.
>
> We should realize more keenly that in a republic all the citizens must be efficient, and that it is our duty to counteract the influences of all those who would keep the immigrant in ignorance so that he might remain their prey.
>
> Our program of Americanization might be defined then as an attempt to give to all those within our border a common national ideal, a point of view that is essentially American, a loyalty to America that gives the pledge of allegiance to the United States in terms of service. It should include an effort on our part to make the English language our common tongue, to create a greater social solidarity, to raise the general level of intelligence, to protect all the children of all the people and see that they are raised and educated to emphasize the high value and real meaning of American citizenship.

Despite a decision in 1917 that the Americanization of Americans was at least as important as work with the foreign-born and a change of name of the committee to the Council for Better Citizenship, in the 1920s the chamber's work continued to concentrate primarily on immigrants.[28]

The "Americanization" movement was much slower to get underway in Utica. A representative of the State Department of Education initiated the first activities under that specific rubric in December 1919 at the Italian Settlement House. The following year the Utica School Board directed the public schools to enter the field. The school system soon had classes in thirteen different industrial establishments, branch libraries, homes, churches, clubs, and community centers, as well as one at the Hotel Utica for the Greek waiters who worked there. Often, as in the case of the Polish Roman Catholic parish, local groups organized classes and then requested a teacher from the public schools. From the outset the enterprise was under the Department of Immigrant Education headed by an energetic and creative directress. The program spanned four years, with a curriculum that underwent several revisions in attempts to fit it better to the characteristics of adult immigrants. In order to improve the quality of instruction, the department offered in-service training in methods for teaching adults and elementary economics to its teachers in 1922. The need for special preparation in economics arose out of questions frequently asked by immigrant students.

The following year the administration formed a student council made up of representatives of each school class to help set the policy and direction of the department. Five members of the first council of twelve were Italians. By mid-decade the program produced its first graduation class from the four-year course of study. They formed an alumni association to keep their interest alive, to maintain contacts with the program, and to help publicize it among fellow immigrants. At this point the department was registering slightly over 2,000 immigrants from twenty-six countries a year. This represented a 132 percent increase in registration from the first year of operation. Average attendance increased from 38 to 43 percent of total enrollment.

By June 1927 the sixty-six graduates averaged 7 years in the United States and 3.5 years in the evening school.[29]

The immigrant education program was never overtly hostile to the national cultures of its students or their interests in maintaining them. Rather, with a few exceptions such as programs of lantern slides of Syria and Italy and essays written on their Old World backgrounds, the program simply ignored the various national cultures as irrelevant to its primary focus. The program's goals were "All Utica English Speaking" and the building of a sense of commonality and identification with America. Nothing pleased the directress of the program more than to be able to report the testimony of one student: "In evening school I have met people from all nations and find them all good."

The schools sought to produce this sense of solidarity and esprit de corps through an extensive program of social events. The intent was to foster mixing of the various national groups in order to break down prejudice and suspicion built upon isolation and ignorance. The school program ignored Old World themes because the director feared that the school could not give equal treatment to all and would thus only reap more discord and jealousy. To this end, social gatherings carried responsibility for an important part of the educational experience. Classes from different schools entertained each other. Larger gatherings including the whole student body sometimes met to watch operattas and pageants, to listen to guest speakers, and to socialize. In addition to the student drama, the program published a newspaper which united students in a common activity. The paper carried pieces promoting American institutions and inspirational material, as well as student essays and personal news such as announcements of marriages, births, and other special events in the lives of students and recent graduates. It maintained a tone of intimacy and community.[30]

Lay interest in Americanization was slower to manifest itself in Utica than it was in Rochester, and when it appeared it was in response to and supportive of public school initiatives. Organizations as varied as Rotary, Kirotex Club (a young businessmen's club), Kiwanis, Daughters of the American Revolution,

Harmony Club, Catholic's Women's Club, Elks, Tabernacle
C.E., Vis Unita Club, Daughters of Columbus, St. David's Club,
Exchange Club, Plymouth Men's Club, and Sonta Club entered
into the social and cultural activities of the immigrant education
program with the intent of producing new levels of mutual
understanding and a broader sense of community. In addition,
the Utica Americanization Council, formed in 1922, supported
and promoted Americanization through night school and settlement houses and coordinated the activities of various member
organizations. The council maintained a Citizens' Bureau as a
clearing house for information about problems affecting foreigners. The council also proposed to investigate the home conditions of citizenship applicants and report its findings to the
judges of the naturalization court. It apparently did not carry
through with this potentially oppressive plan of snooping. The
activities of the council during the 1920s and early 1930s centered around support of the public school's immigrant education
program, assuring the dignity of the naturalization procedure
by providing appropriate ceremonial activities and intervention
in the naturalization procedure to help immigrants with special
problems. For example, it helped to obtain pardons for criminal
convictions which prevented otherwise worthy immigrants
from becoming citizens.[31]

Preoccupation with the forces motivating reformers can
easily lead to unwarranted assumptions that the persons who
were the objects of their concern were passive, uncritical, perhaps unwilling recipients of this beneficence and that the inputs
defined in terms of the interests of the reformers were translated directly to outputs received by the clients. In fact, the
colonies were selective in their utilization of these agencies.
They could and did resist offerings which they viewed as irrelevant to their goals or offensive, such as the Protestant pro-
seletyzing. This gave the colony a kind of veto power in certain
circumstances. Each agency was dependent on voluntary attendance to justify its existence to its financial supporters. Private
charities competed for the attention of the colonies. Successful
programs provided the basis for an appeal for a larger budget in
succeeding years. Low attendance figures raised questions among

the American sponsors. Protestant missions, with their small numbers of converts, were particularly vulnerable. Popular recreational, educational, health and social programs lessened, but never eliminated, doubts among the religious groups supporting the mission. Agencies competed to find new offerings that would prove popular, thereby strengthening their reason for existing.

Workers and directors might have their own agendas, but if they proved unpopular in the competition for attention from the colonies they could be pushed through only at considerable risk to the enterprise. Public agencies had some slight advantage in the stability of their funding, though the difference was in degree, not kind. They too engaged in the head-counting practice. The evening schools devoted considerable attention to publicizing their achievements to the school commissioner and to the public. Accountability meant attracting clients. This gave the colonies some control over the activities of the agencies. While they seldom shared in the planning or initiation of programs, they could and did help determine which ones survived.[32]

When compared with the variety and flexibility of the educational and other supportive activities generated within the Italian colonies, the endeavors from the outside to help the immigrant adjust to urban living in America were clearly late and often unimaginative. Furthermore, they were limited in their potential impact by an imperfect perception of the real nature of the urban problems and reliance on a largely mythical and inadequate rural metaphor. These programs, while they may have provided enjoyment for many children, had little relevance to the fundamental problems of immigrants or others grappling with life in industrial, urban America.

12

THE PASSAGE REVIEWED

Most historical studies of Italian immigrants have stressed the strains and conflicts between their cultural backgrounds and their experience in America. From this perspective, the story is often one of suffering and alienation, in which the immigrants are portrayed as essentially passive, impotent victims of social and economic forces in the American environment. Such works often present the immigrants as having had little that was positive to contribute to the unfolding of their destiny here except for such vague and nebulous virtues as a strong back and a sunny disposition. According to this view, like the balls in a pinball machine, the immigrants were propelled through their physical and social environment by external forces which were activated by their presence but which they could not influence. My account has largely eschewed this well-studied story of exploitation, discrimination, and rejection in order to take the immigrants on their own terms. I have portrayed the immigrants as active agents, capable of initiative as well as of accommodation, and as possessors of a viable culture which shaped their perceptions of their American experience, in many ways giving them a sense of continuity between past and present.[1]

Italian emigration was a selective process initiated as part of a reaction to the threat of a reduction of a complex status system into one based on simple exchange values associated with the wage-labor system. The emigrants give testimony through their mobility to a deep concern for their future places in society rather than to their immediate poverty. In Italy they had already expressed through their societies and associations bourgeois values such as individual advancement through hard work, thrift, education, acquisition of property, and autonomy in their occupational and economic lives.[2]

Once in America, the immigrants found that this important part of their world view was compatible with a similar popular tradition here. But they had to learn new ground rules and make appropriate tactical adjustments since the game was played on a different field. As long as newcomers anticipated imminent return to Italy, they employed strategies the roots of whose logic lay in the Old World. Later, when they recognized that their futures lay in America, strategies shifted to meet this realization. Once committed to America, they had to learn English and a constellation of behavior patterns appropriate to life in an urban industrial society. The magnitude of this task and the degree to which immigrants achieved it should not be underestimated.

Yet the important point is that the logic supporting these changes was rooted in a world view brought with them from Europe. The immigrants did not have to change their general convictions about the nature of man and society. This similarity of values in both cultures could have drawbacks as well, for one who failed, did so in the eyes of both societies. There was little opportunity to invoke the sanction of an alternative set of values in defense of one's position in the society, since the Italian immigrant ideology held that social mobility and ethnic preservation were compatible. Irving Child found that the second generation experienced difficulty in defining these goals in a mutually reconcilable fashion, but this was not the case with the immigrants.[3]

In America the immigrant found new opportunities for personal mobility and advancement. The growth of colonies created a host of commercial and service markets which offered the more energetic and talented opportunities to acquire proprietorship status. The need for communication and mediation between the colony and the broader community also opened new avenues for those who could learn to function in American society. On more modest levels, those who established permanent residence in this country could measure their personal advancement against a variety of standards. Movement up the occupational and skill ladders within the working class and the acquisition of property were popular gauges at the time and are currently used by scholars studying social mobility in the nineteenth and twentieth centuries. Education and self-improvement were important themes expressed by worker societies in Italy. They continued to be prominent in America, while status acquired through the education of their children became increasingly important in the mobility ideology. This avenue to greater status was not lacking in Italy prior to mass emigration, but Joseph Lopreato's work suggests that it may have become more important with repatriation of the first and second waves of emigrants.[4]

Italian children seem to have fared at least as well as their classmates in schooling, although much work remains to be done before we shall have an adequate statistical assessment of the school careers of children of various social and ethnic groups. Extended schooling as an avenue of mobility only emerged slowly in the early twentieth century as a practical and realistic alternative for sizable numbers of working-class, especially immigrant, children. Italian children participated in this extension of the working classes into American secondary education.[5] At the elementary level, the data for Rochester suggest that Italian parents did not sacrifice their children's education for the sake of the wages they might earn any more readily than their neighbors did. With the exception of a tendency to be overage for grade level, Italians were at least equals to other children in their schools.

Of course, the use of children's earnings to support family mobility through the acquisition of property was both an Italian and an American working-class tradition, which illustrates the potential for paradox in both value systems. Stephen Thernstrom demonstrates the pervasiveness of mobility through acquisition of property in the second half of the nineteenth century among both native-born and immigrant unskilled workers. Josef Barton's pioneering quantitative study of the use of the school by immigrants in Cleveland suggests a complex relationship between exploitation of schooling and factors such as family and community organization, public versus parochial education, and the occupational status of one's father. Scholars must do more research in a number of different cities to identify

the mechanisms by which one or the other of the competing
values in the mobility ideology were selected and to establish
any unique patterns associated with a particular group. Exploration has only begun on the degree to which Italians were
able to realize their goals for individual mobility through schooling, the reasons for choosing this approach, and the extent, if
any, to which they differed from other similarly placed groups.[6]

The melting-pot metaphor has hindered the study of immigration by masking areas of fundamental agreement between
the American and the immigrant cultures. It led scholars to con-
fuse what were only superficial cultural changes for a transformation of deeper values. Its allusions to homogenization also
tended to hide the fact that Americans did not expect, and
many would not accept, full amalgamation of the newly arrived
immigrants.[7] It presented the debate between pluralism and
assimilation in absolutes of black and white, making a closer
and more sensitive analysis of the phenomenon difficult. The
simplistic image of the caldron minimized the complexity of
the process and the importance of the institutions involved in
cultural maintenance and change. Finally, it suggested to many
an inevitable, automatic, and total transformation in which the
immigrant culture gave way to the superior appeal of the culture of the new land or the ruthless aggression of the "Americanizers." In 1930 the Italians were not "Americans" in the
middle-class mold. The existence of a colony symbolized the persistence of structural divisions along ethnic lines.

Yet the colony itself was a mosaic of cultural patterns expressed in the variety of societies and associations, which ranged
from those adhering strictly to the traditions of the Old World
to those which sought to reproduce for a growing Italian middle
class the patterns common in the broader community. The end
of a steady cultural reinforcement from Italy caused by the
cessation of immigration in 1924 had not yet taken its full toll.
The colonies were culturally and materially prosperous. The
Depression, residential changes forced by a dynamic urban environment, the continuous squeeze of small enterprise by big
business, and the growing taste for American consumer goods,
rapid expansion of educational opportunities and compulsion

to attend school, and the increasing dominance of the second and third generations all were to alter fundamentally the life of the colonies. In the late 1920s the colonies had reached a high point they would never experience again.

In a study of post–World War II Sicilian immigration to Australia, Constance Cronin makes a useful distinction between the public and private sectors of the lives of immigrants. Cronin's interview approach revealed that longtime immigrants and those who were occupationally mobile were both highly satisfied with the public institutions of Australia and appeared to be well assimilated into their public-sector behaviors. Still, they retained their Sicilian ideals and way of life at home and associated socially only with other Sicilians.[8]

Such a finding is not inconsistent with this study. I have shown that the Italian version of "Americanization" envisioned just such a dichotomy in their lives and held that they could become "Americans" without a wholesale surrender of their own heritage. A small study done in Rochester after World War II found a pattern very similar to Cronin's. The immigrants studied showed assimilation in the public sector of their lives and a number of instances of cultural survivals in their private lives. The children of these immigrants made sizable moves toward American patterns in their private lives, as well as continuing their parents' assimilationist tendencies in the public sector.[9]

Lacking the anthropologists' or sociologists' opportunities for on-site observations and data gathering, the historian is severely handicapped in his attempts to study private-sector phenomena such as internal organization and authority patterns in families, or friendships and personal associations. Yet it is important for historians to seek new ways to approach these topics since America is presently experiencing a revival of interest in ethnicity which desperately needs a more profound historical perspective.

According to Michael Novak, a prominent spokesman for the movement, this "new ethnicity" derives from feelings of dissatisfaction with "acceptable" identities available in contemporary society and seeks an affirmation and legitimation of the pluralism presently suppressed in own society. The literature of the

movement tends to be strident and accusatory, assigning much
blame to the arrogant cultural aggression of WASPS. Richard
Sennett and Jonathan Cobb have written in a similar style in
The Hidden Injuries of Class.[10] Part of Novak's work explores
the "hidden injuries" of suppressed ethnicity. I do not doubt
that both varieties of injury exist. Yet the task of distinguishing
between these and other possible sources of discontent is only
in its early stages. Alienation, frustration, rage, and hurt are not
the exclusive property of ethnics. Nor was ethnic culture always
alien to success in the New World. Recognition of the unhappy
cost of life in urban and industrial society can be found in all
classes and cultural groups. It is not enough for spokesmen of
the new ethnicity to point to such feeling among ethnics as
proof of a continuing ethnic influence.

I do not wish to repeat the objection common among critics
of Novak that his ethnic characteristics are in fact largely class-
determined, but to suggest that there are multiple levels of
culture which call forth varying degrees of meaning and commitment and derive from several origins. My study has placed
special emphasis on the areas of agreement between Italian immigrants and the American communities they entered. Failure
to recognize these similarities in ethos has led American observers to credit too much of what seemed favorable in the
adjustments the immigrants made here to presumed redemptive
qualities in the American enviroment, and hid the more likely
origins within the Italian-Americans themselves.[11]

If the renewed interest in ethnicity is to produce a deeper
understanding of the contribution of ethnicity to American
life, scholars will have to move beyond oversimplified, ahistori-
cal, and often filiopietistic assertions about the nature of cultural persistence and develop new ways of sorting out class and
other nonethnic influences on the psyches and cultures of
ethnic groups. Simple gross measures of differential frequencies
of cultural and social characteristics across ethnic lines, with
nonexistent or very poor controls for potential nonethnic influences, are suggestive but hardly provide a basis for a confident
analysis of what is ethnic about ethnic groups. The demonstra-
tion of the existence of an "ethnic" pattern in voting, for

example, may be all that a political strategist wishes or needs to know. For those interested in ethnicity, it should raise questions concerning the origin of the pattern and its relationship—if any—to the group's ethnic heritage. Class, religion, demography, ecology, and ethnic heritage all interact to produce the cultural and social patterns of an ethnic group.

Future research in this area will have to provide greater sensitivity to the dynamics of this interaction and explore new ways to understand the nature of the contribution of the various forces. Help may come from a source heretofore almost totally ignored in work in this area—education. How were the various elements of an ethnic culture selected, combined, interpreted, and finally kept alive and transmitted across generations? Such questions deal with the educational mechanisms of a society. The link between the culture of one generation and that of another is in the broadest sense educational. It is in the study of the educational function of the institutions which shape, perpetuate, and transfer culture that we may hope to find the means to expand our understanding of ethnic influences in America.

NOTES

Introduction

1 Table 5.12, p. 96, presents more comparisons of the population characteristics of the three cities for 1890–1930. See U.S. Bureau of the Census, *Census of Population 1960*, vol. 1, pts. 22, 23, 27, 32, 34, and 40 for the 1960 figures. By comparison, the standard metropolitan statistical area of New York–New Jersey had 10.3% Italian stock. Boston had 7.8%, Newark 9%, Trenton 8.2%, and Philadelphia 5.7%. Only New Haven, Conn., with 15.8%, and Jersey City, N.J., with 13.6%, had significantly higher proportions of "Italians" among major metropolitan areas on the eastern seaboard than Rochester and Utica.

2 Luigi Villari, *Italian Life in Town and Country* (New York, 1902), p. 36.

3 Denis Mack Smith, *Italy: A Modern History* (Ann Arbor, Mich., 1959), pp. 230–31. Leo Schelbert also has identified nationalistic sentiment as a prominent force shaping the view of emigrants. He observes that "seen from their country of origin, emigrants are ungrateful, disturbed, and misguided people." Schelbert, "On Becoming an Emigrant: A Structural View of Eighteenth- and Nineteenth-Century Swiss Data." *Perspectives in American History* 7 (1973): 441–44.

4 Phyllis Williams, *South Italian Folkways in Europe and America* (New Haven, Conn., 1938); Leonard Covello, *The Social Background of the Italo-American School Child: A Study of the Southern Italian Family Mores and Their Effects on the School Situation in Italy and America* (Lieden, 1967), pp. xxi, 8, 475.

5 Rudolph J. Vecoli, "Contadini in Chicago: A Critique of The Uprooted," *The Journal of American History* 51, no. 3 (December 1964): 404–17, and "The Italian Americans," *The Center Magazine*, July/August 1974, p. 31; Marcus Lee Hansen, *The Immigrant in American History*, ed. Arthur M. Schlesinger (New York, 1964). Luciano J. Iorizzo and Salvatore Mondello, *The Italian Americans* (New York, 1971), largely ignore the influence of Italian culture on the New World experience, while Humbert S. Nelli, *Italians in Chicago, 1880–1930: A Study in Ethnic Mobility* (New York, 1970), assigns it a negative role and concentrates on the American enviroment in explaining the positive adjustment by immigrants to their new surroundings. Andrew Rolle, *The Immigrant Upraised: Italian Adventurers and Colonists in an*

Expanding America (Norman, Okla., 1969), carries this further and attributes much of the desire for, and success in, social mobility to the
salubrious environment of the American West.

6 Herbert Gutman's *Work, Culture and Society in Industrializing
America* (New York, 1976) has helped sharpen my presentation of
this perspective.

7 Representative works are Stearns, *Lives of Labor: Work in a Maturing
Industrial Society* (New York, 1975); Gutman, "Work, Culture and
Society in Industrializing America, 1815–1919," *American Historical
Review* 72, no. 3 (June 1973): 531–88; E. P. Thompson, *Making of the
English Working Class* (London, 1963); idem, "Time, Work Discipline,
and Industrial Capitalism," *Past and Present* 38 (1967): 56–97; and
Yans-McLaughlin, "A Flexible Tradition: South Italian Immigrants
Confront a New Work Experience," *Journal of Social History* 7, no. 4
(Summer 1974): 429–45. An anthropological exploration is Emilio
Willems, "Peasantry and City: Cultural Persistance and Change in
Historical Perspective, A European Case," *American Anthropologist*
72 (1970): 528–43. For a statement of the issue as it pertains to
family organization, see Joseph F. Kett's review of Edward Shorter,
The Making of the Modern Family, in *Harvard Educational Review* 46,
no. 3 (August 1976): 498–501.

8 Nelli, *Italians in Chicago*, pp. 5, 170–71. Nelli was also poorly served
by his acceptance of Edward Banfield's amoral familism thesis, which
posits that there could be no voluntary associations in southern Italy.
Apparently, he never checked to see if this corollary of the hypothesis
was consistent with the evidence. For a critique of Banfield's position,
see pp. 15, 65–68 and 284–85 below. Jack C. Ross, *An Assembly of
Good Fellows: Voluntary Associations in History* (Westport, Conn.,
1976) is the most recent major work on voluntary associations.

9 Michael Katz, *Class, Bureaucracy and Schools* (New York, 1971)
brings together much of the revisionist interpretation.

Chapter 1

1 The study of emigration commonly proceeds from recounting the general political, economic, and social conditions of the country of origin
to the deduction of the most probable victims of the system, and
finally to the assumption that it was these victims who were the ones
who left in response to the exploitation and oppression catalogued in
the first instance. There are important exceptions, however. Simon
Kuznets, in his essay "Immigration of Russian Jews to the United
States: Background and Structure," *Perspectives in American History*
9 (1975): 35–126, makes the selectivity of the emigration process a
central concern. Limited by the Old World evidence available for this
task, he has taken the imaginative approach of comparing the profile

of Jewish immigration as recorded by the U.S. government with the profile of the Jewish population in Russia constructed from an 1897 census.
There is a great deal of ambiguity and sloppiness in an analysis which relies
on such diverse types of data. However, the significance of Kuznets' questions makes his efforts worthwhile even after necessary qualifications.
Leo Schelbert, on the other hand, adopts a case-study approach in which
he recreates from local Swiss records the biographies of individual immigrants who illustrate various dimensions of his typology of emigration.
Schelbert, "On Becoming an Emigrant: A Structural View of Eighteenth-
and Nineteenth-Century Swiss Data," *Perspectives in American History* 7
(1973): 441–95. My approach falls somewhere between these two. The data
are almost entirely Italian and are usually taken from the local centers of
emigration. Yet the concern is with aggregates rather than the single, perhaps idiosyncratic, individual.

2 John S. MacDonald, "Migration from Italy to Australia" (Ph.D. diss.,
   Australian National University, 1958), pp. vi, 63, 74ff. MacDonald
   restates the thesis in several journal articles; see, for instance, "Some
   Socio-Economic Emigration Differentials in Rural Italy, 1902–1913,"
   Economic Development and Cultural Change 7, no. 1 (October 1958):
   71–72.

3 MacDonald, "Migration," chap. 4, especially pp. 88–116; Josef J.
   Barton, *Peasants and Strangers: Italians, Rumanians, and Slovaks in an
   American City, 1890–1950* (Cambridge, Mass., 1975), pp. 27–47. Also
   see Barton, "Immigration and Social Mobility in an American City:
   Studies of Three Ethnic Groups in Cleveland, 1890–1950" (Ph.D. diss.
   University of Michigan, 1971), pp. 16–30.

4 MacDonald, "Some Socio-Economic Emigration Differentials," pp. 55,
   72ff.

5 MacDonald, "Migration," pp. 111, 295–302, 322, 344–47, 387–88.

6 Joseph Lopreato, *Peasants No More: Social Class and Social Change in
   an Underdeveloped Society* (San Francisco, 1967), pp. 211–12, 222–23.
   This exclusion of the lowest stratum of a society from voluntary migration has been noted by other scholars. Maurice R. Davie suggested
   that the ability to finance the transportation was the controlling factor,
   in his *World Immigration with Special Reference to the United States*
   (New York, 1936), p. 249. This has been challenged by MacDonald,
   who argues that sponsorship in the chain migration phenomenon
   muted the steamship fare as an obstacle to migration. A conclusion
   of this chapter is that psychological and cultural resources are just as
   necessary as money for the transatlantic passage. They are symbolically
   acknowledged by Lopreato in one of his strata, which is categorized as
   people who "are getting somewhere" (p. 187).

7 "Registro della domanda di nulla osta per ottenere passaporto per
   l'estero," 1901–14, Archivio Comunale, Termini Imerese.

8 Francesco Renda, *L'emigrazione in Sicilia* (Palermo, 1963), pp. 40–52;
   MacDonald, "Migration," pp. 303–04; "Stato degli utenti pesi e misure,"

1874 and intermittently through 1932, Archivio Comunale, Sant'
Agata di Militello. Sant' Agata grew from a small, insignificant village
in the commune of Militello into a major commercial and market center during the late nineteenth and early twentieth centuries.

9 Sidney Sonnino, *I contadini in Sicilia*, vol. 2 of Leopoldo Franchetti
and Sidney Sonnino, *La Sicilia nel 1876* (Florence, 1877), pp. 120–24,
271–72; Salvatore Francesco Romano, *La Sicilia nell'ultimo ventennio
del secolo XIX* (Palermo, 1959), pp. 118–23.

10 Salvatore Francesco Romano, *Storia dei fasci Siciliani* (Bari, 1959),
pp. 74–75, 241–42.

11 Sonnino, *I contadini*, p. 69; *Inchiesta Parlamentare sulle condizioni
dei contadini nelle provincie meridionali e nella Sicilia* (Rome, 1909–11),
12: 72–73; Francesco Renda, *Il movimento contadino nella società
Siciliana* (Palermo, 1956), pp. 163–201, relates the slow radicalization
of the Società Cincinnati at Palagonia. A recent anthropological study
of a commune in Matera describes a similar cultural ethos which extended back into the nineteenth century. An increasing population and
gradual redistribution of communal lands into private hands created
a situation which fostered competition between families and promoted
an individualistic spirit. The author speculates that many small gradations in status developed with the passage of more land into private
hands. The gradual intrusion of the state and outside economic forces
into the local village produced new clerical and professional positions.
This growth, in turn, encouraged expansion of the building trades
and retail establishments. With more ranks it became "possible for
individuals to pursue calculated strategies of social mobility." One
strategy presumably would be to seek capital outside the system
through emigration. J. Davis, *Land and Family in Pisticci* (London,
1973), pp. 87–89.

12 Adolfo Rossi, "Vantaggi e danni dell'emigrazione nel Mezzogiorno
d'Italia," *Bollettino dell'Emigrazione*, no. 13 (1908), pp. 68–71,
80–83; J. S. MacDonald, "Agricultural Organization, Migration and
Labor Militancy in Rural Italy," *The Economic History Review* 16,
no. 1 (1963): 62, 66, and "Some Socio-Economic Emigration Differentials," p. 58; Lopreato, *Peasants No More*, pp. 221–22; Giovan
Battista Raja, *Il fenomeno emigratorio Siciliano: Con speciale riguardo
al quinquennio 1902–1906* (Palermo, 1908), pp. 28–42.

13 Romano, *Fasci*, pp. 60–63; Romano, *Sicilia*, pp. 27–28; Giuseppina
Scanni, "L'Emigrazione delle donne e dei fanciulli dalla provincia di
Caserta," *Bollettino dell'Emigrazione*, no. 13 (1913), pp. 11–12ff.

14 "Registro della domanda di nulla osta per ottenere passaporto per
l'estero," 1901–26, Archivio Comunale, Serradifalco.

15 Sonnino, *I contadini*, pp. 120–24, 271–72, 472–89; Jessie V. Mario,
"Le miniere di zolfo in Sicilia," *Nuova Antologia*, 1 February 1894,
pp. 450–51; Erminio Ferraris, "La miniera di Monteponi presso
Iglesias," *Nuova Antologia*, 16 July 1907, pp. 290–99; Angelo M.

Vaccaro, "I zolfatai della Sicilia," *Giornale degli Economisti,* 2
February 1891, pp. 170-87; Romano, *Fasci,* pp. 69-72.

16 These generalizations are the product of an analysis of data from 1901
manuscript census schedules for 122 emigrant households and 389
nonemigrant households. The schedules are housed in the communal
archives. See p. 46 below for evidence of attempts to restrict
literacy and franchise.

17 Romano, *La Sicilia,* p. 46; *Bollettino dell'Emigrazione,* no. 18 (1910),
pp. 504-11; Scanni, "L'Emigrazione," p. 10; Sonnino, *I contadini,*
pp. 451-54; Pietro Kacava, "Sulle condizioni economico-sociali della
Basilicata," *Nuova Antologia,* 1 March 1907, p. 111; Rossi, "Vantaggi," p. 57.

18 Reports of the *Consular Officers of the United States: Emigration and
Immigration* (Washington, D.C., 1887), pp. 255, 269, 272, 279-80,
290.

19 Coletti, *Dell'Emigrazione Italiana* (Milan, 1912), p. 259; "Ruolo
matricolare comunale dei militari," 1878, Records of the elementary
school, 3a maschile, 1888-89, 1889-90, 1890-91, 1893-94, and 4a
and 5a maschile 1893-94. Archivi Comunale and Scuole, Valledolmo.
Draft evasion does not seem to be a contributing factor to the emigration of the educated. Presumably, they are in the best position to
hire substitutes, and thus, if any influence is at work here, it is in the
direction of increasing the migration of poor and presumably less
well-schooled males. Timothy L. Smith suggests that the tendency for
the better-educated to emigrate was general among the various national
groups involved in immigration to America in the late nineteenth and
early twentieth centuries; see his "Immigrant Social Aspirations and
American Education, 1880-1930," *The American Quarterly* 21 (Fall
1969): 527-31.

20 Lista della leva, Laurenzana, Potenza, 1884, 1886, 1888, 1890, 1892,
and 1894. Archivio Comunale, Laurenzana, and Archivio di Stato,
Potenza. Draft evasion, again, does not seem to have been a dominant
motive for those known to be abroad. Some emigrants were exempted
for physical reasons or family obligations. Others submitted to the law
by registering with an Italian consul abroad. The overall impression is
one of young men seeking to reconcile their immediate self-interests in
emigration with the need to conform to the law brought on by the intention to repatriate.

21 Luigi Vallari, "L'emigrazione italiana negli Stati Uniti d'America,"
Nuova Antologia, 16 September 1909, p. 297; Robert F. Foerster,
The Italian Emigration of Our Times (Cambridge, 1919), p. 330. T. L.
Smith has documented the existence of this value system, often associated with the "Protestant ethic" in East European peasant cultures
and in those of Catholic, Orthodox, and Jewish, as well as Protestant
faiths, pp. 531 ff.

Chapter 2

1   The interpretation of a totally crippling ethos of familial centeredness
    characterizing southern Italy is fully developed in Edward Banfield,
    The Moral Basis of a Backward Society (Glencoe, Ill., 1958). Ban-
    field has lately come under increasing attack for his methodology,
    his causative analysis, and his overgeneralization from evidence derived
    from a restricted and perhaps distinctive area. See Sydel F. Silverman,
    "Agricultural Organization, Social Structure, and Values in Italy:
    Amoral Familism Reconsidered," *American Anthropologist* 70 (1968):
    1-20; Joseph Lopreato, *Peasants No More: Social Class and Social
    Change in an Underdeveloped Society* (San Francisco, 1967), pp. 245-46,
    252-57 and passim; J. Davis, "Morals and Backwardness," *Comparative
    Studies in Society and History* 12 (July 1970): 340-59; and Anthony
    H. Galt, "Carnival on the Island of Pantelleria: Ritualized Community
    Solidarity in an Atomistic Society," *Ethnology* 12, no. 3 (July 1973):
    325-39.
        The argument presented here is not an attempt to deny the importance
    of the family in southern Italian culture. Rather, it is suggested that
    Banfield is ahistorical in his analytic ordering of the observations he
    makes. This allows him to ignore the contradictory and extrafamilial
    elements in the society. He also tends to homogenize a society which
    Lopreato found to contain a number of distinct strata, each with its
    own world view. Humbert S. Nelli, *Italians in Chicago, 1880–1930*
    (New York, 1970), is a recent example of the application of this inter-
    pretation to Italian immigration to America. This leads him to concen-
    trate largely on the American environment in explaining positive
    adjustments by immigrants to life in America. As an example, he
    argues that mutual benefit societies here do not represent "transplanted"
    institutions, since such institutions in Italy were middle-class, northern,
    and urban (p. 170).
        The use of Banfield's characterization of southern Italian society for a
    description of the values and ethos of pre-World War I immigrants
    requires energetic scholarly gymnastics that are not discussed in the
    literature taking this tack. One must accept the validity of Banfield's
    description of the village he studied, generalize it to all of southern
    Italy, project it largely unchanged back sixty or seventy years over two
    wars and many social, political, and economic changes, and then across
    the Atlantic with the immigrants. Herbert Gans then projects these
    characteristics ahead into the second and third generations, in his *The
    Urban Villagers* (New York, 1962), pp. 197-226.
        This exercise requires one of two possible assumptions. Either the
    culture was exceedingly durable and resistant to change—(Banfield's
    argument, developed more fully in a later work, suggests that it has
    within it protective mechanisms which undermine the power of en-
    vironmental and social conditions to effect change. See my discussion

below in Chapter 4) or, that there have been, over time and across
national boundaries, few social, economic, and ecological changes that
could fundamentally alter the culture. See William Muraskin, "The
Moral Basis of a Backward Sociologist: Edward Banfield, "The Italians
and the Italian-Americans," *American Journal of Sociology* 79, no. 6
(1974): 1484-96, for evidence that this is still a lively issue.

2 Sidney Sonnino, *I contadini in Sicilia*, vol. 2 of Leopoldo Franchetti
and Sidney Sonnino, *La Sicilia nel 1876* (Florence, 1877), pp. 19-23,
285, 316-17, 322, 427-42 and 457-59. Francesco S. Nitti, *Scritti
sulla questione meridionale*, vol 4, no. 1: *Inchiesta sulla condizioni dei
contadini in Basilicata e in Calabria* (Bari, 1968) pp. 328-30. D. Mack
Smith, "The Latifundia in Modern Sicilian History," *Proceedings of
the British Academy* 51 (1965): 117-18.

3 The Italian government kept a close watch over popular organizations,
collecting statistics, constitutions, and reports from local officials on
the activities of the societies, as well as "their influence among the
masses." The following analysis is based largely on these materials,
found in the provincial archives of Palermo, Enna, Caltanissetta,
Messina, Potenza, and L'Aquila, as well as the examination of over
seventy-five constitutions of such organizations.

4 Francesco Brancato, *La Sicilia nel primo ventennio del Regno D'Italia*
(Bologna, 1956), pp. 268-69. Salvatore Francesco Romano, *La Sicilia
nell'ultimo ventennio del secolo XIX* (Palermo, 1958), pp. 331-35.
Maestranze, descendants of medieval craft guilds, were prominent in
Sicily as late as the end of the eighteenth century, when there were
seventy-four in Palermo alone. Each served a specific trade whose members often congregated around a church dedicated to the patron saint
of their trade. The associations regulated entry, practice, and competition in the trade; provided support for members in distress or in prison;
insured proper funerals for deceased members; made provision for
widows and orphans; and afforded artisans a measure of protection
against the power of the barons. I have not found direct ties between
the *maestranze* and the mutual benefit societies, though they share
many obvious similarities in structure and purpose. See Giuseppe
Scherma, *Delle maestranze in Sicilia: Contributo allo studio della
questione operaia* (Palermo 1896) and Ferdinando Lionti, *Antiche
maestranze della citta di Palermo* (Palermo 1886).

5 "Elenco delle associazioni esistenti nel territorio della giurisdizione
del suddetto circondario-Mistretta." See lists for the Circondari of
Pati, Castoreale, and Messina, Gabinetto della Prefettura—Messina,
fasc. 193, Archivio di Stato, Messina. Aldolfo Rossi, "Vantaggi e danni
dell'emigrazione nel mezzogiorno d'Italia," *Bollettino dell'Emigrazione*,
no. 13 (1908), p. 65. Romano, *La Sicilia*, pp. 331-35. Also see generally,
files under the title "Worker Organizations" in the collections for
"Capo di Gabinetto" in the Archivio di Stato at Palermo, Messina,
Caltanissetta, and Potenza. Francesco Renda asserts that the mutual

benefit societies outside the major cities seldom transformed themselves into *fasci.* Yet his own evidence undermines his contention that
nothing of the older organizations is recognizable in the new fasci. He
reprinted the constitution of a *fascio* which lists as its first four objectives goals common to most mutual benefit societies. The document
then goes on to call for aggressive action in the areas of wages, hours,
and conditions of labor, as well as solidarity in the political struggles.

Overall, it is a very conservative document when compared with the
clearly socialist-inspired statutes from the Palermo and Catania areas
and from the radical mining commune of Grotte. Common sense would
argue against this assertion that in the matter of a few month the
fasci sprang up all across the island from an organizational void. A contemporary observer felt that the fasci represented a shifting emphasis
toward resistance and self-defense. As we shall see below, resistance
and cooperatives were not lacking among the mutual benefit societies.
My own work supports this thesis. For example, a society of *zappatori*
(workers with the hoe) in Valguarnera became identified in 1893 as
the leading fascio organization. Yet it continued to list itself as a
mutual benefit society during and after the Fasci period. Francesco
Renda, "Origine e caratteristiche del movimento contadino della
Sicilia Occidentale," *Movimento Operaio* 7 (3–4 August 1955): 659–61;
Salvatore Francesco Romano, *Storia dei Fasci Siciliani* (Bari, 1959),
pp. 15–32; Romano, *La Sicilia,* pp. 469–72, 482; Enea Cavalieri, "I
Fasci dei Lavoratori a le condizioni della Sicilia," *Nuova Antologia,*
1 January 1894, pp. 130–31; Ciacchie Angiolini, *Socialismo e
socialisti in Italia* (Florence, 1919), p. 77. For activities of the Fasci
and other mutual benefit societies in Valguarnera, see "Elenco degli
individui che compongono La Società disciolta degli zappatori chi . . .
[sono?] i principi dei fasci dei lavoratori in Valguarnera [1894]" and
related reports, charters, and membership lists in Pubblica Sicurezza,
busta 8, Archivio di Stato–Caltanissetta.

6 For example, consider the occupations of the members of three of the
   five societies in Valguarnera in 1893–94. One society of 120 members
   was overwhelmingly made up of contadini. The other two, with 48 and
   110 members, were almost exclusively artisans, small merchants,
   teamsters, and the like. One of the remaining, the "Società Agricola"
   had 84 members, while the other, "Sons of Labor," listed 104 members. Thus, in this commune of less than 14,000, there were 466
   members of workers' societies. Shortly after this date a mass emigration
   began. By 1920 some 4,000 residents of the commune were reported
   as being abroad. See membership lists and reports in Pubblica Sicurezza,
   1893, busta 8, Archivio di Stato–Caltanissetta and Giacomo Magno
   Parroco, *Memorie storiche di Valguarnera Caropepe.* 2d ed. (Catania,
   1965), pp. 92–97.

7 Ross, *An Assembly of Good Fellows: Voluntary Association in History*
   (Westport, Conn., 1976), p. 16.

8   *Statuto della società degli operai di Villarosa* (Castrogiovanni, 1888).
9   *Statuto per L'Associazione di Mutuo Soccorso degli Operai di Avigliano* (Potenza, 1870).
10 *Statuto delle Società degli Operai di Villarosa; Statuto per L'Associazione di Mutuo Soccorso degli Operai di Potenza* (Potenza, 1870); and *Società di Mutuo Soccorso Tra gli Operai di Matera—Statuto e Regolamento* (Matera, 1874).
11 *Società . . . Matera; Statuto . . . Avigliano* and *Statuto per la Società di Mutuo Soccorso per gli Operai di Stigliano* (Matera, 1873).
12 *Statuto della Società Operaio di Lavello* (Melfi, 1870); *Statuto della Società Filarmonica ed Operaia per Mutuo Soccorso di Viggiano* (Potenza, 1971); and *Statuto dell'Associazione Operaia G. Mazzini in Miglionico* (Matera, 1886).
13 *Società Operaia di Mutuo Soccorso Sotto il Titolo Vittorio Emanuele Principe Ereditorio D'Italia in Brindisi di Montagna* (Potenza, 1889).
14 Report of the "Sotto Prefetture al Prefetture," 1901 R. Prefetture—Gabinetto,busta 192, Archivio di Stato—Palermo; "Constituzione e Statuto della Società Anonima Cooperativa 'La Coltura' fra falegnami e muratori residenti in Chiusa Sclafani" (1908), MS in Archivio di Stato—Palermo; *Statuto Sociale Dell'Azienda Concioni di Girgenti* (Girgenti, 1912), reprinted in Giovanni Raffiotta, *Storia della Sicilia Post—Unificazione* (Palermo, 1959), 3: 308; *Lega Generale fra Gl'Impiegati di Commercio Palermo: Statuto Sociale* (Palermo, 1892); Handbill of the Societa degli Impiegati Civili di Palermo 1901, in Gabinetto di Prefettura, busta 192, Archivio di Stato—Palermo; *Statuto e Regolamento della Società di Mutuo Soccorso fra i Militari dell'Arma dei Reali Carabinieri Congedati e Giubilati in Palermo* (Palermo, 1902).
15 "Minute Book" of the Società Agricola di Mutuo Soccorso di Alcara Li Fusi, 8 September 1891, 18 September 1892, and 15 January 1893; Report on the "Associazione Clericale nel Circondario di Termini," R. Prefettura Gabinetto—busta 124, Archivio di Stato—Palermo.
16 *Giornale di Sicilia* (April 1899), pp. 24-25.
17 *Società . . . Brindisi di Montagna.*
18 *Statuto . . . G. Mazzini in Miglionico; Statuto . . . Avigliano.*
19 "Minute Book" Società Agricola di Alcara Li Fusi, 8 January 1893; "Registro per le deliberazioni aduso della Società Agricola di Mutuo Soccorso di Alcara Li Fusi," 19 January 1892.
20 *Statuto . . . Villarosa; Statuto per la Società di Mutuo Soccorso per gli operai di Stigliano* (Matera, 1873).
21 *Statuto . . . Villarosa; Statuto . . . Avigliano; Società . . . Matera* (1874); *Società Matera* (1867).
22 "Minute Book" *Società . . . Alcara Li Fusi*, 16 January 1914.
23 *Statuto . . . Villarosa; Statuto . . . Avigliano; Società Matera,* (1874); *Società . . . Matera* (1867); "Minute Book" *Società . . . Alcara Li Fusi*, 16 January 1914.
24 Nitti, *Scritti,* pp. 328-30.

25 See the differences in assessments of the various fasci made by the Carabinieri and the local communal officials in R. Prefettura-Gabinetta, 1894, Archivio di Stato—Palermo and the reports of the Carabinieri Reale, "Statistica delle società operaie estanti in questo primo circondario," Potenza, 24 December 1872, Gabinetto di Prefetto, 288, Archivio di Stato—Potenza. "Minute Book" Società . . . Alcara Li Fusi, 8 March 1914; Signor Francesco Sole to the Prefetto di Basilicata, 30 July 1874, Gabinetto di Prefetto, 1874, Archivio di Stato—Potenza.

26 Robert T. Anderson, "Voluntary Associations in History," *American Anthropologist* 73 (1971): 209–22. Constance Smith and Anne Freedman, *Voluntary Associations: Perspectives on the Literature* (Cambridge, Mass., 1972), briefly summarizes the literature on the role of voluntary associations and social change. On the English Friendly Societies, see J. M. Baernreither, *English Associations of Working Men*, trans. Alice Taylor (London, 1889, 1966), pp. 155–295; P. H. J. H. Gosden, *Self-Help: Voluntary Associations in the 19th Century* (London, 1973), and Ross, *An Assembly of Good Fellows.*

27 *Statuto . . . Potenza; Statuto . . . Avigliano;* report of the "Sindaco Municipio di Episcopia Provence di Basilicata," 24 May 1889, Gabinetta di Prefettura, 441, Archivio di Stato—Potenza; Aldolfo Rossi, "Vantaggi e danni dell'emigrazione nel mezzogiorno dell'Italia," *Bollettino dell'Emigrazione* 13 (1908): 43–44; letter from supplicants in Cleveland to President of "La Società Agricola di Mutuo Soccorso in Alcara Li Fusi," 15 June 1919.

28 Rossi, "Vantaggi," pp. 25, 31, 91, and passim. George R. Gilkey, "The United States and Italy: Migration and Repatriation," *The Journal of Developing Areas* 11 (October 1967): 30–31.

29 "Le società italiane all'estero nel 1908," *Bollettino dell'Emigrazione* (1908), n. 24. There are obvious flaws in this survey, and thus the figures can only be taken as a general indication of activities of the emigrants. There appears to be some double counting of membership in instances where there was a local federation of societies. In the United States at least, important areas of Italian settlement are not included. For example, no figures for upstate New York cities are reported. See B. Frescura, "La mostra degli italiani all'estero all'esposizione internazionale di Milano nel 1906," *Bollettino dell'Emigrazione* n. 18 (1907): 100, for an account of the activities of these societies.

30 Benjamin Franklin was known to Italian laborers. His life and proverbs were the subject of a little book directed toward Italian workers. The work, written in both Italian and dialect, stressed religion, honesty, charity, sincerity, character, thrift, education, sobriety, and hard work. Carlo Leoni, *Libro pegli operai* (Venice, 1866). Workers in Laurenzana, Potenza, a commune which provided several early leaders for the Italian colony in Utica, N.Y., actually founded a "Benjamin Franklin Workers M.S. Society" in 1892. By 1895 it was reported to have 150 members. *Elenco delle società di mutuo soccorso*, p. 182.

Chapter 3

1   Leonard Covello, *The Social Background of the Italo-American School Child: A Study of the Southern Italian Family Mores and their Effect on the School Situation in Italy and America* (Leiden: E. J. Brill, 1967), pp. xxii–xxiii, 250, 273–74ff.

2   D. Mack Smith, "The Latifundia in Modern Sicilian History," *Proceedings of the British Academy* 51 (1965): 113; idem, *Italy, A Modern History* (Ann Arbor, Mich., 1959), pp. 55, 57; Maggiorino Ferraris, "La lotta contro l'analfebetismo," *Nuova Antologia*, 1 April 1907, p. 527; Will S. Monroe, "Progress of Education in Italy," U.S. Bureau of Education Report, 1906 (Washington, 1907), 1: 73–90.

3   Ministero della Pubblica Istruzione, Direzione Generale dell'Istruzione Primeria e Popolare, *L'istruzione primaria e popolare in Italia con speciale riguardo all'anno scolastico 1907–08* (Rome, 1910), 1: 108. These statistics are particularly impressive since they come after the 1904 law mandating six years of schooling in communes with over 4,000 inhabitants.

4   Sidney Sonnino, *I contadini in Sicilia*, vol. 2 of Leopoldo Franchetti and Sidney Sonnino, *La Sicilia nel 1876* (Florence, 1877), p. 196. *L'istruzione primaria e popolare*, 1: 102, 106; Walter A. Montgomery, "Education in Italy," *Bulletin of the Bureau of Education*, no. 36 (Washington, 1919), p. 5.

5   *L'istruzione primaria e popolare*, 1: 109, 816–19. From the way the statistics are presented, it is impossible to determine whether the school directors were also counted as teachers. It was assumed here that such double counting took place. If that is an error and if the directors also taught, then the teacher/student ratio for the private schools would be even more favorable.

6   Ibid., pp. 422–23.

7   Ibid., pp. 164, 567–69, 655–57.

8   Ibid., pp. 159, 160; Alessandro Lustig, "Le condizioni igieniche delle nostre scuole," *Nuova Antologia*, 1 June 1907, pp. 467–72. Davis quotes a communal counselor on the horrid state of schools in a village of about 8,000 in 1896: "The rooms in the boy's school are more suited to wineshops than school. The girls' rooms are like punishment cells: They are so lacking in light and air that in winter one of the teachers . . . is forced to teach school in her own home. It is a crime." Yet the construction of a new school building already proposed thirty years before did not come about until two more decades had passed. *Land and Family in Pisticci* (New York, 1973), p. 84.

9   Monroe, "Progress," pp. 77, 79–81; Amministrazione Provinciale Scholastica di Messina, "Graduatoria dei concorrenti ai posti vacanti nel ruolo provinciale degli insegnanti elementari e elenco dei posti vacanti" (Messina, 1914); *Germinal Corriere quindicianale del Circondario di Nicosia* (Nicosia), 1, no. 2, 1 July 1909; *L'istruzione primaria e popolare*, 1: 508.

10 "Relazione sulle scuole municipali di Palermo fatto al consiglio communale da Emanuele Paternò di Sessa" (Palermo, 1885), p. 37; Monroe, "Progress," p. 81; *L'istruzione primaria e popolare*, 1: 118-19; Gaetano Salvemini, "Il problema della Scuola popolare in provincia di Reggio Calabria," *Nuova Antologia*, 1 February 1910, pp. 529-33; Luigi Villari, *Italian Life in Town and Country* (New York, 1903), pp. 237-39.

11 Salvemini, "Il problema," pp. 529-30, 531; Emidio Agostinoni, "La lotta contro l'analfebetismo in Abruzzo," *Nuova Antologia*, October 1907, pp. 658-60; Luigi Izzo, *La finanza pubblica nel primo decennio dell'unita italiana* (Milan, 1962), pp. 93ff. *L'istruzione primaria e popolare*, 1: 187.

12 Salvemini, "Il problema," p. 531. See Table 3.6, items 5, 6, and 7, for the relationship between communal ownership of schools and illiteracy.

13 *L'istruzione primaria e popolare*, 1: 165-66; Enea Cavalleri, "I Fasci dei Lavoratori e le condizioni della Sicilia," *Nuova Antologia*, 1 January 1894, p. 138; Robert F. Foerster, *The Italian Emigration of Our Times* (Cambridge, 1919), pp. 88-93. Communal revenues declined starting in the latter part of the nineteenth century, as communal land holdings which previously produced rental income were sold off or illegally encroached upon by large landowners. Other sources of revenue never replaced the rent. The local land tax, largest and most ready source to replace the lost income, was seldom fully exploited in southern communes, whose administration was in the hands of local landholders. F. Voechting, *La Questione Meridionale* (Naples, 1955), pp. 110-17. Davis, *Land and Family*, p. 84, gives an example of a commune where this process retarded the development of schools.

14 *Inchiesta parlamentare sulle condizioni dei contadini nelle provincie meridionali e nella Sicilia*, 8 vols. (Rome, 1909-11), 2: 876, 4: 531, 5: 850; Aldolfo Rossi, "Vantaggi e danni dell'emigrazione nel mezzogiorno d'Italia," *Bollettino dell'Emigrazione*, no. 13, (1908), p. 67; Salvemini, "Il problema," p. 531; *L'istruzione primaria e popolare*, 1: 35; Ferraris, "La Lotta," p. 527.

15 Monroe, "Progress of Education," pp. 78-79; Giovanna Russo, *Bell e Lancaster in Sicilia: saggio storico pedagogico con documenti inediti* (Palermo, 1911); *L'istruzione primaria e popolare*, 1: 122, 124-43; Norman Douglas, *Old Calabria* (London, 1923), p. 185; Andrea Caronna Giarraffa, *La scuola elementare popolare maschile* (Palermo, 1885), passim. Fifteen years after the unification of Italy and the new national heroes it produced, history lessons in the first elementary class still centered around the exploits of Christopher Columbus. It was prophetic relevancy for young Sicilians, who would soon join the mass migrations to the New World themselves.

16 Giovanni Scaminaci Piccione Dei Frangipane, *Note ed osservazioni sulla scuola primaria di Castelvetrano* (Palermo, 1893), pp. 7, 11, 12ff.

17 Salvemini, "Il problema," p. 528.

18 Ibid., pp. 528-29; Rossi, "Vantaggi e danni," p. 47.

19 Salvemini, "Il problema," p. 528.
20 Vicenzo Ragusa, *Le scuole—officine: conferenza agli operai di Palermo
    nel Febbraio 1884* (Palermo, 1884), pp. 10ff.; *Giornale di Sicilia*,
    20-21 April 1899.
21 *Giornale di Sicilia*, 3-4 April 1899, 6-7 April 1899, 9-10 April 1899;
    Monroe, "Progress of Education," p. 89.
22 Salvemini, "Il problema," pp. 521-26.
23 Dei Frangipane, *Note ed osservazione*, pp. 5-6; R. Prefetto di Palermo
    al Ministero Interno, 30 May 1893, R. Prefettura-Gabinetta 1861-1905,
    busta 16; R. Questura al R. Prefetto, 14 November 1900 and 1 Decem-
    ber 1900, R. Prefettura-Gabinetta 1861-1905, busta 183, Archivio di
    Stato—Palermo.
24 Roger Thabault, *Education and Change in a Village Community:
    Mazierse-en-Gatine, 1848-1914*, trans. Peter Tregear (New York, 1971),
    pp. 67-68, 94, 128ff.
25 Margaret Carlyle, *The Awakening of Southern Italy* (London, 1962),
    p. 11; *Associazione pro biblioteche popolari di Palermo: regolamento
    per le biblioteche scholastiche nelle scuole elementari* (Palermo, 1909);
    Statuto (Palermo, 1909); "Relazione per l'anno 1909; Convengo meri-
    dionale delle biblioteche popolari e delle sezioni dell'U.M.N." (May
    1910).
26 "Il nuovo patronato scholastico in Castelvetrano," *La Vita Nuova*,
    16 January 1913; G. B. Ferrigno, "La biblioteca communale," ibid.
27 "Statuto organico del Circolo Cattolico di S. Mauro Castelverde,"
    typescript, n.d., R. Prefettura-Gabinetta 1861-1905, 1902, busta 192,
    Archivio di Stato—Palermo; "Prima lettera pastorale di Monsignor
    Mariano Palermo al clero e popolo della Diocesi di Piazza Armerina"
    (Palermo, 1887), Pubblica Sicurezza 2, Archivio di Stato—Caltanissetta,
    pp. 20-21; Salvatore de Lorenzo, *Cultura popolare religiosa in Calabria*
    (Reggio Calabria, 1913), reprinted in Pietro Borozomati, *Aspetti
    religiosi e storia del movimento cattolico in Calabria 1860-1919* (Rome,
    1967), pp. 443-558.
28 Rossi, "Vantaggi e danni," pp. 75-76; Agostinoni, "La lotta," pp. 656-
    57; *L'istruzione primaria e popolare*, 1: 422-23.
29 Salvemini, "Il problema," p. 526; Antonio Mangano to Pasquale Villari,
    letter printed in *Nuova Antologia*, 1 September 1907, p. 5.
30 "Terza relazione annuale del commissariato generale sui servizi dell'-
    emigrazione . . . ," *Bollettino dell'Emigrazione*, no. 7 (1904), pp. 55-58;
    "Relazione sui servizi dell'emigrazione per il periodo Aprile 1905-
    Aprile 1906."
31 *Bollettino dell'Emigrazione*, no. 7 (1906), pp. 37-38; "Commissariato
    generale dell'emigrazione e la lotta conto l'analfabetismo degli
    emigranti," *Bollettino dell'Emigrazione*, no. 6 (1919), pp. 5-15;
    L'istruzione primaria e popolare, 1: 449-50; "Uncle Sam's Debt to the
    Italians," *Il Pensiero Italiano* (Utica, N.Y.), 26 September 1914;
    Ferraris, "La Lotta," pp. 526-27.

The postwar educational program reflected a consensus among many Americans and Italians that agriculture was the most suitable activity for peasant immigrants and the best way of alleviating problems of Italians in urban settings. It also was motivated by Italian colonial schemes in Africa.

32 Douglas, *Old Calabria,* p. 48; Camillio Corradini, "Il compito dell'-esercito nella lotta contro L'analfabetismo," *Nuova Antologia,* 16 March 1907, pp. 310–11.

33 Monroe, "Progress of Education," pp. 81–83. Philippe Aries traces the history of the emergence of this dual educational system in Europe, with primary education for the lower classes and the separate secondary system for the middle class, in his *Centuries of Childhood* (New York, 1962), pp. 306–14, 334–36.

34 Monroe, pp. 82–83, 79–81.

35 Ministero di Agricoltura, Industria e Commercio, Direzione Generale della Statistica e del Lavoro, Ufficio Centrale di Statistica, *Notizie sommarie sugli istituti per l'istruzione media e normale negli anni scolastici dal 1909–10 al 1911–12* (Rome, 1916), pp. 69–89; "Verbale di deliberazione del consiglio comunale di Melfi, 3 July 1892," Archivio di Stato—Potenza; "Verbale di deliberazione del consiglio comunale di Termini Imerese, 17 September 1901," R. Prefettura-Gabinetta, busta 199, Archivio di Stato—Palermo.

36 Report to the Minister of Agriculture from the R. Prefettura—1891, Sezione Amministrativa—*"statistiche" no. 3805, Archivio di Stato—Cal*-tanissetta; *Annuario-societa dei licenziati della R. Scuola Mineraria di Caltanissetta,* 1 (1885): 33–35, 37–38, 111; *Notizie sommarie sugli istituti,* pp. 72 ff. The poor showing of Calabria in technical education is in part a product of the absence of schools in this field. Luigi Izzo, *La popolazione calabrese nel secolo XIX: demografia ed economica* (Naples, 1965), pp. 69–70.

Chapter 4

1 Oscar Handlin's essay "Old Immigration and New," in his *Race and Nationality in American Life* (New York, 1957), is a forceful critique of the alleged differences between the groups of immigrants. Also see Maldwyn Allen Jones, *American Immigration* (Chicago, 1960), pp. 177 ff. The place of this idea in American social thought and its influence on immigration restriction legislation can be found woven through John Higham, *Strangers in the Land: Patterns of American Nativism, 1860–1925* (New York, 1963).

2 Edward C. Banfield, *The Unheavenly City Revisited* (Boston, 1974), pp. 65–66.

3 Eric R. Wolf, *Peasant Wars of the Twentieth Century* (New York, 1969), pp. xii–xv, is an anthropologist's definition of *peasant* and

the distinction made between peasants and farmers.

4 In light of recent studies that emphasize the peasantlike character of New England puritan settlements, Banfield's assertions of differences between these immigrants and later peasant settlers require an analysis and justification which is lacking. See as examples Kenneth Lockeridge, *A New England Town, The First Hundred Years* (New York, 1970), and Sumner Chilton Powell, *Puritan Village: The Formation of a New England Town* (New York, 1965). Banfield does not make clear where enough townsmen could be found to make the eighteenth- and nineteenth-century emigrations different from later movements, or how the peasants from northern and western Europe were different than those from southern and eastern Europe. The classic work on early migration is Marcus Lee Hansen, *The Atlantic Migration, 1607–1860* (Cambridge, 1940).

5 It would be an anachronism to attempt to place the immigrants in Banfield's class categories. He defines the classes by contemporary features, many of which are inappropriate for the immigrants living in another era and society. Banfield, *Unheavenly City*, pp. 56–60.

Chapter 5

1 Aldolfo Rossi, "Vantaggi e danni dell'emigrazione nel Mezzogiorno d'Italia," *Bollettino dell'Emigrazione*, no. 13 (1908), pp. 9–10, 52, 57, 61, 68–71; Giovan Battista Raja, *Il femmeno emigrazione siciliano con speciale riguardo al quinquennio 1902–1906* (Palermo, 1908), pp. 28–35 ff. *Reports of the Consular Officers of the United States: Emigration and Immigration* (Washington, D.C., 1887); Giuseppina Scanni, "L'emigrazione delle donne e dei fanciulli dalla Provincia di Caserta," *Bollettino dell'Emigrazione*, no. 13 (1913), pp. 14–15; Emilio Sereni, *Il capitalismo nelle Campagne* (Turin, 1948), p. 394.

2 Giuseppe Bruccolire, *La Sicilia di oggi* (Rome, 1913), p. 94; Robert E. Park and Herbert A. Miller, *Old World Traits Transplanted* (New York, 1921), p. 146; John S. MacDonald and Leatrice D. MacDonald, "Italian Migration to Australia: Manifest Functions of Bureaucracy Versus Latent Functions of Informal Networks," *Journal of Social History* 3, no. 3 (Spring 1970): 249–75; and "Chain Migration, Ethnic Neighborhood Formation and Social Networks," *The Milbank Memorial Fund Quarterly* 41, no. 1 (January 1964). In the latter article the MacDonalds assert, following a popular tradition in Utica, that "the great majority of the Southern Italians came from Laurenzana and adjacent towns in Basilicata" who settled in that New York State city. In fact, both the parish records and the naturalization records agree that the greatest number came from Apulia. By comparison, Basilicata falls behind all but one of the southern regions in the size of its contribution to the immigration to Utica.

3 "Registro della domanda di nulla osta per ottenere passaporto per
   l'estero," Archivi Comunali, Termini Imerese and Villarosa.
4 Ibid., and "Census of Italians in St. Paul, Minnesota by Rev. N. C.
   Odone—1907," Odone Papers, Immigrant Archives, University of
   Minnesota, Passport lists from Nicosia (1904–12), Serradifalco (1904–
   26), and Villarosa (1911–14). All communes in the interior of Sicily
   display this mixed pattern of heavy migration to half a dozen or so
   more prominent destinations, and at least equally heavy departures for
   less popular ones.
5 Naturalization petitions, Oneida County Clerk's Office. The identification of Old World origins of immigrants is one of the more intractable
   problems that plagues the student of historical migrations. Naturalization records used above prove to be one manageable source for this
   information on Italian immigrants. They are obviously selective, in
   that they only include those who settled more or less permanently and
   are usually compiled many years after the arrival of the individual
   applicants. Where possible, this study has relied on marriage records
   kept at Italian parishes. The form in common use at the turn of the
   century called for the place of baptism of each of the principals of the
   marriage to be recorded. Rochester priests consistently interpreted
   this as calling for a designation of the commune in which the sacrament
   took place. This record is interpreted here as the "commune of origin."
   In Utica this item often merely consisted of the useless designation
   "Italy." This necessitated the use of the naturalization data. The
   utilization of this data rests on the assumption that the origins of
   partners making marriages in America represent a reasonable approximation of the total immigrant population in the city under study.
   This author has found nothing in his research to challenge this assumption.
6 Rudolph J. Vecoli, "Contadini in Chicago: A Critique of 'The Uprooted,'"
   Journal of American History 51, no. 3 (December 1964): 406, 408,
   412–13, 416–17.
7 Bianco, *The Two Rosetos* (Bloomington, Ind., 1974), p. 21.
8 Blake McKelvey, *Rochester: The Quest for Quality, 1890–1925* (Cambridge, 1956), p. 7; U.S. Bureau of the Census: *Fifteenth Census* (1930);
   Population (Washington, D.C., 1932), vol. 3, pt. 1, pp. 300–04, pt. 2,
   pp. 1316, 1359.
9 Karl E. and Alma F. Taeuber, *Negroes in Cities* (New York, 1969),
   pp. 195–245, is a convenient survey and methodological discussion of
   this and other measures of residential concentration. Stanley Lieberson,
   in his *Ethnic Patterns in American Cities* (New York, 1963), uses the
   index of dissimilarity extensively. His figures, even when he uses ward-
   size units as he does for pre-1930 data, are not exactly comparable.
   He uses native whites as the base against which to measure the degree
   of concentration of each ethnic group. Thus, he is measuring the degree
   to which a group's residential patterns deviate from those of native

whites. This study measures the individual group's clustering against the total population. Lieberson's choice of a more select baseline results in generally higher index values for the ten cities in his study (see his appendix F).

10 Robert W. DeForest and Lawrence Veiller, eds., *The Tenement House Problem: Including the Report of the New York State Tenement House Commission of 1900* (New York, 1903), 1: 151–52.

11 McKelvey, *Quest,* pp. 36–41, 242–43, 244–47; *La Luce,* 1 August 1903.

12 McKelvey, *Quest,* pp. 54–72, 272–90; U.S. Bureau of the Census: *Thirteenth Census* (1910); *Manufactures* (Washington, D.C., 1912), 9: 711–12, 759–60, 763.

13 Josef J. Barton, *Peasants and Strangers* (Cambridge, Mass., 1975).

14 Virginia Yans-McLaughlin, "A Flexible Tradition: South Italian Immigrants Confront a New Work Experience," *Journal of Social History* 7, no. 4 (Summer 1974): 429–45, and "Patterns of Work and Family Organization: Buffalo's Italians," *The Journal of Interdisciplinary History* 11, no. 2 (Autumn 1971): 299–314; Louise C. Odencrantz, *Italian Women in Industry: A Study of Conditions in New York City* (New York, 1919), p. 29, and Robert A. Woods and Robert J. Kennedy, *Young Working Girls* (Boston, 1913). In 1909 and 1910, *The Survey* published a series of articles on female employment in various cities.

15 Louise A. Tilly, "Comments on the Yans-McLaughlin and Davidoff Papers," *Journal of Social History* 7, no. 4 (Summer 1974): 452–59. The 1901 manuscript census schedules are in the communal archives at Villa Vallelonga.

16 Warner and Burke, "Cultural Change and the Ghetto," *Journal of Contemporary History* 4 (October 1969): 173–87; Chudacoff, "A New Look at Ethnic Neighborhoods: Residential Dispersion and the Concept of Visibility in a Medium-Sized City," *The Journal of American History* 60, no. 1 (June 1973): 76–93. The residential pattern of Italians in Omaha and my three cities conforms in a general way to those reported for Chicago by Humbert S. Nelli, *Italians in Chicago* (New York, 1970), pp. 22–54. Joseph P. Lyford, *The Airtight Cage* (New York, 1966).

Chapter 6

1 Irving Child, *Italian or American? The Second Generation in Conflict* (New Haven, Conn., 1943). Child's study deals with the psychological costs and rewards of assimilation on the part of second-generation Italian-Americans.

2 *Il Messaggero,* 1 August 1926; *Il Pensiero Italiano,* 3 July 1914. An editor in Utica assured the colony that a few years spent away from Italy could not "destroy the vigorous and determined impression that

distinguishes us." He reassured them that "the Italianness, which we enjoy, is blood filtered in our beings through centuries." He was not so sanguine about the children living here, so he called for a school to ensure their Italian heritage; it would also help the immigrants to learn new ways appropriate to their lives here (*La Luce*, 30 August 1902). A Rochester paper supported a Sons of Italy campaign to establish scholarships for Italian children in the United States as a means of destroying the stereotype of Italians as an inferior race. The recipients of such help, by advancing their schooling, would become exceptions who would destroy the rule and carry on the honor of the race and mother country. *La Stampa Unita*, 3 November 1922.

3 *Il Piccolo Messaggero*, April 1926, pp. 19-22.

4 *La Stampa*, 16 March 1923, 5 March 1926, 4 April 1924; *L'Avvenire*, 30 May 1903, 12 January 1901; *La Stampa Unita*, 12 March 1926. On a national level this spirit of participation in and contribution to a great new civilization found expression in the activities of the Italy America Society. In 1928 Mario Cosenza, president of the Italian Teachers Association, announced to the membership that:

> the grandeur that was Rome is closely related to the grandeur that is America . . . .
>
> We are here in America, on the threshold of newer, mightier, better things. We have achieved a material prosperity such as the world has never seen. We are now ready to enter upon the development of a civilization such as the world has never seen. Into this newer civilization we, as Americans, want to bring what is best and most significant in the old, but ever new, civilizations of other countries. To this newer civilization we desire to contribute that Roman and Italian quality of mind, that composite of qualities embracing sturdiness, tenacity, courage, clear vision and loyalty; that accuracy of expression; that love of beauty and of song; that enthusiasm, that fine, keen-edged, penetrating intellect which, in every age and in every art and science, seems to have been the leaven that hath leavened the whole mass.
>
> To this newer, stronger, and finer civilization which is coming to birth in the United States, we must sincerely desire that the contribution made by the Italian mind and the Italian genius be second to none. [*Bulletin and Italiana* (of the Italy America Society) 11, no. 8 (August 1928): 173-74]

The Polish-American press advocated a similar definition of "Americanization." See Adam Urbanski, "Americanism and the Polish-American Press, 1916-1925 (Ph.D. diss., University of Rochester, 1974), especially chaps. 4 and 5.

5 *La Luce*, 26 April 1920, 23 August 1902, 7 March 1904, 30 April 1904; *L'Avvenire*, 26 April 1902, 28 February 1903; *La Stampa*, 25 July 1929; *La Stampa Unita*, 4 January 1924.

6 *L'Avvenire*, 26 April 1902; *La Luce*, 10 September 1904, 14 January
   1905; *La Stampa Unita*, 4 January 1924.
7 *L'Avvenire*, 30 May 1903, 2 December 1905; *La Luce*, 20 August 1904;
   La Stampa, 18 and 25 March 1921. Clement Lanni frequently pointed
   out press use of Americanization exams and ceremonies as humorous
   "local color stories." He stressed that while the misstatements and
   clumsy English of prospective citizens may have amused American
   readers, such stories tended to discourage immigrants from applying
   for citizenship for fear of subjecting themselves to such ridicule. Still,
   Lanni, a staunch Republican, could not resist telling one of these
   stories himself. Among Italians in Rochester a stock answer to the request for the name of the mayor, governor, or even the president was
   "George Aldridge." To those familiar with the power and career of
   this long-time Republican city boss, the answer has a certain black
   humor about it. Clement G. Lanni, "The history of the Italians of
   Rochester from 1876 to 1926," *The Rochester Historical Society
   Publication Fund Series* 6 (1927): 187-88.
8 *L'Avvenire*, 15 April 1905, 8 February 1902, 9 July 1904; *La Stampa
   Unita*, 23 May 1924, 12 October 1927, 12 January 1923; *La Luce*,
   16 August 1902, 23 August 1902, 10 May 1911.
9 Andrea Caronna Giarraffa, *La scuola elementare popolare maschile*
   (Palermo, 1885); *La Luce*, 9 January, 15 October 1904; *L'Avvenire*,
   28 October 1905; *La Stampa*, 12 October 1926, 20 (27?) April 1928.
10 *L'Avvenire*, 18 March, 16 September 1905.
11 *Il Messaggero*, 15 May, 15 July 1926. This concern for the good reputation
   of Italy and recognition of her contributions to civilization culminated in
   New York City in the establishment by the Italian community, in cooperation with Columbia University, of the "Casa Italiana." This institution carried on a program that promoted Italy and Italian culture. The Casa also
   collected materials for the serious study of Italian history and served as a
   general information center on contemporary Italy. In the 1930s it turned to
   the study of Italian life in New York City as well. Federal Writers' Project
   (W.P.A.), *The Italians of New York* (New York, 1938), pp. 116-18. For the
   initiative behind the founding of "Casa Italiana," see *Revista d'Italia ed'America* 3, nos. 13-14 (January-February 1925): 51-52, and "La casa italiana
   presso la Columbia University," *Revista d'Italia ed'America* 4, no. 3 (March
   1926): 70-71. *Il Pensiero Italiano*, 14 June 1919.
12 *La Stampa*, 2, 9 April 1926; *Il Messaggero*, 1 May 1926; *Il Piccolo
   Messaggero*, January 1926.
13 *La Stampa Unita*, 2 December 1921; *La Luce*, 25 April 1903. Joshua
   A. Fishman has observed that the English language never had the kind
   of intimate association with American nationalism which characterizes
   many European tongues. Americans accept it pragmatically as the common medium of communication rather than "because it is beautiful,
   divine or indivisible from American traditions." Even the most ardent
   Americanizers seem to have realized this distinction, for with the single
   exception of the short, intensive Americanization craze immediately

after World War I, their promtion of English has been entirely based on utilitarian grounds. *Language Loyalty in the United States* (The Hague, 1966), pp. 29–30.

14 Rev. Andreis to Rev. S. N. Odone, Baltimore, Md., 11 January 1900, Odone Papers, Immigrant Archives, University of Minnesota.

15 *La Luce,* 7 March 1914. By October the paper was searching for alternative methods of preserving Italian in the colony, pointing to a flowering of the Italian language in centers across the American continent. Nearby Syracuse University hired a professor of Italian whose offerings were increasing in popularity. *La Luce,* 3 October 1914.

16 Jerre Mangione, *Mount Allegro* (New York, 1952), pp. 22, 51–55.

17 *La Stampa Unita,* 9 September 1927; *La Luce,* 26 December 1903. Rizzo is an interesting example of the importance of sorting out generations and dates of arrival, as well as economic and educational backgrounds, in dealing with immigrant attitudes toward "Americanization." He was educated in a Protestant institute and normal school in a mining area of Sicily which, in the late nineteenth century, was known for its social radicalism promoted by a Waldensian minister. After service in the Italian Quartermaster Corps in World War I, he held the position of principal and teacher of Italian language and literature at a technical school. In 1923 his socialist background made it obligatory for him to leave the country. When he criticized the colony for its attitude toward the Italian language, he was a newly arrived intellectual speaking to second-generation sons and daughters of working-class immigrants.

Rizzo attempted to publish a literary magazine in the 1920s, wrote short stories, and acted as a free-lance journalist. In the 1930s he attended an American high school and the University of Rochester while he specialized in teaching Italian language and literature concurrently at several Rochester schools. He also served as "educational director" of the Eleonora Duse Italian Women's Club. The club, led by his wife, concentrated on the diffusion of Italian culture in a pluralist formula of "Italian Americanism." *"L'Italiana* 2, no. 6 (June 1939): 23–24. For the interplay between socialist organization and the Waldensians in Grotte, see Salvatore Francesco Romano, *Storia dei Fasci Siciliani* (Bari, 1959), pp. 70–72.

18 *La Luce,* 3 October 1914; *La Stampa Unita,* 9 September 1927; *La Stampa,* 24 August, 14 September 1923, 2 July 1926. In 1909 the Milwaukee, Wisconsin, school board introduced Italian into schools where enrollment was 75 percent Italian and at least 100 children requested it. Sixty students were the minimum necessary for the upper elementary grades. Twenty of the students were non-Italian. The initial enrollment in 1909 was 609. In 1915 there were Italian classes in two schools taught by three teachers to 1,109 students. In Utica during the 1920s, this story was used as an example of what 7,000 Italians could do in a largely German community through unity and dedication to their mother tongue. G. E. DiPalma-Castiglione, "Vari centri italiani

negli stati di Indiana, Ohio, Michigan, Minnesota e Wisconsin," *Bollettino dell'Emigrazione,* no. 6 (1915).

19 *L'Avvenire,* 12 March, 4 June, 12 November 1904, 4 November 1905; *La Luce,* 13 September 1913, 14 November, 5 December 1914; *La Stampa Unita,* 30 July 1920, 12 January 1923; *Il Messaggero,* 1 May 1926; *La Stampa,* 16 April 1920.

20 *La Stampa,* 5 May 1922; Robert F. Foerster, *The Italian Emigration of Our Times* (Cambridge, 1919), pp. 486–91. In one sentence Foerster does state that "frequently the emigrants are urged to refrain from naturalization abroad; or satisfaction is taken in the circumstance that they commonly do refrain." Yet the whole tenor of his presentation supports his later conclusion about the concern of the Italian government for facilitating the rapid resumption of citizenship by repatriated emigrants. "It assumes, what doubtless is true, that there must be many emigrants whose naturalization in other countries is primarily for personal convenience, and not the sign of a new allegiance of the heart. It does not desire to discourage such naturalization." See also Tommaso Tittoni, *Italy's Foreign and Colonial Policy,* trans. Bernardo Quaranta di San Severino (London, 1914), p. 185 and passim.

Certainly Italian government discouragement of naturalization did not show itself in the press of the three colonies. Regular reminders of military obligations which Italians owed Italy might be considered one exception. The periodic announcements made by the Italian consuls of military call-ups for various age-groups may have actually promoted naturalization.

21 *Il Pensiero Italiano,* 5 October 1918, 4 and 11 January, 21 June 1919; *La Stampa,* 27 May 1921.

22 *L'Avvenire,* 5 and 25 April 1903; Mangione, pp. 213–31. This interpretation of the development of an Italian-American identity is compatible with Theodore C. Blegen's presentation of Norwegian-Americanism as "a gradual normal process of change, adaptation and growth." Both interpretations see immigrant life as dynamic rather than static. *Norwegian Migration to America: The American Transition* (Northfield, Minn., 1940), pp. 70–74.

The realization of a long-term commitment to life in the United States appeared in Utica as early as 1902 in a remarkable newspaper column which surveyed with satisfaction the progress and success made by the colony thanks to the industry of the early settlers. The author asserted that they were at first ignored, then actively opposed. Yet they acquired property, opened stores, and moved aggressively into many areas of life in America. Italian industry soon won respect in many circles. By this date, part of the colony had already entered into the process of assimilation that was to produce the future American type. The column ended with an appeal to all fellow Italians to make themselves successful, a task compatible with both the new and the old cultures. *La Luce,* 23 August 1902.

Chapter 7

1   A few careful observers were cognizant of the contribution which a
    steady flow of new arrivals made in producing an appearance of stability
    in immigrant colonies and the resultant obscuring of both individual
    and group changes taking place among the earlier arrivers. See Kate
    Holladay Claghorn, "Our Immigrants and Our Selves," *The Atlantic
    Monthly* 86, no. 516 (1900): 538.
2   George Schiro, *Americans by Choice* ([Utica], 1940), chap. 2; Blake
    McKelvey, "The Italians of Rochester, an Historical Review," *Rochester
    History* 22, no. 4 (October 1960): 2–5.
3   "My Experience as an Immigrant," *The Common Good* 6, no. 4 (Jan-
    uary 1913): 104–07; 6, no. 6 (March 1913): 187–89; 6, no. 9 (June
    1913): 271–74.
4   Schiro, p. 93
5   "Incorporation papers—membership corporations," on file at the office
    of the New York Secretary of State, 30 December 1889, 36p–77;
    Schiro, chap. 2; *Utica City Directory.*
6   "Incorporation papers," 27 February 1895, 54p–59; Schiro, chap. 2;
    Utica City Directory. The first successful and long-lived society to be
    founded in Kansas City was the "Società de Mutuo Soccorso Italo-
    Americani," established in 1891 by "Professor" Langieri. It continued
    to prosper during the 1920s. *Il Messaggero,* 1 May 1926.
7   "Incorporation papers," 7 October 1914, 135q–102; 22 September
    1904, 59q–125; *L'Avvenire,* 31 January 1903, 12 March 1904; *La Luce,*
    30 July 1904.
8   "Incorporation papers," 28 August 1900, 38q–28; 7 October 1914,
    135q–102.
9   "Incorporation papers," 15 April 1904, 57q–109; 7 October, 1914,
    135q–102; *L'Avvenire,* 3 June, 1 July 1905.
10 *L'Avvenire,* 8 June, 21 December 1901, 2 August, 3 October, 31
    October 1903; *La Luce,* 23 August, 20 September 1902, 17 September
    1904; *L'Avvenire,* 4 January, 27 September, 6 December 1902, 2
    August 1903.
11 Jack C. Ross, *An Assembly of Good Fellows* (Westport, Conn., 1976),
    p. 16; "Le Società Italiane negli Stati Uniti dell'America del Nord nel
    1910," *Bollettino dell'Emigrazione,* no. 4 (1912), pp. 27, 36–37;
    L'Avvenire, 13 June 1903, 19 March 1904; *La Luce,* 2 and 16 January
    1904; *L'Avvenire,* 17 June 1905; *La Luce,* 1 November 1902;
    L'Avvenire, 15 November 1902, 1 January 1904; *La Luce,* 17 October
    1903, 3 September 1904, 20 May 1911.
12 The number of residents from a given commune is not necessarily
    directly related to the speed with which exclusive territorial groups
    formed. The largest single group in Rochester, those from Valguarnera,
    Sicily, did not found a society for their *paesani* until 1933. For evidence
    on the competition among societies in Utica, see the references in note

10 above. The story of the San Bartolo society was recounted in an interview with its longtime president Joseph Fortino, 20 December 1967.

13 Robert F. McNamara, *The Diocese of Rochester: 1868-1968* (Rochester, 1968), pp. 210-11; *The Rochester Directory* 66 (1915): 1515a; "Incorporation papers," 13 December 1917, 162q-69, 29 March 1916, 148q-56.

14 "Incorporation papers," 2 September 1886, 28p-73, 29 October 1886, 28p-115, 15 November 1894, 53q-63, 18 November 1898, 30q-78; *La Luce*, 1 November 1902; *L'Avvenire*, 17 January, 8 November, 6 and 20 December 1902, 13 June 1903, 11 October 1902; "Incorporation papers," 11 March 1914, 130q-104, 27 November 1914, 137q-5; Schiro, *Americans by Choice*, pp. 99-100; *L'Avvenire*, 1 May 1901, 25 December 1902, 15 August 1903, 15 August 1903, 15 April 1905.

15 *L'Avvenire*, 15 December 1900, 5 October, 16 November 1901; *La Luce*, 28 December 1901; *L'Avvenire*, 21 June, 22 November 1902, 2 August 1903, 2 December 1905; *La Luce*, 28 March 1903; *L'Avvenire*, 17 June, 1 July, 12 August 1905.

16 *L'Avvenire*, 8 February, 23 August, 22 November 1902; *La Luce*, 16 August, 22 November 1902, 7 December 1901; *L'Avvenire*, 17 August 1901, 29 March, 10 and 17 May, 26 April 1902, 13 February 1903; *La Luce*, 18 January, 12 April, 24 May, 9 and 16 August 1902; *L'Avvenire*, 22 November 1902.

17 Schiro, p. 87; *La Luce*, 17 September 1904; "Incorporation papers," 11 April 1906, 60q-79; *L'Avvenire*, 18 November, 9 December 1905, 30 January 1904.

18 *L'Avvenire*, 29 April 1905, 24 November 1900; *La Luce*, 17 September 1904.

19 *L'Avvenire*, 6, 13, and 20 May 1905; *Utica City Directory.*

20 *L'Avvenire*, 12, 19, and 26 August, 9 September, 7 and 28 October, 1 and 22 July 1905. It is interesting that the paper used the word *genetliaco* which usually referred to the birthday of a royal personage, in connection with Dr. Palmieri's party for his daughter.

21 *Il Messaggero dell'Ordine*, 16 April 1932; *Il Messaggero*, 1 and 15 February 1930, *La Stampa Unita*, 19 June 1920, 13 January 1922, 30 May 1924, 2 January 1926; *La Stampa*, 13 February 1925.

22 B. Frescura, "La mostra degli Italiani all'estero, all'esposizione internazionale di Milano nel 1906," *Bollettino dell'Emigrazione*, no. 18 (1907), p. 101; Marie J. Concistre, "Adult Education in a Local Area; A Study of a Decade in the Life and Education of the Adult Italian Immigrant in East Harlem, New York City" (Ph.D. diss., New York University, 1943), pp. 236, 242-45; *Atlantica* 13, no. 4 (June 1932): 166.

23 *Il Pensiero Italiano*, 18 July 1914; *La Luce*, 12 December 1914, 13 and 20 February 1915. By the 1920s there had been a schism in both the New York State and the national organizations which led to the

founding of a competing society, the Independent Order of the Sons of Italy. By the end of the decade the new organization was making significant headway in Utica and Rochester, where four lodges appeared by 1926. At the same time the Sons of Italy were in the initial stages of organization in Kansas City.

24 *La Luce*, 20 February 1915.

25 Ibid., 25 September 1915.

26 Ibid.

27 *La Luce*, 27 June 1903; William Pizzoglio, "St. Mary of Mount Carmel Church, Utica, New York: Its History and Progress from the Beginning to the Present 1896–1946" ([Utica], 1947): *La Luce*, 10 September 1910, 17 and 24 June, 1 and 15 July 1911, 7 November 1914.

28 *La Stampa*, 23 July, 13 and 27 August, 3 and 10 September, 10 December 1920.

29 Ibid.

30 Ibid., 25 March, 29 July 1921, 1 September 1922, 12 January 1923.

31 *La Stampa*, 12 January, 12 October 1923; *Il Piccolo Messaggero*, February 1926; *Il Messaggero*, 15 January 1929.

32 *La Stampa*, 9 January 1925; *Il Piccolo Messaggero*, February 1926.

33 *La Stampa Unita*, 4 January, 14 and 28 March, 4, 18 and 25 April, 2, 9, 23 and 30 May 1924.

34 McKelvey, "The Italians," pp. 15–19; Lanni, "The History," p. 198; *La Stampa Unita*, 10 December 1926; interview with George Schiro, January 1968; *Il Messaggero*, 15 August 1926, 15 March 1929; *La Stampa Unita*, 22 October 1920; Pizzoglio, "Mt. Carmel," p. 26; "Jubilee Book, Our Lady of Mt. Carmel Church—Rochester," pp. 21–22. In 1927 about one-half of the membership of Rochester's Italian Business Men's Association was reported to be "college men." It held its third annual dance during the Christmas holidays so that the numerous Italian college students who were home on vacation could join the festivities. *La Stampa Unita*, 15 December 1927.

35 *La Stampa Unita*, 8 May 1920, 4 April 1924, 19 November 1926, 4 November 1927, 8 November 1928, 29 May 1929; McKelvey, "The Italians," p. 16.

36 *La Stampa Unita*, 24 June 1921, 2 January 1926; *Rochester Italian Directory* (Rochester, 1931).

37 I am indebted for guidance on this point to a number of colleagues who worked on a project studying immigration, education, and social change directed by Timothy L. Smith. The importance of nationalism among Slovak immigrants and the role they played in the movement to create an independent Slovakia are well recounted in Mark Stolarik, "The Role of American Slovaks in the Creation of Czecho-Slovakia" (M.A. thesis, University of Ottawa, 1967). William Galush first alerted me to this difference in the meaning of nationalism among various immigrant groups. His unpublished paper, "Education in the Immigrant Ghetto: The Development of Two Polish-American Communities,"

pp. 29–31, 36, documents the decline in Old World patriotic nationalism after World War I as a central theme of organizational life. The new
postwar orientation tended to center on local activities and concerns.
The differing intensities of nationalism in the religious life of Poles and
Italians can be judged from Victor R. Greene, "For God and Country:
The Origins of Slavic Catholic Self-Consciousness in America," *Church
History* 35 (December 1966): 446–60, and Rudolph J. Vecoli, "Pre-
lates and Peasants: Italian Immigrants and the Catholic Church," *Jour-
nal of Social History* 2 (1969): 217–68. Joseph P. O'Grady, *How the
Irish Became American* (New York, 1973), pp. 190 ff., presents a
similar interpretation of the impact of the struggle for independence in
Ireland on the Irish community in America.

Chapter 8

1 *L'Avvenire*, 7 March 1903; *La Luce*, 16 July 1904.
2 *L'Avvenire*, 5 April 1903; *Herald* (Rochester), 7 February 1893.
3 *La Luce*, 14 February 1903, 16 April, 21 May, 2 and 23 July, 22 October 1904, 3 June 1911; *L'Avvenire*, 24 May 1902, 20 May 1905; *Bollettino dell'Emigrazione*, no. 7 (1904), pp. 145–47, no. 5 (1907),
   pp. 68–69, and no. 13, p. 125. Development of economic institutions
   lagged in the more slowly growing colonies of Rochester and Kansas
   City. Neither colony had an agent of the Bank of Naples before 1907.
4 *L'Avvenire*, 26 April 1902, 28 June 1903; *La Luce*, 15 November 1902.
5 George Schiro, *Americans by Choice* ([Utica], 1940), pp. 145–46; *La
   Luce*, 24 September 1904; *Il Messaggero*, 15 October 1927. Rochester's
   first Italian manufacturing enterprise opened in 1883 as Antonio Man-
   cini and Company Confectioners. Ten years later the first macaroni
   company opened under Domenico Lanni. In 1926 there were eight
   such factories in the city. Clement Lanni, "The History of the Italians
   of Rochester from 1876 to 1926," *The Rochester Historical Society
   Publication Fund Series*, 6 (1927): 191–92.
6 *La Luce*, 16 April, 19 December 1904; *L'Avvenire*, 19 May 1904, 2
   August, 26 September 1903. The *Utica Saturday Globe*, 21 October
   1911, printed pictures of five Italian constructed and owned commercial
   buildings as evidence, in an article titled "Italians in Utica—Their
   Progress Has Been Rapid."
7 *L'Avvenire*, 13 June 1903, 22 February, 1 and 8 March 1902; *La
   Stampa Unita*, 19 November 1920, 12 October 1927; *La Stampa*, 20
   June 1924. Luigi Villari did not think highly of the Italian doctors he
   met in the American colonies. Most were mediocre and a few even
   ignorant and lacking medical diplomas, though he did admit that some
   were serious and talented. He found that almost all lawyers were from
   the second generation. "L'emigrazione italiana negli Stati Uniti
   d'America," *Nuova Antologia*, 16 September 1909, p. 297.

8   Jerre Mangione, *Mount Allegro* (New York, 1952), pp. 226-27; *Il Messaggero dell'Ordine,* 16 April 1932.

9   *L'Avvenire,* 19 August, 28 October 1905, 16 May 1903; *La Luce,* 13 February 1904; *Il Messaggero,* 15 October 1927; Lanni, "The History of the Italians," pp. 191-92; Personal correspondence with David S. Lanni (a grandson of Clement), December 1965; *L'Avvenire,* 22 February 1902, 11 April, 21 November 1903.

10 *L'Avvenire,* 27 February 1904; *La Luce,* 22 and 29 April 1911, 1 January 1903, 2 January, 21 May, 16 July 1904, 28 May 1910. In Kansas City, Giuseppe De Maria illustrates the opportunities open there to a few ambitious and talented immigrants of humble background. Born in Salaparuta, province of Trapani, Sicily, in 1885, he came to the United States at age fourteen to join an older brother. After some time in Louisiana, he moved north to Kansas City where, starting as a fruit peddler, he soon moved into the wholesale business. He was one of the founders of the Middle West Building and Loan Association, an Italian enterprise, and served for some years as a director of the Merchants Bank. The latter position suggests something of his place in the broader commercial community. In the colony he was active in founding several societies, including a religious one and a mutual benefit organization among his fellow *Salaparutani.* Finally, he was a member of the group that united the various societies in the colony under the "Supreme Inter Social Council." When he died in 1935, he had four sisters living in Kansas City, one in Italy, and a brother in Merriam, Kansas (*Il Messaggero,* 15 December 1935). Luciano J. Iorizzo relates several careers built on the new opportunities created by immigrant colonies in "A Reappraisal of Italian Leadership in Central New York Immigrant Communities—Some Preliminary Observations," in Istituto di Studi Americani Università degli Studi di Firenze, *Gli Italiani negli Stati Uniti* (New York, 1975) pp. 207-32.

The contention that most prominent and successful Italians in America were immigrants from the northern portions of the peninsula is largely a myth fostered in part by successful Italians in response to the prevailing stereotypes and prestige system existing both within and outside the Italian-American community. In 1906 the Milan Exposition of Italians Abroad published a monograph detailing the achievements of Italians in the United States. The work included short biographies of 138 prominent and "successful" Italian immigrants. One hundred and three of these give the Italian origins of the individuals. Northerners are probably somewhat overrepresented in comparison with their actual numbers in the total collection. Given the status associated with a northern background, those who were silent on their origins probably included few northerners. Also, at this early date they enjoyed a temporary advantage because of the fact that migration to America from the North started earlier than that from the South; thus the northerners here had had a longer time to establish themselves. Even considering this, the overwhelming number of the biographies are of southern Italians. The percentages using the standard Italian division of the country are: North—17.5%; Central—9.7%; and South—72.8%. *Gli italiani negli Stati Uniti D'America* (New York, 1906).

11 *L'Avvenire,* 8 and 22 February, 8 March, 28 June, 9 May 1902; *La Luce,* 31 May 1902. G. E. Palma di Castiglione, "L'immigrazione italiana negli Stati Uniti dell'America dal Nord dal 1820 al 30 giugno 1910. Nota statistica con quattro quadri," *Bollettino dell'Emigrazione* 12, no. 2 (1913): 109.

12 *L'Avvenire,* 27 September, 18 October, 8 November 1902; *La Luce,* 11 October, 8 November 1902.

The Italian political experience in America has been contrasted with that of the Irish in cities where the latter lived in numbers sufficient to permit them control of the political machines. The comparison ignores important differences in time of arrival (thus length of residence here), proportion of the groups in the electorate, language skills, and the state of the political machinery at the time each group arrived. The Irish came in large numbers at a time when urban political machines were still in their infancy. Italian found a fully developed, powerful system in the hands of others. More interesting comparisons emerge from situations where the Irish did not have the resources sufficient to dominate the machines. There, the behavior of Irish politicians is much closer to that of the Italians described here. See Dennis J. Clark, *The Irish in Philadelphia* (Philadelphia, 1973), pp. 171–72.

13 *L'Avvenire,* 26 September, 3, 17, and 31 October, 7 November 1903.

14 *L'Avvenire,* 28 November 1903, 2 April, 25 September, 1 October 1904; *La Luce,* 24 September, 1 and 8 October 1904.

15 *L'Avvenire,* 2 and 30 September, 7, 14, 21, and 28 October, 4 and 18 November 1905.

16 Lanni, "The History of the Italians," pp. 193–95; Blake McKelvey, "The Italians of Rochester: An Historical Review," *Rochester History* 22, no. 4 (October 1960): 17–18; *La Stampa,* 20 April, 11 May 1928. Utica Republicans ran an Italian for the state assembly in 1914.

17 *L'Avvenire,* 27 October, 3 November 1900, 9 February, 17 August 1901, 15 November 1902; *La Luce,* 14 December 1901, 25 October, 20 December 1902; O. Fritiof Ander, "The Swedish-American Press in the Election of 1892," *The Mississippi Valley Historical Review,* 23 March 1937, pp. 533–54; idem, "The Swedish-American Press in the Election of 1912," *The Swedish Pioneer Historical Quarterly* 14, no. 3 (July 1963): 103–26. Although the Italian papers behaved in ways that must have pleased Republican agent Lewis Hammerling, there is no evidence that his heavy-handed tactics or his American Association of Foreign Language Newspapers were responsible for the political commitment of the Utica papers. Their political preferences were well established before Hammerling's rise to national prominence as an intermediary between the Republicans and the Foreign Language Press.

See Robert E. Park, *The Immigrant Press and Its Control* (New York, 1922), chapter 15, for a discussion of Hammerling's role in purchasing editorial loyalty to the Republican party. A. William Hoglund suggests that ambitious Finnish-Americans before 1920 also consistently supported the Republican party, which they saw as the party of the doctrine of "getting ahead," in his *Finnish Immigrants in America 1880–1920* (Madison, Wis., 1960), p. 116.

18 *L'Avvenire*, 6 October 1900, 17 and 31 August 1901; *La Luce*, 16 November 1901; John W. Briggs, "The Italian Immigrant Press in America; A Survey and Guide for Collecting," an unpublished paper on file at the Immigrant Archives, University of Minnesota.

19 Briggs, "The Italian Immigrant Press." I was not able to locate a file of *Lotta Operaia* or *Il Pagliaccio*. Fairly complete files of the other papers exist on microfilm at the Immigrant Archives, University of Minnesota and at the Utica Public Library.

20 Briggs, "The Italian Immigrant Press." Most of *La Stampa Unita* is available on microfilm at the Immigrant Archives or at the Rochester Public Library. A file of *La Stampa* is housed at the Center for Research Libraries in Chicago.

21 Carl Wittke, *The German-Language Press in America* (Lexington, Ky., 1957), chap. 11; Park, *The Immigrant Press*, pp. 87–88. Milton Gordon's distinction between cultural and structural assimilation is helpful here. Immigrant editors recognized the need for their readers to learn a great deal about and to live with much of the American culture. At the same time, they envisioned the Italian colonies remaining separate entities in which a set of Italian-American institutional structures, in large part replications of American institutions, would provide services parallel to those offered to Americans. The Italian press was such a parallel institution. Gordon's analysis of assimilation can be found in his *Assimilation in American Life: The Role of Race, Religion and National Origins* (New York, 1964), pp. 60–83. E. C. Sartorio, in his *Social and Religious Life of the Italians in America* (Boston, 1918), p. 50, roundly condemns the Italian press for adopting a two-faced position on America. He claims to "have seen Italian newspapers with laudatory articles on America written in English, which no Italian would read, and with an article in Italian in the same issue, that the American would not understand, painting America in the blackest colors." Angelo DiDomenica concurred in Sartorio's belief that the Italian press retarded "Americanization" by their scornful and derisive attitudes toward America and things American. See his *Protestant Witness of a New American* (Philadelphia, 1956), pp. 95–96. My study found no such stance in the presses of the three colonies discussed here. The editors could be very critical of America's failure to live up to its promise, but the contemptuousness cited by these authors did not surface. Perhaps, as converts to both a new religion and a new nationalism, they were overly sensitive to any criticism, whether justified or not.

22 *L'Avvenire*, 6 September 1902, 27 October, 17 November 1900, 17
   December 1904; *La Luce*, 14 December 1901.
23 *La Luce*, 3 October 1914, 1 October, 19 March 1904; *L'Avvenire*, 15
   April 1905; *Il Messaggero*, 1 May 1926; *Il Pensiero Italiano*, 13 October
   1914; *La Stampa Unita*, 12 October 1927, 11 April 1924.
24 *La Luce*, 7 November 1914; *L'Avvenire*, 3 June 1905.
25 *La Stampa*, 25 June, 23 and 30 July, 6 and 13 August 1926.
26 *La Luce*, 22 July 1916, 3 January 1903, 10 February, 3 March 1906,
   6 February 1904; *Il Messaggero*, January 1926; *La Stampa*, 12 October
   1919; *L'Avvenire*, 3 December, 26 June 1904, 15 August 1903.
   Many have commented on the popularity of Joseph Pulitzer's style
   of journalism among immigrants. An emphasis on sensationalism,
   scandal, and personal tragedy was common to the reporting in the
   press of the three colonies. The phenomenon is an intriguing one. Did
   the steady diet of personal tragedy, disaster, and crime serve to raise
   the spirits of the immigrants by protecting them from potential home-
   sickness and confirming their decision to emigrate? Was it a form of
   self-reassurance about a highly emotional and uncertain decision?
   Colleagues working in the immigrant presses of the Poles, Slovaks, and
   Rumanians report finding the same biases in the selection of news. For
   examples from the Italian press, see: *L'Avvenire*, 25 March, 5 July
   1905, 11 April 1903; *Il Pensiero Italiano*, 8 August, 1 July 1914.
   Surely a commune such as Valguarnera, which had a large group of
   immigrants in Rochester, would have at least one repatriated citizen
   who, knowing both communities, could serve as a correspondent to
   keep the immigrants abreast of the "news" from back home. That no
   such reporting developed is further testimony to the limited nature of
   campanilismo. News undoubtedly came with each arrival of a relative
   or friend and from family correspondence. Again, it appears that the
   significant Old World ties were familial rather than territorial.
27 *La Stampa*, 6 October 1922, 3 April 1920.
28 Park, *The Immigrant Press*, chap. 5; See Ruth Mary Keene, "Acculturation of the First and Second Generation Italians in Rochester, New
   York," (M.A. thesis, University of Rochester, 1946), pp. 86–87, 99, for
   a discussion of the high degree of Italian acceptance of American material possessions.
29 John W. Briggs, "The Italian Press in America," in Lubomyr R. Wynar,
   ed., *History of the Ethnic Press in America* (forthcoming).
30 McKelvey, "The Italians of Rochester," p. 4.
31 *L'Avvenire*, 10 November 1900, 11 January 1902, 12 September 1903;
   La Luce, 19 March 1904.
32 *L'Avvenire*, 11 January 1902, 10 January, 14 February, 12 September
   1903, 6 and 20 February 1904; *La Luce*, 10 January 1903, 19 March
   1904.
33 *L'Avvenire*, 26 August 1905.
34 *L'Avvenire*, 11 June 1904. The Italian Baptist Association recognized

the intermediary role of the Italian press. In a 1918 convention, the association approved a report which included the statement: "The owners of these papers are generally considered the kings of the Italian colonies, by both Italians and Americans. The American politicians elevate them to the sky, because they need them at election times. These and other prominent Italians can obtain any favor from the officials of the city. Sometimes people arrested for crimes are released through the 'pull' of these men." "Report of the Americanization Committee," quoted in DiDomenica, *Protestant Witness*, pp. 95–96.

Chapter 9

1 Representative works in this revisional approach are: Michael Katz, *The Irony of Early School Reform: Educational Innovation in Mid-Nineteenth Century Massachusetts* (Cambridge, Mass., 1968), and his *Class, Bureaucracy and Schools: The Illusion of Educational Change in America* (New York, 1971); David Tyack, *The One Best System: A History of American Urban Education* (Cambridge, Mass., 1974); and Marvin Lazerson, *Origins of the Urban School: Public Education in Massachusetts* (Cambridge, Mass., 1971).

2 *L'Avvenire*, 12 October 1901. Throughout his tour of Italian-American colonies, Bishop Scalabrini stressed the importance of establishing Italian parochial schools. He recognized the interest among Italians in learning English and the culture of the new land and gave his blessing to the effort. In addition, he pleaded with the immigrants not to neglect their Italian heritage in their rush to learn American ways. Italian schools would allow them to do both. See Marco Caliaro and Mario Francesconi, *L'apostolo dagli emigranti, Giovanni Battista Scalabrini vescovo di Piacenza; la sua opera e la sua spiritualità* (Milan, 1968), pp. 282–83.

3 *La Luce*, 30 August, 20 September 1902, the second of the three editorials is no longer extant; *L'Avvenire*, 13 December 1902. The New York City school received contributions from the King of Italy and the Children's Aid Society, long an active charity in the city.

4 William Pizzoglio, *St. Mary of Mt. Carmel, Utica, N.Y. – Golden Jubilee, 1896–1946*, pp. 11, 12, 14; A Frangini, *Italiani nel centro dello stato di New York – strenna nazionale – cenni biografici* (Utica, N.Y., 1912), 59: 37; *L'Avvenire*, 14 February 1903; William P. H. Hewitt, ed., *History of the Diocese of Syracuse: Story of the Parishes, 1615–1909* (Syracuse, N.Y., 1909), pp. 253–54.

5 *La Luce*, 18 January 1902, 24 September 1904.

6 *L'Avvenire*, 13 February 1905; *Il Pensiero Italiano*, 9 September 1914. The desire for Italian schools indicated a concern with cultural preservation rather than cultural exclusiveness. It was not that children were learning English but that they were failing to learn Italian which troubled

the proponents of an Italian school. A charity school in New Jersey represented its ideal of a "complete education." Music and embroidery were part of the curriculum, while Italian and American sisters taught their respective languages. The school was for orphans and was also open to others at reasonable rates. *L'Avvenire*, 18 March 1905.

7   *La Luce*, 18 January 1902, 24 September 1904; Pizzoglio, *Golden Jubilee*, pp. 20–21; Frangini, *Italiani nel centro*, p. 38; Diocese of Syracuse, "Report of Schools," 1908, Chancellery Archives; *L'Avvenire*, 13 and 20 February, 5 March, 10 September 1904.

8   *Golden Jubilee Book—Holy Rosary Parish*—1942.

9   Norman T. Lyon, *History of the Polish People in Rochester* (Rochester, N.Y., 1935), pp. 26–27 ff. McQuaid wished the curriculum of his schools to be in English to ensure that the children would gain an excellent command of the language. He did recognize the advantage of having a few nuns who could speak the language of the immigrant children. He had several sisters learn German and planned to send two nuns to an Ialian convent school where he believed they would easily learn Italian. Poles were an exception to McQuaid's desire to staff parish schools from his diocesan order of nuns. Only a Pole, he thought, could ever learn to speak Polish well. Therefore, he did seek Polish sisters for schools in Polish parish schools. Sister Norlene Mary Kunkel, C.S.F.N., "Bishop Bernard J. McQuaid and Catholic Education" (Ph.D. diss., University of Notre Dame, 1974), pp. 142–43, n. 44.

10 Robert F. NcNamara, *The Diocese of Rochester, 1868–1968* (Rochester, N.Y., 1968), pp. 201–02, 272, 187; idem, *The American College in Rome, 1855–1955* (Rochester, N.Y., 1956), p. 817; *The Catholic Journal, Historical-Pictorial Edition* (Rochester, N.Y., 1914), pp. 123, 125. See Rudolph J. Vecoli, "Prelates and Peasants: Italian Immigration and the Catholic Church," *Journal of Social History* 11, no. 3 (Spring 1969): 217–68, for a broader exploration of the relationship between the American Catholic church and Italian immigrants. The impact of Italian nationalism and anticlericalism, which plays an important part in Professor Vecoli's account, did not surface in an explicit form in the sources used in this study. This may in part be due to the lack of extant socialist publications in the three colonies. Also, the fact that these colonies lacked any important numbers of European-educated intellectuals and professionals helps to account for the absence of a strong spirit of Italian nationalism and anticlericalism, which strained the relationship between the church and Italian leaders in larger American colonies.

11 Aaron Abell, "Elementary and Secondary Catholic Education in Rochester," *The Rochester Historical Society Publication* 17 (1939): 138–39; McNamara, *The Diocese*, pp. 163, 189, and personal conversation on the topic of leadership in establishment of schools in Italian parishes; *Golden Jubilee—Holy Rosary Parish;* Pizzoglio, *Golden Jubilee*, p. 15. An extensive search of the chancellery archives in Syracuse failed to unearth any evidence of episcopal prodding of the Utica parish

to build a school. This, of course, does not rule out the possibility of intervention through verbal directives.

12 McNamara, *The Diocese*, p. 162; the data is derived from an examination of the annual financial statements for the three parishes through 1918, on file in the library of St. Bernard's Seminary, Rochester, New York. More recent records of these parishes are still in the chancellery offices of the diocese and were not opened to me. I was unable to examine any records of the Sisters of St. Joseph and can only infer from the parish budget entries that the order's charity was made necessary by the limited resources of the parishes.

13 Utica Public Schools, *Annual Report*, 1900. Annual financial reports.

14 Annual reports of St. Marie of Mount Carmel Church, on file in the Diocesan archives at the chancellery in Syracuse; *Golden Jubilee— Holy Rosary Parish*. Kansas City's first Italian parochial school, which cost $10,000, was tuition-free except for a short period in the early 1920s.

15 See list of contributors to the school fund in the Fall 1904 issues of *L'Avvenire* for an indication of the nature of the support for this project.

16 Abell, "Catholic Education," pp. 142-44; McNamara, *The Diocese*, pp. 64-68; personal interview with Sister Eligia, 20 December 1967; personal interview with Sisters Irmina and Maria Antonio, 24 January 1968. There were Italian teaching orders which provided Italian nuns for parish schools in America. The Daughters of Mercy, centered in Savona, had a house in Pennsylvania and were teaching in the Italian parishes of the Diocese of Scranton. The Maestre Pie Fillippini opened their first school at Trenton, N.J. in 1910. N.S. Odone to Archbishop Dowling, July 23, 1925, Odone Papers, Immigrant Archives, University of Minnesota, and *Solemn Dedication and Blessing of Holy Trinity School* [Trenton], in Immigrant Archives.

Jay P. Dolan has shown that a spirit of competition between the parochial and public schools produced a tendency on the part of the Catholic school to emulate the best in public schooling in order not to be found lacking in any comparisons. The process eventuated in the "Americanization" of the parish school. Dolan, *The Immigrant Church: New York's Irish and German Catholics, 1815-1865* (Baltimore, Md., 1975), p. 113.

17 *The Catholic Journal*, p. 123; compare with the call to preserve Italianness and the love of the distant homeland expressed by the first Italian pastor at Utica in *La Luce*, 18 January 1902. Bishop McQuaid's early interest in using American priests to work with Italians stemmed, according to the diocesan historian, from his desire to "inculcate a systematic American Catholicism upon the casual Mediterranean immigrant." McNamara, *The Diocese*, pp. 201-02.

18 Interview with Sister Eligia; "Diocese of Syracuse—Report of Schools" (1908); *La Stampa*, 30 August 1923.

19 *L'Avvenire,* 18 March 1905; *La Stampa,* 30 August 1923.
20 *La Stampa Unita,* 19 and 26 June 1920; The Public Schools of Roches-
    ter, *Bulletin of General Information* (April, 1913), pp. 36, 38.
21 *La Stampa,* 27 May 1921. One would expect a slight bias here toward
    the parochial school, since the religiously disinterested and the converts
    to the active Protestant missions in Kansas City who sent their children
    to public schools would not be included in this sample; "Notitiae"–
    St. Mary of Mount Carmel parish, 1916–18, Archives of the Diocese of
    Syracuse; "Report of the Superintendent of Schools," Diocese of
    Syracuse, 1919–20; *Annual Report of the Public Schools of Utica,
    New York 1919–20; Attendance Registers,* Mount Carmel School,
    Rochester, 1910–11, 1916–17.

    While doing research for his book on Italians in Utica, George Schiro
    produced figures which suggest that by 1938 only 8 percent of the
    children of Italian descent were in parochial schools. After the first
    surge in the building of parochial schools, the parishes did not expand
    their facilities nearly as rapidly as the public schools. Schiro, *Americans
    by Choice,* (Utica, N.Y., 1940), pp. 130–32.

    It is interesting that among eighth-grade graduates the sex ratios were
    reversed in the public and parochial schools. In 1920 Utica's Mount
    Carmel had 38 percent boys and 62 percent girls in this highest grade.
    The Italian contingent in the same grade of the public schools consisted
    of 63 percent boys and 37 percent girls. Perhaps Italian parents viewed
    the parochial school as a vehicle for sheltering daughters from too much
    free and unsupervised exposure to public life.

    Some may find these estimates of the ratios of public-parochial school
    attendance surprising. Italians have been thought to have chosen public
    schooling overwhelmingly. A sample of immigrants' children in Cleve-
    land reveals that more than nine out of every ten Italians and Rumanians
    attended public schools. Slovaks, on the other hand, largely patronized
    their parochial elementary schools before switching to public institu-
    tions for their middle and secondary schooling. Careful studies of a
    number of other colonies will be necessary before we can determine
    whether Cleveland or the three cities examined here more accurately
    represent the experience of Italians in America. Josef J. Barton,
    Peasants and Strangers (Cambridge, Mass., 1975), pp. 149, 150.
22 *Annual Report of the Superintendent of the Public Schools, City of
    Utica–1900,* pp. 19–21; "Annual Report" 1904-05, pp. 19–20;
    L'Avvenire, 17 November 1900.
23 *Annual Report–1900,* p. 16; "Attendance Register," Wetmore School–
    1901–10, Union Street School–1901–10, Brandegee School–1911,
    Mary Street School–1902–03, 1905–06, 1919–23; *Annual Report–
    1909–10,* p. 19, *1912–13,* pp. 21–23.
24 Carrie Westlake Whitney, *Kansas City Missouri: Its History and Its
    People, 1808–1908* (Chicago, 1908), pp. 337–41; *Kansas City, Mo.
    Directory* (1914); *La Stampa,* 29 May 1925, 4 June 1926.

25 *La Stampa,* 21 March, 2 and 24 May, 19 September, 3 and 31 October,
    7 November 1919, 11 June 1920, 15 April, 13 May, 12 August 1921, 6
    January, 19 May 1922, 8 June, 26 October 1923, 20 June, 12 October
    1924, 2 October, 6 November 1925; *Forty-Fifth Annual Report of the
    Board of Education of the School District of Kansas City, Missouri–
    1915–1916,* pp. 298–99.

26 *The Evening School* commenced publication in June 1922 and appeared
    about four times an academic year throughout the remainder of the
    decade. *The Fifty-Fourth Report of the Board of Education of the
    City of Rochester, N.Y.–1905, 1906, 1907,* p. 30; "Proceedings of the
    Board of Education of the City of Rochester–1916," 2 October, p. 46;
    "Proceedings–1918," 7 October, p. 59; "Proceedings–1920," 24
    September, p. 54; *The Fifty-Fifth Report–1908, 1909, 1910,* p. 140;
    Herbert S. Weet, "Citizenship and the Evening Use of School Buildings:
    The Social Centers and the Civic Clubs," *The Common-Good of Civic
    and Social Rochester* 4, no. 5 (February 1911); The League of Civic
    Clubs, *Rochester Social Centers and Civic Clubs: The Story of the
    First Two Years* (Rochester, N.Y., 1909), pp. 36, 43.

27 Marvin Lazerson, "Urban Reform and the Schools: Kindergartens in
    Massachusetts, 1870–1915," *History of Education Quarterly* 11, no. 2
    (Summer 1971): 115–42; *Annual Report–Utica–1899,* p. 29.

28 *Annual Report–Utica–1904–05,* p. 62; *1905–06,* pp. 32–37; *1911–12,*
    pp. 119–22. The annual reports of the kindergarteners reveal a strong
    concentration on play, object learning, nature study, paper cutting,
    weaving, cardboard modeling, formal and free color work, singing and
    the annual planting of a garden. *Annual Report–Utica–1909–10,*
    pp. 28–29, and 1916–17, pp. 26–27, are representative.

29 Charles Edgar Finch, "The Foreign Child in the Rochester Schools,"
    The Common-Good 5, no. 12 (September 1912): 25–26. In 1912 Finch
    was principal of a school with a heavily East European and Italian
    student body. He went on to specialize in immigrant education and to
    teach a course on the subject at the University of Rochester; "The
    Public Schools of Rochester: Bulletin of General Information" (April
    1913), p. 27; "The Fifty-Sixth Report–Rochester–1911, 1912, 1913,"
    pp. 97–101; Helen B. Montgomery, "The Last Ten Years of the Roches-
    ter Schools," *The Common-Good* 5, no. 1 (October 1911): 9–10;
    "Fifty-Fourth Report–Rochester–1905, 1906, 1907," p. 29.

30 The data on the foreign-class teachers are drawn from the personnel
    files of the Rochester city schools. The teaching staff of the foreign
    classes did not differ ethnically or in sex composition from the general
    elementary school staff. See Edward Willard Stevens, Jr., "The Political
    Education of Children in the Rochester Public Schools, 1899-1917:
    An Historical Perspective on Social Control in Public Education" Ed.D.
    thesis, University of Rochester, 1970), pp. 201–05. Stevens did not
    have a single Italian teacher in the sample of staff members from the
    period he analyzed.

31 See the "Grade Course of Study" in the "Annual Report—Utica—1911–
    12," pp. 117–251. The course outline, and, more importantly, the in-
    troductions to and commentaries on the various subjects by the city
    supervisors, indicate no thought that modifications might be in order for
    various groups of students. The guide recognizes that some differences
    in the pace of learning are to be expected and encourages teachers to
    be aware of the fact that some students will learn faster than others.
    Beyond this lone warning, the document is a singular prescription as-
    umed suitable for everyone. "Annual Report—Utica," 1905–06, p. 145;
    1906–07, p. 137; 1907–08, p. 138; 1909–10, p. 108; 1911–12, p. 114;
    1916–17, p. 89; 1923–24, p. 33; 1930–31, pp. 20–39.

32 Department of Public Schools, Utica, N.Y., *Tentative Course of Study
    for Schools in Foreign Districts, 1916–1917*, pp. 1–4. A decade earlier,
    educators in New York City adopted a similar program of eliminating
    the "frills," such as "paperfolding, construction of paper boxes, the
    knotting of cord, sight reading of music, illustrative drawing," in order
    to be able to concentrate on the basics. Julia Richman, "What Can Be
    Done in the Graded School for the Backward Child," *The Survey* 13
    (November 1904): 129–31.

33 State Department of Education, *A Report of the Survey of the Utica
    School System*, pp. 80–81. The schools are not identified in this study.
    However, from internal evidence it could only be the principal of the
    Brandegee School writing here.

34 Ibid., pp. 82–84. Approximately one-third of the students of this
    school were of Italian background.

35 McNamara, *The Diocese of Rochester*, p. 266; Kunkel, "Bishop Bernard
    J. McQuaid," pp. 98, 142–43.

36 *La Stampa Unita*, 8 January 1926, 18 March 1927; *La Stampa*, 24
    September 1920, 29 July 1921; *La Luce*, 31 October 1914, 4 Septem-
    ber 1915, 15 June 1907; *La Stampa Unita*, 10 March 1922, 23 February
    1928; *Il Messaggero*, 1 February 1929. The level of reporting of educa-
    tional subjects in the Italian press compares very favorably with the
    contemporary American press. For example, the *Utica Daily Press* in
    mid-April 1904 carried a series that was representative of its reporting
    on education. The articles describe the debate over whether schools
    should be named after famous Americans rather than designated by a
    number or street name as the major educational question of the year.

37 *La Stampa Unita*, 16 September 1921, 12 January 1923, 31 March
    1922, 6 March 1930; *Il Messaggero*, 15 June, 1 September 1926.

38 *La Stampa Unita*, 26 June 1920, 22 February 1924; *Il Messaggero*, 15
    June 1926, 15 March 1930; *Il Pensiero Italiano*, 3 and 18 July 1914;
    La Luce, 25 June 1910, 17 June 1916; *L'Avvenire*, 9 July 1904; *La
    Luce*, 5 July 1902; *Il Messaggero*, 1 and 15 April 1926, 15 June 1926,
    1 January 1929; *La Stampa Unita*, 20 December 1934, *L'Avvenire*,
    13 June 1903; Schiro, *Americans by Choice*, pp. 105–07, 133.

39 *La Stampa*, 13 and 20 June 1923; *La Luce*, 23 April 1910, 10 January

1914, 30 June 1906, 27 August 1904, 17 April 1915, 21 February 1914, 15 November 1902; *La Stampa Unita,* 1928 passim.

40 *L'Avvenire,* 28 March 1902, 15 February 1905; *La Stampa,* 10 February 1928; *La Luce,* 23 May 1914; *La Stampa,* 24 September 1920, 31 October 1919; *La Stampa Unita,* 31 March 1922.

41 *La Luce,* 7 November 1914.

42 *La Stampa,* 29 July 1921; *La Luce,* 6 December 1913; *La Stampa Unita,* 31 March 1922.

43 *La Stampa Unita,* 19 January 1923.

44 *La Stampa,* 15 January 1926, 6 April 1918; *La Luce,* 10 January 1914; *La Stampa Unita,* 17 January 1929, 4 April 1924, 26 January 1928; *L'Italiano* 2, no. 8 (August 1939): 20-21, 2 no. 9 (September 1939): 13.

45 *L'Avvenire,* 12 October 1901, 4 January 1902, 22 August 1903, 19 November 1904, 28 May 1904; *La Luce,* 22 October 1904, 2 April 1910, 13 May 1916; *La Stampa,* 26 August 1921, 29 December 1922, 12 January 1923, 15 June 1903, 10 February 1928; *La Stampa Unita,* 2 January 1926, 30 September 1927.

46 *L'Avvenire,* 7 September 1901, 24 October 1903, 2 and 30 April, 8 and 29 October, 5 and 26 November 1904, 4 May, 8 July 1905; *La Luce,* 17 October 1903, 28 January 1905, 27 September, 16 August 1913.

Chapter 10

1 Leonard P. Ayres, *The Public Schools of Springfield, Illinois* (New York, 1914), pp. 52-53. At the time of the study, Springfield was a growing city of over 50,000 inhabitants, of which 13 percent were foreign-born. Two-thirds of these were of British or German extraction; Frank V. Thompson, *Schooling of the Immigrant* (New York, 1920), p. 33.

2 Sister Mary Fabian Matthews, "The Role of the Public School in the Assimilation of the Italian Immigrant Child in New York City, 1900–1914" (Ph.D. diss., Fordham University, 1966), p. 176; "Annual Report—Utica," 1904, pp. 26-30; Leonard P. Ayres, *Laggards in our Schools* (New York, 1909), pp. 105-06; Forest Chester Ensign, *Compulsory School Attendance and Child Labor* (Iowa City, 1921), pp. 129-69, has a history of New York State attendance legislation.

  In Omaha, the rate of nonattendance cases in the school population for the years 1930-32 ran between 4 percent and 5 percent of the school population up to the age of thirteen. For ages thirteen, fourteen, and fifteen, the percentages were 7.2, 10, and 15.8. At age sixteen it returned to the 5 percent level. T. Earl Sallenger, *Studies in Urban Sociology* (New York, 1933), p. 87.

  A study of school children in Minneapolis and St. Paul, Minnesota, reveals one of the hazards involved in making comparisons of student performance between school systems, or even between individual schools within a single system. As a result of different administrative procedures regarding registration, the entire school population of St. Paul was "retarded," or at best average, by Minneapolis norms. At the same time, within the Minneapolis system the highest-ranking students in every grade except the sixth in one school were given grades below the median for pupils of the same grades in another school. It seems logical to assume that the school with such "inferior" students, largely children of Jewish immigrants, had a different and more rigorous grading standard, which accounted for a major portion of the school's "academic deficiencies." The possiblity of the existence of unequal and prejudicial standards, both between schools and within a single school or classroom, should be kept in mind in evaluating the evidence below. I have attempted to minimize this factor by choosing groups for comparison which are as close to the Italians as possible. Still, the ultimate influence of prejudice remains undetermined. Rivera Harding Jordan, *Nationality and School Progress: A Study in Americanization* (Bloomington, Ill., 1921), pp. 49, 51.

3 The proportions of families with male and female children of various ages who had children in school suggest some sex-related differences. Girls' enrollment drops off in the oldest age category.

	1905		1915		1925	
Families with children ages:	Male	Female	Male	Female	Male	Female
6–14	88.1	90.7	93.8	97.4	96.9	97.5
15–16	21.4	28.0	57.1	29.6	71.4	63.3
17–18	27.3	28.6	10.0	16.0	30.0	33.3
19+	2.9	0	7.0	0	5.5	2.0

4 Karl E. Taeuber and Alma F. Taeuber explore these phenomena of selective out-migration of high-status whites from areas of black in-migration, the resulting change in the character of the white population, and the comparative social standing of the new black residents, in their *Negroes in Cities: Residential Segregation and Neighborhood Change* (New York, 1969), pp. 154–65 and passim.

5 Ayres's 1908 study of 20,000 New York City school children found that Italians had the greatest percentage of children who were "retarded." The standard of retardation was a rather liberal one, where children over nine-years-old in the first grade, over ten in the second grade, over eleven in the third grade, and so on were so classified. The overall retardation was 23 percent. For specific nationalities the figures were:

German	16%
American	19%
Mixed	19%
Russian	23%
English	24%
Irish	29%
Italian	36%

Source: Ayres, *Laggards,* pp. 106-08.

Ayres does not compare Italians with other recent arrivals from peasant and rural artisan backgrounds. More than two decades later, a study of "slow progress by predominant ethnic groups" found Italians still the most overage students, with the Poles have almost comparable figures. J. B. Maller, "Economic and Social Correlatives of School Progress in New York City," *Teachers College Record* 34 (May 1933): 655-70. The U.S. Immigration Commission found that children of immigrants born in America had a substantial advantage over their peers born abroad in escaping the "laggard" label. Neither Ayres nor Maller seems to have controlled for the distinction. See David K. Cohen, "Immigrants and the Schools," *Review of Educational Research* 40, no. 1 (1970): 13-27, for a summary of these "retardation" studies.

6   Statement of Herbert S. Weet reported in *Post Express* (Rochester), 17 June 1915.
    Colin Greer, *The Great School Legend: A Revisionist Interpretation of American Public Education* (New York, 1972), pp. 122 and passim. Greer does briefly note, in a paraphrase of David Cohen, that a variety of factors independent of the school may influence academic outcomes and that data on age retardation do not yield measures of the comparative impact of such factors. Yet he repeats only a part of Cohen's analyses of the retardation studies. He neglected material from studies which suggest that the retardation was far more the product of social and economic characteristics of the children's backgrounds than of the quality of the schools. More regrettably, he does not consider the possibility that "laggardness" was not an adequate measure of academic failure. Age retardation and successful progression through the grades, or learning from the school experience, are not necessarily and irrevocably linked. Cohen, "Immigrants," p. 13.

7   "Annual Admission Records," Rochester Public Schools—Schools no. 10 and no. 20 (FF 16 FC 1.16 and FF 23 FC 1.23) and "School Registers," School no. 6 (FF 6 FC 1.6 and FF 7 FC 1.7).

8   Attendance Registers, Mount Carmel School—Rochester, 1909-10 through 1935-36. Josef Barton reports that most Italian, Slovak, and Rumanian children in Cleveland entered school at age six. Italians and

Slovaks left school at sixteen years of age, while the Rumanians more often stayed on for an extra year of schooling. The discrepancy between my findings on entry age and Barton's may reflect differences between school systems. More likely, it represents an increasing acceptance of American patterns by the immigrants. Members of Barton's sample began their formal education about a decade after my students entered school. The pattern of increasing attendance at the younger and older ends of the scale in the New York State censuses (Table 10.1) supports this interpretation. *Peasants and Strangers* (Cambridge, Mass., 1975), pp. 161–63.

9   *Il Pensiero Italiano,* 12 December 1918, carries an appeal to Italians not to let the pressure of ready employment opportunities override the educational interests of their children. The paper pointed to experimental work-study plans as possible compromises; *Report of the General Survey Committee of the Industrial Education Survey of the City of Utica* (Utica, N.Y., 1919). Occupations of two-thirds of these youths were given in the report. The breakdown was:

Workmen or apprentices in machine trades	13.8%
Carpenters or carpenters' apprentices	1.1%
Those in textile lines	5.4%
Chauffeurs	3.4%
Those in electrical field	1.1%
Plumbers or sheet-metal workers or apprentices	1.5%
Common laborers	39.0%
Teamsters	2.3%
Delivery boys	7.2%
Office clerks	16.1%
Store clerks	8.8%

While a number of those in the categories of Textile lines and Electrical field may have been common laborers, it is nonetheless clear that there was a wide variety of economic activities open to these "school dropouts."

Early twentieth-century figures for Utica show that 38 percent of the children starting elementary school completed the full course. The average figure for thirty-nine city school systems across the country was 48.3 percent. The number remaining to age fifteen out of all starters was 41.1 percent for Utica, as compared with an average of 41.3 percent for all cities. Ayres, *Laggards,* pp. 159–69.

These data should not be extrapolated directly to Rochester. Children there tended to stay in school for a longer time. Attendance patterns for older children in Utica more closely approximate overall state averages.

Percentage of Children in School: Utica,
Rochester, and New York State, 1930

Ages	Rochester	Utica	New York State
7-13	97.1	97.8	97.7
14-15	97.3	90.2	93.9
16-17	70.6	56.4	59.4
18-20	23.2	20.6	20.4

Source: Fifteenth Census of the United States: 1930 Population
III, pt. 2, p. 292.

10 Transcripts of family court records—Rochester, 1925–29, held by the
Rochester School System; "The Reasons the Children Were Not in
School," *The Common Good* 5, no. 5 (February 1912): 28ff. See
Federal Writers Project (WPA), *The Italians of New York* (New York,
1938), chap. 4, for a typical example of the simple conversion of
Italian truancy rates into parental attitudes toward schooling and desires to profit from the children's labor.
11 Weekly reports of attendance officer John E. Day, September 1929–May
1931. Day was a wily and experienced truant officer, having served in
that capacity in Utica from 1895 to 1931.
12 Transcripts of Family Court—Rochester.
13 Ibid.; "Reports"—John E. Day; *La Luce*, 4 April 1903, 23 April 1904,
15 March 1902. The variety of attendance patterns appearing in a
family characterized by lack of parental guidance and support for
schooling offers some insight into the kind of possible responses. Antonio M. did not register until December 1904. After twenty-six days
of attendance and at the age of sixteen, he left the second grade to go
to work. His younger brother Daniele, age eleven entered school at the
beginning of the term in September and compiled the second-best
attendance record in his class. (The best record was achieved by a
thirteen-year-old Italian boy in a class of mostly non-Italians.) A
twelve-year-old sister did not appear at school until January. Once
registered in the first grade, she had an average attendance record. Six-
year-old twin brothers appeared on time for the start of kindergarten
in September but had mediocre and erratic attendance. A seven-year-
old sister joined the twins in kindergarten in late November, and once
there she attended regularly. School attendance in a family such as this
appears to depend more on the inclinations of the individual children
than on any positive or negative encouragement from the parents. This

material is from "Annual Admission Registers," School no. 10—Rochester, 1904-05 (FF 16 FC 1.16).

14 *The Fifty-Third Annual Report—Rochester 1903-04*, p. 9; *The Fifty-Fourth Report—Rochester, 1905, 1906, 1907*, pp. 7-8; Attendance Registers—School no. 9—Rochester, 1914-15 (FF 11 FC 1.11).

15 Schiro, *Americans by Choice*, pp. 132-33; Lanni, "The History of the Italians," pp. 190-91. The sharp drop in the number of immigrants' children attending high school compared with their numbers in the elementary schools was a common phenomenon in other cities. A 1915 survey of ethnicity in Cleveland revealed that, while 56 percent of the first-grade students were from foreign-speaking homes, only 23 percent of those in the twelfth grade identified themselves in that category. Also, it is important to note that the senior class was one-tenth the size of the entering elementary class. Overall, 10.8 percent of the student body was at the high school level. There were wide differences in the proportions of students found at the secondary level for various ethnic groups. These ranged from a high of over 15 percent for "Hebrew" children to a low of 1.7 percent for "Slovenian." More importantly, five recently arrived national groups (Italians at 2.3%, Slovaks at 2.5%, Hungarians at 2.6%, Polish at 3.1%, and the Slovenes) were clustered together at more than 7 percentage points under the average for all children in the city. This study must be used with caution, however. The criterion for determining ethnicity was student reports of language spoken in their homes. Thus, the "English-speaking" group, 14.4 percent of whom were in high schools, must have included children of immigrants who switched to the use of English in the home. One might also expect that the older students would be more sensitive to social pressures and thus less willing to admit to coming from a foreign-language home. Also, the most recent arrivals would be expected to have generally younger families, and thus would be overrepresented at the elementary level. Germans, the largest foreign-language group, and one with a longer history of immigration, on the other hand, fall very close to the city-wide average for the breakdown between elementary and secondary students. Herbert Adolphus Miller, *The School and the Immigrant* (Cleveland, 1916), p. 25.

The early twentieth century was a period of rapid expansion of secondary education in America. The proportion of high school students in the total school population in Rochester increased from 4 percent to 27 percent between 1900 and 1929. The percentage of high school students more than doubled in the first ten years of the decade. Yet even this expansion was probably an underexpression of the popular interest in secondary education. In 1900, 925 students were crowded into the single public high school. In 1903 and 1905 two new buildings were opened. Each was filled to its designed capacity in its first year of operation, and the high schools went on half-day sessions awaiting the completion of another building a decade later. Thus, the new schools were unsuccessful in alleviating overcrowding at the secondary level. Instead, they appear to have generated new interest in education at that level. The evidence suggests that the size of the high school population was artificially controlled by the inadequacy of the physical facilities available in the system. The middle classes were the first to benefit from this expansion of educational opportunity. Only in the 1920s did the lower classes among the native-born and immigrant urbanites begin to move in numbers into the expanded secondary programs.

The following tables give some indication of the growing popularity of secondary schooling. The data represent only public school children, and since a greater proportion of the parochial school population was at the elementary level, the tendency is to overstate slightly the size of the high school population in the total student body of a city. Also, close comparisons between the two cities should not be made, since the proportion of parochial students may have varied in the two cities.

Percentage Distribution of Day Students
in Elementary and Secondary Schools

Utica	1900	1910	1920	1930	
Secondary	5.7	8.1	9.5	15.5	
Elementary	94.2	91.8	90.4	84.4	
Rochester				1929	1932
Secondary	4.2	9.2	17.4	29.4	39.1
Elementary	95.7	90.7	82.5	70.5	60.8

Percentage of Increase in School Population by Decade

Utica	1900–10	1910–20	1920–30	
Secondary	44.7	38.1	51.4	
Elementary	20.2	26.2	15.5	
Rochester			1920–29	1929–32
Secondary	61.2	63.4	54.4	29.4
Elementary	10.2	24.5	9.8	-9.1

Source: "Annual Report to the Public Schools of Utica, New York," 1900, 1909–10, 1919–20, 1929–30; Herbert S. Weet, "The Development of Public Education in Rochester, 1900–1910," pp. 225–26, and Stanley V. Levey, "The Last Twenty-five Years in the Public Schools,"

The Rochester Historical Society Publications 17 (1939): 265. Selwyn Troen reports the proportions of students in the high schools of St. Louis as 2.96 percent in 1900, 7.10 percent in 1910, and 10.65 percent in 1920. It appears that an important stimulus for the increase in popularity of secondary schooling came from new programs in general education, commercial education, manual training, and the domestic arts. These new offerings quickly gained in enrollment at the expense of the old classical and scientific curricula intended as preparation for college. Curricular change broadened secondary schooling to attract those who had no plans for going on to higher education. Troen, *The Public and the Schools: Shaping the St. Louis System, 1838-1920* (Columbia, Mo., 1975), pp. 187-90. Also see Marvin Lazerson, *Origins of the Urban School* (Cambridge, Mass., 1971), pp. 139-48.

16 Joseph Wilfrid Tait, *Some Aspects of the Effects of the Dominant American Culture Upon Children of Italian-Born Parents* (New York, 1942), p. 52. Historians have largely ignored Tait's work, perhaps because it is fairly technical and does not conform to the popular impression of the impact of the school on the immigrant child. He did find slight increases in inferiority feelings and extroverted behavior, and decreases in social adjustment and emotional stability, as the proportion of Italian to American students decreased. Yet, this same increase in contact with American children had no effect on the awareness of rejection or on the Italians' attitudes toward their families' foreign background. To the degree that the immigrant child experienced emotional trauma arising from schooling, the significant cause may lie more in his or her relations with American classmates rather than in the schooling itself. Also, increased contacts lessened prejudice and increased tolerance toward the Italian on the part of the American child (pp. 30-48).

See Oscar Handlin, *The Uprooted* (New York, 1951), pp. 244-49 for an interpretation of the school as a divisive force irreparably dividing the generations. Phyllis H. Williams's *South Italian Folkways in Europe and America* (New Haven, Conn., 1938), pp. 129-34, presents a view of schooling and the Italian family that is, on the whole, compatible with the evidence presented in this chapter.

Chapter 11

1 Kirschner, "The Ambiguous Legacy: Social Justice and Social Control in the Progressive Era," *Historical Reflections* 2 (Summer 1976), pp. 68-88 is a brief summary of the competing interpretations.

2 *Utica Saturday Globe,* 11 October 1902, 21 October 1911; *Utica Sunday Journal,* 30 December 1894, 19 March 1899; *Utica Daily Press,* 23, 24, 27 May 1904, 4 June 1900; *The Union and Advertiser* (Rochester), 22 July 1893; Peter Roberts, *The New Immigration* (New York,

1912), p. 327; Bernard J. Lynch, "The Italians in New York," *The Catholic World* 48 (April 1888): 67–73. Lynch conceded that the Italians were slow to support the church financially. He attributed this to their Italian experience with a state-supported church. Twelve years later the same journal presented a much less favorable and optimistic view of the character and potential of the Italian immigrant. See Laurence Franklin, "The Italian in America: What He Has Been, What He Shall Be," 71, no. 421 (April 1900): 67–80.

The following stories are typical of the detached sensationalism of the American press. Under the caption "Razor Wielded as Weapon—Bloody Fight in East Utica," the paper described the assault from behind on a hard-working Sicilian family-man by an unemployed, transient dandy who tried subsequently to flee to New York City. The resulting wound was described in bloody detail. The victim received a sympathetic treatment which recognized "good" and "bad" Italians. A second story, entitled "Usual Italian Sunday Row," was written in a semi-jocular style. The author noted that the participants had introduced some variety this time by using an axe and shovel in place of the customary knives. *Utica Daily Press*, 4 June 1900, 25 April 1904.

3 Blake McKelvey, *Rochester: The Quest for Quality, 1890–1925* (Cambridge, 1956), pp. 154–55; idem, "The Italians of Rochester, An Historical Review," *Rochester History* 22, no. 4 (October 1960): 5–6; *La Luce*, 27 September 1902.

4 *Primo annuario delle Missioni Battiste Italiane negli Stati Uniti; Pubblicato per cura della Associazione Battista Italiana* (New Haven, Conn., 1912), p. 58; "Winter Bulletin—Colgate University—The Theological Seminary," ser. 8, no. 1 (January 1908): 14; [Rev. Ernesto G. Merlanti], "Church of the Evangel—Report on Merger with the North Presbyterian Church into Christ Presbyterian Church," 1959; Antonio Mangano, "Dedication in Rochester," *The Watchman-Examiner* 17, no. 3 (17 January 1929): 91–92.

5 *Primo annuario delle Missioni Battiste Italiane*, pp. 70–71; "Minute Book of the Pastor's Conference of the Oneida Baptist Association": vol. 1 (1902–1918), 13 March 1905, 13 March 1906, 16 May 1910; vol. 2 (1919), 10 March 1919, housed at the American Baptist Historical Society Archives. See G. E. DiPalma-Castiglione, "Vari centri italiani negli stati di Indiana, Ohio, Michigan, Minnesota e Wisconsin," *Bollettino dell'Emigrazione*, no. 6 (1915), p. 36, for a statement on the ubiquitousness of these combination mission, social work, and educational establishments.

6 *L'Avvenire*, 27 May 1905; *La Luce*, 4 July 1914, "Minutes of the Eighty-Ninth Anniversary of the Oneida Baptist Association" (1909), pp. 22, 36–37; "Minutes of the 91st Anniversary . . ." (1911), pp. 50, 58; "Minutes of the 92nd Anniversary . . ." (1912), pp. 37, 44; "Minutes of the 93rd Anniversary . . ." (1913), p. 28; "Minutes of the Oneida Baptist Association" (1923), p. 28 (1924), p. 32 (1929), pp. 18,

24; Charles A. Brooks to Rev. C. J. Oxley, 25 January 1922; "Petition of Members of the Italian Baptist Mission of Utica to Baptist City Mission Board of Utica and Vicinity, State Convention and Home Mission Society," 15 July 1924; Frank A. Smith to H. B. Rice, 25 July 1924, 15 September 1924, 21 January 1925; Frederic Kronmeller and H. F. Bantham to The Baptist Mission Board of Utica and Vicinity, 3 May 1926; "Report," Budget Committee, 1927, to the Baptist Mission Board of Utica and Vicinity; "Minutes of the Baptist Mission Board of Utica and Vicinity," 2 May 1916, 2 January 1917, 7 January 1919, 1 April 1919, 2 September 1919, 2 December 1919, 6 January 1920, 14 April 1920, 18 June 1920, 2 May 1932, 6 February 1933, 5 June 1933; "Report," Rev. Antonio Perrotta to the Baptist Mission Board of Utica and Vicinity, March 1930, April 1930. The above manuscript material is in the American Baptist Historical Society Archives, Rochester, N.Y.

7 *The Italian Mission in the Heart of America, Now the Christ Presbyterian Church and Northeast Community Center: A Report in Stewardship During Dr. Bisceglia's Ministry, June 1, 1918–May 31, 1965* [Kansas City, 1965], p. 22; *Il Messaggero,* January 1926, p. 7, April 1926, p. 11, 15 April 1927, vol. 34, nos. 10–11 (October–November 1958), pp. 6, 12; *La Stampa,* 15 June 1923.

8 *Il Messaggero,* February 1926, p. 7, April 1926, pp. 11–12, 1 May 1926, 15 July 1926, 15 April 1927, 1 August 1927, 15 June 1928, and October–November 1958, pp. 10, 13, 14.

9 *Il Messaggero,* April 1926, pp. 14, 15, April 1927; "Report of the Budget Committee—1927," Baptist Mission Board of Utica and Vicinity; "Minutes of the Baptist Mission Board of Utica and Vicinity," 2 September 1917. The Methodist Institutional Church in Kansas City seems to have been headed by a non-Italian. However, it was closely identified in the colonial press with Elisabetta Guzzardo, a teacher at Karnes School and an active youth-worker at the church. *La Stampa,* 4 April and 30 October 1919, 16 July 1920.

10 "Minutes of the Oneida Baptist Association," 1912, p. 58, 1923, p. 28, 1929, p. 24; "Membership records, 1910," Central Chapel, Kansas City, Mo.; Baptism and marriage registers, Central Chapel, September 1918–30; comments of Dr. Roy E. Williamson in "Minutes, Baptist Mission Board of Utica and Vicinity," 6 April 1922.

Enrico C. Sartorio contended that "The Italian work [by Protestants] must prepare them to step into an American church as soon as they move away from the Italian colony." *Social and Religious Life of Italians in America* (Boston, 1918), p. 124. See Anne Parsons, "The Pentecostal Immigrants: A Study of an Ethnic Central City Church," *Journal for the Scientific Study of Religion,* vol. 4 (1965), for a contemporary study of the relationship between religious conversion, individualism, and social change.

11 In 1927 the Institute in Kansas City sent fifty-eight boys to Rotary

Summer Camp. Only 40 percent of these have surnames that appear
in the church membership rolls. In 25 percent of the cases, a given
name and surname from the camper list appears in the membership
records. *La Stampa,* 29 June 1923, 12 October 1924.

Rudolph Vecoli makes this same point concerning the tendency of the
Catholic church to copy Protestant strategies, in his "Prelates and
Peasants: Italian Immigration and the Catholic Church," *The Journal
of Social History* 2, no. 3 (Spring 1969): 252-53. Also see Jay P. Dolan,
The Immigrant Church (Baltimore, 1975), pp. 130ff.

12 Abbe Felix Klein, *In the Land of Strenuous Life* (Chicago, 1905),
p. 110; Robert F. McNamara, *The Diocese of Rochester,* 1868-1968
(Rochester, N.Y., 1968), pp. 197-202, 203; Di Palma-Castiglione,
"Vari Centri Italiani," p. 35.

McQuaid's benign neglect stopped short of allowing the nationalistic
sentiments of any group in his diocese to challenge the authority or
traditions of American Catholicism. His initial policy of trying to
assign all work among Italians to American priests may have reflected
his perception of the differences between the Italian immigrants' and
the American church's views of the proper roles for faithful adherents.

13 McNamara, *The Diocese,* pp. 266, 275-76, 310-11, 345.

14 These articles are reprinted in *La Stampa,* 31 January, 6 and 21
February 1930.

One instance of lay Catholic initiative in founding such organizations
among Italians brought a protest that carried as far as the bishop. A
Utica pastor objected strenuously to the action of the local Christ
Child Society in forming a "Young Ladies Catholic Italian Club," on
the grounds that it competed with the parish in raising special collections and because it was outside his authority. Rev. John Marchegiani
to Bishop McEvoy, 3 August 1931, Archives of the Diocese of Syracuse.

15 *La Stampa,* 25 June, 23 July 1920, 20 March 1925, 2 March 1928,
9 and 30 April, 14 May, 16 July 1926, 10 February, 2 March, 3 August
1928, 18 July 1929, 17 January, 14 March 1930.

16 "The New House Keeping Center," *The Common Good* 4, no. 4 (January 1911): 8-9. A Polish housekeeping center was abandoned because
of limited funds. Annual Report of the Secretary of the Board, 1914-
15, box 1, Lewis Street Center Papers.

Speaking thirty years after its founding, Helen Rochester Rogers, one
of the founders of the center, stressed a more balanced objective. She
recalled its purpose as that of bringing understanding of Americans to
Italians and of Italians to Americans. Of the two sets of misunder-
standings she felt the latter involved the greater confusion. The practical housekeeping format was borrowed from a New York City prototype.
Miss Rogers stressed the importance of the residential concept and the
fact that all the housekeeping classes were given in a house of the
same kind and under the same market and community conditions

which the students faced every day. The lessons in cooking, cleaning, and shopping had immediate application because they utilized the same stoves, sinks, and markets the mothers and daughters used daily. Helen Rochester Rogers, "History of Lewis Street Center Given at Thirtieth Anniversary Dinner, November 16, 1937," M. S. Lewis Street Center Papers, University of Rochester Archives.

Not all settlements were dependent on initiative from outside the colony. The New York City Mulberry Community House was founded in 1921 "by energetic members of the [Italian] colony who sensed the hunger for education among their neighbors and determined to satisfy it, at least in part." The house had 1,462 adults in English classes held in private homes, especially for mothers. Nearly 2,000 were enrolled in practical citizenship courses in 1923. Other educational features included cooking, dressmaking, and millinery classes for girls, and the circulation of the equivalent of 25,000 books in three years. Playgrounds, a gymnasium, rooms for study, music lessons, and a free employment bureau filled out the program. *The Interpreter* 3, no. 4 (April 1924): 12-13.

17 "The New House Keeping Center," pp. 8-9; Mrs. Charles Melford Robinson, "What I Found on Lewis Street," *The Common Good* 4, no. 10 (July 1911): 13-16; *The Common Good* 6, no. 12 (September 1913): 355; *Lewis Street Center—1907-1957* (50th anniversary pamphlet). Annual reports.

18 *Democrat & Chronicle*, 25 September 1907; *MS* by Dr. Alvah Strong Miller [ca. 1926], box 1; Monthly Reports of the Housekeeping Center Dispensary 1916-17, box 2; Monthly Report of the Resident Head-worker, 1912-17, box 3; Annual Report of the Secretary of the Board of the Housekeeping Center, 1916-17, box 1. Note the pride the center took in Mabel H. Kittredge's praise of their programs for not allowing "institutionalism" to displace the home education ideal. Kittredge was a national leader of the Housekeeping Center movement. Charles P. Ray, "American and Italian Woman: A Decade of Progressive Reform at the Practical Housekeeping Center of Rochester, N.Y., 1907-1917" (senior thesis, History Department, University of Rochester, 1976), traces the upper- and upper-middle-class character of the Center Board of Directors. Most members were from professional and commercial families listed in the local blue book.

19 McKelvey, *Rochester,* pp. 95, 102-07; Herbert S. Weet, "The Development of Public Education in Rochester: 1900-1910," *The Rochester Historical Society Publication* 17 (1939): 203-05; *The Fifty-Fifth Report of the Board of Education of the City of Rochester, 1908-1910,* p. 140; *The Fifty-Sixth Report . . . , 1911-1913,* p. 335; [Edward J. Ward], *Rochester Social Centers and Civic Clubs: The Story of the First Two Years* (Rochester, N.Y., 1909); Ran Stannard Baker, "Do It for Rochester," *The American Magazine* 70, no. 5 (September 1910):

683-96; Herbert S. Weet, "Citizenship and the Evening Use of School
Buildings: The Social Center and Civic Club," *The Common Good* 4,
no. 5 (February 1911); George M. Forbes, "Buttressing the Founda-
tions of Democracy," *The Common Good* 5, no. 4 (January 1912);
McNamara, *The Diocese*, pp. 268-70; Edward Willard Stevens, Jr.,
"The Political Education of Children in the Rochester Public Schools,
1899-1917; An Historical Perspective on Social Control in Public
Education" (Ed.D. thesis, University of Rochester, 1970), pp. 246-51.
Marvin Lazerson, *Origins of the Urban School* (Cambridge, Mass., 1971),
pp. 223-28, is an account of the social center movement in Massachusetts.

The centers were widely attacked. Conservative Protestants and Catholics objected to an incident when Jewish girls danced in a Sunday
program. Political conservatives found it hard to accept the proposition
that socialists should be accorded the same reception given to spokesmen for the Democratic, Republican, and Prohibition parties. This
disparate group of critics, led by a Catholic priest who even opposed
free textbooks in schools as a possible opening wedge for state socialism, kept up a constant agitation against these "socialistic centers."
Politicians found the consistent good government prejudices against
professional politicians annoying, while businessmen were undoubtedly
uncomfortable with the open—and often heated—anticapitalist and
antitrust discussions held in the civic clubs. Ultimately, disparaging
remarks about the state of Rochester's churches, along with some
untimely socialist propaganda, provided the pretext for closing down
the civic clubs. For an interpretation of the role of socialist Kendrick
Shedd in the political hassle over the social centers, see John Dutko,
"Socialism in Rochester: 1900-1917" (M.A. thesis, University of
Rochester, 1953), pp. 145-64.

20 [Ward], *Rochester Social Centers*, pp. 11-12, 64, 70; *The Common
   Good* 5, no. 3 (December 1911): 21.
21 [Ward], *Rochester Social Centers*, pp. 64 and passim; *The Common
   Good* 5, no. 3 (December 1911): 21.
22 *Il Messaggero*, 15 October 1927, *The Common Good* 6, no. 1 (October
   1912): 18, 20; Jasper H. Wright, "The Housekeeping Center Crop,"
   The Common Good 5, no. 7 (April 1912): 16-17.
23 *Il Messaggero*, April 1926, p. 12, and 15 November 1929.
24 *Il Messaggero*, 1 November 1927. The quotation of Mrs. Nisbet continued:

> All children are our children and it is our duty to the children of
> poor parents to place them in the presence of as much real beauty as
> possible. Too little beauty starves the appreciation of children. Taste-
> less gorgeousness, i.e., ignorant showy efforts at beauty, gorge a child's
> appreciation. It takes more thought and ability to express beauty for
> a child's use than for a grown person's.

The predominating characteristic of beauty created for children
should be sunlight, and such beauty should be in a form that they
can absorb unconsciously. Beauty created for children, whether it be
gardens or pictures or books, should be the most perfect that it is
possible to make, but suited to their ability to grasp.

The perspective of the immigrant and his problems in urban America
discussed in these pages can best be described as a view filtered through
an amalgam of the "Arcadian Myth" as presented in Peter J. Schmitt,
Back to Nature: The Arcadian Myth in Urban America (New York,
1969), and the deep faith in the superiority of rural communities and
institutions suggested in R. Richard Wohl, "The 'Country Boy' Myth
and Its Place in American Urban Culture: The Nineteenth-Century
Contribution," in Moses Richin, ed., *Perspectives in American History*
(1969), 3: 77–156.
　　Robert Wiebe identifies this cluster of rural and village ideals as the
initial values that shaped the middle-class response to the emergence of
of modern urban industrial society. These values were still informing
charity work in the three cities two to three decades after they are reported to have given way to concerns for professionalization and ef-
ficiency. Wiebe, *The Search for Order* (New York, 1967); Roy Lubove,
The Professional Altruist (Cambridge, Mass., 1965); and Kenneth L.
Kusmer, "The Functions of Organized Charity in the Progressive Era:
Chicago as a Case Study," *Journal of American History* 60, no. 3
(December 1973): 657–78.
25　*The Fifty-Second Annual Report of the Board of Education of the
　　City of Rochester, N.Y., 1900, 1901, 1902,* p. 52; *The Fifty-Third
　　Annual Report . . . , 1903–04,* p. 9; *The Fifty-Fourth Report . . . ,
　　1905, 1906, 1907,* pp. 7–8, 114–15; *The Fifty-Fifth Report . . . , 1908,
　　1909, 1910,* pp. 104–05; *The Fifty-Sixth Report . . . , 1911, 1912,
　　1913,* pp. 274, 279; Florence Cross Kitchett, "A New Kind of School
　　Exhibit," *The Common Good* 6, no. 11 (August 1913): 319–22; Weet,
　　Citizenship," pp. 5–7; Horace J. Wolf, "Rochester's Welcome to the
　　Jewish Immigrants," *The Common Good* 4, no. 8 (May 1911): 16–18;
　　George E. Smith, "Gentlemen All," *The Common Good* 7, no. 4 (Jan-
　　uary 1914): 55–57.
26　Rochester Public Schools-System Unit for Adult Education, *Adult
　　Education in the Public Schools* (Rochester, N.Y., 1922), pp. 4–8;
　　"Proceedings of the Board of Education of the City of Rochester for
　　the Year 1917," 15 October 1917; *The Public School Programs:
　　Democrat and Chronicle Reprints,* no. 3 (1926), pp. 92–93; Charles E.
　　Finch, *The Rochester Plan of Immigrant Education* (Albany, N.Y.,
　　1916), pp. 3, 4, and passim.
　　The state of New York was slow to become interested in immigrant
education. In 1915 the State Department of Education made a brief
survey of the situation. The following year it published Finch's

pamphlet and several bulletins for the use of local public schools. Only in 1917 did it finally appoint a full-time supervisor to assist localities in improving night school programs. See John L. Riely, "Administration and Organization of Immigrant Education in the State of New York," *Bulletin,* University of the State of New York, no. 765, 1 September 1922, p. 3. Lazerson, *Origins of the Urban School,* pp. 214-23.

27 Weet, "Citizenship"; Smith, "Gentlemen All"; "Schools to Teach Polish and Italian," *The Common Good* 5, no. 3 (December 1911): 27; *The Common Good* 4, no. 1 (October 1910): 4-5; 5, no. 11 (August 1912): 26-27; 6, no. 1 (November 1912): 40-41.

28 *Publications,* The Rochester Chamber of Commerce, 1916, p. 4; 1917, p. 7; *La Stampa Unita,* 12 and 26 November 1920, 6 and 13 January 1922, 2 July, 17 September 1926, 4 February, 18 November 1927.

29 *Annual Report of Public Schools of Utica, New York,* 1919-20; 1920-21, pp. 40-43; 1921-22, pp. 36-38; 1922-23, pp. 33-35; 1923-24, pp. 54-57; 1924-25, pp. 57-59; [S. Alice Smith], *Review of the Work in Immigrant Education* (Utica, N.Y., 1927).

30 *Annual Report . . . Utica, New York,* 1922-23, p. 33; 1924-25, pp. 57-59, *The Evening School* 1, no. 1 (June 1922), and passim.
   The program of immigrant education was remarkably even-handed considering the hardline views of the superintendent of schools at the time. In 1933 he went on record as advocating the forced naturalizing of all aliens under threat of deportation. "Minute Book of Americanization Council Inc., 1922-1949," 8 June 1933.

31 *Annual Report . . . Utica, New York,* 1924-25, pp. 57-59; "Minute Book of Americanization Council Inc., 1922-1949." The council had an Italian businessman, Rocco Perretta, as its first treasurer and a Pole as a member-at-large. Otherwise it was an entirely "American" organization.

32 Alan Davis emphasizes the importance of free choice by potential clients in shaping settlement-house programs, in his *Spearheads for Reform* (New York, 1967). Attendance reports at the Housekeeping Center reveal this process of testing the popularity of programs. The agency expanded those which found support from the colony and dropped those that did not. The bathing facilities were very popular in the early years but lost patrons in later years as Italians equipped their homes with baths. The library also found much favor. Recreational activities, sports leagues, and the band attracted large numbers of youths, while the garden program, so important to the reformers, attracted little interest. Reports of the Resident Headworker, box 3; Monthly Reports of the Dispensary, box 2. Lewis Street Center Papers.

Notes to Chapter 12

1 Clement L. Valletta applies a similar emphasis in his *A Study of*

Americanization in Carneta (New York, 1975). He argues that immigrants in a small American town which they established and dominated
found elbowroom and a fair degree of freedom in which to work out
their own destinies, much as they did in the colonies I have described.

2 Timothy L. Smith identified future orientation as a characteristic
common to many immigrant groups on Minnesota's Iron Range, in his
"New Approaches to the History of Immigration in Twentieth Century
America," *American Historical Review* 71 (1966): 1265-79.

3 A study of forty Italian families in Rochester after World War II gives
some indication of the extent to which they accepted American consumer goods, appliances, bathrooms, and richer diets. In the case of
food consumption patterns, the study supports Phyllis H. Williams's
contention that these changes in diet were attempts to emulate patterns
of the wealthy in Italy as much as a conscious adoption of American
standards. Ruth Mary Kenne, "Acculturation of the First and Second
Generation Italians in Rochester, New York" (M.A. thesis, University
of Rochester, 1946), pp. 82, 86-87. Theodore Saloutos touches briefly
on the impact of the Greeks' intention to return home on their immigrant organizations in America, in his "Causes and Patterns of Greek
Emigration to the United States," *Perspectives in American History*
7 (1973): 408-09, 418-20. See also Child, *Italian or American* (New
Haven, Conn., 1943).

4 Joseph Lopreato, *Peasants No More: Social Class and Social Change in
an Underdeveloped Society* (San Francisco, 1967), pp. 175-79, 184.
Davis, *Land and Family in Pisticci* (New York, 1973), pp. 8-9, 52-53,
57 ff., shows this interest in schooling in a contemporary Italian
commune.

5 Richard Ulin has demonstrated that by the mid-1950s male Italians in
a suburban Massachusetts community had not caught up to their
"Yankee" high school peers in grades achieved. This research is rigorous
in testing the significance of differences found between the two groups
and casual in the assignment of part of the cause for the differences to
the continued impact of a detrimental Old World heritage. Ulin should
not be severely criticized for his portrayal of southern Italian society,
however. He was not studying that society directly and could not know
that the available secondary literature was one-sided and inaccurate in
its identification of the origins and character of the emigrants. He is
more culpable, though, for his decision to eliminate from the study
other ethnic students, the very groups which offer the most fruitful
possibilities for discerning features of school performance that were
rooted in class determinants or experiences common to immigrants
generally. Parsimony dictates that more proximate influences be tested
before moving to more distant sources of explanation.

To show that Italian youth, largely from the lower social and economic
levels, are different in some ways from "Yankees", a group overwhelmingly from families in the upper status categories, even after controls

are applied for social and economic status, is not sufficient ground to
assume that those differences can be attributed to the unfortunate
persistence of southern Italian cultural patterns. (Ulin defines social
and economic status by father's occupation. He made an unreported
number of adjustments when this criterion did not, in his judgment,
accurately represent the true family status.) Inclusion of other ethnic
and lower-class groups might well have pointed to important un-
measured intervening variables. In an aside, Ulin mentions that while
the proportion of Italians choosing the college preparation curriculum
was considerably smaller than for "Yankees," it was somewhat larger
than those of the other ethnic groups in the high school. Would the inclusion of these students in the analysis have washed out the "Italian"
character of the differences he found? He has demonstrated that
Italians shared characteristics which were not as prominent among
"Yankees." The unfortunate failure to include other relevant reference
groups prevents him from knowing whether these characteristics are
uniquely Italian or whether other similarly placed groups shared them.
Ulin, *The Italo-American Student in the American Public School; A
Description and Analysis of Differential Behavior.* (New York, 1975
[1958]).

6 Several recent studies have documented the very limited reach of
secondary education in the nineteenth century. Michael B. Katz points
to the contradiction between the rhetoric that promised increasing educational opportunity for workers' children associated with the founding of public high schools, and the fact that very few workers' children—
and practically no sons of Irish immigrants—attended the new schools,
in his *The Irony of Early School Reform: Educational Innovation in
Mid-Nineteenth Century Massachusetts* (Cambridge, Mass., 1968),
pp. 39–40 and passim. Stephan Thernstrom's *Poverty and Progress:
Social Mobility in a Nineteenth Century City* (Cambridge, Mass., 1964),
pp. 11 and passim, gives further testimony of the irrelevance of secondary education to the mobility of the working classes. This study of
unskilled laborers in a small industrial city between 1850 and 1880
uncovered little social mobility promoted through education. Significantly, not a single son of an Irish immigrant in the sample Thernstrom
studied moved up through the "channels so often stressed in impressionistic accounts of immigrant life—politics and religion"; both areas required more than a few years of common schooling. Also see Clyde
Griffen, "Workers Divided: The Effect of Craft and Ethnic Differences
in Poughkeepsie, New York, 1850–1880," pp. 49–97, and Stephan
Thernstrom, "Immigrants and WASPs: Ethnic Differences in Occupational Mobility in Boston, 1890–1940," pp. 125–64, in Stephan
Thernstrom and Richard Sennett, eds., *Nineteenth Century Cities:
Essays in the New Urban History* (New Haven, Conn., 1969). See
also Josef J. Barton, *Peasants and Strangers* (Cambridge, Mass., 1975).

Barton is the first scholar in this emerging school of historical analysis systematically to study the role of education in the mobility of sons of immigrants. Ruth Mary Keene's study, though limited by a small and selective sample, suggests considerable movement through education into higher status occupations on the part of second-generation Italians by 1946 (pp. 47-49).

Finally, there is the question of whether a distinct pattern of occupational and educational achievement associated with parochial schooling existed. Barton suggests that such a possiblility might account for differences he found between ethnic groups in Cleveland. My study identified no elements in the curricula or organization of the parochial schools which would lead one to suspect that they might be impeding the achievement of their students in either of these two areas. Andrew Greeley's and Peter Rossi's comparison of parochial and public schooling suggests that the determining elements lie, not in one or the other schoolhouse, but in the deeper relationships a child and his family had with the ethnic, religious, and broader communities. This study surveyed Catholics, most of whom were educated before World War II. Children of immigrants were an important part of the sample. *The Education of Catholic Americans* (Chicago, 1966), pp. 140, 146-57.

7 Americans were no more ready for total assimilation of the recently arrived immigrants than most Italians were. Sociologist Emory Bogardus's work on the concept of social distance in the 1920s supplies important evidence on this point. An American-born, largely middle-class sample of 1,725 respondents reveals that only 15 percent were willing to admit Italians into close kinship by marriage. Slightly over 25 percent would admit them "to my club as personal chums." Less than 35 percent would welcome them "to my street as neighbors," and fewer than 55 percent would admit them "to employment in my occupation." Finally, slightly over 71 percent thought that Italians should have the opportunity to acquire United States citizenship. Five and one-half percent of the sample was of Italian descent; presumably they would view their own national group more favorably and thus slightly inflate the low level of general "American" acceptance of Italians. Other eastern and southern Europeans and Asians were viewed even less favorably by Bogardus's respondents. Emory S. Bogardus, *Immigration and Race Attitudes* (Boston, 1928), pp. 23-26. For Bogardus's model of this process, which results in only partial acceptance of newcomers and their children, see "A Race-Relations Cycle," *American Journal of Sociology* 25 (1930): 612-17. The classic study of hostile attitudes toward immigrants during this period is John Higham, *Strangers in the Land: Patterns of American Nativism, 1860-1925* (New York, 1963).

8 Constance Cronin, *The Sting of Change: Sicilians in Sicily and Australia* (Chicago, 1970), pp. 266-68.

9 The concept of the persistence of ethnicity in the United States was

popularized by Nathan Glazer and Daniel Patrick Moynihan, in *Beyond the Melting Pot: The Negroes, Puerto Ricans, Jews, Italians, and Irish of New York City* (Cambridge, Mass., 1963, 1970), and reinforced by the work of Michael Parenti, in "Ethnic Politics and the Persistence of Ethnic Identification," *American Political Science Review* 61 (September 1967), and Andrew M. Greeley's *Why Can't They Be Like Us? "* (New York, 1969); Kenne, "Acculturation," passim.

10 (New York, 1973).

11 *The Rise of the Unmeltable Ethnics* (New York, 1973) is Novak's book-length treatment of the "new ethnicity." Also see his "The New Ethnicity," *The Center Magazine* 8, no. 4 (July/August 1974): 18–23, and his newsletter EMPAC. Novak's critics include Gunner Myrdal, "The Case Against Romantic Ethnicity," *The Center Magazine* 8, no. 4 (July/August 1974): 26–30; John Higham, "Another American Dilemma," in his *Send These To Me* (New York, 1975); and Robert Alter, "A Fever of Ethnicity," *Commentary,* June 1972.

BIBLIOGRAPHICAL NOTE

The following references are representative of the most important books and journals used in this study and do not comprise a comprehensive list of works cited in the text.

Popular sources on southern Italian society include: *Atti della Giunta per l'Inchiesta Agraria e sulle Condizioni della Classe Agricola,* 13 vols. (Rome, 1881-86); *Inchiesta parlamentare sulle condizioni dei contadini nelle provincie meridionali e nella Sicilia,* 15 vols. (Rome, 1909-11); Sidney Sonnino, *I contadini in Sicilia* (Florence, 1877), as well as numerous articles on social and economic topics in *Nuova Antologia.*

Important modern studies include: Luigi Izzo, *La popolazione calabrese nel secolo XIX: demografia ed economia* (Naples, 1965); Francesco Renda, *Il movimento contadino nella società Siciliana* (Palermo, 1956); Salvatore Francesco Romano, *La Sicilia nell'ultimo ventennio del secolo XIX* (Palermo, 1958); also by Romano, *Storia dei Fasci Siciliani* (Bari, 1959); Francesco Brancato, *La Sicilia nel primo ventennio del Regno D'Italia* (Bologna, 1956); and Denis Mack Smith, *Modern Sicily After 1713* (New York, 1968).

Popular and conflicting interpretations of contemporary southern Italian society are Edward Banfield, *The Moral Basis of a Backward Society* (Glencoe, Ill., 1958) and Joseph Lopreato, *Peasants No More: Social Class and Social Change in an Underdeveloped Society* (San Francisco, 1967).

Statistics on schooling in Italy can be found in the Ministero della Pubblica Istruzione (Direzione Generale dell'Istruzione Primeria e Popolare), *L'istruzione primaria e popolare in Italia con speciale riguardo all'anno scolastico 1907-08,* 2 vols. (Rome, 1910), and Ministero di Agricultura, Industria e Commercio, Direzione Generale delle Statistica e del Lavoro (Ufficio Centrale di Statistica), *Notizie sommarie sugli istituti per istruzione media e normale negli anni scolastici dal 1909-10 al 1911-12* (Rome, 1916). Will S. Monroe, "Progress of Education in Italy" (U.S. Bureau of Education), *Report,* 1906 (Washington, 1907), and Walter A. Montgomery, "Education in Italy" (U.S. Bureau of Education) *Bulletin,* 1919 (Washington, 1919), provide descriptions of the basic structure of Italian schooling.

The Italian government collected voluminous statistics on mutual benefit societies. Ministero di Agricoltura, Industria e Commercio, Direzione Generale della Statistica, *Elenco delle società di mutuo soccorso* (Rome, 1898), is a representative publication of this data.

333

The most comprehensive study of Italian emigration in the late nineteenth and early twentieth centuries remains Robert F. Foerster, *The Italian Emigration of Our Times* (Cambridge, 1919). Other valuable early accounts are Francesco Coletti, *Dell'emigrazione italiana* (Milan, 1912); Giovan Battista Raja, *Il fenomeno emigratoriao siciliano: con speciale riguardo al quinquennio 1902-1906* (Palermo, 1908); and especially the numerous articles, reports, announcements, and statistics in the *Bollettino dell'Emigrazione* published by the Italian government commencing in 1902. More recent studies include Francesco Renda, *L'emigrazione in Sicilia* (Palermo, 1963) and John S. MacDonald, "Migration from Italy to Australia" (Ph.D. diss., Australian National University, 1958). MacDonald has restated his central thesis in several articles, including "Some Socio-Economic Emigration Differentials in Rural Italy 1902-1913," *Economic Development and Cultural Change* 7, no. 1 (October 1958), and "Agricultural Organization and Labor Militancy in Rural Italy," *The Economic History Review* 16, no. 1 (1963). Josef J. Barton has refined MacDonald's analysis and applied it to other emigrant groups, in his *Peasants and Strangers* (Cambridge, Mass., 1975).

Australian scholars have made the most significant contributions to the study of chain migration. Among these are Charles A. Price, *Southern Europeans in Australia* (Melbourne, 1963); John S. and Leatrice D. MacDonald, "Chain Migration, Ethnic Neighborhood Formation and Social Networks," *The Milbank Memorial Fund Quarterly* 41, no. 1 (January 1964); and "Italian Migration to Australia: Manifest Functions of Bureaucracy Versus Latent Functions of Informal Networks," *The Journal of Social History* 3, no. 3 (Spring 1970).

Background material on Rochester, N.Y., and a brief history of Italians in the city can be found in Blake McKelvey, *Rochester: The Quest for Quality, 1890-1925* (Cambridge, Mass., 1956); the same author's "The Italians of Rochester: An Historical Review," *Rochester History* 22, no. 4 (October 1960); and Clement G. Lanni, "The History of the Italians of Rochester from 1876 to 1926," *The Rochester Historical Society Publication Fund Series*, vol. 6 (1927). An instructive though limited sociological study is Ruth Mary Keene, "Acculturation of the First and Second Generation Italians in Rochester, N.Y." (M.A. thesis, University of Rochester, 1943). The journal *The Common Good of Civic and Social Rochester* printed many important articles on social and economic topics in the early twentieth century. Robert F. McNamara, *The Diocese of Rochester, 1868-1968* (Rochester, 1968), is a useful history of the Catholic church in Rochester. George Schiro, *Americans by Choice* ([Utica], 1940), is the only study of Italians in Utica. Giovanni Schiavo, *The Italians of Missouri* (Chicago, 1929), is the only book-length study touching on the colony in Kansas City.

Italian-language newspapers were an important source for each of the colonies. The principal ones are now microfilmed and on deposit in the Immigrant Archives, University of Minnesota. The Rochester and Utica public libraries also have film copies of the papers from their respective colonies. In addition, the local history divisions of the libraries in each city yielded a wealth of information in the form of pamphlets, bulletins, and other locally published materials, as well as plat maps, city directories, and English-language newspapers.

Archival research provided an important base for this study. In Italy, I concentrated largely on communal and provincial archives. The latter were generally well organized and adequately indexed. With the exception of Messina, where earthquakes have destroyed many documents, the provincial archives I visited were rich sources of information concerning social conditions preceding and during the period of heavy emigration. Communal archives, unfortunately, are unprepared to receive scholars, and local officials often try to dissuade them from doing research in their records. Anyone contemplating work in these collections must be ready to face rebuffs and, if admitted, to sift through piles of unorganized and unindexed material. These archives are very spotty, having been decimated by neglect, natural disasters, wars, and Red Cross scrap-paper drives. Yet the rewards can be very great for those who persist. The following is a list of those archives in Italy which contributed most significantly to this study:

ARCHIVES

Italy

Archivio Comunale, Alberobello (school records, draft lists)
Archivio Comunale, Alcara Li Fusi (school records, election lists, tax records)
Archivio Comunale, Melfi (school records, draft records, passport lists)
Archivio Comunale, Militello Rosmarino (school records)
Archivio Comunale, Nicosia (passport records)
Archivio Comunale, San Cataldo (passport records)
Archivio Comunale, Sant'Agata di Militello (tax records)
Archivio Comunale, Serradifalco (passport records)
Archivio Comunale, Termini Imerese (passport records)
Archivio Comunale, Valguarnera Caropepe (school records)
Archivio Comunale, Valledolmo (school records, draft records)
Archivio Comunale, Villarosa (school records, passport records)
Archivio Comunale, Villa Vallelonga (manuscript census schedules)
Archivio di Stato, Enna (Gabinetto della Prefettura)
Archivio di Stato, L'Aquila (Gabinetto della Prefettura, Pubblica Sicurezza)
Archivio di Stato, Messina (Gabinetto della Prefettura)
Archivio di Stato, Caltanissetta (Pubblica Sicurezza, Sezione Amministrativa)
Archivio di Stato, Palermo (R. Prefettura-Gabinetto)
Archivio di Stato, Potenza (Gabinetto del Prefetto, Pubblica Sicurezza)
Società Agricola di Alcara Li Fusi (minute books, correspondence)

Statuti for over seventy-five workers' societies in Italy provided important material for a part of the analysis in chapter 2. These documents are for the most part found in the state archives listed above. Communal libraries occasionally yielded a short run of a local newspaper or a few pamphlets; however, generally they were disappointing.

I utilized a number of archival collections in the United States. They are listed below, along with an indication of the types of records consulted.

United States

American Baptist Historical Society Archives (Baptist Mission Board of Utica and Vicinity, The Monroe Baptist Association, Associazione Battista Italiana, Baptist Pastors' Conference, Utica, Oneida Baptist Association, American Baptist Home Missions' Society)

Holy Rosary Parish, Kansas City, Mo. (marriage registers, baptism registers, school records, historical file)

Immigration History Research Center, University of Minnesota (Odone Papers, Italian language press collection, Italian parish jubilee booklets)

Italian Institute and Central Chapel, New Northeast Community Center and Christ Presbyterian Church, Kansas City (marriage registers, baptism registers, membership lists, minutes of officers' meetings)

Jackson County Clerk, Missouri (marriage license records)

Monroe County Clerk, New York (New York State manuscript census schedules)

New York State Secretary of State (incorporation records, membership corporations)

Oneida County Clerk (Naturalization Office, naturalization records; New York State manuscript census schedules)

Our Lady of Mount Carmel Parish, Rochester, N.Y. (marriage registers, baptism registers, school records)

Public schools, Kansas City, Mo. (attendance records, permanent pupil record file)

Public schools, Rochester, N.Y. (attendance records, personnel files, family court records, board deliberations, historical files, annual reports, school census)

Public schools, Utica, N.Y. (attendance records, permanent record file, annual reports, attendance officer reports)

Roman Catholic Diocese of Rochester (parish files)

Roman Catholic Diocese of Syracuse (parish files, priest files, school files)

St. Anthony of Padua Parish, Rochester, N.Y. (marriage registers, baptism registers, school records)

St. Lucy's Parish, Rochester, N.Y. (baptism registers, marriage registers, school records)

St. Mary of Mount Carmel Parish, Utica, N.Y. (marriage registers, baptism registers, school records)

University of Rochester Archives (Lewis Street Center Papers)

Utica City Clerk (marriage license records)

My final resource is an archive of a different sort. I profited from visiting
the physical locations in both Italy and America that were the scenes for
the action described in this book. I walked through the major parts of the
original colonies in the three cities, including visits to the schools,
churches, business districts, and residential areas. Time and urban renewal
have radically transformed or dismantled many of the physical structures
created by the growing colonies. For the most part, those who have torn
down the old have not built anew, so it is possible to acquire a sense of
distance, spatial relationships, and terrain. Those buildings which remain,
yield added meaning for the spirit of hope, confidence, and commitment I
was discovering in the written record. The brief hours during which Italian
libraries, archives, and communal offices are open for business left me
with a great deal of time in which to explore the towns and countryside.
In L'Aquila, the sight of peasants coming from all directions with their
sheaves of wheat on mules, in wagons or small three-wheeled trucks, to be
thrashed in a harvester which had been jacked up off the ground to keep it
stationary and deprive it of its intended function as both cutter and
thrasher of the grain, suggested the continuing strength of the agriculturalists' spirit of individualism in the face of technology and corporate
agriculture.

INDEX